# The Light of
# Zen in the West

# The Light of Zen in the West

incorporating

## The Supreme Doctrine

and

## The Realization of the Self

HUBERT BENOIT 1904–1992

*Translated by*
GRAHAM ROOTH

**sussex**
ACADEMIC
PRESS
*Brighton • Chicago • Toronto*

*The Supreme Doctrine* was originally published as two separate volumes in 1951 and 1952. They were entitled *La Doctrine Suprême: Réflexions Sur Le Bouddhisme Zen*, and *La Doctrine Suprême: Études Psychologiques Selon La Pensée Zen.* respectively. *The Realization of the Self* was originally published as *De la Réalisation Intérieure.* in 1979. A revised version containing Part IV appeared in 1984.

*First published 2004, reprinted 2014, in paperback, in Great Britain by*
SUSSEX ACADEMIC PRESS
PO Box 139
Eastbourne BN24 9BP

*and in the United States of America by*
SUSSEX ACADEMIC PRESS
Independent Publishers Group
814 N. Franklin Street, Chicago, IL 60610

*and in Canada by*
SUSSEX ACADEMIC PRESS (CANADA)
8000 Bathurst Street, Unit 1, PO Box 30010, Vaughan, Ontario L4J 0C6

*British Library Cataloguing in Publication Data*
A CIP catalogue record for this book is available from the British Library.

*Library of Congress Cataloging-in-Publication Data*
Benoit, Hubert.
 [Selections. English]
 The light of Zen in the West : incorporating The supreme
doctrine and The realization of the self / Hubert Benoit ;
translated by Graham Rooth.
 p. cm.
 In English; translated from French.
 Includes bibliographical references and index.
 ISBN 978-1-84519-015-6 (alk. paper)
 1. Zen Buddhism—Doctrines. 2. Zen Buddhism—Psychology.
 3. Self. 4. Phenomenology. I. Rooth, Graham. II. Title.
BQ9268.3.B56 2004
294.3'420427—dc22                          2004000507

Typeset and designed by Syssex Academic Press, Brighton & Eastbourne.
Printed by Edwards Brothers Malloy, Ann Arbor, USA.
This book is printed on acid-free paper.

# Contents

# THE REALIZATION OF THE SELF

*Introduction*
**Part One**   *Traditional Metaphysics*

**Part Two**   *Cosmic and Human Phenomenology*

**Part Three**   *The Agony and Death of Human Egotism*

## Contents

# Translator's Preface

A Zen nun, the late Nancy Amphoux, suggested that I try reading *The Supreme Doctrine*. This was towards the end of the 1980s when she and her husband Jean Baby, who were running a Zen *dojo* in Bristol at the time, inspired in me an enduring interest in Zen Buddhism. The book impressed me, though I found a great deal of it incomprehensible. I took extensive notes, and then forgot about them until I came across them by chance about ten years later, and obtained another copy of the book. I still found it difficult and wondered whether it might be easier in the original. In fact the original remains a difficult text but there were a number of places where I felt it shed significant light on the English. This was the point where I decided that it would be justifiable to attempt a new translation, believing it to be an important book which deserved to reach a new generation of readers.

Aldous Huxley, who admired Benoit's work (*The Supreme Doctrine* was among the books on oriental philosophy and religion which Huxley asked a friend to replace after a disastrous fire destroyed his library in 1961), referred to 'the crabbed, abstract style which made his first book so hard to read' (Letter 602 from *Letters* 1969, ed. Grover Smith). There is no escaping the fact that Benoit deals with difficult and unfamiliar abstractions, but I hope I have been able to reduce some of the stylistic features of the original which had the effect of obscuring Benoit's meaning.

*The Realization of the Self* was mostly written a quarter of a century later with a fourth section appearing in 1984. In it Benoit provides a summary of the metaphysical scaffolding which he had found helpful in his attempts to fathom the mystery which surrounds enlightenment. It is a brief book and readers may find it useful to read it as an introduction to the main work, providing they are willing not to be shocked by an unashamedly metaphysical framework. He wrote most of *The Realization of the Self* in the last decade of his life and it contains a distillation of his ideas.

Benoit published very little in addition to his books, but it was possible to trace two papers which have been included in this centenary volume: 'Buddha and the Intuition of the Universal', originally published by the *Hibbert Journal*, 1959, vol. LVII, pp. 113–16; and 'Notes in Regard to a Technique of Timeless Realization', translated by Aldous Huxley, from *Vedanta and the West* (March–April 1950).

Benoit's major publications, all of which were translated into English, began appearing in 1949 with *Métaphysique et Psychanalyse: Essais sur le Problème de la Réalisation de l'homme*. This was followed by *De L'Amour: Psychologie de la Vie Affective et Sexuelle* and *La Doctrine Sûpreme Selon la Pensée Zen*, both in 1951. His last major work was *Lâcher Prise: Théorie et Pratique du Théorie du Détachement selon le Zen* (1954). He also translated *The Zen Doctrine of No Mind* by D. T. Suzuki into French.

I am grateful to have had the opportunity of translating Benoit and I hope he would have approved of this version. It has been a struggle at times and I have often felt that I was engaged in a dialogue with someone who was himself struggling to find ways of expressing complex and elusive ideas. It is easy to forget just how much of a pioneer Benoit was, as he developed his own approach to the great existential questions in the early post-war years. It also comes as a surprise to recognize how much his work foreshadowed those developments in how we think about the human condition which led to the emergence of the Humanistic and Transpersonal psychologies, and subsequently to more inclusive forms, perhaps best represented currently by the Integral Psychology of Ken Wilber and his many associates at the Integral Institute.

Benoit was undoubtedly an important recent contributor to the slow process whereby the spiritual dimension is re-emerging in the Western psyche at a new, integrated level and it is appropriate that the centenary year of his birth should be celebrated by a major new publication of his works in English. That this has been possible is in large part due to the enthusiastic support and encouragement for the project provided by Anthony Grahame, Editorial Director at Sussex Academic Press.

It is always easier to follow where others have led, and I acknowledge my debt to those earlier translators who helped Benoit reach English-speaking readers: Terence Gray and John F. Mahoney, who produced the first English translations of *La Doctrine Suprême* and *De la Réalisation Intérieure*, respectively. Such mistakes as remain, however, belong to me.

Except where otherwise indicated, all footnotes have been inserted by the translator.

Graham Rooth
*February 2004*

# Original Preface by Swami Siddheswarananda

WRITTEN 1955

It is impossible not to be aware of Dr Benoit's arrival on the intellectual scene. There can be no doubt that a time will come when the impact of his work will rival that of Bergson's.* The reader can justifiably ask my reasons for making such a bold claim; books like *Creative Evolution* only appear once in a hundred years. If I wanted to provide a full explanation, I would have to write another book myself! I refrain from doing so while begging the reader not to look on my laudatory assessment as an example of Oriental exaggeration. The truth of what I have just said will be confirmed in time to come. Dr Benoit introduces an entirely new way of approaching the problem of human destiny; and unlike Bergson in this respect, he does so by developing his teachings along traditional metaphysical lines.

What entitles me to introduce this work is my personal admiration for Dr Benoit, both as a man and as a thinker. He is one of those great spirits that I have been privileged to meet during the fourteen years that I have lived in Europe. Without any doubt he leaves an indelible mark on our thought processes, and consequently upon the structure of our character. What he teaches are the principles and conditions of an intelligent life. We are at the present time in a very serious impasse due to the defective way in which our civilization functions. The inevitable

Except where indicated, the footnotes are the Swami's own.

This Preface appeared in the 1951 and subsequent editions of *La Doctrine Suprême*.

* Henri-Louis Bergson (1859–1941), the leading French philosopher of the early 20th century. *L'Évolution créatrice* was published in 1907 and introduced his concept of the *élan vital*. (Tr.)

result of this impasse has been the current anguish and distress, which *1955*
is a universal malady. We do not know how to confront life. In her
remarkable study of anguish, Dr Juliette Boutonnier rightly observes:
'our civilization, which often fails to teach us how to live, is no better at
teaching us how to die. It provides morphine to ease suffering during
the final stages of life, and that is virtually all.'*

Dr Benoit's foreword to his earlier book, *Metaphysics and
Psychoanalysis*, could apply with equal justification to this work for
which I am writing this modest preface today: 'If a modern Western
reader finds the ideas in this book surprising, this is not because they
are in any way daring or original. It is because the traditional metaphysics from which they are developed, that patrimony of ancestral
wisdom which has been a human birthright through the millennia, has
been gradually forgotten and is nowadays practically ignored by the
majority of people, particularly in the West.' . . . 'I realized that there
existed, beyond the individual systems of philosophical thought, an
impersonal truth.'[†] The book in which these lines are to be found has
hardly attracted any notice. Some of the fundamental ideas expounded
in the present volume were expressed in one form or another in the
previous work. Dr Benoit now presents for the first time the traditional
doctrine of Zen Buddhism in a form which makes it accessible to the
Western reader. Such readers will be delighted to discover that the
purely Chinese aspect of Mahayana Buddhism, Zen Buddhism, which
has appeared enigmatic and virtually impenetrable to the Western
mind, is presented here in a way which does away with its exotic features and employs a dialectical approach which is easier to grasp. As a
practitioner of psychological analysis, Dr Benoit brings the profound
insights of clinical observation to his thinking; and this, together with
his personal experience, gives the book a freshness and directness of
approach which no academic study could ever possess.

It is not for me to say what influence Dr Benoit's works will have on
orthodox psychology of the kind approved of by academia and the psychoanalytic establishment. Professor Dalbiez has taken on the
Herculean task of separating psychoanalysis from Freudian doctrine. Dr
Benoit, in his book on psychoanalysis as well as in the present one (in
which he presents his latest conclusions), has tried to understand human
psychological function by comparing the state in which we *are* to the
state in which we *could* be if our conflicts were fully resolved. This potential level of functioning is not just a fanciful hypothesis. Psychoanalysts

---

* *L'Angoisse*. Dr Juliette Boutonnier. Presses Universitaire de France, Paris.
[†] 1949: *Métaphysique et Psychanalyse*. Paris, La Colombe.

in general adopt a pragmatic point of view in clinical practice and try to help their patients resolve their inner conflicts and re-discover the adaptation which they lost when they lost contact with reality. Dr Benoit does better than this: as a practitioner he relates all his cases to a norm, to what would be 'normal'. The nature of this norm constitutes the fundamental question and this is where Dr Benoit's enormous contribution has to be acknowledged. Without in any way deviating from scientific method, he uses historical and intellectual material to demonstrate that the 'normal' state is a reality. In this study of Zen Buddhism he provides a detailed account of the state which really should be called 'normal'. People who are not normal in this sense suffer. The normal human being is someone who is liberated from suffering. Individuals whose pathology is such that they require the clinical attentions of a psychoanalyst are classified as suffering from neurosis or psychosis, but no great distance separates the neurotic who requires clinical attention and those of us who are considered to be normal in its usual sense. However, when we consider normal in its absolute sense, we are all abnormal. Dr Benoit uses the terms 'natural' or ordinary to designate the condition of someone whose conflicts are unresolved but whose imbalance is not such as to require medical treatment. We call ourselves normal, but in Dr Benoit's terminology the terms natural and ordinary apply to us in so far as we do not belong to the group of pathologically abnormal cases that require psychiatric and psychoanalytic treatment. A huge gulf separates the ordinary person from the 'normal' person.

The agnostic spirit of science refuses to accept any statement which cannot be verified or checked. When we say that normal in the above sense describes a real state we are making an assertion that has to be verified and put to the test by the intellect. There are criteria that enable us to do this, which can be applied adequately without our opinions and 'beliefs' getting in the way, and it is essential that these are given due prominence. There are not all that many examples of 'normality' for us to take into consideration, but it would be quite contrary to the spirit of science if we were to refuse to accept the idea of normal individuals simply because evidence on a statistical scale is unavailable. It is supremely important that all scientific endeavour should be carried out in a spirit of open-minded investigation. If our investigations are pursued impartially, we will discover people whose lives personify the historical and intellectual facts which persuade us that the concept of 'normality' is indeed correct. Dr Benoit has had the courage to state that only someone who has attained *satori* (or *sambodhi*) is normal. Hitler burned six million Jews; for a period of time a section of humanity which had become deranged considered anyone abnormal whose point of view was different from that imposed by the Nazi state. From a statistical point of view, anyone with healthy views was insignificant. Similarly, it is the height of folly to think that because we are all more or less abnormal someone who has achieved satori must be abnormal. For those of us who live in a state of mental tension founded on illusion, the doctrine of 'letting go' which this book puts forward will seem at first to be misguided, like some kind of mystical nonsense. We have to detoxify ourselves with patience, ridding ourselves of our present concept of 'normal', and we have to understand its meaning in the light of undeniable historical and intellectual facts in order to grasp the idea of the 'realized' individual who has attained satori, and to recognize that this is what is meant by a normal person.

The intellectual and historical facts are consistent with one another. The historical facts are not restricted to a particular time. The state of satori is not a temporal reality: it is atemporal.* The truth of gravitation existed before Newton. Newton only discovered it, and when he did so it became an obvious historical fact, capable of being tested and verified: a temporal, historical fact which accords with the atemporal.

Our original state is 'Buddha nature'. The historical evidence which has given us the possibility of confirming the truth of this within ourselves is provided by those individuals who attained atemporal realization. They have simply discovered a pre-existing truth. The point where eternity and durational time intersect is the instant. This process, which is unconscious in those of us who have not realized the atemporal, becomes conscious in people who have attained satori. The experience cannot be called psychological in the sense that it cannot apply to our current limited psyche with its uncontrolled, erroneous way of functioning. But it is psychological – or parapsychological – if we think of the extended psyche of those who have attained satori, the *jîvan-muktas,* the living Liberated Ones.†

This book on Zen Buddhism studies 'normality', the state of someone who has become normal as a result of the satori experience. The concept of what constitutes normality is essential for correcting the errors present in anyone who is abnormal. We need to use the 'normal' as our reference point in order to understand and assist the different kinds of ordinary people.

---

* I recommend the reader to refer to Dr Benoit's article on atemporal realization, which Aldous Huxley translated into English in 1950 (*Vedanta and the West,* March–April 1950, Los Angeles). See page 297 of this volume.

† Cf. *Essai sur la Métaphysique du Vedânta,* by Swami Siddheswarânanda, Ch. 2, concerning Sri Ramana Maharshi.

In psychoanalysis, there is a relationship between doctor and patient. The relationship under scrutiny in this book is one which connects two poles within the individual person. In his book on psychoanalysis, Dr Benoit differs from his colleagues in basing analysis on traditional metaphysical doctrine.* In this he has moved away from the Freudian school. Psychoanalysis should not be identified with Freudian doctrine. Many people who have studied *Metaphysics and Psychoanalysis* have told me that it is a very original book. Dr Benoit himself would take issue with this way of seeing it. I have a letter from him in which he expresses his distaste for any theory which is a 'personal construction'. The personal is the particular. When the particular separates out from the universal we enter the domain of error. Truth is traditional and eternal (*sanâtana*). It is atemporal. The synthesis of the temporal and the non-temporal (or negation of the temporal), in other words the synthesis of the manifested and the non-manifested, takes place in the Atemporal. The atemporal is the third term which resolves the contradiction between the temporal and its negation.** According to the Vedânta, the Atemporal is *turîya*,[†] or the fourth state of consciousness. It is the *prajnâ, or shûnyatâ, or âlaya vijñâna* of Mahayana Buddhism. Observing experience in both categories, manifested and non-manifested, is a difficult endeavour. Observation should be impartial, uncontaminated by any individual projected opinions or beliefs. When these conditions are established, the next task, also difficult, is to create a synthesis of both terms. This kind of synthesis is not a simple mental process. It is a way of functioning in one's life where 'thinking' and 'feeling' are no longer separated. (To understand this process of synthesis, read Dr Benoit's chapter on the mechanisms of distress). Only a synthesis of this kind can free us from error. To achieve this we must develop lucidity of mind to the highest degree.

In psychoanalysis the doctor's role is to enable the patient to become conscious of his conflicts. Relationship problems are put under the spotlight. Error is present when relationships are misunderstood or

* A profane science evolves, while a traditional sacred science does not. The latter is Truth and so, like all truths, it is atemporal and hence eternal.

** Dr Benoit provides a very clear explanation in this book of the dialectical process whereby the opposition between thesis and antithesis is resolved in a synthesis, which is the ternary term. It is this synthesis which leads us through the operation of independent Intelligence to an understanding of true, intellectually self-evident facts. The realization of this synthesis gives rise to the 'quaternary', which for us is the self-evident historical fact of the reality of people who have achieved satori. (Cf. *Métaphysique et Psychanalyse*).

[†] The transcendental Reality beyond the three modalities of consciousness. (Tr.).

unaware. Error is the medium which allows a whole range of hallucinations and illusions to operate. Over the course of treatment the awakening of Intelligence takes place. Given that this awakening has such an important part to play in getting rid of the kind of error whose clinical variants are so familiar to specialists in the field, how much greater, *a fortiori*, must be the role of Intelligence when we are attempting to liberate ourselves from all forms of error, and obtain the transformation of our life which represents, according to Dr Benoit, the transition from the ordinary or natural state to 'normality'.

This book is written for those who aspire to become normal. It provides ideas which are necessary if we are to become aware of the relationships at work within us, of the relationship between self and not-self, of how the ego functions and the part it plays in dealing with the problem of 'compensation'.* It explains what the Delphic oracle meant by: 'Man, know thyself!' It teaches us how we can have objective knowledge of the mind's conditioning and of the modalities in which the self's processes operate. Awareness of relationships enables us to condition our mental processes intelligently. In this the question of will takes on great importance. The problem of the will is directly connected to the action of intelligence. The will takes on a definite direction as it gives form to action. It is the unity of desire and action – or the power of acting; when will is united to intelligence it is none other than *buddhi*. Its action is an upward movement, from error to truth. The term used by Dr Benoit to indicate *buddhi* in French is 'Intelligence Indépendente' (Independent Intelligence).

How to awaken *buddhi* or Independent Intelligence, or Divine Reason, is the subject of this book, which could well have been entitled 'The Science of *Buddhi-Yoga*'. Dr Benoit writes as a true apostle of the doctrine of Independent Intelligence. Neither he nor the author of this preface makes any claim to have attained satori. We simply belong to that category of seekers who attach as much importance to the intellectual witness of people who have attained satori, who have become 'normal', as we do to the facts which history provides. As far as I am concerned, I have had the privilege of knowing three men who, without a shadow of doubt, had experienced satori. Dr Benoit would not have been able to write this book without the certainty provided by his own experience of self-evident truth. He has shown his admiration for Hui-neng, the Sixth Patriarch, by producing a careful translation of Professor

---

* See Chapter 22.

† D. T. Suzuki, *The Zen Doctrine of No-Mind – The Significance of the Sutra of Hui-neng.* Ed. C. Humphreys. London: Rider, 1949 (trans.).

Suzuki's recent work, 'The Zen Doctrine of No-Mind',[†] which expounds Hui-neng's message. The fact that the Sixth Patriarch lived in the 7th century AD, while the men I have known were still alive recently, is of no significance when one is studying the state of illumination; *sambhodi* is atemporal, and whoever understands the importance of Independent Intelligence cannot separate it from its field of action. Its field of action is life; the fulfilment of life is the historical fact which we are offered by a Hui-neng, by a Ramana Maharshi, and it is one which makes it impossible to deny or contradict what our intellect tells us is evident truth. This book is a witness to Faith in Professor Suzuki's sense. It is not someone's individual construction or set of beliefs. It is the itinerary of a soul searching for the truth. In some respects this book is an autobiography.

# Original Foreword by Aldous Huxley

Philosophy in the Orient is never pure speculation, but always some form of transcendental pragmatism. Its truths, like those of modem physics, are to be tested operationally. Consider, for example, the basic doctrine of Vedanta, of Mahayana Buddhism, of Taoism, of Zen. "Tat tvam asi – thou art That." "Tao is the root to which we may return, and so become again That which, in fact, we have always been." "Samsara and Nirvana, Mind and individual minds, sentient beings and the Buddha, are one." Nothing could be more enormously metaphysical than such affirmations; but, at the same time, nothing could be less theoretical, idealistic, Pickwickian. They are known to be true because, in a super-Jamesian way, they work, because there is something that can be done with them. The doing of this something modifies the doer's relations with reality as a whole. But knowledge is in the knower according to the mode of the knower. When transcendental pragmatists apply the operational test to their metaphysical hypotheses, the mode of their existence changes, and they know everything, including the proposition, "thou art That", in an entirely new and illuminating way.

The author of this book is a psychiatrist, and his thoughts about the *Philosophia Perennis* in general and about Zen in particular are those of a man professionally concerned with the treatment of troubled minds. The difference between Eastern philosophy, in its therapeutic aspects, and most of the systems of psycho-therapy current in the modem West may be summarised in a few sentences.

The aim of Western psychiatry is to help the troubled individual to adjust himself to the society of less troubled individuals – individuals who are observed to be well adjusted to one another and the local institutions, but about whose adjustment to the fundamental Order of Things no enquiry is made. Counselling, analysis, and other methods of therapy are used to bring these troubled and maladjusted persons back to a normality, which is defined, for lack of any better criterion, in statistical terms. To be normal is to be a member of the majority party – or in totalitarian societies, such as Calvinist Geneva, Nazi Germany, Communist Russia, of the party which happens to be in power. For the exponents of the transcendental pragmatisms of the Orient, statistical normality is of little or no interest. History and anthropology make it abundantly clear that societies composed of individuals who think, feel, believe and act according to the most preposterous conventions can survive for long periods of time. Statistical normality is perfectly compatible with a high degree of folly and wickedness.

But there is another kind of normality – a normality of perfect functioning, a normality of actualised potentialities, a normality of nature in fullest flower. This normality has nothing to do with the observed behaviour of the greatest number – for the greatest number live, and have always lived, with their potentialities unrealised, their nature denied its full development. In so far as he is a psychotherapist, the Oriental philosopher tries to help statistically normal individuals to become normal in the other, more fundamental sense of the word. He begins by pointing out to those who think themselves sane that, in fact, they are mad, but that they do not have to remain so if they don't want to. Even a man who is perfectly adjusted to a deranged society can prepare himself, if he so desires, to become adjusted to the Nature of Things, as it manifests itself in the universe at large and in his own mind-body. This preparation must be carried out on two levels simultaneously. On the psycho-physical level, there must be a letting go of the ego's frantic clutch on the mind-body, a breaking of its bad habits of interfering with the otherwise infallible workings of the entelechy, of obstructing the flow of life and grace and inspiration. At the same time, on the intellectual level, there must be a constant self-reminder that our all too human likes and dislikes are not absolutes, that yin and yang, negative and positive, are reconciled in the Tao, that "One is the denial of all denials", that "the eye with which we see God (if and when we see him) is the same as the eye with which God sees us, and that it is the eye to which, in Matthew Arnold's words

> each moment in its race,
> Crowd as we will its neutral space,
> Is but a quiet watershed,
> Whence, equally, the seas of life and death are fed.

This process of intellectual and psycho-physical adjustment to the Nature of Things is necessary; but it cannot, of itself, result in the normalisation (in the non-statistical sense) of the deranged individual.

It will, however, prepare the way for that revolutionary event. That, when it comes, is the work not of the personal self, but of that great Not-Self, of which our personality is a partial and distorted manifestation. "God and God's, will," says Eckhart, "are one; I and my will are two." However, I can always use my will to will myself out of my own light, to prevent my ego from interfering with God's will and eclipsing the Godhead manifested by that will. In theological language, we are helpless without grace, but grace cannot help us unless we choose to cooperate with it.

In the pages which follow, Dr Benoit has discussed the "supreme Doctrine" of Zen Buddhism in the light of Western psychological theory and Western psychiatric practice – and in the process he has offered a searching criticism of Western psychology and Western psychotherapy as they appear in the light of Zen. This is a book that should be read by everyone who aspires to know who he is and what he can do to acquire such self-knowledge.

# Foreword by
# Asanga Tilakaratne

The idea of publishing a fresh translation of Hubert Benoit's two works on Zen – *The Supreme Doctrine* and *The Realization of the Self* – from a psychoanalytic point of view, is good news for those who take human freedom seriously. While all religions are interested in this matter, the seriousness with which Buddhism has addressed this issue has been widely acknowledged. The Buddhist concept of suffering as the human predicament and its cessation in nirvanic freedom, and the Freudian concepts of illness and health, have been found to have something in common before and after Benoit. The unique characteristic of Benoit's presentation of Zen is that he articulates it in a language and metaphor intelligible to the contemporary mind informed of psychology, philosophy and science.

In this foreword, I shall first try to locate Benoit's discussion in the larger soteriological context of Buddhism, and subsequently highlight some of its theoretical and practical implications.

The beginning point for Benoit is the human condition and its problems. He underscores the need for radical change in what he calls "our natural condition". This, undoubtedly, is quite near to Buddhism. In one of his early discourses the Buddha, at the beginning of his quest for enlightenment, is reported to have thought in the following manner:

Alas, this world has fallen into trouble, in that it is born, ages, and dies, it passes away and is reborn, yet it does not understand the escape from this suffering [of] aging-and-death. When now will an escape be discerned from this suffering [of] aging-and-death?*

In attaining Buddhahood by "conquering the evil ones" (to use a traditional phrase) in his own mind the Buddha found a solution to the

---

* *The Connected Discourses of the Buddha*, Bhikkhu Bodhi, Wisdom Publications, Boston, 2000, p. 537.

problem. This involved a total transformation of his vision and outlook, and resulted from the purification of mind.

Understandably, Buddhism is rich in analyses of the human mind. Perhaps Buddhism is the most psychological of all religious traditions for it attributes a very important place for purification (*'visuddhi'* in Pali) of one's mind in the process of achieving liberation (*vimutti*). According to the analysis found in the early discourses of the Buddha the defiled character of one's mind is what is ultimately responsible for one's suffering (*dukkha*) in the *samsara* (wheel of existence). This requires anyone interested in getting rid of suffering to analyze, understand and purify one's mind as a priority.

A unique characteristic of Buddhism is that it rejects the concept of everlasting soul, a key element in the concept of the human being across religions belonging to both theistic and non-theistic traditions. The biggest theoretical challenge for the Buddha was to articulate his teaching without allowing the concept of *atma* to creep in. In the context of the ancient Indian religiosity the challenge for the Buddha was to steer clear of the two extreme positions: namely, eternalism, that *atma* is eternal; and annihilationism, that human life is discontinued at death. The 'middle position' of the Buddha was to explain reality without reference to an agent characterized in either eternalist or annihilationist terms.

It is clear that the Buddha accepted such concepts as *samsara* and *karma*, which were very much part and parcel of the brahmanic and non-brahmanic Indian tradition. In those traditions, however, these concepts were articulated through the concept of *atma* believed to be the agent behind these phenomena. The challenge for the Buddha was to articulate these concepts without referring to a doer or an experiencer understood as constituted by an everlasting *atma*. There were misunderstandings regarding the Buddha's position already during the time of the Buddha. Brahmins accused him saying that he was an annihilationist. The disciples grappled with the idea and at times went perilously close to the view rejected by the Buddha. In one such case, a monastic disciple called Saati thought it is consciousness that runs through without undergoing change. The Buddha corrected him, saying that consciousness as taught by him is causally conditioned.*

In the history of Buddhism, it is clear that the biggest challenge faced by the followers of the Buddha was to be faithful to the *anatma* (no-soul) stand of the Master while, at the same time, accepting the validity of

---

* *The Middle Length Discourses of the Buddha*, Tr. Bhikkhu Bodhi, Wisdom Publications, Boston, 1995, pp. 349–61.

such concepts as *samsara* and *karma*. The personalist view (*pudgala-vada*), the idea of karma-seed (*karma-bija*), and store-consciousness (*alaya-vijnana*) are some historical efforts by various schools of Buddhism to overcome this challenge. None of these theories, however, seem to have been able to do successfully what is required of them for all of them have as their point of reference a concept of substratum or an underlying essence.

Coming to the later stages of Buddhism: a doctrinally significant factor in the emergence of Mahayana is the need to apply the concept of *anatma* to the religious life itself which was meant to eradicate the *atma* view. The perception was that the early Buddhists in their practice geared to achieve personal liberation were motivated by the *atma* view itself. The paradox was sought to be resolved by applying the view that everything – including the path, the person who practices the path and the defilements that he is determined to eradicate – are all in actual fact devoid of any self-nature and hence are empty. This is the key point made in such well-known Mahayana sutras as the Diamond-sutra, the Heart-sutra and the Vimalakirti-nirdesa-sutra. It is in this light that we have to make sense of the statements of the type quoted below, which occur frequently in these sutras:

> There is no such thing as myself realizing enlightenment. Why? Because bodhi (or enlightenment) is not an object which can be realized. . . . all Buddhas and great bodhisattvas achieved their goals because they were free from the idea of winning supreme enlightenment.*

Zen Buddhism as articulated by early Chinese masters is the culmination of this way of thinking. According to an episode well known in Zen, Hui-neng (638–713), a mere kitchen help at that time but later the sixth patriarch of Zen, responded to his senior colleague, who asserted that one must guard one's mind diligently so that dust may not accumulate on it, by asking where is the mind that dust settles on and hence requiring purification. This response is believed to be the origin of the Southern school of Zen, which held that enlightenment is sudden and not something to be achieved by prior planning and exertion.

In presenting Zen to the modern reader, Benoit does not particularly lay emphasis on this methodological issue. In fact he directly mentions it only once, towards the end of his work (p. 334). This shows that he is not interested in the intricacies of theoretical debates that went on for centuries between the two sections. He, nevertheless, makes clear, throughout his entire work, that he advocates the sudden approach to

---

* *The Vimalakirti Nirdesa Sutra* (chapter seven).

realization. He further makes clear that he does not believe in 'progress' in religious life, which is indicative of the gradual approach to realization, but in 'evolution' (p. 339).

What Benoit is interested in is the solution to the human predicament. It is his conviction that Zen has something substantial to offer. The fact that he sees some striking similarities between Zen and psychoanalysis makes him present the two systems as complementary to each other. But there are differences between the two and the comparison has limits. Can Zen be taken away from its soteriological context? Benoit refers to the advice by a Zen master to his student that he should eat when he feels hungry and sleep when he feels sleepy. The deeper meaning is that one must engage in such day-to-day activities with 'right attitude', one of being free of any 'I-making' or 'mine-making'. The camouflaged advice is not a plea for carrying on one's usual activities and still being 'religious'. It is good to note in this context that in the early discourses the Buddha gives the identical advice to person called Baahiya who insisted that he wanted guidance in summary form. The Buddha said:

> Baahiya, Thus must you train yourself: In the seen there will be just the seen; in the heard just the heard; in the sensed just the sensed; in the cognized just the cognized. Thus you will not be [carried by that lust].*

The advice is not as simple as it sounds at the practical level. It is also interesting to note that the Buddha gave this advice to one who was far advanced in his path to purity.

Today, some five decades after Benoit's original writing, the educated knowledge in Buddhism of traditionally non-Buddhist countries is no longer in its infancy. After an initial infatuation with Zen, people have discovered many other forms of Buddhism. Notable among such are the insight (*vipassana*) meditation as taught in the Theravada, traditionally found mainly in Sri Lanka, Myanmar and Thailand; and the Tibetan tradition, found in almost all western countries as a result of the Tibetan diaspora with the annexation of Tibet by China. While it is important to have works trying to articulate Buddhist wisdom through a kind of 'non-religious' language there are many who feel that they need to see these traditions in their deeper religious perspective.

The key virtue of Benoit's presentation of Zen is that it is addressed to those open-minded people who do not have a special commitment

---

* *Udana: Verses of Upliftmnet.* Tr. F. L. Woodward, Pali Text Society, London, 1948, p. 10.

to any particular religion. Even if the reader belongs to a particular religion he does not need to forsake his religious views; for Zen, when 'purified' of any sectarian elements, is universally applicable. As Benoit says, one does not need to burn the Gospels in order to read Hui-neng (p. 6). There are, however, limits to this viewpoint. Benoit is quite right insofar as most readers do not plan to go beyond the level of intellectual appreciation of the system and perhaps piecemeal application. Nevertheless, any further involvement would require keeping one or the other text aside. I do not think that one can be faithful to both simultaneously without contradicting oneself. This should not mean that a comparison within a limited space is unacceptable. But it does mean that one must be conscious of the limits of such exercises.

The sudden realization upheld by the Southern school of Zen is obviously not the received view of Zen. Furthermore, the Southern Zen school itself was not quite unanimous about the nature and the extent of practice required for enlightenment. For example, teachers such as Tsung-mi (780–841) in China and Chinul (1158–1210) in Korea, who identified themselves with this particular school, held that sudden realization is only the initial awakening; real enlightenment would only come with gradual practice. These teachers often warned their students against misuse of the system, for there were many who faked enlightenment. Benoit's presentation is clearly based on one school of Zen, although that particular Zen happens to be more influential of the two. Not only Zen but also any religious system has the danger of being misused and misinterpreted. This particular type of Zen seems to be more vulnerable. If this is a problem at all, it is obvious that Benoit is not responsible for it. The iconoclastic character found in Zen admonitions is certainly attractive and ultimate realization seems to be so easy. Nevertheless we must not forget the fact that many Zen masters spent much of their time in wall-gazing meditation. Legendary Bodhidharma is believed to have spent seven long years 'gazing at the wall'! Satori does not need to be made easier than it actually is!

In understanding Western analysis of the human mind, knowledge of psychoanalysis is of great significance. Likewise Zen can never be ignored by those who take Buddhism as a viable solution for the ills of contemporary society. Zen has played a crucial role in making the Buddhist way of thinking familiar to the West. Both have come a long way to achieve professional status in their respective fields. As systems of thought seriously concerned about human predicament and aiming at human well-being, the two systems have ample room for cooperation. Benoit's work is a commendable contribution to exploring the possible areas of such interaction. It needs to be taken more as an inspirational and instructive volume than a factual presentation of two towering movements in the making of contemporary man. It is clear that both the author and the translator have been motivated by far loftier goals transcending the narrow limits of academia. All those who take seriously the collective well-being of humanity deserve this volume.

Asanga Tilakaratne, Ph.D.
Professor of Buddhist Thought
Postgraduate Institute of Pali and Buddhist Studies (University of Kelaniya)
Colombo

# THE SUPREME
# DOCTRINE

# Part One

*of*

## The Supreme Doctrine

# Reflections on Zen Buddhism

# Foreword to Part One

This book contains a number of essential ideas intended to improve your understanding of the human condition. I am assuming that you accept that you still have something to learn on the subject. I mean this quite seriously. To get by in everyday life, we have to function on the inside *as if* we had resolved or eliminated the great existential questions. Most people never think about these issues because they are convinced, explicitly or implicitly, that they understand them. So if you ask people why they want to exist, how they explain the so-called instinct for self-preservation, some are going to answer that it is just a fact of life, and why see a problem where there isn't one? As far as they are concerned, there is no such question and they live their lives in that belief. Others will say: 'I want to live because this is what God wants; it is his Will that I should want to exist so that I may use my life to gain salvation and do the good works that He expects of one of His creatures.' These are people who follow an explicit belief in their lives; push them further, for instance by asking why God should want them to gain salvation, and they will end up replying that human reason cannot and need not understand what lies at the heart of things.

In this they agree with the agnostic viewpoint that we will never know ultimate reality; the wise course is to resign oneself to this ignorance, which, in any case, need not prevent one enjoying life. Though some will deny this, we all live according to a 'metaphysics' of our own which we consider right. This is a practical metaphysics consisting of positive beliefs, our 'principles', the hierarchy of values we live by; and a negative belief, which is that it is impossible to know the ultimate reality of anything. Most people trust their metaphysical system, whether it is explicit or implicit, and this means that they are quite sure that they have nothing more to learn in this area. Where they are most ignorant, they are most confident, this being where the need for confidence is greatest.

Since my topic is the human condition and its problems, open-minded readers will not be easy to find. If I had written about pre-Columbian civilization or some technological subject, I am sure I would be accepted as having something to teach. But what I have to say concerns my readers at the deepest and most personal level, and there is every chance that this will provoke resistance and cause people to close their minds and tell me to mind my own business.

But this is an area where I cannot give you anything unless you agree that you still have something to learn. I have written this book for people who accept that their understanding of the human condition might be improved, and who are also prepared to give me the benefit of the doubt for the time being and assume that I understand more than they do and really do have something to teach them. And there is also the most difficult condition of all, which is that they should not be resigned to the idea that ultimate reality is unattainable: instead they should accept as a working hypothesis the possibility of what Zen calls 'satori', meaning a change in our inner functioning which finally enables us to enjoy our absolute essence.

So if you accept these three ideas: that you can deepen your understanding of the human condition, that I can help you in this task, and that radical change in our natural state is possible, then it may not be a waste of time for you to read this book. If not, however, you will certainly be wasting your time and I would not recommend that you read it.

You may wonder whether this book could make you accept ideas which you do not accept at present. But this is simply not possible: we can influence one another in the realm of emotion, by inducing feelings and associated ideas; but we cannot do this in the pure realm of intellect, which is the only place at present where we already enjoy freedom. I can reveal insights from this realm which are latent in you: but they are already there, and all I do is rouse them from their slumber. Nothing belonging to pure intellect can be 'introduced' into you. For example, you might seem to become decidedly more sympathetic to the idea that satori is possible, as a result of reading my book: if this were to happen, you can be quite sure that it would only happen in proportion to a sympathy which was already there, in a more or less dormant state.

You do not have to be in total agreement with the three ideas mentioned above for my book to have some prospect of being useful, although there has to be some minimal measure of agreement. But the most important consideration is that your attitude should not be hostile *a priori*. If it were hostile, I would never convince you nor would I even make the attempt: metaphysical ideas cannot be demonstrated and each of us can only accept them to the extent that we understand intuitively that they explain phenomena in us which are otherwise inexplicable.

So far I have been dealing with the one basic misunderstanding which we must avoid, but there are also some less important ones to consider.

You will get very little out of this book if you take it to be a sort of digest setting out 'everything you need to know about Zen.' For a start a popularized version of this kind of subject is inconceivable; no text will provide a quick initiation into Zen. And my book is really intended for people who have already given a lot of thought to Eastern and Far-Eastern metaphysics, read what they could of the essential material, and are now seeking to develop an understanding appropriate to the Western mind. My intended reader will have read *The Zen Doctrine of No-Mind* by Dr D. T. Suzuki in particular; or, failing that, his earlier books.

I do not claim that my books conform to a Zen 'orthodoxy'. The ideas I express in them are only derived from what I have read on the subject. In any case, 'orthodoxy' is not a valid concept as there is nothing systematic in Zen, which compares all teaching to a finger pointing at the moon. It warns unceasingly against the mistake of attributing Reality to the finger, which is only a means, and in itself is of no importance.

I do not call myself a follower of Zen either; Zen is not a church of which one is or is not a member. It is a universal point of view, offered to everyone, imposed on no one; it is not like a political party which one has to enrol in and commit oneself to. I can make use of the Zen approach in my search for truth without arraying myself, literally or metaphorically, in Chinese or Japanese garments. Labels vanish and there is no East/West dilemma in the realm of pure thought. I am a Westerner in terms of the way I think but that does not stop me meeting Orientals on an intellectual plane and sharing in their understanding of the general human condition. I do not have to burn the Gospels to read Hui-neng.*

This book is written as it is because I think as a Westerner does. Dr Suzuki has said that Zen 'detests any form of intellectualism'. Zen masters do not answer questions with a lengthy discourse; they prefer to reply by saying something disconcerting, or by silence, or by repeating the question, or hitting the questioner with a stick. But my impression is that enlightenment for the Westerner does require some intellectual input, though kept within strict limits. The ultimate viewpoint, that of reality, is clearly inexpressible; and the teacher would

---

* The sixth Chinese Patriarch (638–?713) from whom all later Zen schools and lineages derive.

harm the pupil if he let him forget that the whole problem is precisely one of leaping the gap which separates verbal truth from real knowledge. But rational explanation is necessary to coax Westerners to the edge of this gap. Zen says, for example: 'There is nothing complicated to do: seeing directly into one's own nature is enough.' It took me years of reflection before I began to see how this advice could be given substance and put into practice in our inner life. And I think that many of my fellow Westerners find themselves in the same situation.

The style of my book may be Western in one sense, but the nature of the Zen approach prevents it having the kind of clearly ordered structure that the rationalist in us finds so appealing. Each paragraph is set out logically, but this is not true of the chapters or the book as a whole. The easy flow of logic is repeatedly interrupted; it does not really matter what order the chapters are taken in. There are some phrases which seem to contradict themselves from one chapter to the next, if they are taken at face value. Western readers need to be warned about this; anyone who begins to read with the implicit assumption that they will find a convincing demonstration set out in strict sequence from start to finish, will try and fit the book into their preconceived framework. It will not be long before they fail and give up the struggle.

It is worth repeating that this difficulty derives from the very nature of the Zen approach. With most doctrine-based teachings, the point of view offered implies that one looks at things from a fixed perspective; if I look at a complex object from one angle only, what I perceive is projected onto my retina as lines and surfaces whose relationship to each other is constant. But Zen does not attach any importance to theory in itself, to the angle from which it studies the book of Reality. Zen is only interested in Reality. It has no objection to moving around this complex object to extract whatever information it can, so that a formless synthesis may develop within the mind. Because Zen does not idolize any one particular formulation, it is free to explore every conceivable formal idea without bothering about apparent contradictions: using ideas *without becoming attached to them* allows Zen to possess them without being possessed by them. So the Zen point of view does not look at things from just one angle: it takes in all possible angles.

Understanding emerges as a synthesis in the mind. My readers must realize that this text is not meant to be a medium for transmitting a synthesized understanding from my mind into theirs. Everyone has to make their own synthesis in their own mind in the way appropriate for them, just as I had to. No one else can do this work for us. What my text does is suggest suitable elements for this synthesis. The order in which they are organized does not always follow a logical sequence, but take it as you find it, without longing for some neat formal structure, which might simulate an intellectual synthesis, but would never be the real thing, formed in the depths of your being.

# CHAPTER ONE

# *Zen Thought: An Overview*

SINCE TIME BEGAN, people have reflected on the human condition and have been dissatisfied with the way we are. With varying success they have engaged in what amounts to self-criticism and identified defects in how we function. This kind of critical analysis can be crude, but there are teachings in which it achieves considerable depth and subtlety, with a very precise recognition and description of the undesirable aspects of ordinary human psychological functioning.

Compared with this diagnostic wealth, the work on treatment is notably unimpressive. When schools which teach about the human condition and its problems have described and analysed the dysfunctional nature of the ordinary person, they then have to consider how this state of affairs can be remedied. This is where their teachings become confused and lacking in substance. Almost all teachings lose their way at this point, though this is not always immediately apparent. Zen – more specifically the Zen of certain masters – is the exception.

There have been other teachings through which people have attained realization. But only Zen in its pure form provides a clear exposition of the problem and a clear refutation of wrong methods.

The essential mistake of all wrong methods is that the remedy they propose does not focus on the root cause of human misery. Their analysis of the human condition does not consider the factors which control inner phenomena in sufficient depth; it does not pursue the chain of cause and effect right the way back to its beginning, to the original, first phenomenon. It stops prematurely, while still at a symptomatic level.

Someone who approaches matters in this way, whose analysis cannot penetrate beyond the symptom, will only be able to think in terms of putting every problem right by artificially contriving a new symptom which is the exact opposite of the target symptom. An example of this would be someone who comes to the conclusion that displays of anger, pride, sensuality, and so on are responsible for their woes; so they decide that the remedy lies in making an effort to display gentleness, humility and asceticism, etc. A more thoughtful person might conclude that mental agitation was responsible, and decide to calm the mind with appropriate exercises.

Some doctrines instruct us that we are miserable because we always want things, and are attached to our possessions. We are then advised, depending on how intelligent our teacher is, either to give away all our possessions, or to learn to detach ourselves inwardly from what we continues to possess externally. There are other doctrines which maintain that lack of self-mastery is the key to human suffering, so they teach various yogas, methods of training which focus on producing progressive changes, whether in the body, the emotions, in knowledge, attention, or in altruistic behaviour.

So far as Zen is concerned, this is no better than training for a performing animal, and the result will be some form of enslavement, accompanied by the uplifting illusion that one is becoming free. The reasoning which underpins all these approaches is simplistic: 'This way of doing things is causing problems, so from now on I am going to do just the opposite.' Formulating the problem like this, by taking a *form* of activity judged to be bad as one's starting-point, confines the seeker within the *formal* domain. This precludes any possibility of integrating consciousness by transcending form: if I am confined within the dualistic plane, no change in polarity, no switch from negative to positive, will free me from the dualistic illusion and restore me into Unity. This is like the problem of Achilles and the Tortoise, which is insoluble within the constraints imposed by the way in which it is formulated.

Zen thought penetrates and cuts through all our phenomena without dwelling on their particular features. It knows that there is nothing wrong with us: we suffer because we do not understand that things are perfect just as they are, and are therefore under the illusion that something is wrong and needs to be put right. This is not the same as saying that all our ills come from an illusory belief that we are lacking something. That would be a nonsense because the ills referred to lack reality in an absolute sense, and an illusory belief, one not based on reality, cannot be the real cause of anything. In any case, careful introspection fails to reveal that I have this positive belief that I am in some way lacking something (perhaps it is not surprising that I cannot find positive evidence for an illusory belief in something which is not there!). But what I do observe is that my inner phenomena behave *as if* such a belief were present. The fact that this is so does not mean that this particular

11

belief is present: it happens because the direct intellectual intuition that nothing is lacking has not been aroused, and still *sleeps* in the depths of my consciousness. That intuitive knowledge is actually there, because I am lacking in nothing, especially that; but it is still dormant and ineffective.

My apparent ills result because my *faith* in a Perfect Reality is asleep. All I have active within me are beliefs in what is conveyed to me by my senses and mind operating in the dualistic plane (so these are beliefs in the non-existence of One Perfect Reality). They are illusory mental formations which lack reality, and result from my faith being asleep.

I am 'a man of little faith', more accurately someone who has no faith, or, better still, someone whose faith is dormant, who does not believe in anything he does not perceive in the world of form. (This way of thinking about faith, as present but asleep, helps us understand why our deliverance depends on our being 'woken' by a master, or a teaching, or a revelation. That we still sleep implies that the measures needed to waken us have yet to be taken.)

*To summarize, everything seems to be going wrong in me because the fundamental idea that everything is perfectly, eternally and totally positive is dormant in the centre of my being, instead of being awake, alive and active.* We are now touching on the primary distressing phenomenon, from which all other distressing phenomena are derived. Our dormant faith in the Perfect Reality that is One (outside which nothing 'is') is the primary phenomenon from which the whole distorted sequence flows. It is the causal phenomenon, and no therapy for illusory human suffering can be effective if it is directed elsewhere.

To the question, 'What must I do to achieve deliverance?' Zen replies: 'You don't have to do anything because you have never not been free, and in reality there is nothing from which you have to be delivered.' This reply can be misunderstood and can seem discouraging, because the word 'do' is ambiguous. In ordinary usage, 'do' can be split into two components, idea and action; and the term is applied to the act of carrying out what has been conceived. This is the sense in which Zen is right; there is nothing for us to 'do': everything will sort itself out harmoniously and spontaneously in our 'doing' precisely when we stop trying to modify it in some way or another, confining our efforts instead to arousing our dormant faith, in other words, to the task of conceiving the primordial idea necessary for our understanding. This whole idea is like an unmoving sphere; it does not lead to any particular action, nor is it driven by any dynamic of its own. It is the purity at the heart of not-doing, through which the spontaneous activity of real natural life will pass unaffected. Waking and nurturing this concept is not 'doing' something in the ordinary meaning of the word. The effect this awakening in the mind has in daily life is to reduce and gradually stop all the useless manipulation to which we subject our inner phenomena.

Obviously one can say that the work involved in conceiving an idea is a kind of 'doing'. But, given this word's usual connotations, it is best to avoid a potentially harmful misunderstanding by speaking in Zen terms and making it clear that the work which can put an end to human anguish is strictly confined to the pure intellect. It does not involve 'doing' anything in particular in one's inner life: on the contrary, it involves relinquishing the wish to introduce change of any kind.

Let us take a closer look at this. Work to awaken faith in the unique and perfect Reality which is our 'being' has two phases. There is a preliminary phase when discursive thought conceives all the ideas necessary for a theoretical understanding that this dormant faith exists in us, that it can be awoken, and that only by awakening it can we put an end to our illusory suffering. During this preliminary stage, the work we carry out can be called 'doing' something. Obtaining this theoretical understanding will not of itself modify our painful state in any way: it must next be transformed into an understanding which is lived and experienced by our whole organism, so that it is both theoretical and practical, abstract and concrete. Only then will our faith be awoken.

This transformation, this going beyond form, cannot be the result of any direct work undertaken by ordinary people, whose eyes are closed to anything beyond the formal domain. Obviously there cannot be a 'way' leading to deliverance, because in reality we never were in a state of bondage, nor are we now; there is nowhere to 'go', and nothing to 'do'. The experience of total liberty and infinite happiness does not depend on any kind of directed action. What has to be done is indirect and negative; and what has to be understood, which takes work, is that all possible, imaginable 'ways' are deceptive and illusory. Only when persistent effort has brought about an absolutely clear understanding that 'doing' *anything* to liberate oneself is futile, and only when the very idea of any imaginable 'way' has been stripped of all value, will 'satori' shine forth, as the realization that there is no 'way' because there is nowhere to go, because from the very beginning of time one was at the sole centre and origin of all things.

'Deliverance', which is what we call the disappearance of our illusion that we are enslaved, that we are not free, follows inner work chronologically, but is not in fact caused by it. Inner work in the domain of form cannot act as a cause in relation to what is prior to all forms, and therefore prior to it; it is simply the instrument through which the **First Cause** works.

In short, the celebrated 'strait gate' does not exist in the domain of form any more than the 'way' upon which it supposedly opens; that is, unless one wishes to apply this name to the realization that there is no way, no gate, and nowhere to go. This is what the Zen masters reveal to us, the great secret which all along is staring us in the face.

# CHAPTER TWO

# *Good and Evil*

TRADITIONAL METAPHYSICS DESCRIBES the universal process of creation as the concurrent and conciliated interplay of two opposing and complementary forces. So creation results from the interaction of three forces: positive, negative, and conciliating.

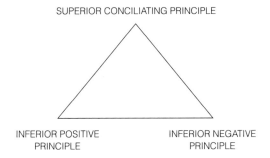

SUPERIOR CONCILIATING PRINCIPLE

INFERIOR POSITIVE PRINCIPLE

INFERIOR NEGATIVE PRINCIPLE

This 'Law of Three' can be represented by a triangle, with the superior or conciliatory principle at the apex. The two inferior principles, positive and negative, occupy the bottom corners and are the two great cosmic forces of Chinese philosophy, *Yin* and *Yang* (Yin is negative, feminine, damp, and cold; Yang is positive, masculine, dry and hot); they are also represented by two dragons, red and green, whose unceasing struggle gives rise to the 'Ten Thousand Things'.

The T'ai Chi diagram consists of equal black and white parts, Yin and Yang respectively. They are contained within a circle, which is the Tao or Superior Conciliating Principle. Both parts contain their opposite as a small point, showing that nothing in creation is absolutely positive or absolutely negative. The primordial Yin/Yang dualism includes every conceivable opposition: summer-winter, day–night, movement–immobility, beauty–ugliness, truth–delusion, construction–destruction, life–death, etc.

T'AI CHI DIAGRAM

There is a Hindu version of this triadic relationship which illustrates the last pair of opposites particularly clearly: under the authority of Brahma, creation is the simultaneous work of Vishnu, Protector of Beings, and Shiva, Destroyer of Beings.

The creation of the perceived universe unfolds in time, so the action of the two inferior principles is *temporal*. But the principles are not themselves temporal because they cannot be subject to the limits which they create by their own action; they are intermediaries, and they are positioned between the Superior Principle and the created universe which is its manifestation. So universal creation unfolds in time, but is itself an atemporal process and it cannot be said to have or not have a beginning or an end, since these words are meaningless outside time. Modern scientific theory agrees with metaphysics on this point, attributing neither beginning nor end to the material universe.

All this must be fully understood if we are to get rid of the childish idea that an anthropomorphic Creator set the universe in motion. In the same way, my body was not just created on the day I was conceived; it is being created all the time. Every moment of my life the cells which make up my body are involved in a continual process of death and renewal, and it is this balanced struggle between Yin and Yang which goes on creating me until the moment I die.

The two inferior principles function as perfect equals in this atemporal triadic process as it ceaselessly creates our temporal world. Since their collaboration is necessary for the emergence of all phenomena, however small, neither can be considered superior to the other either qualitatively or quantitatively. Sometimes one or the other may predominate in a particular phenomenon, but the two Dragons maintain a state of dynamic equilibrium across the whole body of space and time throughout the universe. Hence the triangle with which traditional metaphysics represents the Triad of creation is always an isosceles triangle with a strictly horizontal base.

Since the two inferior principles are equal, the same applies to their manifestations when one views them in the abstract. If Shiva and Vishnu are equal, why should life be superior to death? Considered in the abstract, this is perfectly obvious. From the same point of view, why should construction be considered superior to destruction, affirmation to negation, pleasure to suffering, or love to hate, etc?

If we relinquish the theoretical and abstract realms of pure intellectual thought and come down to the world of everyday psychology, two observations strike us: first, we have an innate bias in favour of positive manifestations such as life, creation, kindness, beauty and truth. This is easy to understand as the intellectual expression of an affective preference which is itself the logical outcome of our innate desire to exist. But there is a second observation which is not so easy to explain, relating to the qualities which metaphysicians usually attribute to realized individuals. These people are liberated from all irrational determinism, are inwardly free, and they live according to Reason. They are identified with the Supreme Principle and in perfect alignment with the cosmic order; and free from the irrational need to exist and the consequent preference for life over death. The puzzling observation is that those who study metaphysics recognize intuitively that the realized person is without question someone who acts lovingly and creatively, not hatefully and destructively. This is not to say that the 'realized' person has a particular enthusiasm for constructive activity, for such people have passed beyond the dualistic feelings experienced by ordinary people; but we cannot see their actions in any other way, other than as loving and constructive. Why the bias which has disappeared from the mind should seem to persist in behaviour after enlightenment is a question which must be answered if we want to fully understand the problem of 'Good' and 'Evil'.

Many philosophers have rightly been critical of our emotionally-coloured notion of Good and Evil, and the claim that these are absolute values. However they then not infrequently promote some system which rejects what is right as well as the mistaken aspects and, having dismissed and passed beyond the idea of Good and Evil, either fails to provide practical guidance or stands morality on its head. It is not difficult to criticize our affect-laden view of Good and Evil; but it is difficult to do this in a way which integrates it into an understanding in which everything is conciliated, without destroying it in the process.

Let us first take a look at the mistaken way in which we usually approach this problem. We observe positive and constructive phenomena, and negative and destructive phenomena both outside and within ourselves. Our wish to exist leads us to prefer construction to destruction. Being animals endowed with the capacity for abstract thought and generalization, we begin to conceptualize construction and destruction in abstract terms, which brings us in other words to the idea of there being a positive and a negative inferior principle. At this level of thinking, affective *preference* becomes intellectual *bias*, so only the positive aspect of the world is considered good and legitimate, while the negative aspect is evil and the object is to eliminate it as completely as possible. Hence the nostalgia for a paradise free from any negative aspect.

At this incomplete stage in the development of thought, the existence of these two inferior principles is recognized, but not that of their conciliating Superior Principle. So the two Dragons are only seen as antagonistic, but not complementary: they are seen to be fighting, but the collaborative aspect of their struggle goes unrecognized. There is an inescapable but irrational wish to see 'Yes' triumph once and for all over 'No'. We call our constructive impulses 'qualities' and our destructive impulses 'faults', and think that correct personal development requires the complete elimination of 'faults' so that only 'qualities' are left to provide our motivation. People think about 'saints' as they do about 'paradise', so the saint is imagined as someone in whom only perfect positivity holds sway, whom we should take as our model.

At its best, this will result in a kind of training based on reflex conditioning in which negative impulses are inhibited and positive ones are favoured. This kind of development is clearly incompatible with atemporal realization. The two poles must achieve a conciliated synthesis for this to occur, which means that they must eventually collaborate harmoniously without ceasing to oppose each other.

When there is no concept of the Superior Principle, and only the two inferior principles are recognized, personal and absolute characteristics are inevitably attributed to them, in other words they are *idolized*. The positive principle becomes 'God', and the negative principle becomes the 'Devil'. Without an apex, the base of the Triadic triangle cannot remain horizontal and tilts through ninety degrees: the positive angle becomes God and swings up to the zenith ('paradise'), while the negative becomes Devil and swings down to the nadir ('hell'). God is conceived as a perfect anthropomorphic positivity, and is just, good, beautiful, affirmative, and constructive. Satan is a total anthropomorphic negativity, unjust, wicked, ugly, negating, and destructive.

Since the dualism represented by these two principles contradicts the intuition which we otherwise have, that there is a Unique Principle encompassing everything, the existence of Evil and Satan confronting God is a practically insoluble problem, and it gives rise to all kinds of philosophical acrobatics. Among these is an idea which we will see to be well-founded in due course, and this is that God actually intends the Devil to exist, not the contrary. This obviously gives God primacy over the Devil, but nothing in this dualistic perspective explains how God can need the Devil's existence and still remain a perfectly free agent.

There is a close relationship between the dualistic 'God/Devil' concept, and the *aesthetic* sense which distinguishes humans from other animals. The aesthetic sense is the ability to discern the affirmation/negation dualism in the formal domain, in forms. Satan is deformed, a negative form disintegrating into formlessness. Humans have an emotional preference for the creation of form (construction) as opposed to deformation (destruction). The human body is considered 'beautiful' when its form has reached the peak of its development (construction), when it has emerged furthest from the formless and not yet begun to return to it. It is not surprising that every morality can be understood as an aesthetic of subtle forms ('a fine gesture'; 'ugly motives', etc.)

This dualistic conception of 'Good' and 'Evil', without the Superior Conciliating Principle, is what the human mind arrives at spontaneously and naturally in the absence of any metaphysical initiation. It is incomplete and to that extent erroneous; but there are also interesting truths contained within its limitations. The intellectual bias in favour of Good may be erroneous, based as it is on ignorance, but the same ought not to be said of the innate affective preference for Good. This exists on the non-rational affective level where things are neither according to Reason nor against it. There must be a cause, a *raison d'être*, underlying this preference which our rational intellect should not reject *a priori* but should rather try to understand.

I will try to clarify this. As far as pure intellect is concerned, the two inferior principles are strictly equal in their complementary antagonism, so why should they seem unequal from the practical affective viewpoint, with the positive principle unquestionably superior to the negative? If, when we draw the Triadic triangle, we call the base angles 'relative yes' and 'relative no', why do we feel constrained to call the apex 'Absolute Yes', and not 'Absolute No'? If the base angles are 'relative love' and 'relative hate', why is 'Absolute Love' and not 'Absolute Hate' at the apex? Why does the word 'creation' evoke construction, not destruction in our minds, although the concept implies both processes?

A simple mechanical phenomenon can be used to explain all this. If I throw a stone, two forces are involved: an active force from my arm and a passive force (inertia) located in the stone. They are opposing and complementary, and their collaboration is necessary for the stone's trajectory. Without the active force supplied by my arm, the stone would not move; without the force of inertia supplied by the stone's mass, there would be no trajectory. The stone I throw furthest will be the one whose inertial mass best balances my arm's active force.

If we compare the two forces, neither causes the other: the stone's mass exists independently of my arm's force, and vice versa; and looked at like this, neither is superior to the other. *But the active force causes the passive force*; my arm is effective through *action*, the stone's inertia operates as *reaction*. And what is true of the forces involved in this tiny event is equally true at all levels of creation in the universe. If one considers the two inferior principles in the abstract as if they existed independently of their activity, they do not cause one another; they have independent status under a First Cause from whose viewpoint they are strictly equal.

But, the moment we think of them in action, the workings of the active force appear responsible for what the passive force does (it is in this sense that God wills the Devil's existence, and not the contrary). In the creative interplay of the two principles, it is the positive one which releases the activity of the negative one, and this gives rise to its unchallenged superiority. This is not a chronological primacy (action and reaction being simultaneous) but a causal one. One way of expressing this is that the instantaneous flow of energy from the Superior Principle reaches the negative principle by passing through the positive. So the two principles are 'noumenally' equal, but 'phenomenally' unequal with the positive being superior to the negative: the force which moves the sister of charity is strictly equivalent to that which moves the murderer, but help given to orphans is undeniably superior to murder. Despite this, in abstract terms both deeds are equivalent, being no more than symbolic representations of the positive and negative forces, which are equal.

We can now understand that every constructive phenomenon expresses the workings of the active force (action), and every destructive phenomenon the workings of the passive force (reaction). This is why realized individuals are always as constructive as the circumstances permit: being effectively free of conditioning, they no longer 'react', they act; and being active, they are constructive.

Destructive behaviour on the part of a wicked person may seem to be initiated and caused by the operation of an active destructive force. In fact, the initial purpose is constructive, in this case self-affirmation; the wrong associations conditioned in ignorance are responsible for the predominantly destructive outcome of what must necessarily have started out as a constructive activity. If I try to lift a stone which is too heavy for me, the stone fails to rise and I collapse: but my initial active force was nonetheless directed upwards.

So realized individuals do good, and the good they do is simply the consequence of inner work which has led to their Divine Reason being actively involved the whole time in carrying out their own triadic synthesis. Good is simply what happens when a liberating understanding has been integrated into the whole being; and has abolished any belief in the illusory primacy of the positive inferior principle or principle of Good. *Realized individuals only do good, and this is precisely because they no longer idolize it and are no more attached to it than to evil.*

Their behaviour is different from that of people who have disciplined themselves to be saints: the end result of a saint's rigid and systematized behaviour may be more destructive than constructive. The opposite is true of the 'realized' person: in their behaviour constructiveness outweighs destructiveness, without this being something they actively seek. The activity which generates it is flawless, while their behaviour adapts and changes continuously in response to circumstances.

*In short, truly ethical behaviour is a direct result of atemporal realization. The way of liberation cannot be 'moral'.* Before satori, all ethical systems are premature and impose constraints which hinder its attainment. This does not mean that someone whose goal is liberation should try to block their affective preference for good. It should be accepted with the same all-embracing intellectual neutrality which is directed towards the whole of their inner world; but this harmless affective preference should not be allowed to develop into an intellectual bias which would be an obstacle to inner peace.

None of this amounts to a condemnation of spiritual or idealist doctrines which teach people of goodwill the supreme value of virtue, kindness, and love etc. That would be another irrational intellectual bias: people can only think and act in the light of their understanding. All I am saying is that such teachings by themselves cannot lead to satori. Everyone is equally entitled to aspire to satori; but to achieve it, their level of understanding must enable them to transcend any teaching whose approach to Yin and Yang entails a built-in theoretical bias. Zen proclaims: *'The Perfect Way knows no difficulty, except that it rejects all preferences. A difference of a tenth of an inch, and Heaven and Earth are separated.'*

# CHAPTER THREE

# *Salvation as Idolatry*

There is one mistake which is a particularly serious obstacle to atemporal realization, and that is to think that there is something compulsory about it. According to many spiritual systems, religious or otherwise, mankind has a duty to achieve 'salvation': the temporal is devalued and salvation is invested with an intensely imagined reality. That there is a form of *idolatry* in this is obvious because realization is both thought of as something which excludes other things, in other words it is treated as an object among other finite objects in the domain of form, and at the same time it is held to be uniquely 'sacred', and immeasurably superior to everything else. So all the enslaving, prescriptive reality otherwise invested in worldly enterprises crystallizes around 'salvation', which becomes the most enslaving and prescriptive enterprise of all. Realization signifies liberation, which leads to the senseless paradox of people subjecting themselves to a compulsory duty to be free.

The issue of salvation becomes the focus of mankind's distress, and people are terrified of dying before they have been saved.

A misunderstanding as serious as this is bound to cause problems, and it leads to anxiety and agitation, with feelings of unworthiness, and an egotistical clinging to the idea of oneself as a distinct and separate entity. In other words, it precludes such factors as peace of mind, self-acceptance, indifference to the idea of oneself as a distinct entity, and a reduction in emotional activity: in short, that easing of the whole inner climate which is a precondition for the release of satori.

This is a mistake which can be rectified with a little thought. The existence of a duty implies that there is some authority which imposes it. Religious believers say that God is the authority who imposes the duty of salvation. But what kind of 'God' is this? If God imposes something on me this implies that He is separate from me and needs some action on my part. How can divine harmony be perfect if it is incomplete?

The same mistake is made by people who have developed intellectually to a point where they no longer believe in a personal God. At least they give the impression of not believing in one, though in fact they do.

They have an image of satori and of their post-satori selves which is their personal 'God', and this is an idol which is demanding, disturbing and implacable. They feel compelled to achieve realization and self-liberation, and the prospect of failure frightens them, while any encouraging experience fills them with elation. This amounts to spiritual ambition, which is inevitably associated with the ridiculous idea of having to become a 'Superman', all of which becomes a further demand and source of distress.

Predictably and disastrously, this mistake leads to the need to teach others. Our attitude towards other people reflects our attitude to ourselves. If I believe I must obtain salvation for myself, I cannot help feeling that I must help other people do the same. If the relative truth which I have grasped is associated with an obligation to express it through the way I live – and I may or may not be conscious of the idolatry which gives rise to this sense of obligation – I am forced to the conclusion that I have a duty to communicate my truth to everyone else. In its extreme form, this leads to the Inquisition and the Dragonnades;* its milder expression can be seen in the innumerable churches of all sizes which have worked throughout history to influence the minds of people without anyone inviting them to do so.

This whole mistaken approach is completely refuted in Zen, and nowhere else, as far as I am aware. Zen tells us that we are free right here and now, that there are no chains binding us; there is only the illusion of chains. We will enjoy freedom the moment we stop believing we have to free ourselves, the moment we throw off the dreadful burden of salvation as a duty. Zen shows the emptiness of belief in a personal God, and its undesirable consequences. It says, *'Don't put another head on top of the one you already have*; and *'Do not seek the truth; just stop thinking opinions have any value.'*

Some people are bound to ask why one should bother to obtain satori. Such a question implies the ridiculous supposition that the struggle to achieve satori can only be driven by some compelling sense of duty. Satori represents the ending of the anguish at the centre of my whole psychic life, the distress from which all my experiences of happiness provide no more than a brief respite. Does it make any sense to ask me why I should strive to obtain such a complete and final relief? My answer, if the questioner persisted, would be: 'Because it will make my life so much pleasanter.' And, with right understanding, the possibility that death could come today or tomorrow and interrupt my efforts prematurely does not frighten me: the problem of my suffering

---

* A phase in the persecution of Protestants in France in the 1680s.

ceases with me, so why should I worry about not being able to solve it?

Right understanding neither forbids nor obliges one to teach others; forbidding teaching would be as misguided as making it obligatory. But whoever fully understands that realization is not a duty will confine themselves to replying only if questioned. If they do take the initiative in speaking, they will simply mention certain ideas discreetly, and they will not experience any *need* to be understood. It is like someone with good food to spare who leaves the door open: if a passer-by sees the food and comes in to eat it, that is good; someone else seeing it may choose not to come in, and that is just as good. Emotions, cravings and fears have no place in right understanding.

# CHAPTER FOUR

# *Zen Existentialism*

Someone says: 'My life is dull and monotonous; it's not *living*; at most it's simply *existing*.' Everyone understands what this means, which shows that we are all aware of this distinction; and everyone feels that 'living' is superior to 'existing'. This opinion is generally held so clearly and categorically that people come to believe that 'existing' is nothing, and 'living' is everything. The distinction between them can disappear altogether, so that the two terms are used interchangeably. 'Life' seems so uniquely important that it now incorporates 'existence', which has been wholly divested of any independent significance.

Among the whole complex mass of phenomena that comprise an individual, which are the ones that belong to 'living' and which to 'existing'? The answer lies in the difference between the animal and plant kingdoms. Animals and plants are not completely different organisms; animals have everything that plants have (the vegetative* aspect of life), and something more (the way they relate to their environment). Despite their differences, similar phenomena occur inside plants and animals, fundamental processes such as the circulation of sap or blood, respiration, birth and death of cells, and anabolism and catabolism. But plants are fixed to the ground, while animals are mobile and can carry out a whole range of activities, which can be summarized by the word 'agency'.

Yet, when people express a marked preference for 'living' as opposed to 'existing', they are not drawing a distinction between their vegetative phenomena and their actions. What they are contrasting lies within the realm of agency: there are actions, such as eating, resting, and sex in response to straightforward animal lust, which fulfil biological needs and affirm us (in the sense that they maintain the process which creates us) as organisms similar in all respects to other animals. This is affirmation of our life as seen from the universe's perspective, affirmation of us as cogs in the cosmic machine, and of us to the extent that we are

---

* See the Glossary.

'universal'. But these activities are not the only ones we engage in: every day we do other things which are not dictated by our biological needs, and may even be harmful to them. Their purpose is to make us appear different from everyone else, in other words to affirm us as someone distinct and special.

My present focus is the line which separates these two types of activity.

My egotistical condition, which implies a fiction of personal divinity, leads me to devalue the vegetative aspect of life and everything I have to do for it, all of which I disparage as mere existing. I only find meaning in actions which distinguish me and set me apart: this constitutes 'living' as far as I am concerned, and this is what I value. The universal in me means nothing to me: what matters to me is me as an individual. As far as my fiction of personal divinity is concerned, it would be ridiculous to base the meaning of my life on vegetative phenomena and the activities which sustain them, while it makes perfect sense to find meaning in activities which affirm me as separate and distinct. This view is deeply rooted in the human psyche.

*Looked at objectively, this belief is clearly irrational.* It contains the implicit assumption that my specific organism is the centre of the cosmos (only the central point of a hollow sphere can be unique, every other point being at the same distance from the centre as an indefinite number of other points). But only the First Cause of the Cosmos is its centre; and my particular organism is manifestly not its First Cause. It is one link in an immense cosmic chain of cause and effect: I can only see its real meaning if I place it in its real context, with all its real connections to everything else. This means looking at it from the point of view of the Universe, as universal man, not as individual man; as someone like everyone else, and not as someone different from everyone else.

People do what they have to in order to 'exist', but only because this is what makes 'living' possible; they sleep and they eat, but only because they could not otherwise succeed in their egotistical affirmation of themselves as separate and distinct. They get through the common, everyday things so that they can do things which make them special; this is 'existing' in order to 'live'. To subordinate existing to living like this is to go against the real order of things, because this is basing reality on illusion. The ordinary egotistical person is always in a state of unstable equilibrium, like an upside-down pyramid.

The following remarkable little parable is one of many to be found in the Zen literature: '*A man was standing on a hill. Three travellers passing in the distance noticed him and argued about him. One said: 'He must have lost his favourite animal.' Another said: 'No, he must be looking for his friend.' The third said: 'He's just up there enjoying the cool air.' The three travellers could not agree and went on arguing until they reached the top of the hill. One of them asked the man: 'My friend, I suppose you are standing on this hill because you have lost your favourite animal?' 'No, sir, I have not lost it.' The other asked him: 'You have lost your friend, then?' 'No, sir, I haven't lost my friend either.' The third asked: 'Aren't you here to enjoy the cool air?' 'No, sir.' 'Since you answer all our questions with "No", please tell us why you are here?' The man on the hill answered: 'I am just here.'*

The ordinary person reading this will tend to think that 'just being here' is meaningless. 'The man on the hill is a fool; he's not *doing* anything there.' (In other words, he is not looking for egotistical affirmation there. I am reminded of Rimbaud's* ironic phrase: *'L'action, ce cher point du monde!'*)

'Exist' comes from the Latin *ex(s)istere*, 'to stand forth, emerge, be visible or manifest', based on *ex-* plus *sistere*, 'to take up a position.'† It suggests movement out of, separation from the Principle which is immanent in, and transcends everything in, existence. Existing is manifestation emerging (as a centrifugal impulse) from Original Being. It is dualistic, the *'sistere'* component being positive and the *'ex'* negative. People feel there is both good and bad in existing: that there is something in it which they possess and something which they lack. So within the existential condition there is an implicit tendency to self-completion, to make good the lack, and to neutralize the *'ex'*, by developing consciousness of the Principle from which human existence emerges.

But human intellectual development proceeds in a way which makes it possible to satisfy the need for egotistical affirmation with an illusory substitute, which is always temporary, before it can experience the plenitude of *'sistere'*: in other words, before it is able to recognize that, as an emanation of the Principle, its filial relationship to it is one which endows it with the same nature and limitless attributes. Fascination with egotistical affirmation has already crystallized strongly in the mind by the time intellectual development has reached a stage where awareness of identity with the Principle becomes a possibility. Because affirmation is a false substitute for *'sistere'* it cannot neutralize the *'ex'*. So the individual who focuses on affirmation and ignores the *'ex'*, which represents the constraints of temporality, is caught in a destructive dualism, torn between the *'ex'*, which is behind and cannot be abolished,

---

* Arthur Rimbaud (1854–1891). French poet whose work had a profound effect on modern poetry.
† Cf. *Oxford Dictionary of English Etymology*.

and an illusory *'sistere'* which seems to be in front in the many guises of egotistical affirmation, and is forever unattainable.

If we were to accept the relative reality that existence offers, we would be aware of our identity with the Principle, from which we emerge. But egotistical man does not accept it. His mind scorns and rejects existence and grasps at the illusory egotistical affirmation provided by activity as a distinct and separate entity. The mind acts the part of the Principle, which it has usurped in a self-aggrandizing way, in relation to this mirage emanating from itself. Thus man seeks inner peace in a way which makes it impossible to find.

Everything must be re-examined if we are to find inner peace. We have to acknowledge the nothingness of all our opinions and all our value judgements, and so free ourselves completely from our fascination with egotistical affirmation which is impelling us away from the centre. We must come to understand the nothingness of egotistical 'living' and the reality of universal 'existing'. We must renounce every false heaven and return to earth, to live consciously, to live in the world (Rimbaud: *'Nous ne sommes pas au monde'*). Reconciled to *'ex'*, we can then fully enjoy the *'sistere'*. To accept that our organism is a mere phenomenon, a fleeting emanation from the original source, something of no particular interest, whose individual destiny is quite insignificant, this is to *be* the originating source of everything.

It can be helpful to look at the human organism and its anatomy and physiology as a whole, and ask what purpose its various components serve. Digestion and respiration and their associated organs supply the blood with nutrient material. The circulation delivers nutrition-rich blood throughout the organism, and maintains bones, joints and muscles; the bones and joints provide essential scaffolding for muscle action. The central nervous system initiates and controls muscle contraction; it is responsible for instigating and executing movements. The autonomic nervous system is responsible for the smooth functioning of the organs on which the voluntary musculature depends for its maintenance. The endocrine system is linked to the autonomic nervous system and has the same harmonizing purpose. *In short, everything except the genital apparatus is directed towards the muscles and their movements; 'existing' is directed towards living, towards action; the human machine seems designed for action.*

But what purpose do this machine's activities serve? We have seen that ordinary people only consider action useful and worthwhile if it supports and affirms their ego. But what seems useful from a solely individual viewpoint appears illusory when viewed from a universal perspective: one cannot imagine that the human machine exists simply so that Mr So-and-So can affirm himself as Mr So-and-So as opposed to Mr Somebody Else. So, if we exclude the possibility of human activity having a purely egotistical purpose, what purpose is served by the activity of this machine designed for action, the human organism?

A whole range of activities play an obvious part in maintaining the machine: obtaining food, shelter, and clothing for itself or for other machines like itself. Other activities, which distinguish the human from the non-human animal, are just as useful but less obviously so: scientific discoveries, artistic creations, and the intellectual search for truth, in other words, the pursuit of the good, the beautiful and the true. The good and the beautiful contribute by tending to improve the conditions of existence; the true also does this by easing human anxieties and so promoting peace and harmony during the human organism's existence.

*Viewed objectively, then, the machine acts in a way that tends to maintain its existence, and existence itself seems to be the only purpose of existing.* Does this come to the same thing as saying that existence has no purpose? (Here I will ignore the possibility of there being any cosmic usefulness in human existence. If there were, it would be quite beyond ordinary human understanding and experience). Reproduction has been left out of the discussion, but does not conflict with what I am saying, since its purpose is to maintain the existence of humankind as a species.

In so far as action is used to affirm me in my egotistical identity as separate and distinct, it is illusory. If I eliminate that aspect, I see that my activity, for which my whole action-oriented organism seems expressly designed, has for its sole purpose the organism's existence. Its only purpose is to avert death, the cessation of existence. 'Living', which was so highly esteemed, turns out to be the servant of its poor relation, 'existing'. Action issues from existence and serves it, so existence is the principle and ultimate source of action and therefore infinitely superior to it (every principle being immeasurably superior to its manifestation).

Looked at like this, existence, as the cause of all my activity, of all my phenomena, is none other than the First Cause of the microcosm which is my organism. It is also the First Cause of the universal macrocosm, in other words it is the Absolute Principle and Origin. The *apparent* senselessness of existence willing itself and seeming to have no other purpose is the *apparent* senselessness which the Absolute Principle presents to discursive intelligence, which originates from it and, since it originates from it, cannot apprehend or imagine it.

If I think of my existence in this way as the first cause of my organism, I see that it transcends all my phenomena and is wholly independent of my organism's life or death. It is mine, my own personal existence until I die (immanence of the Principle), though it does not belong to the separate entity me, but only to the universal me, a link in a chain, identical to every other link. In other words, my existence is not touched by the death of my organism (transcendence of the Principle).

The explanation just given enables us to understand that the fear of death, which is present in ordinary people and forms the centre of their whole psychology, is related to the irrational way in which existence is discounted. Egotistical individuals tremble at the prospect of relinquishing existence, which seems paradoxical at first when one considers how little they value it in comparison with 'doing' and 'living'. We have seen that the Absolute Principle is present in 'existing': it is the All to which mankind can only respond absolutely – no half measures are possible. If it is ignored, its value can only be zero; acknowledged, it is infinity. When anonymous existence is felt to be valueless, the individual is not conscious of sharing in the nature of the Principle, and is consciously nothing, and therefore unable to cope with the subtraction death represents (it seems to be a negative infinity). If, on the contrary, anonymous existence is seen to be of infinite value, then the individual shares fully in the nature of the Principle, and is conscious of being infinite. Death is a subtraction which takes nothing away.

It is also clear that the questions about an after-life over which egotistical individuals agonize are illusory. Questions of this kind are based on a misleading belief in the reality of individual 'living' and on ignorance of universal 'existing'.

Some so-called existentialist philosophies run into difficulties, because among other things, they confuse 'existing' and 'living'. This confusion leads to unfortunate consequences: 'existing' is only conceived in phenomenal terms and any idea of the First Cause is dispensed with, so the fact that existence intends itself results in a real, as opposed to apparent, categorical absurdity (like the idea of a physical eye which can see itself); their concept of living entails the same senselessness. Despite this, the idea of living is fundamental to these philosophies; action, 'doing', 'engagement', all become dogmatic imperatives. Once the Principle is no longer involved, a fragmented and destructive dualism of this kind is inevitable.

Let us go back to the distinction I drew between 'existing' and 'living', and the line which separates them inside the domain of action. I have indicated that this line separates the actions serving my vital needs and those serving egotistical affirmation. If I examine all this in relation to my consciousness, my first impression is that 'existing' consists of an unconscious part, comprising vegetative phenomena, and a conscious part, comprising the actions which serve my vital needs. But if I go further into it, I can see that these actions are just as unconscious as the vital phenomena, since consciousness attaches no value to their objectives. I cannot claim that I am consciously maintaining my existence, because I am entirely unconscious of its reality. Let me quote a dialogue from the Zen literature:

> MONK: *'Is there a special way of working in the Tao?'*
> MASTER: *'Yes, there is.'*
> MONK: *'What is it?'*
> MASTER: *'When you are hungry, eat; when you are tired, sleep.'*
> Monk: *'That is what everyone does; so is their way the same as yours?'*
> MASTER: *'It is not the same.'*
> MONK: *'Why not?'*
> MASTER: *'When they eat, they do not simply eat, their minds are busy with all kinds of imagination; when they sleep, they do not simply sleep, they give free rein to a thousand idle thoughts. That is why their way is not my way.'*

Ordinary people are only conscious of images; so it is not surprising that they are not conscious of existing, which is real and has three dimensions. To summarize, I am unconscious of that aspect of myself which is real and what I am conscious of in myself is illusory.

To obtain satori is nothing other than to become conscious of the 'existing' which is at present unconscious within me. It is becoming conscious of the unique and originating Reality of this universal vegetative life, which is the Absolute Principle manifesting in my person (it is in this respect that I am both self and infinitely more than self; immanence and transcendence). This is what Zen calls 'seeing into one's own nature'. Hence the insistence with which Zen comes back to how we meet our vital needs; when the pupil enquires about the way of Wisdom, the master replies: 'When we are hungry, we eat; when we are tired, we lie down.' This shocks the conceited egotist who dreams of spiritual feats and an ecstatic personal relationship with a personal God created in his own image.

It would be a mistake to think that acknowledging the full value of vegetative life and the behaviour sustaining it must require some kind of concrete inner effort at the feeling level. The Zen master is too intelligent to advise ordinary people to use auto-suggestion to create the belief that they are finally in contact with Absolute Reality when they are satisfying their hunger. This would simply replace their previous day-dreams with a theoretical image of cosmic participation which would change nothing at all. It is not a question of re-establishing the value of vegetative life: what is necessary is that at some point there should be unmediated perception of this life's infinite value *as a result of egotistical life having undergone a complete loss of value.* Correct inner work does not consist of 'doing' something, it is an 'undoing' something, undoing all the illusory egotistical beliefs which keep the 'third eye' tightly shut.

In fact everything I have said so far about the unconscious nature of the vegetative aspect of life was only an approximation. It is more accurate to speak of 'unconscious awareness' or 'indirect or mediated awareness'; and to think of satori not as an awareness arising *ex nihilo*, but rather as the metamorphosis of a mediated into an immediate awareness. By indirect awareness I mean that I am getting information indirectly about reality at the vegetative level from my direct perception of the shifting threats to the phenomena of vegetative life. When I feel hungry, this is a direct perception of the threat which starvation poses to my vegetative existence. If I did not have some kind of awareness at this level, I would not be aware that its manifestation in the domain of phenomena was under attack. In other words, hunger provides me with an indirect awareness of this vegetative existence. The same is true when my ego is affirmed or denied: the associated feelings of joy or sadness correspond to variations in the intensity of the continuous threat which the outside world presents to my vegetative existence as a totality. So these too are moments when I become indirectly aware of its existence.

To summarize, all positive and negative fluctuations in my affective life derive ultimately from the pure and perfect joy existing at the level of vegetative existence. This is not experienced directly; it is only sensed indirectly as fluctuations in the security of vegetative life.

Let me emphasize that perceiving the perfect joy of vegetative existence would not bring about a fear of death, but would have the opposite effect of neutralizing it once and for all.

The fear of death presupposes some representation of death in the imagination; but the effect of perceiving three-dimensional existential reality in the present instant would be to annihilate all imaginings about past or future which lack present reality. After satori there is perfect joy in existence as it is, right up to the very last moment when the mind ceases to function and all human joy and sorrow come to an end.

I recognize that I am not directly conscious of my existence, that is to say of myself existing, but only of how my existence varies at the phenomenal level; and that my present belief in the absolute reality of these variations prevents me being aware of what *is* beneath these variations (which does not vary: this is noumenal existence, the fundamental source and origin of my phenomenal existence). I have to understand that changing phenomena such as joy or sadness, or life or death, are perfectly equivalent from the perspective of what *is* beneath these variations. This understanding must penetrate into the very centre of my being if I am finally to become aware of what *is* beneath the variations, by which I mean the noumenon of my existence, my Reality.

Zen says that we are enslaved by our desire to exist. The human intellect develops in such a way that our earliest perceptions are not perceptions of our existence; they are of biased and incomplete images. These indicate that existential consciousness is completely absent at this stage; but their effect is to implant a desire for this consciousness in the psyche. It is part of the human condition that we have to pass through the desire to exist in order to reach the existential consciousness which will abolish it, and it is an obstacle which can only be destroyed if the failure of every attempt to satisfy this desire is correctly interpreted and understood.

So many people are terrified of making a mess of their lives! Yet in reality there is nothing to make a success of, and nothing to make a mess of. But a measure of worldly fulfilment is necessary in a negative way for satori. Until we have been able to do our best to satisfy our desire to exist, we cannot transcend it. This is the sense in which real existing can only be reached through illusory living. Existing precedes living in reality, in the sense that the Principle must precede its manifestation; but, within the framework of durational time, the individual must journey through consciousness of 'living' before attaining consciousness of 'existing', which is identical during the life of the human organism to consciousness of 'being'.

# CHAPTER FIVE

# *The Mechanisms of Distress*

When we observe ourselves honestly and impartially, we discover that we are not consciously and intentionally creating our own thoughts or feelings: they are simply phenomena which happen to us. It is easier to observe this with feelings than with thoughts; yet if I look carefully within myself, I realize that my thoughts are also just happening to me. I can choose what topic to think about, but I cannot choose the thoughts themselves, and have to take them as they come.

Since I do not create my thoughts or feelings intentionally, I am forced to acknowledge that I cannot be the intentional author of what I do, in other words that I cannot do anything freely.

However, these negative observations concerning real will and consciousness lead on to the idea that these faculties might possibly emerge in us, and to the question of how this might be brought about. This question is of particular concern because I sense a fundamental distress within me which is connected with this lack of self-mastery. My mental sufferings bear direct witness to this distress, and the moments of respite which my joys provide are short-lived.

My investigations into methods of self-liberation show that the teachings which consider liberation or 'realization' possible during one's lifetime fall into two groups.

Most of these teachings are based on the following mistaken theory: real consciousness and will are *lacking* in ordinary people, and they are not present at birth. They have to be acquired and developed by special inner work. It is a long, difficult work which results in a *progressive evolution*, whereby will and consciousness are developed gradually. By degrees a process of self-transcendence takes place, and students work slowly up through the stages of development, gaining ever higher forms of consciousness which gradually bring them closer to the highest level of consciousness (objective, cosmic, or absolute consciousness).

Zen doctrine is radically opposed to this, and denies that real consciousness and will are absent. It teaches that we lack nothing and have within us all we need; and that, from the beginning of time, we are Buddha nature. We are provided with everything that we need for our temporal machine to be controlled directly by the Absolute Principle, in other words our own Creative Principle, so that we may be free. We are like machines which have all the components needed for them to work perfectly. But we will see that there is an innate aspect of human development which results in a discontinuity, a non-union, which separates its workings into two components, soma and psyche. Unless these are united, we do not enjoy the privileges of absolute essence, though it is already fully ours. It is no good objecting that something must be missing and that this explains the non-union: the machine is complete, perfect down to the smallest detail, no bit missing which has to be manufactured and fitted to make it work properly. All that is needed is for the two separate components to be brought together.

A chemical analogy would be when one has all the ingredients necessary for a particular reaction, but before it can take place they have to be brought into contact with one another. Or there is another analogy which Zen provides: there is a lump of ice inside us which has all the properties of water, but unless heat melts it these properties remain latent.

This formulation implies that realization is instantaneous, and comes as a blinding flash. Either there is no union between the two parts and our divine essence is inaccessible; or direct contact is restored and, given that there is absolutely nothing lacking, there is then nothing to stop us entering instantaneously into full possession of our divine essence. *The inner work which brings this direct contact into being is difficult, long and gradual; but it is the preparation for deliverance which is gradual, not deliverance itself.* The effect of preparation is to bring freedom closer in time, but not even the minutest hint of freedom can be enjoyed before that instant when it is fully achieved. Until then, all this work achieves is some reduction in the suffering which not being free causes. It is like when a prisoner is laboriously filing away at the bars of his window: his work is gradually bringing him closer and closer in time to his escape, but until it is completed he is still a prisoner in all respects. He does not become free bit by bit: for a period of time he is not free at all, and then he becomes completely free at the point when the bars give way. The only progressive benefit he gets from his efforts is that his distress at being a prisoner is alleviated; he is just as much a prisoner from one day to the next, but he suffers less because his instantaneous deliverance is getting closer in time.

There is another way of illustrating this, which Jesus used when he spoke with Nicodemus. Jesus said a man had to die in order to be born again. A special form of inner work results in the 'old' man drawing closer to death gradually, but this death and the re-birth into another state could only be two aspects of a single, instantaneous, inner event. The old man may be more or less in the throes of death, but he cannot be more or less dead; the 'new' man is either born or not yet born, but he cannot be more or less born. *Zen calls this unique, instantaneous inner event 'satori', or 'the opening of the third eye', and maintains that it happens abruptly.*

> *'At a stroke I have completely crushed the cave of phantoms.'*
>
> *'A taut thread, a light touch, and an explosion shakes the earth to its foundations; everything hidden in the spirit explodes like a volcanic eruption or bursts forth like a flash of lightning.'*

Zen calls this 'going back home'. *'You have found yourself now; right from the very beginning nothing has been hidden from you; you yourself closed your eyes to reality.'*

The fundamental divergence between the two approaches, which are referred to in the East as the 'progressive' and the 'abrupt' or 'sudden' methods, has major implications for the theory and practice of inner work towards liberation.

Let us now take a detailed look at how we can apply Zen teaching in general to the ordinary human condition, this inner lack of union I have been discussing, and all the consequences this has for how we function.

First, though, I need to outline briefly what it means for someone to be 'realized' and 'perfected', in full enjoyment of their divine essence. As psychosomatic organisms, such people are composed of a soma, or animal machine, and a psyche, but in their case the latter is pure thought, or Independent Intelligence. It functions independently of any influence deriving from the animal machine, so its activity is not determined by the machine, but by the superior influence of Absolute Truth. So their psyche can also be called Divine Reason or Cosmic Intelligence. A force which proceeds from this Intelligence and penetrates the animal machine unites the two components in a tripartite synthesis linked to the Absolute Principle and sharing in its essence. A substance within the animal machine combines with another in Intelligence to provide the Absolute Substance of the whole 'realized' person.

The substance within the animal machine derives from Nature, which created the machine, and I will refer to it as 'negative pro-divine substance'. The substance within Independent Intelligence originates in 'supernatural' Truth and will be referred to as 'positive pro-divine substance'. The force entering the machine from Independent Intelligence can be thought of as a correct and appropriate form of love for oneself: technically speaking, it is the hypostasis,* a neutralizing or conciliating force which makes it possible for the two pro-divine substances to combine and for the Divine or Absolute Substance to appear. Another way of looking at this is to think of the positive and negative pro-divine substances as masculine and feminine, as the sperm and ovum of being. Their union takes place when a force from Independent Intelligence penetrates the machine in a kind of inner coitus, an act of love which gives birth to the 'new man'.

We will now look at normal human development, and see how it relates to realization.

## A. The Earliest Stages of Existence in the Ordinary Human Being

Independent Intelligence is still not functioning, so the positive pro-divine substance has not appeared yet. The machine exists, but it is in a state of incomplete development; the brain, and the mind which is dependent on it, are under construction, but the process is still unfinished. The negative pro-divine substance is not present either, because the animal machine must be completed fully before it can be produced. Because its mind has not reached a sufficient level of development, the child is unaware of the distinction between self and not-self, and remains immersed in the external world without awareness of its own boundaries.

## B. When the Machine is Complete, the Pro-Divine Negative Substance Appears

Development of the animal brain is completed during the second year of life. The machine is fully assembled and the pro-divine negative substance is now present. The mind has completed its development as an animal mind capable of concrete perceptions, in other words it has reached the level of the non-human animal. However Independent Intelligence, the capacity for functioning under the influence of

---

* A theological term applied to the three distinct aspects of the Holy Trinity. Benoit uses it here by analogy with the theological concept of Christ integrating (conciliating) the human and the divine.

Absolute Truth, is still not present. As yet there is no positive pro-divine substance. Negative pro-divine substance, as in the non-human animal, is present on its own.

The development of the animal mind makes concrete awareness of the distinction between self and not-self possible. This new awareness constitutes an unavoidably traumatic event. Before this stage, the child lived with the implicit, unconscious conviction that the driving principle of its own existence was the driving principle of the universe: nothing existed independently of him and there was no threat to his own existence. Then suddenly the child becomes aware through distressing encounters with 'the world as obstacle' that he does not bring the universe into being and that there are things which exist independently of him. The conscious fear of death appears at this stage, fear of the danger to self represented by not-self. This sets off a war in the psyche between self and not-self at the level of affect; the child wants to exist and wants to destroy anything outside himself which is not favourable to his own existence. He expresses this when he wants to do things on his own and refuses help. He affirms himself by saying no.

Self must be understood to comprise everything favourable to the individual's existence; not-self includes whatever threatens that existence, and also anything which is not obviously favourable and might therefore conceal a potential threat. At the affective level the situation is now straightforward: there are two opposing camps, two factions separated by a barrier, locked in a life or death struggle. When the child's mother is good, she is part of the self, and a powerful defence against death, and an ally behind which the child feels secure; when she is bad ('I don't love you any more; you're not my little boy any more'), she becomes part of the not-self, the powerful defences collapse, and the child screams, terrified of death (although it obviously has no clear idea yet of what death is).

In this straightforward situation where there is a duel to death with not-self, the subject's involvement is entirely biased and partial. Without Independent Intelligence there cannot be a vestige of impartiality, and never any question of 'putting oneself in the other person's shoes'; strategic and practical considerations are the only constraints on attack and defence. The child's attitude towards the not-self is an unqualified 'No!' whose explicitness and forcefulness will depend on the nature of the conflict. The causes underlying the child's behaviour are wholly irrational and affective.

## C. The Emergence of Independent Intelligence and the Pro-Divine Positive

Independent Intelligence appears, in humans only, with the 'age of reason', when the mind becomes capable of abstract, general, and objective perceptions. It becomes possible to put oneself in someone else's place and to conceive of a Good which is not necessarily identical with whatever affirms self over not-self; and value can be attached to events which are irrelevant to one's struggle against not-self. The instinctive tendency to safeguard the growth of one's own organism is now joined by an emerging preference for constructive activity in general, an inclination to participate in the constructive aspect of the cosmos. The child can now think in general terms of the Good, the True and the Beautiful, and feel drawn towards them.

However, by the time Independent Intelligence arrives, all the individual's powerful affective mechanisms have already been established on the basis of a wholly biased and partial view of his or her place in the universe. The abstract part develops very late in humans, at a time when the animal component is already firmly organized around an individualistic and biased approach to life. The mind of Spirit appears much later than animal mind, which is fundamentally opposed to it: the former affirms the Whole, where the one and the many are reconciled, while the latter can only affirm the one by denying the many which are outside the one.

Animal mind is unable to rise up to the pure mind of Spirit. Pure mind should reach down towards it, but instead yearns for objectivity and turns away from the animal's biased and partial preoccupations, drawn towards pure ideas such as Eros, and the love of God, which are its own creation. So a gulf separates the two parts, and they will co-exist like this, side by side, without uniting. As long as they fail to unite, absolute consciousness will remain unattainable. While the abstract part is cut off from the animal part, it can only conceive of forms without substance, images which lack a dimension. It conceives of an ideal, universal image, a 'divine' image, incorporating the good, the true, and the beautiful. In the absence of universal consciousness, this image is projected onto the temporal image which the subject forms of himself, and the result is an ideal, narcissistic self-image, or 'ego'.

Since the two parts are unable to unite naturally, the individual does not participate in the essence of the Absolute Principle, and begins to worship this unreal image, the ego. Without the abstract part loving the animal part appropriately, the individual only has a poor substitute, self-love, which is the love of the abstract part for an ideal self image.

The effect of the non-conciliated duality of the two parts is that the individual contains and is impelled by two different dynamic systems which interact in various ways, sometimes re-enforcing, sometimes opposing one another.

**Type 1.** *Independent Intelligence is weak. Both systems are mutually supportive. The politics of prestige.*

These dualistic types lack inner unity but there is a need for it within them which derives from their absolute essence. They dupe themselves, inwardly putting on an act to convince themselves that inner union is already theirs. To achieve this, they cheat by modifying their ideas to bring them into harmony with their animal or their abstract parts.

This first type can be seen among people whose Independent Intelligence is weak. Their perception of the abstract and general is not strong enough to prevent the concrete and particular appearing more real. They live in the concrete world. From a temporal perspective, this means that they live in *duration* and not in the eternal. Because duration is their frame of reference, they want self to win out over not-self *in the final reckoning*; in other words, they can accept setbacks as they occur without suffering intolerable damage to their egotistical image of themselves as 'divine'. They look for temporal success, and seek self-affirmation through their achievements in the temporal realm. The abstract and animal aspects of their make-up pull in the same direction, with the former intensifying the effect of the latter. Such people are not torn apart by internal conflict; they rationalize their preferences; they cheat by bringing their ideal principles into line with their will for power, or, more accurately, they present their practical problems to themselves in such a way that reason gives its blessing to the underlying impulse.

**Type 2.** *Strong independent intelligence. Conflict between the two systems. Fear of failure. Distress.*

People whose abstract side is strongly developed are intellectually more in touch with the abstract and general than with the concrete and particular. In their quest to overcome not-self, individual successes count for less than the idea of success in general. They are not thinking within the framework of duration, but of eternity; and because in fact they live in duration, and eternity and duration intersect in the *instant*, they live in the instant. They want it all, and they want it immediately: they are not interested in defeating not-self *eventually; victory must be in the instant.* Their demand is success within the temporal framework, in the eternal instant.

But this kind of complete victory in the eternal instant over some aspect of not-self is clearly impossible; it is impossible to do anything in time which does not involve duration. They are at risk of experiencing a sense of negation in the very centre of their being, and they have to find a way of avoiding this: so they reason things through and persuade themselves that, in this particular instance, they should relinquish their claim to omnipotence ('these particular grapes happen to be sour'). They adapt themselves to the limitations imposed by their temporal existence, and claim in the meanwhile that they have chosen freely to accept them. But they do not, and cannot, really accept them: *they merely resign themselves* to them, which is to say that they act as though they accepted them, but without doing so.

The distinction between acceptance and resignation is of fundamental importance. To really accept a situation is to think and feel with all one's being that one would not change it even if one could, that there would be no reason to do so. But when the inner state is one of unconciliated dualism, and reason and affect are disconnected, it is impossible to give wholehearted acceptance to the existence of the not-self by which one feels negated. All this type of person can do is simulate acceptance. In other words they opt for resignation, which contains *de facto* acceptance and theoretical rejection. These two elements are not conciliated, and nor can they be, because they are in different compartments, and there is no way across the gap which separates them.

People like this manage to keep the necessary sense of inner unity by a defence mechanism which makes them blind to the fact that they hold a theory which rejects their temporal condition (this is a kind of mental scotoma). They persuade themselves that they do accept, and that they are philosophical and reasonable; they put on an act and the end result is that they delude themselves. In fact their reasonable intentions are rational and in accord with the real order of things in the cosmos. But these are people who *are wrong to be right*, because they are right in a way which is premature – it is a sham based on two lies: they cheat when they withdraw an instinctual demand, which then goes on growing underground in its original direction, and they cheat when they claim that they do so *because it is reasonable,* when the real reason is they do not want the experience of seeing themselves negated by not-self. This is to behave like an angel without being one.

Where the animal part said 'no', the abstract part says 'yes'. But this is no absolute 'Yes', it is only a relative 'yes'; not the 'Yes-noumenon', only a 'yes-phenomenon', which is just as illusory from the absolute perspective as the animal part's 'no'. The eventual attainment of Absolute Yes will come about through the union of relative 'no' and 'yes' in a tripartite synthesis.

Being unaware of all this, they are pleased with their 'yes' and see it as evidence that they have mastered their animal part, and themselves, when this is simply not the case. They imagine that saying this kind of 'yes' more and more is a good idea, and think that they are adapting to reality when their adaptation is just a form of play-acting. They split themselves into two personalities: there is the 'yes' personality, the 'angel', which is the one they very much prefer and try to be conscious of as much as they can. This is the aspect they call their *real self*. In the meantime, the 'no' personality, the 'beast', is spurned and repressed. What awareness they might have of it is kept as vague as possible; when it cannot be ignored, they say that *it is not them*, and 'I don't know *what* came over me; *it* was stronger than *me*.'

The 'no' personality had the place to itself at the very beginning when the little child was first becoming aware of the opposition between self and not-self, and was denying not-self with its whole being. It gradually loses ground thereafter as adaptive mechanisms build up and consolidate. It is repressed more and more deeply, buried beneath densely proliferating layers of adaptive mechanisms: it is suffocated slowly and systematically. So the voice which was driven to rebel against the temporal state is gradually gagged and reduced to silence. Sham reasonableness stifles spontaneity.

With people in whom the instinctual drives are weak, this stifling of the 'no' personality can sometimes lead to what might be considered a 'positive' outcome. Although the 'animal' in them has not really been killed, and cannot be finished off as long as they are still alive, it is *just as though it were dead;* and the end-product is someone who is called 'civilized' and 'adapted'. How can this come about? How can people come to believe that they accept their temporal state, when the reality is that the condition of being finite and mortal is emotionally unacceptable? How can life be lived on this basis? The answer lies in the workings of the imagination, and the mind's ability to re-fashion a subjective world in which the individual is experienced as the sole driving principle. They would never resign themselves to not being the unique principle driving the real universe were it not for the consolation they derive from their ability to create their own individual universe by their own efforts.

Next we will consider the personality type where the strength of the instinctual forces overwhelms the adaptive mechanisms, which are then unable to stifle the 'no', the animal. There is a dramatic or tragic quality to the lives of these people which makes this type particularly interesting. There is a period during which the mechanisms work effectively; reason and persuasion exercise powerful control, and the imagination, like a kind of stabilizing gyroscope, spins away rapidly and efficiently. A particularly clever adaptive mechanism is often used, where the 'divine image' is projected onto the image of some aspect of the outer world, which is then worshipped like an idol. Examples of this would be when another person, or a 'just cause', or a personalized God, become objects of adoration. This mechanism apparently resolves the self versus not-self dualism, and everything is fine as long as it lasts.

But problems arise when the adaptive mechanisms lose their effectiveness, and the idolizing process breaks down or fails to get established. A point is reached where the animal is unable to carry on suppressing its wish to overcome not-self, and the fox who said the grapes were too sour is starving, and can hear his 'animal' growling angrily in the depths of his being.

This is the moment when distress and the so-called *fear of failure* appear. If we take a closer look at what is occurring within the individual when this happens, it will become clear that the expression 'fear of failure' is inexact. The phenomena under consideration originate in the abstract part of the individual. This part is intellectual, not affective, so strictly speaking it is incapable of fear. We have seen that the people we are studying want something impossible, which is to gain success of a temporal nature *in the eternal instant*. The only way they can avoid the sense of being negated by the world of concrete experience is to stop demanding the impossible, and this is what they do.

Their abstract part has no *fear* of concrete failure, but this is better understood as the result of a powerful pre-determined mechanism which prevents them imagining it, or thinking of it as a possibility; so the *idea is refused*. To achieve this refusal and denial of the possibility of failure, the fight against not-self has to be refused and denied, since it can only result in failure, given the total and instantaneous nature of the outcome demanded. So, because a complete and instantaneous victory cannot be guaranteed, the abstract part feigns ignorance of not-self's material existence and takes refuge in a world re-fashioned by its own imagination.

For some time, the animal part accepts what its loftier friend is doing; it has benefited from some of the advantages which giving up the duel between self and not-self has brought, such as the friendship and approval of others, which guarantee some support against not-self. But life gradually disappoints hopes of reward for having been kind and wise; misfortunes occur which are felt to be unfair; the animal part no longer believes in these chimeras, decides it has been duped for long enough, and is no longer willing to avoid battle for the sake of a pacifist attitude which brings nothing. It becomes deaf to promises of deferred benefits which never seem to materialize, and all it wants to do is wage war. In its new frame of mind, it considers that the abstract part has deserted and shown cowardice in the face of danger, and has collaborated outrageously with the enemy.

Someone in this situation can be compared to a besieged fortress where the soldiers, who can only feel and act, want to save their skins; while their leader, who can only think, dismisses all talk of fighting and orders them to lay down their arms. The army cannot *understand* this ridiculous order, but at the same time it cannot fight as it would like to without an order or at least some authorization from a higher level. It feels abandoned and this terrifies it. It experiences anguish. This is not the same as fear of an impending defeat: it is the fear of death, the ancient fear which resides in one's being from the very first encounter with not-self, and the same fear which the little child feels whenever it feels that it does not have its mother's support.

So distress is a phenomenon which has two important phases. It begins with the head, (reason, the 'angel') which pretends not to know that the dangerous not-self exists, and escapes into fantasy. In doing so, it is giving implicit support to not-self in everyday reality, which effectively moves it into the enemy camp. Next the animal part, the 'beast', is thrown into a panic, and its fear is not a relative fear in the face of some relative impending defeat, but total fear before the total danger of death which not-self represents to a self rendered powerless by the head's defection. So there are two distinct elements in what is incorrectly referred to as 'fear of failure': intellectual denial of failure, and affective anguish at the prospect of death, not failure.

The mistaken belief implicit in the so-called fear of failure explains how the vicious circle of anguish is locked into place. The people we are concerned with do not understand that they are trembling before death, and that this is happening because their head has abandoned their organism to escape the ubiquitous threat of not-self. They think that their distress is caused by some concrete negative aspect of the external world, which might be something quite insignificant, such as someone's poor opinion of them. They are responding to this particular aspect of the world as though it signified death and total destruction (since death is the real object of their fear), so it presents as a total negative Reality, a negative absolute, and hence as something indestructible. This vision of the world as absolute and indestructible object has the obvious effect of reinforcing the abstract part's refusal to acknowledge the struggle. So the vicious circle snaps shut.

One can understand why distress is the unavoidable fate of people who are in a sense the best and most richly endowed, whose abstract and animal parts are both strongly developed. In contrast to them, there are two types who will never experience this distress: on the one hand, people whose abstract component is weak will pass their lives in a comfortable state of egoism ('materialists'); on the other, people with a weak animal element will live in a comfortable state of altruistic renunciation ('spiritualists'). 'No' gains the upper hand in the first group, 'yes' in the second; in both types the balance has tipped in one or other direction and then remained fixed in that position. But when both parts are strong, the unfortunate person is fundamentally torn apart, pulled in both directions by unconciliated 'yes' and 'no'. They suffer, but they are at the same time being summoned to the total realization represented by the conciliation of 'yes' and 'no'; the others are comfortable but they are not called to this realization.

It is worth examining the connections between distress and imagination as this will shed light on the precise nature of 'moral' or psychological suffering.

Let us remind ourselves of the two psychological processes which operate in distress: the abstract part shies away from reality because, when it puts in its claim to omnipotence in the instant, it experiences the normal resistance of the exterior world as infinite, unshakable, and absolutely negating. It avoids the situation by fleeing into the realm of imagination. The mind avoids concrete defeat in this way, but though defeat may be postponed indefinitely, the image of defeat stays with the abstract part, which turns away from the practical struggle for existence. The animal part then suffers from the fear of death since the head's defection leaves it paralysed in the face of not-self's aggressiveness.

Imagination clearly plays a double role in distress. It has a protective role in relation to the grandiose, egotistical illusions of the abstract part, and a destructive role in relation to the animal part which it abandons and leaves to its fear of death. It protects the ego, which is illusory, and crushes the machine, which is real.

So it becomes clear on closer inspection that distress is illusory because its causes are illusory (and illusory causes cannot produce real effects). Its immediate cause is illusory, being the imaginative film, which is an artificial creation of the mind. Its efficient cause is just as illusory. The reason the mind turns away from the world as obstacle and takes refuge in the imagination is because it presented the world with an absolute demand; and it did this because of its illusory ignorance of its divine origin. We seek to deify ourselves in the temporal domain only because we are ignorant of our real divine essence. We are born of God, sharing fully in the nature of the Supreme Principle of the Universe, but we are born *amnesic*, forgetful of our origin, under the illusion that we *are* no more than the mortal and limited bodies which our senses perceive. Because of this amnesia, we suffer from the illusory feeling that God has abandoned us (though in reality we ourselves are God), and we busy ourselves in the temporal realm seeking support for our self-deification, without realizing that we would not be seeking Reality if we did not already share in its nature (one cannot lack something without any awareness of it).

So distress is an illusion because its causes are illusory. This can be demonstrated practically as well as theoretically: we can have a direct, intuitive *experience* of the illusory character of psychological distress. If, when I am distressed, I go somewhere quiet where I can relax, and then shift my attention from thoughts to feelings, and, ignoring all mental images, try to perceive this great mental suffering in me so that I can really appreciate it and finally discover what it is, I cannot do it. All I succeed in feeling is a kind of general fatigue, which is the trace left in my body by the anxiety and waste of vital energy generated by the fear of death. But I do not find the slightest hint of genuine suffering. By paying attention to feeling, I withdraw attention from my imaginative film: the more I do this, the less I feel. And I can then *experience* the unreality of distress.

Comparison with physical pain makes this even easier to understand. With a painful boil, the busier my imagination, the less I suffer physically; on the other hand, if my imagination is less active, with my attention shifting from thought to feeling, I become more vividly aware of my pain. This is because this is real, not imaginary, pain.

I am not saying that there is nothing to perceive when suffering is psychological: I am saying that there is an illusory perception, which is not the same thing. If someone sees a mirage in the desert, it is no use saying that they do not see it; they do see it, but it does not exist. In the same way, when I suffer psychologically I perceive something, but I do not perceive anything which really exists.

What is happening inside me when I suffer psychologically? We have seen that the fear of death is present in my feelings. It consumes vital energy and diminishes my innate reserves of energy. So my body and organism are harmed, but it is a different kind of harm from that associated with physical pain, which affects a part of the body and so can be said to affect the body viewed as an aggregate of parts. Psychological suffering, with depletion of energy at its source, harms the body as a totality; it results in a physical sensation which is not a localized pain, but a general malaise, characterized by fatigue, depression and a reduction in vitality. So psychological suffering is accompanied by a generalized depressive malaise at the physical level, while the psyche itself is afflicted by disagreeable and threatening images.

Psychological suffering results from this association between threatening mental images and a depressive somatic state. Because there is no exchange with the outside world, the organism's energy is being depleted without anything being gained in return, and this clearly represents a movement towards death. So the unpleasant images are imbued with a flavour of death and they are perceived as external aggressors whose aim is to kill me. This is the basis of the mirage whose victim I am. I perceive murderers heading towards me and am convinced that they really do exist; yet they are no more real than the water on the horizon in the desert. This is what Zen refers to as '*the cave of phantoms*'.

Let us remember that it is the head which initiates and sets the process going where distress is concerned. Undoubtedly biological depression with a physiological basis can predispose us to it (for example, we can feel gloomy all day after having slept badly the night before); but, even then, distress still depends on the mind: for, if I place my attention on my feelings, what I feel is fatigue but not distress.

Distressed people have their attention fixed on the screen where the imaginative film is playing, which they use to try and escape the real and dangerous not-self; and distress attacks *from behind*, coming from the direction in which they are not looking, towards which their back is turned. The inner movement I mentioned earlier, whereby I displace my attention from thinking onto feeling, is a complete about-turn through 180°, in which I turn away from the imaginative screen and look in the direction from where the distress was coming. I say 'was coming', because, during the moment in which this about-turn is completed, and the imaginative activity initiating the process is abolished, the distress comes to a halt, and all that remains of it is some generalized fatigue. The spectre has an illusory existence only for as long as I look away from the place where I think it exists; the moment I dare to look, I see that there is nothing there.

None of this leads to an immediate cure for distress. One of the mistakes we make is to try and find a remedy for our distress, which is a symptom, without bothering about its underlying cause. However, a theoretical understanding of the mechanisms which underlie distress can help us towards gaining that realization which is beyond time, which alone can save us from our illusory suffering. I cannot devote myself to the work of realization if I have not first fully understood the equally illusory character of the two affective poles, pleasure and suffering.

# CHAPTER SIX

# The Five Modes of Thought and the Psychological Conditions for Satori

Consciousness in ordinary people has five different modes or levels which can be ranked as follows:

*level 1*:  Deep, dreamless sleep. The mind contains no images. Non functioning mode.

*level 2*:  Sleep with dreams.

*level 3*:  Waking state with daydreams.

*level 4*:  Waking state with concrete thought reacting to the real external world.

*level 5*:  Waking state with pure intellectual thought.

Except at level 1, the mind contains an imaginative film whose characteristics vary according to the level involved. This film can be classified according to the kinds of image which compose it: these may be concrete and specific, based on a concrete reality which may or may not be present; or they may be abstract, general images, which are based on abstract reality, to which the terms 'present' and 'not present' are inapplicable. They can also be classified according to how the images are constructed, their associative mode, which can be symbolic, realistic, or pure intellectual.

The imaginative film, which represents *thought* during sleep with dreams, is chiefly characterized by *symbolic* association. In symbolic mode the film's meaning does not lie in its *form*, in how it is expressed. Its meaning lies behind form, which can only point to it. A form merely indicates and is radically separate from the formless substance to which it points (and the latter is at the same time obviously the source of the former).

The waking state with daydreams is intermediate between dream thought and thought in someone who is in contact with the real external world. It can vary between being very close to dream thought and its apparent irrationality, and resembling the reality-oriented, non-symbolic style of the fourth level.

Realistic thought in someone who is reacting to present external reality is comprised of images which go beyond pointing to meanings not contained within the image itself. On this level images are concrete: the claim they make is that they provide direct and real meanings which correspond to concrete reality. So, in contrast to level 2 thought, the meaning of this kind of thought is not so much behind as within the form in which it is expressed. However, this is not to say that none of its meaning lies behind what is expressed overtly. In fact, meaning at this level, which is the relative truth of this kind of thinking, is a manifestation of inexpressible, primordial Truth; and this kind of thinking would have no meaning, in other words would not even exist, without there being a meaning which lay behind its form; it is in virtue of this latent meaning that the form contains its particular relative manifest meaning.

Pure intellectual thought in someone who is reflecting and thinking deeply is different in kind from realistic thought. It is organized along purely intellectual lines. Its images are abstract and differ from those in realistic thought in that they do not correspond to anything that can be perceived by the sense organs. The Hindus consider the mind to be a sixth sense organ: this is valid in the sense that the mind, like the sense organs, can only convey what is relative; but the mind differs from them in that it alone provides us with abstract, general perceptions. In fifth level thought, images are more ambitious in scope than they are in realistic thought; the limited role of pointing indirectly to the truth is now completely discarded, and these images aspire to embody meanings of general significance. Expression through form reaches its peak, and the substance which lies behind form is at a minimum.

These five modalities of thought form a series, and we need to know how they relate as a hierarchy. The current view is that there is a progression from one to five: the state of someone who is engaging with the external world is ranked higher than that of someone who is asleep; and the state of someone who is contemplating general laws is considered superior to that of someone dealing with concrete reality.

This view is partly correct. But first we are going to see what is wrong with it, and to what extent the Vedanta is right in considering deep sleep superior to sleep with dreams, and sleep with dreams superior to the waking state. As one moves from a state without thought (dreamless sleep) through to pure intellectual thought (reflective states), our perception of ineffable Truth increasingly gives the appearance of being embodied in some mental formation. But a mental, or imaginative, form can be compared to the cross section of an object with volume. This can provide information about the object, but it is fundamentally different from it. The more skilfully and accurately the section is prepared, the more precisely it provides information about the object, and the more persuasively it claims to represent it. So there is a sense in which the better the information, the more misleading it is and the less it has to say about the object in reality.

This error is most pronounced in reflective states (level 5), because here the images are thought to correspond to an objective reality with general applicability. In level 4, dealing with concrete reality, the error is less because its images are taken to correspond to a more restricted aspect of reality. Someone who daydreams is still less prone to be mistaken, because less is claimed for daydreams, which are not mistaken for reality. There is even less scope for error with dream sleep; here the images are even more modest, in the sense that they only claim to point indirectly to a truth which they do not contain in themselves.* Finally, someone who is asleep without dreaming is free of error because, when formal thought disappears, so do its claims.

So in one sense there is a degradation between the first and fifth modes, since form increasingly takes over the meaning of thought, and formless originating substance diminishes behind the curtain of images; so there is less and less to underpin images: they are like bank-notes issued against a diminishing reserve.

This way of looking at the sequence of thought modalities as a hierarchy in which there is a progressive reduction in value from level one to level five makes complete sense if we only have to consider people in relation to the eternal instant. But if one thinks of people as beings capable of evolution in durational time, the situation alters. In terms of the instantaneous now, someone who is deeply asleep is less deluded than someone who is engaged in reflective thought. But from the perspective of durational time, the latter is superior to the former, because, in reflective thought, in taking the illusory workings of the ordinary human condition (an egotistical state imprisoned within

---

* Note that the most advanced, esoteric, teachings have always found it necessary to use symbols and myths. (HB)

subject/object dualism) to their fullest expression, the individual draws closer to the moment of satori, when the deluded 'old man' will disappear to be replaced by the 'new man' whose mode of thought, immanent in and transcendent to the five ordinary modes, will express the formless originating Principle.

It will become clear later that the fifth, reflective level cannot by itself release satori; but without it, we would not know how to obtain this release, so it would always be unattainable. By means of this mode of thought, which is the most abstract and ambitious in its claims, and in a sense the most purely erroneous, we can come to understand the futility of all our perceptual resources and of our quest for timeless realization, and to understand what we must do to let go inwardly and thus become available for the explosion of satori.

To summarize, the five ordinary modes of thought can be arranged in two opposite hierarchies. In relation to the eternal instant, thought declines in value from the first to the fifth modes; while, in relation to durational time, and the possibility of human transformation, its value increases.

To digress briefly, there is an analogy between the evolution of the individual and that of mankind. There are those who maintain that mankind has been making progress down the centuries; others consider that scientific and intellectual advances are symptoms of a progressive deterioration. Truth, as always, conciliates the two opposing points of view: in one sense there is a deterioration as human knowledge emerges from its formless state and crystallizes into increasingly skilful, precise forms; in another sense, there are cycles of progress towards a collective explosion analogous to individual satori (though still very different) when an old mankind, learned but not wise, will die; and a new mankind will be born which will be wise but not learned.

Returning to the ways in which we think as individuals, let us now consider them in relation to the satori which we hope one day to achieve. For satori to be released, there are a number of favourable conditions which must first be established in the psyche, and we shall consider these in due course. But there is a preliminary stage where patient intellectual work is required in order to understand what these advantageous conditions are and how they may be created. This stage is the only one where the five modes of thought differ in efficacy, with the fifth being superior to the others. Animals are incapable of satori because they possess the first four levels of thought, but not the fifth. Abstract reflective thought is necessary in order to understand the futility of all direct attempts to achieve the full and definitive satisfaction of human aspirations. Only this level of thought is able to think up various ways of achieving this satisfaction, and then realize that they too are futile, and, finally, after a lengthy labour of elimination, succeed in getting to the heart of the problem.

Reflective thought is only superior during this preparatory phase where theoretical understanding is being acquired. People who have discovered the inner conditions which must be established and enabled to grow within them in order to open them up eventually to the explosion of satori will also have discovered that none of the five modes of thought acting on its own can provide these necessary inner conditions: when it comes to this final stage of inner work, all five are equally ineffective. Dreamless sleep is ineffective because not-self is absent; the other four modes are ineffective because the moment the mind attempts to grasp reality, it becomes a 'formative' instrument which separates the individual from all immediate union with Formless Reality.

The condition which is necessary for the release of satori is a kind of perception which I will now try to clarify. Unlike the five modes of thought, it does not occur naturally and spontaneously in ordinary people.

But first I must digress a little if my attempt is to succeed. We will begin by examining the factors which underlie a common psychological phenomenon, exemplified in the following scene: I am sitting comfortably, reading a book which manages to occupy my attention without reminding me about any of my current worries; I do not identify with any of its heroes and I follow their adventures as a completely detached spectator. My personal life is quiescent and all my hopes and fears are displaced from my mind. The speech which the book gives rise to in my mind is a pure monologue, with no other voice interrupting to make comments or introduce thoughts about my own hopes and fears. My body is nice and comfortable and is not sending any disturbing messages to my mind; everything is 'ticking over nicely'. Then my attention to the book, which has become light and relaxed, disengages from it altogether; at that moment there is such pure calm in me that a true state of suspension is produced (we will see later what this state of suspension involves). Then a sense perception, which might be some object entering my field of vision, or a sound reaching me, abruptly shatters this state, and I see the object or hear the sound as I never see or hear it under ordinary circumstances. It is as though shapes and sounds usually have to pass through a distorting screen in order to reach me, whereas now, during this instant of atypical time, they reach me directly in their pure reality. What is even more interesting is that sensory perception is informing me about the external world and myself simultaneously. During this instant I no longer feel that the world and I are separate, though they remain distinct: not-self and self form a unity, but are still two. Then, after a few seconds during which I become aware of what I have just described, this new way of seeing things vanishes and I revert to my usual state.

If one compares this experience with the descriptions which a number of Zen masters have provided of their satori, a number of striking similarities become apparent: the initial profound calm with a sensation of being in a state of suspension as though both awake and asleep at the same time, the cessation of all mental restlessness (the Zen monk says that he is then 'like an idiot, like an imbecile'), the part played by a sense-perception in triggering a global shift in perspective, the suddenness with which this happens, the impression of clarity and unity brought by the new perspective. But there is also a considerable difference: the experience I have been describing rapidly leaves no more than a memory, while satori inaugurates a new life liberated once and for all from the illusion of egotistical dualism.

What is the significance of these resemblances and differences? Why did this transient mini-satori happen to me in the first place? It happened because my mind entered a state of unusual tranquillity: there was mental activity while I was reading, but its rhythm was regular and uniform, without interruptions; and the images it wove into a film were vague and insubstantial. Finally even these vanished, and my mind was idling in its centre, transmitting nothing to the surface. At that moment the mind's usual contracture had disappeared, although there was still mental activity present (I was not in deep sleep). When my mind was relaxed like that without being asleep, it was capable of receiving, without stirring, a non-dualistic perception of existence which its restless activity usually prevents. This is like a prisoner in a cell whose door is built to open inwards, who keeps on trying to open it by pushing against it: the harder he pushes, the less chance he has of opening it; but if he stops pushing for a moment, the door opens of its own accord.

So why did my mini-satori not last? Because it was triggered by chance conditions; it was thanks to my forgetting my preoccupations for a moment that it became possible for this perfect calm to be realized within me. I had withdrawn from contact with anything which might concern my ego. When I then became aware of my mini-satori by telling myself that this thing had happened *to me*, my whole egotistical life, which had been temporarily excluded from my mind, came bursting back in again, bringing all the usual consequences of its illusory perturbations.

*True, definitive satori pre-supposes the realization of a state of perfect calm in the mind of someone who has not withdrawn from things which matter to the ego, but is on the contrary living them out to the full.*

How can this be possible? What exactly does this calm state of mind consist of? What is in this state of suspension to which I have already alluded? All mental activity cannot be suspended, since the subject stays awake and is not asleep at the time. The mind is functioning, 'ticking over' quietly, without interruptions. Something has stopped, but it is not the mind, only its fits and starts, the irregularities in its rhythm. What do these fits and starts correspond to? They correspond to the emotions. The mini-satori experience described above happened to me because I had been free of emotions for an hour or two; all images relating to my personal life had been displaced from my mind, my book held my attention without in any way disturbing me, and my body was comfortable and silent; I felt neither sorrow nor joy. It was this absence of emotion which was a pre-condition for the smooth, uninterrupted functioning of my mind, which in turn provided the conditions for the sudden release of non-dualistic existential awareness in me.

So what is emotion? We need to know in order to find out how to eliminate emotion from our psyche. (Later we will consider why ordinary people usually react so strongly against the idea of eliminating emotion from subjective experience.)

Emotion represents a short circuit of vital energy between the negative instinctive centre and the positive intellectual centre. Energy disintegrates in this short circuit, and this happens at a point between the two centres which is thought of as a third centre, and referred to as the 'emotional centre'. (After satori this point is no longer a centre like the other two, situated on the same level, but becomes the apex of the triangle which represents its tripartite synthesis). This affective short circuit occurs when the intellectual centre is not insulated.

What does the intellectual centre's lack of insulation correspond to? It corresponds to the mind's passivity in the face of the ultimate problem of the human condition as it manifests in the present instant.

All human activity, internal or external, has one single prime mover: this is our innate need, located in the instinctive centre, to be a distinct and separate entity, in other words our need to 'exist'. We are not conscious of this need *at the moment it is operating in us, as it operates in the given instant.* We can be aware of it at a theoretical level, but we cannot experience it concretely, as a need which is active in the instant. Everything about how we function is influenced by an implicit 'given that I must exist'; the mind can become actively conscious of all the manifestations of this primary need, but consciousness of these manifestations precludes consciousness of the primary need itself.

I will try to put this another way. Behind everything we experience there is a debate going on, illusory proceedings where the matter in dispute is our being or our nothingness. Its ups and downs, the sudden changes in fortune, are what capture our attention, with their seemingly endless novelty and importance. But of the actual proceedings themselves, which carry on monotonously in the background, we remain unaware. We keep a close watch on the ways in which our psychosomatic states manifest, in forms which are continually changing in quality; but there is a quantitative variation which we are unaware of. It lies behind the formal manifestations of our immediate state, and is the variation in strength of what I will refer to as the formless sensation of existing. If I want to, I can perceive this variable formless impression of existing in any given instant by means of a perfectly simple inner act. But I have to will this activity and the moment I stop willing it, I stop doing it, and once again my attention is captured by formal perceptions.

When I deliberately perceive this formless sensation of existing (which varies quantitatively), my mind is at that point active in the presence of the ultimate reality of my condition in the concrete, lived instant, and my intellectual centre is then *insulated*, and I am without emotion. This perception does not happen naturally and has to be deliberate, and the moment I stop it, my intellectual centre stops being active and insulated, and my emotions start up again.

This formless sensation of existing varies quantitatively from annihilation to exaltation, but, unless I make a special effort, I do not pay it any attention, despite it being the thing that *really matters* to me in my present condition of egoistic dualism; what I do pay attention to are the mental forms which manifest my underlying state of exaltation or annihilation.

When my mind is seduced and captivated by the forms in which these states manifest themselves, it is passive. It is this passivity that constitutes non-insulation of the centre, leaving it vulnerable to emotional short circuits, interruptions and distractions, and restlessness (which state of mind the Hindus refer to as 'the crazy monkey').

Whoever wishes to achieve satori must work on progressively isolating the intellectual centre so as to protect it against emotional turbulence. And this must be done without eliminating or artificially modifying those circumstances in practical everyday life which matter to the ego and attempt to influence it. To achieve this, we need to keep on arousing our potential ability to perceive the variably positive or negative formless sensation of existing beneath the mental formations associated with our various states. We have this potential, but our ability to exercise it has a continual tendency to fall back into sleep.

This kind of attention does not lead to rejection of the concrete world of egotistical dualism; on the contrary, it leads us to maintain ourselves in our true centre and fulfil our life by living it at the motionless inner point where the very first dualism, existing/not-existing, appears. It is only when our attention is resting precisely there, in the source and origin of all our restless agitation, that serenity begins. Once serenity is profoundly established, the internal conditions are finally ready for the birth of satori, where dualism is conciliated by integration into a tripartite synthesis.

It is obviously impossible to *describe* this inner presence, which is the immediate, formless perception of our degree of existence at a given instant, precisely because of its formless character. Suppose I ask you: 'How do you feel at this instant?' you might well ask in turn: 'From what point of view? Do you mean physically or psychologically?' I reply: 'From every point of view at once, at the same time?' After a couple of seconds' silence, you might say something like: 'Not so bad', or 'So-so', or 'Fine', or something else. The second half of your silence is not what interests me, because you would have used it to find a way of expressing how you perceived your global state. You would already have slipped out of the inner presence which I am interested in. It is during the first second that you will have perceived the thing that is the real issue for you, all the time. Normally you are unaware of this unconscious perception, and are only aware of forms which derive from it, or forms which are involved in its existence.

Anyone who reads this and tries to have this formless perception had better be careful: there are innumerable ways of thinking one has succeeded when one has not. In all cases the same error occurs, consisting of some complication involving forms; the task has been approached without enough simplicity. *The direct formless perception of existence is the simplest perception possible.* With the correct approach, it can be obtained during, and without interfering with, the most intense external activity. There is no need for me to turn away from what I am doing, but I have to sense myself existing in the very centre of the world of form in which I am active, and in the attention which I give to it.

I commented earlier that ordinary people are most reluctant to consider a reduction in their emotions. They are like caterpillars, which can turn into butterflies providing they go through the chrysalis stage. Caterpillars can only move about at ground level, and are unable to fly and function in the vertical dimension; but at least they can move. The immobility of the chrysalis must seem terrible by comparison. Yet by losing an imperfect kind of locomotion in the short-term, they would gain a superior kind of mobility later on. Emotions are like the cater-pillar's movements which, though not the same as flying, are sufficiently similar to enable one to be mistaken for the other with the aid of a little imagination. People are attached to the pyrotechnics of their internal short circuits; it takes a great deal of honest reflection to understand that these are just fireworks which get us nowhere. True renunciation is not possible as long as we still attach some value to what is renounced.

I am now going to approach the subject of this whole essay by a different route:

The terms 'physical' and 'mental' in ordinary usage correspond to two domains which co-exist within us and seem clearly different to us. I allocate the impressions which mediate my awareness of living to my somatic life or my psychological life; so, for example, when I experience my life negatively, that is to say I feel it to be threatened or under attack, this may be through physical pain or psychological suffering. It is as though my being were in contact with the external world through two different surfaces, one somatic and the other psychological, through which destructive or constructive influences pass into it from outside.

My impressions are triggered by the outside world, but I feel them well up from within myself. Physical pain may by triggered by a punch, but I feel that it wells up from *my* body; my mental distress may be trig-gered by some external event, but I feel it welling up from what I call *my* soul. If I try to see where these impressions are coming from within me, I fail; my pain arrives in consciousness from a source where it was unconscious. The same applies to psychological distress; I can see clearly that the distress is connected with some mental image, but where did this image originate from before it sprang into consciousness? The answer is the same in both cases: from an unconscious source. To me it seems an inescapable conclusion that this source is the source of my life and I think of it as single and undivided, because my intuitive impres-sion is that I am *one*, a single and undivided synthesis beneath the duality of my reactive manifestations.

If I investigate the flux of my somatic and psychological lives in this way by moving my attention 'upstream', I see that these two currents come together at the mid-point of a single source. I can then understand why soma and psyche continually react upon one another; and the concept of a third term, the notion of 'being' as synthesis, unites what appeared to be separate. I realize that I have misunderstood how my two lives react on one another. In reality the exterior world is not in direct contact with either my 'body' or my 'soul' in so far as I am conscious of them; but always with this central crossroads from which my two conscious lives set off; and the contact takes place either *through* the somatic or *through* the psychic aspect which I present to the outside world.

When a stimulus reaches the centre, I will become aware of feelings or impressions arising from it which may be located predominately in either of the two domains (somatic or psychic), but not necessarily in the one through which the contact occurred. How these impressions are distributed between the two domains depends partly on the nature of the stimulus arriving from the external world, but also to a large extent on the make-up of the individual concerned. This corresponds to the distinction that psychiatrists draw between the obsessional neurotic and the hysteric: the former experiences impressions which are predominately psychological, the latter predominately somatic. Digestive problems may not produce any abdominal sensations or feelings in the psychologically-biased individual, but may just give rise to gloomy thoughts; while, for the hysteric, bad news will often translate into a malaise which is mainly, even entirely, physical.

The physical and psychological domains are not really separate, and there is no point spending time on the problem suggested by their apparent reciprocal reactions. It is futile looking for a bridge which might link them; there is no bridge, but they are in direct contact at their point of origin, the unconscious central crossroads of my 'being'. They are both manifestations of the same principle, and there is no need for them to react on one another; when I drink alcohol and the world seems rosy, why speak of soma reacting on psyche? An influence from the external world passes through my somatic aspect and reaches my centre; it then travels through the central crossroads, where it converts into simultaneous reactions in my somatic and psychological domains (general warmth, physical lightness, etc. in the former; cheerfulness in the latter). Good news, or the excitement and pleasure of meeting friends again, can produce exactly the same effect without any alcohol entering the system. This is because, although the influence affecting my centre arrived on this occasion via my psychological aspect, it worked in the same way and produced the same double reaction.

We have seen that this central crossroads of my 'being' is unconscious. It is the originating Unconscious from which all my consciousness flows. It should not be thought of as an absence of consciousness, but as Absolute Thought, which is prior to every conscious manifestation, and the source from which every conscious manifestation springs. It is the 'No-Mind' of Zen, from which all our physical and mental manifestations originate. The concept of the Creative Triad applies again: above the mental and physical poles (the positive and negative forces respectively) sits a higher conciliatory pole. Because of the apparent primacy of the positive over the negative inferior force, this third pole should be referred to as Absolute Mind (as opposed to Absolute Matter), or, as in Zen, as No-Mind (not No-Body).

We need to consider how these fundamental ideas relate to the difference between an ordinary and a realized individual. Both exist by virtue of this central meeting-point where their creative principle resides; there is no fundamental difference between them. Zen maintains that both are identically constituted and that the ordinary person lacks nothing. The realized individual has not acquired something which ordinary people lack. Nonetheless, though both people *are* identical, they differ in their *manifestations*. Why? Might it be because the unconscious central crossroads has become conscious at the moment of satori? This does not make sense: the principle and origin of consciousness must always be above and prior to consciousness, outside it and unconscious. No, the correct answer is different: it is that ordinary people function in every respect as though their central crossroads was asleep and passive; while in the realized individual it is as though it were awake and active.

It is relatively easy to imagine the situation in an ordinary person where this crossroads is in a dormant state: it really is just a crossroads, in other words a location through which all the influences from the external world pass. Through this simple 'space' the influx arriving from outside reaches the secondary centres of the somatic and mental domains, which respond with automatic reactions: the ordinary person whose central crossroads is dormant is an automaton.

In the realized individual the central crossroads is not dormant: Originating Absolute Thought is active there (though this, once again, is always unconscious), interpreting the influx arriving from the external world. Because it conceives the totality of things, it sees the particular influx within the totality of its universal context. So it sees it in its relativity, which means that it sees it as it really is. The secondary centres will now respond to this interpreted, 'illuminated' view of the world (the 'third eye' has opened in the centre of the unconscious), and this means that they will react in a way which is appropriate to reality, because they will no longer be responding to a misleading view of the world, distorted by its lack of context. The ordinary person was a machine whose automatic responses were determined by a particular aspect of the external world; the realized individual is a machine whose automatic responses are determined by the totality of the cosmos as it is represented in a particular aspect. In other words, the individual is now identical with the Cosmic Creative Principle and is manifested, like this Principle, through pure, free invention.

When this Absolute, Universal, Unconscious Thought is functioning at the individual's centre, it constitutes Absolute Wisdom. Obviously it is not in any way comparable with any kind of formal intelligence: this Wisdom is formless, prior to all form, and first cause of all forms.

I have mentioned that Universal Unconscious Thought is dormant in the centre of ordinary people, but that it awakens with realization. In fact, this sleep of Absolute Thought also has different levels, and these can be ranked in inverse order to the five modes of thought in ordinary people. During dreamless sleep in non-realized people, Absolute Thought is effectively in a waking state, or, more accurately, it is not asleep, and in this respect they resemble the realized individual. However, this is not reflected in their consciousness, since they are not conscious during this stage, and it only manifests itself in the harmonious, restorative activity of vegetative life. The moment they begin to dream and the formal mind starts to function, Absolute Unconscious Thought begins to grow dull, and so they are already less 'wise'. When they wake up, Absolute Thought becomes a great deal more somnolent; and this state of torpor increases in proportion as the formal mind proceeds to function in a purely intellectual manner, and thought becomes abstract and generalizing.

However, these moments of maximum torpor will make it possible for a particular development to take place in someone whose abstract intellect is active: over the course of their life, the sleep of Absolute Thought will gradually become less profound, and this means that they will be able to live according to an increasing relative wisdom. It is as though the sleep of Absolute Thought in the instant now were bringing about its awakening in duration. It would not be unreasonable to think of Absolute Thought's positive and definitive awakening (satori) as being released by an instant in which its total sleep will have been accomplished, in other words an instant in which mind will have reached the extreme limits of its dualistic functioning.

To put this in yet another way: someone who sleeps without dreams has withdrawn into their own centre; someone who dreams has already moved out of their centre; the daydreamer is even more 'ex-centric'; someone adapted to external reality and someone engaged in reflection are more and more removed from themselves and distanced from their centre. Someone sleeping without dreams possesses Reality without being aware of it. The further one moves up through the different levels and modes of thought, the less remains of Reality, which becomes more tenuous as the faculties striving to grasp it grow stronger. It is like someone moving away from a source of heat as their sensitivity to it increases. In the instants which precede satori, the subject is at the furthest possible point from their centre. Then, at the moment of satori, the inverse relationship which has applied so far breaks down completely and they are established once and for all in their centre as 'universal' man, though still able to move away from it, as individuals, into the various modes of formal thought.

So satori is attained by turning one's back as completely as possible on one's centre, pursuing this centrifugal direction to its farthest limits, and pushing discursive intelligence, which distances us from Wisdom, to a point where it functions at a level of extreme purity. Formal thought must be carried through until form itself is shattered. This is achieved by requiring the formal mind to strive persistently to go beyond its limits and perceive the formless. In itself this is an irrational endeavour, but one day it will trigger the miracle of satori, not as the crowning achievement of all this irrational striving, but as its final, triumphant failure. It is like someone separated from the light by a wall, who cannot touch the wall without building it higher; then a day comes when all this senseless effort has made the wall so high that it becomes unstable, collapsing suddenly in a final, triumphant catastrophe which bathes him in light.

It is this irrational, essential effort which we make when we force ourselves to perceive our formless sensation of existing-more-or-less during all the events of everyday life. Striving to perceive formless existence is not like the reflex mental efforts that we usually make, which are image-forming contractions or spasms of the mind. It is rather the opposite: it is an effort to relax in order to avoid habitual reflex contracting; it is an effort aiming at perfect simplicity in order to avoid the complexities which we introduce reflexly and habitually into the matter of our existence.

By making this effort we are not learning to *do* something new; we are learning *not to do* something, to give up the useless inner restlessness and agitation that we are accustomed to. We are not learning how to get our mind to act in exceptionally clever and skilful ways, but how to obtain from it the one pure act which is the essence of all the rest, the act which is akin to complete stillness. The mind functioning simply in this way represents the highest accomplishment of ordinary thought, and it breaks through the limits of the fifth level. Setting off from the formless in dreamless sleep, it finds its way back to the formless by completing a full circle, or, more accurately, a full spiral turn, since the point where the circle ends is at a higher level than its point of departure.

# CHAPTER SEVEN

# *Freedom – 'Total Determinism'*

To tackle the problem of freedom productively we must return to the fundamental idea that the architecture of the cosmos in its entirety depends on the two inferior principles, positive and negative, being maintained in a state of strict equilibrium by a conciliating principle which is superior to them.

From the perspective of our present unrealized state, the conciliating principle takes on two aspects. When we consider particular phenomena, we see a partial aspect of the conciliating principle, which we can call the 'temporal conciliating principle'. This is the Demiurge, who presides over the innumerable multitude of individual creations, over constructive and destructive phenomena, the anabolism and catabolism of the cosmic metabolism. When we consider the cosmos in its spatial and temporal totality, we formulate the idea of the Supreme, or Absolute, Atemporal Conciliating Principle which presides over the Unity underlying the multiplicity of phenomena. This Principle is the level at which dualistic manifestation no longer exists, and it is represented at an inferior level by the temporal conciliating principle.

This Supreme Conciliating Principle is the First Cause, prior to all manifestation. It is the end point reached by abstract thought when it moves back up the universal chain of cause and effect.

The presence of the Demiurge between First Cause and phenomena means that we must distinguish between two kinds of determinism. Partial determinism where the temporal conciliating principle determines phenomena, and total determinism where the Supreme Conciliating Principle determines the temporal conciliating principle and, through it, all phenomena.

Each of these two kinds of determinism is manifested through laws. It is worth noting the differences between the laws of partial determinism and the law of total determinism.

63

The laws of partial determinism only operate at the concrete level of time and space, and their individual manifestations seem arbitrary and unpredictable. It may be one person's fate to be wretched throughout their whole life, while someone else is destined to be fortunate. Operating at the level of appearance, partial determinism seems unbalanced, unjust and lacking order.

The law of total determinism applies not only at the level of individual phenomena, but also at the universal level. We can only conceive of it as being perfectly organized. The totality of positive phenomena is perfectly balanced by the totality of negative phenomena. Each and every phenomenon is integrated into a totality where it is exactly counterbalanced by a complementary phenomenon.

The partial determinism of the phenomenal level is apparent, visible and lacking in order, but it is not 'real' because it is partial, and there can only be Reality where the totality is encompassed. But in our ignorance we take what is visible to be the 'real'; we *believe* in the unique reality of partial determinism, and the fact that we refer to it as 'determinism' bears witness to this belief. We also have some innate intuition of Reality, in other words the Supreme Principle, to which we attribute various properties, one of which is *freedom*. Because the only determinism we are aware of is that existing at the partial level, and we are unable to conceive of the total determinism which operates at the level of the Supreme Principle, we contrast the former with the freedom of the Supreme Principle. The end result is that determinism and freedom are seen as opposites, though in reality this is an illusory opposition. What is not illusory is the distinction between partial and total determinism. This distinction is not in any way an opposition, but expresses two different views of one and the same Causal Reality, seen from the individual and universal levels respectively.

Ordinary, egotistical people want to be free and independent, while at the same time thinking of themselves as distinct individuals. I can think of myself in this way as a distinct individual, as a psycho-somatic organism, but then I must understand that my liberation from partial determinism means transcending it and fulfilling it within the Supreme Principle's total determinism. Once I have achieved Realization, my psycho-somatic organism will no longer be governed solely by the apparently disordered laws of partial determinism, but by the all-encompassing law of universal cosmic equilibrium, which is strictly ordered and is the principle and fundamental cause of all the seemingly unregulated laws of partial determinism.

To be liberated by Realization does not mean that my organism breaks free of all determinism. What it means is that my organism will finally be governed by the total determinism of the Supreme Principle, which is my 'own nature'. My organism will still be subject to a causal influence, but this will now be the First Cause, its own Reality. This can be summarized by saying that I am free, not because causation no longer drives my organism, but because there is within me a perfect adaptation between what is caused and what causes, between what is conditioned and the Principle which conditions it. If, at the moment of realization, the constraints upon me vanish, it is not because they have been abolished, but because they have expanded into infinity and coincided with the totality where self and not-self are a unity, so that the word 'constraint' has lost all meaning.

Because they do not understand this, ordinary egotistical people inevitably make the mistake of imagining an act of free will to be something capricious, gratuitous, arbitrary, and disconnected from everything else. This leads them into irrationality and meaninglessness. This kind of freedom is illusory and belongs within the realm of partial determinism, not beyond it. It is a figment of the imagination which is demolished by its own internal contradiction, because it cuts our organism off from the rest of the cosmos. In a recent book on Zen, a Western author asserts that someone liberated by satori can do anything whatever, in any situation. This betrays a radical misunderstanding: a liberated person can only do one thing in any given situation, and that is the one thing completely appropriate to that situation. It is in the immediate, spontaneous production of this unique, appropriate action that the perfect freedom of such a person is expressed. Ordinary, egotistical people, driven by partial determinism, are subject to intervening factors, and produce a reaction to a given situation which will be one of countless inappropriate possibilities. The realized individual, who is responding to total determinism, produces the one strictly appropriate action.

There is a whole hierarchy of actions which fall short of the fully appropriate act of free will and these are more or less inappropriate according to the degree of partial determinism involved. Purely reflex action without the possibility of reflection comes lowest in the hierarchy: it is characterized by spontaneity operating at a level below reflection. This inferior spontaneity gradually disappears as reflective though becomes more active, and action represents an appropriate response to an ever expanding aspect of the context in which it occurs. Reflective thought is transcended after satori: action regains a completely new kind of spontaneity, becoming perfectly appropriate to the temporal and spatial totality of the phenomenal universe.

The hierarchy of actions between these two levels of spontaneity demonstrates an inverse relationship between the extent to which an action is constrained and the inner impression of freedom accompanying it. The more completely an action is determined, the freer it feels inwardly. For example, if I am asked to name any noun whatsoever, the question throws me off balance, and confuses me; I do not know what to say. Being asked to name a musical instrument is less problematic and it is easier for me to give a reply; and if I am asked to name the smallest instrument in a string quartet, the confusion which was unsettling me disappears completely. As I name the violin, I have an inner feeling of freedom which is linked to the fact that I am certain that I have given the right answer. The fewer the possible responses available to me, and the less *outward* freedom I have, the greater my *inner* experience of freedom; in other words, my mind is freer in direct proportion to how precisely my task is defined.

Modern art has evolved in a way which provides a striking illustration of the confusion which grips the human spirit when it rejects all discipline. When no constraints are acknowledged, the experience of freedom found within accepted constraints is lost. With the loss of this sense of freedom, the artist is deprived of a calming influence without which the voice of deepest inspiration cannot be heard. So artists who reject all forms of discipline and pride themselves on breaking the rules cut themselves off from their depths and lose the ability to express themselves. Their voice fails, and they may end up feeling impotent and ineffectual, shackled by their outward freedom.

Spontaneous adherence to some form of discipline is essential to prevent our life becoming a suicidal chaos. On the other hand, while lack of discipline puts our temporal life in danger, this same discipline is an obstacle to Realization. It certainly provides us with a *feeling* of inner freedom; but before satori we are not really free at all. Our feeling of freedom is an illusion, and is no more than a palliative and compensation for our still unconciliated state of dualism. It gives rise to deceptive experiences of joy, and we cannot prevent these experiences using up vital energy.

So there are advantages and disadvantages to discipline, as far as atemporal realization is concerned. It is indirectly advantageous because it supports the kind of fulfilment in the temporal domain without which atemporal realization would be impossible to achieve; and directly disadvantageous to atemporal realization because it promotes the illusion that we are functioning very well inwardly as we are at present.

Those who follow Zen resolve this contradictory situation within themselves by confronting it with an equally contradictory method:

they reject all *specific* disciplines (no 'morality', no asceticism, and no spiritual exercises). As their understanding increases, so does their devotion to the *total* discipline which requires that each and every specific discipline should be implacably rejected. *'Don't cling to your opinions'*; *'The way of perfection rejects all preferences'*, *'Awaken your mind without fixing it on anything'*, etc. They begin to confront and deal with the distress inherent in complete external freedom. By rejecting all opinion, they bring to full realization the state of inner enslavement which characterizes our egotistical condition; they hold themselves in the very centre of this illusory prison of ours until their helpless state of immobility culminates in satori, which disrupts the world of appearances, and reconstructs it in the new light of a real inwardly and outwardly transcendent freedom.

# CHAPTER EIGHT

# *The Egotistical States*

In my centre, my still unconscious centre, primordial man dwells in a state of union with the Origin and Principle of the Universe, and through this with the Universe in its totality, as the One source and origin, wholly sufficient unto itself, neither alone nor not alone, neither affirmed or denied, beyond and above all duality. This is Primordial Being, concealed in my present consciousness beneath a layer of egotistical states.

Because I am currently ignorant of the real nature of these egotistical states, they act as a kind of screen separating me from my centre, from my real Self. I am unaware of my essential identity with the All and I only think of myself as distinct from the rest of the Universe. The ego is what I am when I think of myself as separate and distinct, and it is illusory since I am not distinct in reality; and all the egotistical states are equally illusory.

In the fundamental egotistical state, I experience myself as self opposed to not-self, as an organism whose 'being' is opposed to the 'being' of other organisms. In this fundamental state, everything which is not my organism is not-self. I love my self, and this means that I desire my own existence; I hate not-self, so I want to be rid of its existence. I yearn for my self to be affirmed in its separateness, and for the not-self to be negated, whose claim to existence impinges on the boundaries of my separate self. As far as this fundamental egotistical state is concerned, to 'live' is to affirm self by vanquishing not-self in a material victory gained by acquiring material goods, or in a victory on the subtle level by achieving fame, when not-self acknowledges the self's existence and the separate self achieves 'immortality' by winning glory.

So the ordinary person's fundamental affective state is simple: love of self in opposition to not-self, and hatred of not-self in opposition to self.

This fundamental egotistical egoism can form the basis of five egotistical forms of altruism involving apparent love for another person.

## 1. *Apparent love for others based on projection by the ego**

This is an idolatrous form of love where the ego is projected onto another being. The claim to divine status as a separate entity has shifted from my organism and is now attached to the organism of the other. The affective situation is the same as before apart from the fact that the other has replaced me in my hierarchy of values. I desire the existence of the idolized other, in opposition to everything which is against it. I only continue to love my own organism to the extent that it is my idol's faithful servant; apart from that I no longer feel anything for my organism. I am indifferent towards it and will give my life to save my idol if I have to (I can sacrifice my organism to my own ego attached to the idol; like Empedocles throwing himself into Etna to immortalize his ego).

If the rest of the world is hostile towards my idol, I hate it; but if it is not hostile and if my contemplation of the idol fills me with joy (i.e. with egotistical affirmation), then I love the rest of the world indiscriminately (we will see why later, with the fifth category of apparent love). If the idolized object rejects me to such an extent that I am prevented from investing anything of my ego in it, then this apparent love can be converted into hatred.

## 2. *Apparent Love for Others based on a Localized Extension of the Ego*

Examples of this are a mother's loving attachment to *her* child, a man's loving attachment to *his* native land, etc. This is possessive love. In the case of idolatrous love, the process began with projection of the ego, followed by the need to possess the projected ego by taking material or subtle possession of the idol. In the present case possession of the other comes first (it is a matter of chance that this child is *my child*, and this country *my country*). From the affective point of view, the result is very like idolatrous love; but its joys are less conscious, and fear of loss is often predominant. Idolatrous love provides life with a 'meaning'; possessive love does so as well, but the meaning it provides is often less positive and not so satisfying.

---

* This simplified exposition of the doctrine of projection, known to all classical psychologists, may appear to ignore the detailed analysis of this process expounded by some. Terms such as ego have not, however, a standardized meaning, and the reader may be well-advised to understand the word here as including any aspect of the psyche whose image might be projected. *Footnote from 1998 UK edition.*

## 3. Apparent Love of Others Because They Love Us in One or Other of the Two Previous Ways

The other loves *his* ego in me, but gives me the impression that he loves *my* ego. So I desire his existence in the same way that I desire the existence of everything which desires my existence.

## 4. Apparent Love of Others Because My Ideal Image of Myself or My Idolatrous Love Requires This

I love others because I can only love myself if I am aesthetically pleasing to myself, and loving others is aesthetically pleasing.

Or I love others because I feel a mystical love for a divine image on which my ego is projected, which I believe wants me to love others – and because I desire whatever this divine image, which is identified with my ego, desires.

## 5. Apparent Love of Not-self Because My Ego Is Temporarily Satisfied

Someone filled with a moment of intense egotistical affirmation loves the whole universe. This love without a particular object is not a temporary manifestation of primordial universal love; it is a temporary inversion of the fundamental egotistical hatred of not-self, at a time when egotistical claims are in abeyance. It does not last long. It is like the voluptuous pleasure of interrupted suffering, which is only a comparative pleasure: it does not endure once the suffering with which it is contrasted has stopped.

These five kinds of apparent love for others are different sources of pleasure experienced by my ego in situations which affirm me as a separate entity. If any one of these situations deteriorates, then distress and aggressiveness come to the fore.

The more strongly people are called to atemporal realization, the greater their need to experience these kinds of love, which have something in common with the affective state of an enlightened person (who loves everything), as they appear to connect them to something other than themselves.

Yet, as self-knowledge increases, less value is attached to these kinds of love, which lose their power to compensate. 'Positive' and 'altruistic' feelings are gradually lost. Understanding sees right through these clever shams, and, like it or not, people who aspire to realization are drawn towards the fundamental egotistical state in which they have

always hated that which is not self; this is the state of 'night' and soli-
tude. They experience distress because they have rejected the fight
against not-self (Chapter 5, The Mechanisms of Distress).

Gradually deprived of all their psychological tricks, they find themselves driven on towards the work of realization. They call on impartial
thought increasingly to challenge the legitimacy of the fundamental
egotistical claim, the aspiration to separate and distinct being which
engenders isolation and fear. As the process of purification and simplification proceeds, the ego is constricted and compressed within its last
defences. When the limit to this process of compression is reached, the
ego explodes into satori and, merging into the whole, is fulfilled and
annihilated in the same instant.

# CHAPTER NINE

# *The Zen Unconscious*

In ordinary consciousness, two different perceptual layers are always present, and attention is paid to two different orders of things. Ordinary attention is continuously responding to these two perceptual domains, and is divided between them. The idea that we can only pay attention to one thing at a time is mistaken; we pay attention to two things at once all the time; but, as we will see, in two different ways.

In the foreground of perception, attention is captured by individual aspects of the external world which are either actually present or represented in the imaginative film. This is the level where I live out, in durational time, my own individual contest with not-self, which is ceaselessly changing in quality.

Then there is the other perceptual level where my attention is captured by the state of the ongoing dispute deep within me, taking place in the instant now, concerning 'being' and 'not being'. This dispute is always the same, so this perceptual level is qualitatively very monotonous. In fact there are changes taking place here all the time as well, but these are quantitative. My state on this level is more or less 'white' or 'black', corresponding to a sense of 'being' or 'not-being' respectively. There are also quantitative fluctuations between calm and agitation as well as between white and black, and we will have another look at both of these later on.

It is instructive to consider the ways in which the two levels relate. The deep level is where my non-specific general perception, i.e. my 'state', is active. The surface level, where specific perceptions occur, is affected by the deep level to the extent that my perception of the external world is influenced or altered by imagination. My imaginative film will be full of positive images when my 'state' is 'white' and with negative ones when it is 'black'. An agitated state speeds it up, while a calm state slows it down. The surface level is, of course, governed by external circumstances as well.

The deep level, the 'state', is itself partly dependent on forms present at the surface level. Affirming or invalidating events perceived on that level influence my deep state, while forms imagined in response to my deep state affect it in a positive or negative feedback loop. My state is also dependent on my physiological coenaesthesia:* insomnia and digestive problems darken it, alcohol and opium lighten it.

In short, I am always doing two things at once. I am busy existing in the external world, while at the same time I am inwardly trying to assess whether the matter in dispute concerning my being or nothingness is likely to have a favourable or an unfavourable outcome. My attention is divided between these two activities; this explains why the neurotic often presents with impaired concentration at the surface level and with problems in how the external world is perceived. So much attention is involved in predicting the result of the ongoing enquiry and so little is left for contact with the real or imagined external world that this is experienced as unreal, while the surface mind is felt to be out of control.

My deep state, whether black, white, agitated or calm, is formless. Light illuminates forms but is itself without form. Agitation is similarly without form; forms are agitated to a variable extent, but agitation itself is without form. It follows that all perception at the deep level is without form, though perception at the surface level is formal. Another difference is that surface perception is immediately accessible to me, while perception of my deep state is latent. I can only become aware of it as a more or less pleasant or unpleasant coenaesthesia, reflecting the whiteness or blackness of my state.

These two kinds of awareness correspond to the two levels between which my attention is divided and it is important that I should distinguish between them and designate them by different names. I will refer to surface awareness as *'objectal'* and deep awareness as *'subjectal'*. Consciousness is torn between these two non-conciliated parts as long as the egotistical dualistic condition persists, in which everything is perceived within the framework of subject/object opposition. I use the terms 'subjectal' and 'objectal' instead of 'subjective' and 'objective' because the latter should signify the two conciliated aspects of consciousness in the realized person.

Objectal awareness is obvious, or *manifest*, while subjectal awareness is *latent*. I wrestle with external problems knowing that I do so; but I am unaware of struggling with my deep inner problem. What happens is that my attention is captured differently within the two kinds of consciousness. I have no objection to having my attention captured by external forms; indeed I seem to like this happening. But I resist having my attention captured by my inner state. To put this another way, in

---

* Coenaesthesia is the overall inner perception that we have of our organism.

objectal consciousness I actively permit my attention to be captured, whereas it is captured in spite of me in subjectal consciousness. I am oriented centrifugally, towards the outside; my gaze is directed outwards; but I turn my back on my deep state. That part of my attention which is captured by subjectal consciousness is stolen from me, from behind; the part which is captured by objectal consciousness is proffered by me to the outside world. I am like someone sitting in a cinema with a screen in front and a camera behind: I gaze at the forms on the screen, and turn my back on the camera, my 'state', which is projecting forms and colours onto the screen.

Subjectal consciousness is ignored by classical psychology. It is the latent face of a consciousness which dualism has sundered. The monotonous thought processes which are working away all the time on the issue of my being or not-being are, in a sense, unconscious. But this kind of unconscious is not the originating Unconscious of Zen; it represents the very first appearance of dualism, at the point immediately after the originating Unconscious has become aware of itself. It is the very first dualistic manifestation of this Unconscious. It is not clear whether it should be called unconscious or conscious because it is exactly at the frontier between the originating Unconscious and consciousness. From the point of view of consciousness, it is unconscious (the Freudian viewpoint); but it is subjectal consciousness if considered from the viewpoint of the fundamental Unconscious. The Zen master is considering it from the latter viewpoint when he deplores the damaging effects of dualistic consciousness in ordinary people. He tells us: 'You are unhappy because you are established in consciousness and not in the Unconscious'. He does not consider that the Freudian unconscious is a real unconscious, but rather the deepest and most obscure source of discursive consciousness, that is to say the first modality of dualistic consciousness.

The Zen viewpoint requires us to treat subjectal consciousness as latent consciousness, not as the Unconscious. The fact that it is latent does not reduce its detrimental effect on us. The more active it is, in other words the more involved we are in struggling with our illusory 'being-nothingness' problem, and also the more we are distressed by doubt concerning our being, the more we are deprived of the joyful light of the Origin, and the more our attention is captured by the obscure depths. When a great deal of our attention has been captured in this way, there is not much left for our adaptation to the outside world; this has been referred to as a 'reduction in psychological tone', and is associated with inability to concentrate and all the symptoms of 'psychasthenia'.*

* A neurotic disorder characterized by loss of willpower, debility, doubt, scrupulosity, and meticulosity.

Since subjectal consciousness is latent, a kind of unconscious consciousness, you may wonder how I found out about it and can speak about it. Observation of my surface consciousness and my need to understand why it functions as it does gradually enabled me to infer and understand the existence and nature of this deep subjectal consciousness in which the issue of my being or my nothingness is the subject of an ongoing dispute. Direct intuition of this state deep within me does not reveal any forms in it, but does provide information about its relative brightness (varying from white to black, from light to dark), and about its dynamism (varying from calm to agitation).

This intuitive perception is valuable, because it allows me to observe the relationship between my deep inner state and my behaviour, feelings and actions. Just as the meaning of a dream lies in its latent rather than its manifest content, so the meaning of my life, that other dream, is to be found in my latent, subjectal consciousness, and not in manifest, objectal consciousness. It is the thinking that takes place in my latent consciousness which determines my behaviour and manifest consciousness.

In latent consciousness, where the issue of my being versus my nothingness is being contested, what I want is an acquittal. I want to feel myself 'being', and I am terrified of my nothingness. Let us look at the relationship between the two phenomenal dualisms of my deep state, light/darkness and agitation/stillness, and the fundamental being/nothingness dualism. My inner life is characterized by a seeming identification of light and agitation with being, and of darkness and stillness with nothingness. This means that my inner bias towards being is expressed as a bias towards 'a luminous state in motion'. This bias can be clarified further: the particular characteristics of my life and internal structure do not always permit co-existing light and agitation, and there are times when I have to choose between them. It is then clear from my behaviour that I prefer agitation to light. More accurately, from a negative perspective, while I fear darkness and stillness in the depths of my being, my fear of the latter is stronger; I experience the terrifying impression of not being more strongly in a lack of movement in subjectal consciousness than I do in its 'blackness'. (Similarly a child would rather be scolded than ignored by its mother; it would prefer its mother's attention to take the form of a hug, but, failing that, scolding is better than indifference. In the same way, a masochist's strongest preference, like everyone else's, is directed towards pleasurable excitement, but, if this is unobtainable, he prefers to be excited by suffering than to have no excitement at all).

So everything suggests that my greatest dread is of my deep state being without movement, and that this dread is stronger than my fear of it being dark. What I seem to dread most of all is not feeling that I am alive, and, since movement is the essential criterion of life, this feeling of aliveness has to be conveyed by a sense of activity vibrating within me. My fear of not being happy seems to come second. People in general claim to want happiness, and this aspiration corresponds to a correct intuitive understanding that a realized person's deep state would be luminous and motionless. But there is a discrepancy between this aspiration and the way ordinary people behave. They do not live so as to be happy and they do not aim to acquire a luminous and motionless deep state: their efforts are directed at developing a state which is primarily one of excitation, and only secondarily luminous.

Not surprisingly, happiness eludes ordinary people, since their efforts are not directed towards it. The fact that agitation is preferred to light explains why their happiness is so precarious. When they are enjoying themselves, their agitated pursuit of yet more pleasure matters more to them than does their current enjoyment. The outcome is a limitless demand for pleasure which inevitably comes up against the limitations of the temporal plane and leaves enjoyment in ruins. (Take for example someone who has a great piece of good fortune; their immediate response is to celebrate it and add as many satisfactions as possible to the first one.)

Ordinary people have these two distinct preferences as far as their deep state is concerned, and the second of these, the preference for light, is well-founded. But their fundamental preference for agitation is mistaken and is the cause of all their misfortunes. Their ceaseless wish to sense life vibrant within themselves, in other words, in their current egotistical state, to feel that they are affirmed as distinct entities, explains why they remain plunged in the miseries of dualism and its agonizing contradictions.

Only understanding is capable of delivering humankind from this irrational preference. Understanding brings with it the realization that this terrifying inner stillness is not only nothing to be afraid of, but that it actually represents salvation. It is true that light and stillness cannot be experienced together in the egotistical state; if an initiated person begins to prefer stillness, in other words to seek it, darkness will also be present. The 'Night' of St John of the Cross is both motionless and dark. But this night is very easy to bear when I am established in a stillness which I am no longer afraid of, but in which, on the contrary, I place my hope.

This inner work does not involve 'doing' anything new. All that is required of us, because we have understood, is that we remind ourselves spontaneously that the hope we invest mechanically and naturally in our inner agitation is irrational, while the agitating itself is irrational and damaging. Each time I think these thoughts, which are revealed, not natural, my agitation subsides more or less completely. I stop intending to resolve the being-nothingness issue, and put my trust in my Principle to dispel the phantoms engendered by these senseless proceedings. I do not *do* any more, I *allow* my invisible Principle, which I believe in without seeing, *to be active on my behalf*. My only task is to  maintain and enrich my understanding by honest intellectual work in such a way that the spontaneous effects of this understanding are equally fruitful.

# CHAPTER TEN

# 'Metaphysical' Distress

When some event in my life distresses me, what is actually taking place inside me? My distress is caused by the encounter with not-self, and it expresses my fear of being defeated in this encounter. Since I never stop debating the question of my own being or nothingness in relation to the particular circumstances of my life, the distress I feel expresses my fear that the verdict will go against me. I have attempted to conquer not-self, and now I am afraid that I am not going to achieve this. My fear is that by losing this contest I will come face to face with the negation of my being.

But I would not have tried to conquer not-self and gain a decision in favour of my being if the dispute had not been there deep within me in the first place, if I had not already been possessed by a doubt concerning my being. Consequently, behind the distress I feel at the time when the argument goes against me on a particular occasion, there lies another distress, and this is a permanent distress which is responsible for keeping the whole debate going. Behind the 'physical' or phenomenal distress which is experienced on the phenomenal plane lies a noumenal or 'metaphysical' distress, which lies at a level prior to my phenomenal world.

This metaphysical distress is the originating, or primary, distress, which determines my ordinary, or secondary, distress. I will try to clarify its nature. First of all it is *unconscious*. People who are not realized are only conscious of phenomena; so they cannot be conscious of distress at a level prior to phenomena. The same analysis applies to happiness: I am happy because I sense that I have gained affirmation of self in the conflict between self and not-self, because the dispute is momentarily going in my favour, and I am heading for an acquittal. But, although I am happy because the dispute has taken a turn for the better, the proceedings are still going on in the background behind my happiness, and so the doubt about my being continues, and so does metaphysical distress. Metaphysical distress is as much present in the origins of conscious happiness as it is in those of conscious distress, and in both cases it is equally unconscious. So another characteristic of unconscious metaphysical distress is its permanence. It is always present, and always the same, behind all our affective phenomena and their dualism of joy and suffering. I will also show, on the other hand, that it is illusory and unreal and has no 'existence', although just now the impression might have been given that it had noumenal existence. I will demonstrate that *all our affective phenomena take place as though this metaphysical distress existed in reality.*

Note that metaphysical distress, in combination with the joy and suffering it governs, forms the familiar triangle whose apex represents the conciliatory principle, with the angles at the base representing the inferior positive and negative principles respectively:

MULTIPLE LINE:
METAPHYSICAL DISTRESS

JOY                    SUFFERING

But there is something odd about this triangle: the superior principle has a negative connotation, which is contrary to what we have seen in previous cases. Why? It reflects the fact that Faith is dormant in the unrealized individual, and in someone whose Faith is dormant, the Buddha nature remains unseen. Because they do not see it, unrealized people function as though they lacked Buddha nature, despite the fact that they already possess it. Because Being has not woken in their centre, they function as though a nothingness held sway there which had to be countered. Because perfect existential bliss has not woken in their centre, the effect is that their lives are lived as though the centre were occupied by primordial distress. But this primordial distress is 'non-existent'. From this we recognize that our triangle has been drawn incorrectly; here is a more accurate version:

JOY                    SUFFERING

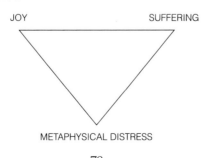

METAPHYSICAL DISTRESS

Ignorance has been responsible for an illusory inversion of the triangle. After satori, this inversion disappears and the triangle becomes:

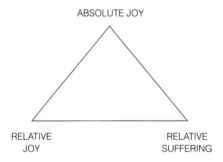

ABSOLUTE JOY

RELATIVE
JOY

RELATIVE
SUFFERING

Metaphysical distress cannot be conscious because it is wholly illusory. It is impossible to bring it into consciousness, because the attempt to do so causes it to vanish completely. To claim that satori results from 'metaphysical' awareness would also be wrong. It is more correct to say that satori occurs when the centre which seemed to be the site of metaphysical distress while it was dormant finally awakens.

All the kinds of distress which can be experienced consciously are secondary; none of them should be classified as primary or metaphysical distress. Sometimes distress is related to the great philosophical problems concerning the human condition, in other words to metaphysical questions; but it is caused by mental images, by phenomena and forms; suffering is experienced on the physical, phenomenal plane, not on the metaphysical plane. Sometimes distress arises from the thought of renouncing some illusory kinds of compensation; and it may perhaps be thought that distress at the prospect of losing one's personality and merging into the universal can legitimately be called metaphysical. But this comes from thinking of renunciation in the wrong way, from not appreciating that true renunciation involves transcending something whose value has already been diminished by the use of understanding to interpret experience. Indeed it is a case of wrongly believing that one is distressed by the universal, when in fact distress is caused by *individual* values to which one is still attached, values which are threatened by a false idea of the nature of Realization. No, it would be wrong to call any consciously felt distress 'metaphysical'; there cannot be distress at the level of the Principle, at the level of the source which creates us.

On the other hand, let me repeat that there cannot be a single consciously experienced distress which does not have unconscious metaphysical distress at its origin: the unconscious, inverted image of dormant existential Bliss. This delusive unconscious image is the effective cause of all our mental pain. Contrary to what we usually believe, distressing life events are no more than the immediate causes of our suffering. A mother who has lost her child is not suffering, as she thinks, because her child is dead. She suffers on account of its death because she believes herself to be abandoned by her Principle, and she suffers because a profound sense of not 'being' has been triggered by what has happened.

Given that we can have no conscious experience of the primary, metaphysical distress, it is important to recognize that some of our secondary distresses are closer to the illusory primordial distress than others. They form a qualitative hierarchy which is related to the depth of our understanding. My distress is furthest from my source if I have no understanding of my inner life, and am completely convinced that my particular concrete concern of the moment is the real cause of my suffering. As I develop a correct understanding of my inner life, I become free of this illusion, and I become less inclined to believe in the causal role of a particular fortuitous circumstance. I am less inclined to connect my suffering with what happens to me as an individual, attributing it rather to the universal aspect of my condition as a human, which I share with every other human being. As this understanding begins to exercise its effect, the dispute concerning *my* individual being versus *my* individual nothingness is brought to an end; in other words, as the universal aspect of the causes of my suffering grows clearer in my understanding, my suffering gradually ceases. As my images lose their mesmerizing intensity, my distress becomes more subtle and moves closer to its source, and in so doing is alleviated.

This is the way in which understanding gradually frees us from suffering; the more profoundly I understand that my distress depends on a condition which is in no way peculiar to me, the more blurred and indistinct the senseless argument about being versus not-being becomes, this great debate which is the source and origin of all my suffering. Understanding does not bring the proceedings to an end with an acquittal, but it scatters its deceptive phantoms. It progressively alleviates all the emotions which arise from this 'cave of phantoms'.

In this way we progress towards satori. The descriptions given by Zen masters indicate that the inner states which precede and herald the release of satori are states of serenity, in other words of affective neutrality. Consciousness has gradually drawn close to the centre where metaphysical distress, the begetter of all forms of distress, seemed to dwell. As the distance to the centre diminishes, the burden of distress grows lighter, becoming so tenuous that it disappears altogether in the final moments which precede satori; and the closer one gets to the supposed site of metaphysical distress, the more obvious it becomes that it is not there, nor was it ever there. The distressing belief system then disappears, and is replaced by serenity; and with this the contraction which kept the 'third eye' closed and denied it the vision of perfect existential joy is finally removed.

# CHAPTER ELEVEN

# Seeing Into One's Own Nature – The Spectator of the Spectacle

I want to take another look at the psychological conditions for satori, and at the need to train ourselves to perceive inwardly, prior to all form, the fluctuations in the strength of our sense of existing, this impression we have of existing more or less. This lies at the heart of the practical inner work whose object is transformation.

Zen instructs us: *'Look directly into your own nature'*. Yes, of course, I understand this, but I know that the task is impossible for me as I am, an ordinary person. For this kind of vision the 'third eye' has to be open, and my third eye seems to be permanently shut. I have come to understand that there is a third eye within me and that there is no opacity obscuring its vision. It is not diseased and it does not need any treatment, but it is closed through habit and I have got to do something if I am to get rid of this habit. The question is, *how* do I get rid of this habit which is the source of all my suffering? I realize that there must be a particular way of looking with my two ordinary eyes, in other words with ordinary attention, which will gradually abolish the spasm affecting the eye-lids of my third eye, and that one day this will suddenly enable me to see into my own nature once and for all.

So I want to know more about this way of looking which is within my capacity as I am at present, unable on its own to allow me to 'see into my own nature', yet able to change my condition so that it stops resisting the opening of the third eye. I know that useful work will involve relaxation, not contraction, but what exactly does this attempt at letting go involve which is going to make me susceptible to the direct action of Atemporal Reality? I know I cannot expect it to bear any immediate fruits, since no inferior manifestation can ever be the cause of a superior one.

The effort to relax in question is a particular kind of looking inwards. It is the glance inside which I mentioned earlier, which I direct at the centre of my whole being in response to the question: 'How are you feeling just now – from every point of view simultaneously?' If someone asks me: 'How are you feeling physically at this moment?' what I introspect is my so-called coenaesthesia, which I will refer to here as *physical coenaesthesia*. If someone asks me: 'How do you feel in your self at this moment?' my inward gaze is directed towards what I will call *psychological coenaesthesia*, which means the same as 'state of mind' or 'mood'. And when somebody enquires: 'How do you feel just now – from every point of view simultaneously?' I look inside myself in such a way as to perceive what I will call my *total coenaesthesia*. It is this last way of looking which represents the essential effort I must make in order that I may one day obtain the sudden release of 'seeing into my own nature'.

Total coenaesthesia is a special kind of inner perception, but it resembles its physical counterpart in two ways which are relevant to our study. First, coenaesthesia is a kind of perception *obtained through relaxation*. For instance, the coenaesthetic sensation of my right arm is a sense of its existence, or of how it feels on the inside, and I cannot obtain this if the arm is contracted. In the contracted state, its feeling is projected onto the surface. I have to relax my arm in order to feel it in its central axis, and when I do so it seems as though feeling were flowing back into its bone marrow. Second, coenaesthetic perception is *formless*. When my arm is contracted, I feel its form; but after it has been fully relaxed for some minutes, and all feeling has flowed back into its central axis, while I can certainly feel my arm and be aware of its existence (this is like the painless sensation that an amputee retains of his missing limb), I no longer feel its form. If I think of it spatially, it feels as big as the whole universe, as if its form had exploded and dissolved into the totality of space. In other words, I perceive it formlessly.

These two features, relaxed perception and formless perception, are common to all three coenaesthesiae. But there is one fundamental respect in which physical coenaesthesia differs from the other two, and that is in the time aspect. I can perceive my physical existence in continuous time, or duration; I can feel my arm (or my whole physical body) from the inside for a continuous period of time. But when I perceive my total coenaesthesia, in other words when I sense my total psychosomatic state from the inside, the experience only lasts for a split second and I cannot hold on to it for any time at all. The perception slips out of my grasp the instant it arrives. It eludes me in its formless purity and immediately slips away into formal perceptions. For example, I can feel 'not very well' for an instant, without this malaise taking any particular form; but then I sense straight away what form my malaise is taking, *in what way* I am not very well; then *why* I think I am unwell; then I have an idea about what I need to get better, and so on . . .

So when I simply try to perceive my existence in its totality, all I succeed in perceiving is the current, instantaneous *state of my existence.* So the gaze that yields this perception both sees and does not see; it sees something of what it looks at, since it sees an instantaneous aspect of it which is not without reality, but it does not see what it looks at in the context of the dynamic reality which sustains all its instantaneous aspects. There is a missing dimension, Time. It is this dimension which has to be mastered if my perception of existing is to be a real subjective awareness, an *awareness of self.*

This difference between total and somatic coenaesthesia is responsible for another difference between them. The element of reality in my global sense of existing depends on the extent to which any given instantaneous perception contrasts with its predecessor, in other words on the extent to which I feel that I exist more or less than I did just a short while ago. If I withdraw from the external world and its stimuli in order to devote myself to repeated attempts at perceiving my existential state, my efforts soon become unproductive. My existential state stops changing once I am insulated from external influences and my instantaneous states become identical, with nothing to distinguish one from another. The time element is represented in the features which distinguish one instant from another, i.e. by the *memory* of the preceding instant which I retain in the present one. When that disappears, so does any formless perception of existing.

Although, as I mentioned above, the time dimension in this context is missing from awareness in ordinary people, it must still be represented there by memory. It must manifest itself in this way in relation to the changes in my existential state, in order for there to be some perception of existing. This perception is in any case *relative*: as an ordinary, unrealized person, I cannot simply feel myself existing. I can only have the formless perception of *existing more or less than I did a moment ago.* (Physical coenaesthesia is different; my perception of my arm's physical existence has something of the nature of the absolute and of the atemporal, hence the phantom limb phenomenon, where an amputee continues to sense the existence of his missing limb.)

So, as I am at present, I can only perceive existing in a way which is *relative and confined to the instant*; it is only an instantaneous perception of existing more or less than I did a moment ago. The sense I have of existing alters continually in response to changes in my relationship with the outside world. It behaves like one of those toys where changes in pressure make a little diver bob up or down in a sealed jar of water; and something like this inside me rises or sinks as I experience the outside world confirming or denying me. My sense of existing more or less is my instantaneous perception of where the little diver has got to compared with where it was a moment before.

I perceive how the diver's positions relate to one another, whether higher or lower than before. *But at present I cannot see it move between these positions.* I only perceive its changes in position indirectly, from the discrepancies between my instantaneous, successive glimpses; I do not perceive them directly. The little diver's changes in position represent alterations in my deep states, and express the deepest level of my vital impulse. They are the first manifestation in the realm of phenomena of my noumenal 'being', of my Principle, of the Supreme Universal Principle which the Vedanta calls the Self. What I perceive are instantaneous, different, contrasting states of my Principle's manifestation, but I do not perceive its manifestation as a continuous process. Only the Principle itself sees itself manifesting in continuity; and my consciousness will not experience its own identity with its Principle until it sees, as a continuous process, that aspect of manifestation which is the spectacle of my own creation, or, as the Vedanta expresses it, when I become the Spectator of my own spectacle.

This concept, 'the Spectator of the spectacle', is often misunderstood; some believe that the spectacle referred to occurs at the stage of internal formal phenomena, in other words that it is the imaginative film of ideas and feelings. This is a serious mistake; it encourages ordinary introspection which increases our tendency to be slaves to our imaginative world. The problem is insoluble if attacked at this lower level: we cannot be the active spectator of our imaginative film. We only *see* it when we are not *looking at* it actively; active looking stops it. We need to become Spectator of the spectacle which takes place at a level above the imaginative film, the level where the first, profound, formless impulse stirs from which all our inner activity in the realm of form subsequently derives. This first movement corresponds to the movement of the little 'diver', and is a shifting upwards or downwards of that global inner state which is the synthesis and source of our psychological and somatic states.

To summarize, obtaining satori requires us to transform instantaneous perceptions of existing more or less than we did a short while ago into one continuous perception, which will simply be the perception of existing. To achieve this, one must train oneself to have more and more of these instantaneous perceptions. To make it easier to understand what happens during this work, imagine projecting a film at the rate of one image every ten seconds, so that each image can be seen distinctly. If the rate of projection is gradually increased, we can see separate images clearly for a while, and then a point is reached when we no longer see them clearly as a series of discrete images, but are still not yet able to see the film as a continuous process. Finally the rate of projection is fast enough for us to see the film clearly in its continuity.

Zen gives an excellent account of the intermediate stage which separates the vision of ordinary consciousness, which is clear but lifeless, from that of post-satori consciousness which is both clear and alive. When this intermediate stage is at its peak, Zen calls it *Tai-i*, the Great Doubt, and describes it as a mental state characterized by total, formless confusion. This state is so complete, and so free of all form, that it is not at all chaotic, but approaches the transparent purity of an immense crystal, behind which nothing is hidden.

This idea that three successive stages are involved can also be found in the following passage from the Zen literature: '*Before someone studies Zen, mountains are mountains and rivers are rivers; when, with the help of instruction from a good teacher, some insight into the truth of Zen has been achieved, mountains are no longer mountains and rivers are no longer rivers; but after that, when the haven of rest has really been reached, mountains are again mountains and rivers are again rivers.*'*

Let us move on to what we understand the practice of inner work to involve at this stage. There is nothing to be added to what has already been said so far about the 'how' of this work, beyond repeating that the difficulty with looking inwards lies in its simplicity. Failure to look in the right way is always due to making things more complicated than they really are: the task is simply a matter of seeing whether there is a global sense of feeling better or worse, whether the little diver has floated up or down.

I want to make it clear that this kind of looking is only useful if the student has understood deeply and is genuinely convinced intellectually that, since obtaining satori is the only possible way of resolving his or her present state of distress, *there is no significance whatsoever in the 'diver' being up or down*. The only thing that matters is developing a continuous perception of its movement, not whether one is happy or unhappy, nervous or confident, etc. Impartial intellectual understanding must be firmly established above affective preferences, which will obviously still persist. A related idea is that the kind of looking we have been discussing obviously presupposes understanding that the

---

* Based on a famous saying by Ching-yüan (11th century), quoted in the *Ching-te Ch'uan Teng Lu (Record of the Transmission of the Lamp)*.

forms taken by our mechanisms are all equally insignificant. There has to have been a preliminary phase during which we analyse our mechanisms, so that we understand the mechanical nature of our inner world. Practical inner work presupposes that all this has been done, and that our complexes have lost their fascination. The work of theoretical understanding must be finished properly before practical inner work can be undertaken.

There is another important question still to be considered: like every ordinary person, I have five different modalities of thought, so which of these will provide the best psychological conditions for my attempts to 'see into my own nature'? The answer is simple: only one of the modalities is compatible with this kind of perception, and that is the fourth one, where the individual is adapted to the real external world.

When the variations in my existential states result from the unreal, non-present external world created by my imagination, in other words occur in response to an imaginative film which I construct outside present reality from material supplied by my store of images, my mind is then fully occupied in its work of construction and is not available for active perception. I can only actively perceive my different existential states when the changes in them are not due to my own agency but occur in response to activity generated by something other than myself, in other words, by not-self, the real, present, external world; and what is going on in the real, present external world only affects my psyche during those periods when I engage with that world, when I adapt to reality.

Even at such moments, it might be objected, the changes taking place in my states must depend on some activity on the part of my mind. This is true, but the activity is reactive. It is a case of reactivity rather than activity. When I adapt to the real, external world, the mechanisms which are going to produce my states are initiated from outside me, not from within me, and that is what matters: the moment that they are initiated from outside me, my own capacity to initiate is available for active perception.

Experience proves the point I have just been making better than any amount of reasoning. If I want to perceive my existential state while daydreaming or thinking about something, I can only succeed in doing so if I interrupt what I am doing, and put my life on hold. Whereas if I want to perceive my existential state at a time when I am doing something real and practical, I realize that I can do so without stopping what I am doing, and that I can feel myself at the very centre of my action. When my attention is turned outwards, my imaginative film is based on the external world as it is. It is reactive and it is initiated by the external world. This reactive imaginative film does not prevent me perceiving my existential state. It is like a wheel turning to the regular rhythm of the cosmos, at whose centre my attention can place itself upon my perception of my existential state in that instant. Active imaginative films, on the other hand, which my mind fabricates without any contact with the actual external world, prevent me perceiving my existential state. So inner work is incompatible with sleep, day-dreaming, and inwardly contemplating; it is only compatible with adaptation to the concrete world as it is.

So we can understand why Zen masters have said again and again that *the Tao is our daily life. One day a monk asked his master to instruct him in Zen. The master said: 'Have you eaten yet?' 'Yes,' replied the monk. 'Well then, go and wash up.'* Zen also says: *'When we are hungry, we eat; when we are sleepy, we lie down. Where does the finite or the infinite come into all this? It is only when the intellect, with its fertile restlessness, enters the scene and carries on in its usual way that we stop living and imagine that we lack something.'*

Inner work consists of an effort to relax, to release what is contracted. It is 'not-doing' opposed to our reflex inner agitating; it is simplicity opposed to our natural complexity. Zen often stresses this simplicity and letting go. This can give us the impression that inner work must be easy, not something one has to bother about too much. Because we know so little about 'not-doing', we assume that we only have to take trouble with our 'doing'. Yet if we try to relax our whole body and keep it in a state of complete relaxation for five minutes, we will see how difficult it is to maintain the level of watchfulness needed to prevent tension building up again in any of our muscles. This is why Zen, despite repeated references to the simplicity of inner work, also says: *'Inner peace is only obtained after a relentless battle against our personality. . . . The battle must rage with total vigour and forcefulness; otherwise when peace reigns, it will only be a sham.'*

This battle against the personality does not take place at the level of forms, and does not, for example, imply struggling against one's failings. It means fighting the mental inertia which is the source of all our inner formal agitation; struggling against this current in order to gradually work our way up to the place where our consciousness is reintegrated into the formless source of our being.

We must now complete our discussion of the ways in which our five modalities of thought are compatible or otherwise with the attempt to 'see into one's own nature'. To do this we need to explore the distinction already made between the *reactive imaginative film*, based on the actual external world, and the *active imaginative film*, which our mind constructs with material from our store of images. There is a parallel between this distinction and one we can observe in our everyday psychological life: we live on two distinct levels at the same time, *sensation* and *imagery*. For instance, most people long for wealth and luxury and expect that these will be a source of self-affirmation; and rich people certainly do get self-affirmation from their wealth. There are two kinds of such affirmation: wealth affirms at the sensory level by providing favourable physical conditions (good food, good rest, relaxing surroundings, etc.) and also at the level of imagery (the feeling that one is 'somebody' because of having all these things). The sensory level corresponds to physical coenaesthesia, the imaginal to psychological coenaesthesia. The sensory level is clearly real, while the imaginal is illusory. The sensory level relates to what the individual has in common with everyone else, in other words to the individual as a universal human being. The imaginal level corresponds to that aspect of individual experience which is concerned with seeing oneself as unique and distinct, and wanting to be so. In other words it corresponds to the individual as self-centred and egotistical with an illusory self-image. (The self-image is illusory because individuals only differ from one another at a formal level, not in their general human condition)

Ordinary people never live on one level only, except during deep sleep; they always live on two levels at once. Mental activity is never confined to producing a reactive film (sensory level) or even to producing an active film on its own (imaginal level); two films, reactive and active, are produced all the time. Attention shifts from one to another, and is only on one at any given moment, but the two films are produced continuously in parallel. It is immediately obvious that my sensory level life is always accompanied by imaginal level activity. The dispute concerning my being versus my nothingness is going on all the time inside me, influenced by everything happening to me on the sensory plane: the confidence or doubt I feel about myself fluctuates according to my physical sense of well-being or malaise, etc.

On the other hand, there do appear to be times when I seem to live solely on the level of imagery. However, we will see that this is not in fact the case and it will become clear that this level is based on the sensory level and is in fact dependent on it and a consequence of it. This can be illustrated by taking a situation where the imaginal level exercises an extreme effect: a rich financier, who has been bankrupted, kills himself to escape having to live a diminished life in which he would no longer be 'somebody'. He destroys his body in order to preserve his self-image.

It seems obvious that this act derives solely from the level of imagery and that the sensory level is subordinate to that level in this example. But let us take a closer look: the man kills himself to avoid being discredited. What makes this intolerable to him is the extreme value which he attaches to his standing in other people's eyes, and the only reason the opinion of other people matters so much to him is that their respect and hence affirmation of him represents their alliance with him in his struggle against not-self. So it protects his organism against death. However paradoxical this may seem, this is someone killing himself to preserve something which potentially protects him against death.

This example helps us understand how the plane of imagery is a kind of illusory edifice which *active* imagination constructs upon the plane of sensation. Everything I like on the imaginal level, which means everything which affirms me on that level, does so because on the whole I consider it favourable to my organism. I say 'on the whole' because affirmation at the imaginal level does not coincide directly with the organismic affirmation which is its source.

Take the case of a powerful business man who works non-stop and becomes very rich; on the sensory level this daily agitation is a negation, and, to put it colloquially, he is leading a dog's life. But he is attached to his situation, because it confers power on him and this represents potential protection for his organism against death. This man is also killing himself, little by little, in order to maintain and increase his protection against death. The affirmation he gets on the imaginal level does not coincide directly with the sensory level affirmation which his wealth has the potential to provide him with; nevertheless, potential though it may be, it is the latter affirmation which determines and underpins the former.

Ordinary people live all the time on these two planes or levels, which correspond to the somatic and psychological domains reviewed in an earlier chapter. Remember that every event in life eventually produces associated reactions in these two realms, but that the contacts with the external world which release them are channelled via one *or* other of them. I may be contacted by the external world through the sensory level (this is the real, present external world) or through the imaginal level (when the external world is represented in memory), but I *experience* both contacts at the same time on both levels.

Although ordinary people live on both levels at once, all the time, I have already mentioned that they only pay attention to one of them at any given moment. During dreams, day-dreams and inward contemplation, attention is fixed on the imaginal plane alone, the active imaginative film. The reactive imaginative film is produced in parallel, but no attention is paid to it. Only when there is adaptation to the actual external world is life experienced on both imaginal and sensory levels, with attention alternating rapidly between them. If I observe myself carefully, I realize that I am always day-dreaming to some extent, usually a great deal, at the same time as I am adapting myself to present reality in order to engage with, and manage, the external world.

Bearing that in mind, we can now get a more accurate idea of the compatibility between fourth modality thought and inner work: in theory, there is complete compatibility, but, in real life it seems incomplete *because I am never unambiguously in the fourth modality*. My attention switches continuously between the fourth and the third modality, in other words I straddle the two kinds of thought. The precise objective of inner work is to establish me through satori in the *pure* fourth modality alone, to really get me adapted to the external world at last, to attain Reality through the elimination of dream.

Experience demonstrates this. As soon as I start to make some correct efforts to perceive my instantaneous existential state, I notice that they put a brake on my imaginative film, which is incompatible with them. More accurately, these efforts cause my illusory film to dissolve by withdrawing attention from it and placing it instead on the reactive, reality-based imaginative film. In short, my efforts dissolve my imaginal life away and purge it from my sensory level life. Inner work eliminates illusory psychological coenaesthesia from reality-based physical coenaesthesia, and my egotistical, illusory life is eliminated from my real, physical life. I realize that within me there exists an 'earth' which is real, my physical life where my perceptions respond to present reality; and there is also an illusory 'heaven', my life where active imagination rules. It is this illusory 'heaven' which prevents me at present from truly possessing either my 'heaven' or my 'earth'. By getting rid of it, inner work will give me back to my earth: through being restored to my earth, I will possess the true Heaven. This is the meaning of the Zen saying: '*Earth is paradise.*'

This understanding, which restores value to physical life and downgrades our imaginative life, could tempt us to force ourselves to focus on physical perceptions and physical coenaesthesia. Inner work of this kind would be sterile and dangerous. It is impossible to expunge our imaginative life artificially; it would only be a senseless sham. The subtle distillation which will eliminate illusion does not take place on the dualistic level where the real and the illusory are manifested, and our form-bound inner manipulations have nothing to offer here. It is only our Principle which can bring about this alchemical distillation, this purification. All we have to do is stop our habitual opposition to the activity of our Principle, and we learn to do so by means of the total, instantaneous, inner relaxing mentioned earlier.

The progressive dissolution of life lived out at the imaginal level brings us closer to deliverance, to our birth into Reality. But, from the pre-satori viewpoint, this dissolution represents the difficult death throes of the old self. Inner work to see into one's own nature also constitutes authentic *asceticism*, purification and mortification. External forms of asceticism are just simulations of the real thing. (Let me spell this out: it is quite clear that genuine asceticism does not require any changes in our external life).

It is important that we should understand the enormity of what we have to give up in our current way of looking at things, and at the same time appreciate the perfectly painless nature of this surrender. As I am today, the imaginal level which I am going to lose is not just enormous, it is everything; it is the salt of my life, it gives it all its meaning; it is the site of my terrors, of my raptures, my enthusiasms, my compassion, and of my hopes. For an ordinary person, life without emotion, without the 'soul's' dualistic sensibility, can only be experienced in *imagination* as the death of one's being; illusory 'heaven', with its storms and its sunshine, seems more precious than anything else, in particular one's 'earth', the body. Indeed the dissolution of life at the imaginal level signifies giving up this illusory heaven once and for all, and renouncing everything which, in our present condition, we look on as sacred or supernatural.

Yet this renunciation is completely painless; the death throes of the old self may be a struggle (this is 'the relentless battle against our personality'), but they are not painful. In practice renunciation only proceeds to the extent that I succeed in dissipating those mirages which make me see worth where there is none, through the shift in my attention which ensures that my sensory level takes precedence. Renunciation does not rob me of valued objects on the level where they are valued. It would be terrible if I were to be deprived of the imaginal level, but I am not: it is I who give it up and I cannot feel regret for what is given up in this way since the illusory existence of the imaginal level only affects me when I inhabit it. Painful inner work is work badly done; it focuses directly on the emotions; correct inner work, the attempt to see into one's own nature, works in us at the point where emotions come into being. How could my escape from emotion be the cause of pain and distress? We have nothing to fear from mental formations as we strive towards the formless in the right way; when light dissipates darkness itself, it dissipates every shadow.

# CHAPTER TWELVE

# Practical Implications of the Zen Approach to Inner Work

In practice it is not easy to understand what Zen means by inner work with satori as its eventual outcome. Indeed, when Zen masters speak directly about it, they make general statements which can seem rather ironic: *'It is sufficient for you to see into your own nature,'* or *'Be completely detached from everything,'* or *'You are Buddhas, so you don't have to become Buddhas, just behave like Buddhas . . . There is nothing else to do except enact one's Buddha role in full,'* etc. That's all very fine, the disciple thinks, but it does not leave me much wiser about how I manage my inner practice. So he tries to imagine what kind of practice could really bring satori closer, and then goes to tell the master. He suffers a series of rebuffs. If he suggests doing good works, the master assures him this would be useless. If he proposes to meditate on sacred texts, the master says: *'Don't let yourself be upset by the Sutra. It is you who should upset the Sutra.'* If he intends to practice emptying his mind, the master indicates that this is just a form of slow suicide. If he suggests some patient, in-depth intellectual study, the master tells him: *'Reflection and discursive thought achieve nothing. Like a lamp in the middle of the day, they don't provide any illumination.'* When the unfortunate disciple finally asks humbly for a glimmer of light, the master replies: *'Thinking that Zen is mysterious is the gravest error and one which many fall into . . . We do not have to avoid contradiction, we have to live it.'*

No doubt Zen Masters are justified when they try to avoid expressing the inexpressible, and, at the same time, indicate that the inexpressible is not at all mysterious. They are right to reply to their pupils' suggestions with negations and hound them from error to error until they reach  a state of mind in which despair is accepted without sadness, and the whole being de-contracts and opens itself to Reality. Despite this I

94

intend to try and do what Zen masters do not do, which is to speak pragmatically about inner work from a perspective which respects the spirit of Zen but is not restricted to abstract generalizations.

Zen teaches that correct inner work is neither a 'doing', nor a 'not-doing'. As it stands, this statement can only succeed in discouraging us unless we understand that 'not doing' on one level corresponds to 'doing' on another, which then makes it possible for us to discover this other level where inner work takes on a positive aspect.

To explain this point, I will refer to something analogous in the way our body functions. When we make a movement, the contraction of each muscle fibre is controlled by the activity of a neurone in the spinal cord whose function is to cause muscle contraction. If there were no means of inhibiting this nerve cell, the muscle would be in a state of continuous contraction. But this neurone is not a free agent, being connected by a long fibre to a neurone in the brain whose activity inhibits the spinal neurone. So, when my muscle is relaxed, this state of rest corresponds, at the level of the spinal neurone, to a 'not doing' (since the muscle contracts immediately the cell 'does' something); but the spinal neurone's 'not doing' corresponds to a 'doing' by the brain cell, since the higher cell's activity blocks activity in the inferior one. Muscular relaxation, which is 'not doing' at a lower level, is 'doing' at a higher level.

Let us now see how vital energy works in us, in our whole being, and consider how two levels can be discerned in this, with non-activity on the lower level corresponding to activity on the higher level. This is the only way we will be able to understand why Zen assures us that we have nothing to 'do', while adding that inner work requires flawlessly attentive activity, 'as if our head was in the midst of flames'.

There is a hidden energy within our organism. This is self-evident from our experience of forces arising ceaselessly within us, forces which move us, and make us think and act. Their source is not directly accessible to us, but we can infer from what we observe of our own subjective phenomena that a source of energy must exist within us. We can only imagine this source as a kind of boundless reservoir containing vital potential energy, which is latent, without movement, invisible and intangible. Although this source is manifestly active in my individual person, it should not be thought of as an individual source. As long as this reservoir of energy remains in a potential and non-manifested state, it should be thought of as universal, since the individual and particular only begin with manifestation. So this source is both Principle and Origin of the Universe as well as being my Principle and Origin, and it corresponds to what Zen calls Cosmic or Unconscious Mind.

Forces from this source are going to well up within me in response to stimuli from the external world. These stimuli may reach me by psychological or physical channels. In either case, the resulting excitation will involve a bipolar tension between the external world and me. For example, when I drink alcohol or eat bread, there is a bipolar tension between what I take in and my own substance. Or again, if I perceive my life to be in danger there is a bipolar tension between that external image and a fantasy within me about my supposed entitlement to immortality.

The vital force which wells up within me in response to an external stimulus represents the first stage in the disintegration of the potential energy of my source. In due course we shall see that there is a second stage. This disintegration can be compared to that of an atomic nucleus. Bergson demonstrated that there were these 'explosive' phenomena within us; but he made the mistake of localizing them in the psyche. They occur at a higher level, above the psychological and physical domains, at the point where the central, common source emerges.

When this force wells up from the source it consists of a certain amount of raw, vital energy, which is still undifferentiated and formless. More accurately, it is intermediate between formal and formless. It is between the source and my phenomena, just as the positive and negative principles of creation lie between the Supreme Principle and the world of phenomena. The microcosm is formed like the macrocosm. Similarly this vital force pouring out from the source can present two aspects, positive and negative. If I experience the external stimulus as affirming me, the force is positive, and feels like a surplus of life at my disposal; it feels like a pressure, urging me towards the not-self (love/desire and love/benevolence). If the external stimulus seems to negate me, the vital force which wells up is negative: it feels like a loss of life, emptiness, 'de-pression', and aversion towards not-self (flight, repugnance, or aggression).

Although this vital energy, pouring forth in its primitive state, has two aspects depending on whether it carries a positive or negative sign, and is to that extent already modified by constraints belonging to the formal world, it is still prior to the formal world and should be considered formless. Similarly, the two principles of creation, positive and negative, which are at the limits of the temporal world, have to be classified as timeless, or atemporal.

We are able to perceive this formless vital force at its birth by direct intuition. We cannot describe it, because it is formless, but we can perceive it. If I have just had some good news, it is possible for me to drive any ideas relating to the cause of my happiness from my mind, and sense directly a kind of bubbling, excess life within me. In the same way, when things have gone wrong, by emptying my mind of associated ideas, I can sense a kind of void within me, like a current sucking me into nothingness. What this indicates is that it is possible for me to place my attention right up against my central source, just where it emerges into manifested creation. What this means is that I can raise my attention within me up to the formless level, where we will see that activity, 'doing', corresponds to 'not-doing' on the formal level of psychosomatic phenomena.

What I have just said is absolutely concrete and practical. Suppose, for example, I have just lost some money and I leave my attention where it normally is (on the formal, phenomenal level), I am then absorbed in vigorous imaginative activity during the course of which I ruminate over present and future concerns. If instead I follow the approach described above and place my attention on this intuitive perception of diminished vitality (I have to put a name to it when I am writing about it, although in reality it is formless), I observe that my imagination stops agitating. This is an experimental fact which anyone can confirm. My activity on the formless level brings about my inactivity on the formal level. The formless level, when my attention is located there, is able to check and inhibit the formal level.

The actual positioning of attention, whether occurring naturally on the formal level or voluntarily on the formless level, determines the fate of outpouring vital energy. Under normal conditions, in our usual state of ignorance, attention always remains in practice on the lower formal level; internal and external phenomena hold us in thrall. When attention is located on that level, the disintegration of vital energy emerging from the source is inevitably channelled into moving the human machine, in other words it *takes form* as somatic and psychological energetic phenomena. The moment formless energy pours forth and begins to take form and flow and disintegrate down the slope of phenomena, it becomes *emotion*. What this indicates is that emotion is a primary inner phenomenon at this stage, still neither somatic nor psychological, but one which will in due course give rise to physio-chemical processes and imaginal activity.

With attention located in this way, a vicious circle is unavoidable: the imaginal activity engendered by the process acts in turn as a source of excitation, stimulating further outpourings of energy which share the same fate as the energy flows which preceded them; and so it goes on.

Contrast this with the situation where my attention, which has been focused on external stimuli, is redirected inwards and is fixed for a moment on formless energy at the point where it first emerges. During this moment, vital energy stops being channelled and disintegrated into formal processes, so it does not produce any activity in the form of actions or thoughts in my machine. It cannot go back into its source, because the first disintegration which gave birth to it is irreversible. So what happens to it? Some teachings, which are insufficiently disengaged from the fascination of form, claim that this force accumulates, taking on the organism's general shape, but in a form which is different and more subtle than the one we are aware of, thus gradually developing into a second, subtle body within the original coarse one (this is the misleading astral body theory).

Zen, which in any case does not 'believe' in anything, does not believe in this. So how are we to conceptualize the fate of this pure vital energy, spared from disintegrating into phenomena? What light does Zen shed on this? In fact we can think of this energy accumulating in us, providing we do not imagine it taking on any form, however subtle: it accumulates without form on the level of the two positive and negative inferior creative principles, which are themselves formless, though all forms arise from them. Accumulating in this situation, it could be described as potential actualized energy: potential because it is no more active at the phenomenal level than the potential energy within the source; and actualized in so far as it is accumulating and available for some event in the future.

That future event is *satori*. Vital energy can be compared to gunpowder: without inner work, small amounts burn up in displays of fireworks which are powerless to effect fundamental changes in structure (fireworks representing the emotions and their psychosomatic effects). Inner work manages to save some of this powder from time to time, storing up little packets of it, and building a sort of time bomb, which will only explode when enough powder has been accumulated in this way. This delayed explosion will have nothing in common with emotional fireworks: emotions wear out the human organism because they are little explosions which take place within its form, but the tremendous explosion of satori will not touch a single cell in the human organism. It will take place in the formless realm and its effect on the formal level will be like that of a catalyst bringing about the conciliation and resolution of temporal dualism and consequently eliminating every inner tension and anxiety once and for all.

Before satori has become possible, during the period when formless energy is accumulating, its build-up results in the emergence of a relative wisdom, or, more accurately, in a relative reduction in our habitual craziness. The fact that some people grow wiser as they get older is due to their paying less attention to internal and external forms, the touch of experience having got rid of some of their illusory beliefs. Without knowing it, they achieve some displacement of attention from the formal to the formless in the way we have just been considering. They do inner work without realizing it. But this lack of awareness means that they do too little to bring about the large accumulation of energy which satori demands.

Let us take another look at the issue of displacing attention. When I was explaining this earlier, I indicated that our attention had to come to rest on a particular intuitive perception, and in fact we have to proceed in this way because it is impossible to remove attention from one object without having another object available to direct it towards. But it would be a big mistake to imagine that the formless intuitive perception towards which we choose to direct our attention possesses any particular merit (this would imply an illusory concept of spiritual as opposed to temporal gains). It is only something to orientate ourselves by, just a means we use to conserve energy which would otherwise be channelled into the formal domain. Displacing one's attention in this way, doing inner work, is not 'doing' something that one would not ordinarily do, it is 'doing nothing', or, more accurately, it is actively inhibiting 'doing' in any shape or form.

This idea of two levels, formal and formless, with 'doing' on the latter corresponding to 'not doing' on the former, enables us to understand the real positive aspect of many of the negative terms commonly used in Zen, e.g. no-mind, no-form, no-birth, emptiness, void, Unconscious, etc.

The practice of using koans* can be understood in the same way. The cryptic formula to which Zen monks repeatedly return their attention has certainly got a form, but one which is so obviously irrational that it rapidly ceases to be perceptible. As an object of attention, the koan itself is not of the slightest interest, but what is interesting and effective is its use to drag the attention away from the formal level.

Displacing the attention is what constitutes this inner work and it really must be a *displacing*, with the attention moving to and fro between formal and formless. It would be impossible to fix attention continuously on the formless (any more than one can on forms). It would be equivalent to suicide. But, more important, stimulation by the external world is absolutely essential to produce the outward flow of formless energy from the central source. So inner work has to be discontinuous

---

* 'An exercise for the mind, beyond thought, prescribed by a Zen master, and of such a nature that it violates the postulates of logic.' *Zen Dictionary* by Ernest Wood, Pelican Books, 1977.

and in this respect it conforms to the law of alternation which rules the whole of creation (day/night, summer/winter, the heart's systole and diastole, etc.).

It is not a question either of wanting to save all our vital energy from disintegrating into phenomena. To spend one's time thinking about the energy going to waste within us would be to fall into the distressing mistake of viewing 'salvation' as a duty. So there would be contraction, not relaxation. Only when I stop bothering about contracting can I relax.

The Zen masters tell us: *'Don't under any circumstances hinder or disturb the course of life.'* Inner work is carried out during the course of our life, but does not disturb it because it runs *parallel to,* not *in* it. Which is to say that it does not deal with the forms and modalities of life, nor does it try to modify them; attention withdrawn from the formal level simply ignores forms. Someone who works according to Zen becomes increasingly indifferent to actions, imaginings, and feelings; they are all part of the form-bound mechanisms from which energy must be preserved. Inner work, using the method of alternation described above, can be carried out all day long without involving the slightest element of spiritual exercise, deliberate discriminative thought, moral rules of conduct, or a wish to do 'good'. The practitioner who disregards the visible world and its phantoms, whether they be attractive or disagreeable, accumulates in the invisible world the charge of energy which will one day explode this whole 'cave of phantoms', and so reveal daily life in its real abundance and plenitude.

# CHAPTER THIRTEEN

# Obedience to the Nature of Things

According to Zen, our nature is Buddha nature; it is perfect, and is lacking in nothing. But we do not realize this, because we are enmeshed in the toils of our mental representations. We seem to be screened from Reality by the activity of our imagination, which functions dualistically.

Imaginative mental activity has a useful role in early life, while the human machine is incomplete and abstract intellect still not fully developed. During this initial period it has a compensatory function without which the limitations of the human condition would be unbearable. Once the human machine has completed its development, imagination continues to serve this useful purpose but it also becomes increasingly harmful, being responsible for wasting energy which would otherwise accumulate inwardly and bring about the crystallization of non-dualistic, intuitive knowledge (satori).

The problem is that the relief provided by imagination is taken for a real improvement in our condition. Any temporary relief of our distress encourages us to think that we are making progress towards getting rid of it altogether. In fact, temporary relief leads to a progressive worsening of the condition it is intended to relieve. But we do not realize this: we cling to an implicit belief in the usefulness of active imagination and ruminations.

One might think that experience would sooner or later contradict such an erroneous belief, but this does not usually happen. So why do we believe so strongly that agitation is useful although experience tells us that it is harmful?

We cling to it because we do not think of ourselves as being anything other than the personal self which we experience in the dualistic mode. We do not know that there is something else within us which is different from this visible self, something invisible working unseen on our behalf. Because we identify with the phenomena we can perceive, and in particular with our imaginative mind, we do not think that we are anything more than this. 'There is no one else who would work on my behalf apart from myself' seems to be our attitude. So, because we are not aware of any other 'me' outside the imaginative mind and the feelings and actions which depend on it, it is to this mind that we turn for delivery from our distress. When there only seems to be one means of salvation, we believe in it because we have to believe in it.

Yet, when I consider my living body, I can see that there are all kinds of marvellous activities taking place within it spontaneously, without any involvement on the part of what I refer to as 'me'. My body is maintained by processes whose ingenuity and complexity defy the imagination. If it is wounded, it is repaired, but by what or by whom I have no idea. The inescapable conclusion is that a benign Principle is tirelessly engaged in continuously creating me on its own initiative.

The organs of my body appeared and developed spontaneously. So did dualistic, sense-mediated awareness. Is it not possible that direct, intuitive, non-dualistic awareness might also appear spontaneously? Zen answers in the affirmative. As far as Zen is concerned, spontaneous normal evolution in man ends in satori. The Principle is at work in me unceasingly, working towards the unfolding of satori (just as the same Principle is working in a tulip bulb towards the unfolding of its flower). But the activity of my imagination impedes the genesis of this profound evolution, continuously dissipating the energy generated by the Principle which would otherwise build up to satori. As an old Zen master said: '*Who conceals Realization? No one except me.*' I am unaware that what I wish for in my essence – to escape dualistic illusion, the source of distress – is being realized within me by something other than my personal self. I do not imagine that I can count on anyone except myself, so I feel it is up to me to do something. I begin to experience mounting distress because of this belief that I am completely on my own. I become unsettled and restless and my agitation gradually neutralizes the beneficial work taking place in my depths. Zen expresses this as follows: '*Not knowing how close they are to Truth, people seek it afar . . . what a pity!*'

The process which impedes this profound spontaneous development is produced by mechanical reflexes. It operates automatically when I do not actively maintain faith in my invisible Principle and its work of liberation. In other words, for these constructive changes to take place there must be an active belief in my Principle and in the fact that its work towards liberation is ever-present and spontaneous. Faith does not move mountains, but it enables them to be moved by the Universal Principle.

The part I play in the development of my satori consists of maintaining this active faith, and in fully realizing and maintaining the idea that my supreme good is developing spontaneously within me.

Zen is clearly passive in some ways and not in others. It is passive when it tells us that we do not have to liberate ourselves, but not passive in the sense that, though we may not have to work directly at being liberated, we have to co-operate in the task by thinking effectively about the process of liberation which is at work deep within us. This is clearly not an idea which nature automatically provides us with. The external world is continually engaged in persuading us that our true good resides in some success in the formal realm which justifies all our restless activity. Intense, patient mental effort is essential if we are to work with our liberating Principle.

A potential pitfall is waiting when we reach this level of understanding: there is a risk that we will think we have to withdraw attention from life, with the result that we go about like a sleepwalker in the belief that the right approach involves continuously bringing the 'idée fixe' that the Principle is at work within us into the forefront of our mind. This could only result in mental disturbance.

A different approach is required. During moments when internal and external circumstances are favourable, we have to reflect on our understanding of spontaneous liberation, thinking as forcefully and concretely as possible of the boundless wonder which is being prepared for us and will one day resolve all our fears and cravings. At such moments, we are repeatedly seeding and re-seeding the field of our faith. We are gradually arousing our dormant faith, and the hope and love which accompany it. Then we go back into daily life and we carry on as usual. Because we have been thinking correctly for a moment, part of our attention remains attached to this level of thought, although the level itself returns into our depths and becomes invisible. Part of our attention remains there while the rest of our attention carries on as usual. Any man who has adored a woman, or been preoccupied with a piece of work in progress, will understand what I mean. When he attends to his ordinary activities, he stops thinking about his love, as if he had forgotten her. But when his thoughts return to her beloved image, he realizes that he has never entirely left her, and that he has stayed with her all the time, as though in a 'second state' of consciousness at a subterranean level of awareness.

As far as our work towards liberation is concerned, this 'second state' is not something we get for nothing. It is something we can only acquire by cultivating specific moments of reflection, on the margins of ordinary practical life. Even so, these moments, though necessary, are not what really matters. The really effective aspect will be what happens when we are back in everyday life: when our faith is aroused and alert at a subterranean level of awareness, it will wrest some of our attention and hence some of our energy from the external world.

As this second, subterranean attention develops, we will notice that our interest in the phenomenal world becomes less compulsive; fears and cravings will lose their intensity. We will be able to learn discretion and non-activity towards our inner world, and so become able to follow the piece of Zen advice which says: '*Let go, let things be as they may. . . . Be obedient to the nature of things and you will be in harmony with the Way.*'

Note that there are occasions when ordinary people do have the correct attitude, when they are discreet and non-active. This happens during deep sleep, which is when they stop their restless attempts to improve themselves, and withdraw into the background. They let go, and 'let things be as they may', in effect abandoning themselves to their Principle and allowing it to work without interruption. It is because we are non-active in sleep that it has such a marvellous restorative effect.

But this wise behaviour during sleep only occurs because of a kind of mental blackout. The pernicious, egotistical, imaginative film has only stopped because the imaginative film based on current external reality has also stopped. The harmful part of the mind only stops because its healthy part (the one which perceives present objects directly) has also stopped. This is why sleep could never bring about realization.

We can attain wisdom without our whole mind having to stop. As our faith in our liberating Principle grows, this weakens our egotistical imaginative film without weakening the film based on present reality. The emergence and growth of our faith enables us to discriminate between the two kinds of imaginative film. So we gradually move towards a state where deep sleep and the waking state are conciliated. This extraordinary development is also one which takes place of its own accord: it is quite impossible for any attempt at inner manipulation to create the slightest real harmony within us. If we think correctly, or more accurately stop thinking in the wrong way, this is sufficient to enable our Principle to work within us, which is the only artisan qualified to carry out this great work.

This can be better understood by means of an analogy. The developing human being can be compared to a child's toy balloon, which expands into the shape of some creature. While the balloon is scarcely inflated at all, it is just a small spherical mass with few distinguishing features, and this stage corresponds to the human being at birth. Then, as the Principle blows into the balloon, its volume increases; at the same time, it begins to lose its simple spherical shape; protuberances and concavities appear, and a figure emerges with unique characteristics. This represents the development of what we refer to as 'character' and 'personality', of what makes me 'me' and no one else. It corresponds to the development of the human machine, soma and psyche.

*Normal* development would then proceed along the following lines if it were not hindered by human ignorance. A point is reached around puberty when the human machine has completed its physical development with the appearance of sexual function, and its psychological development with the emergence of objective, abstract, generalizing intelligence: this corresponds to the point where the balloon is fully inflated and its surface cannot stretch any further. But the Principle goes on blowing into it, producing a state of hypertension. Because the surface cannot stretch any further, the excess pressure forces it to increase its capacity by altering its shape, so that all the protuberances and concavities are gradually evened out. So it becomes progressively more spheroidal, this being the shape which permits the maximum capacity for a given surface. The balloon's irregularities gradually disappear. In the end it becomes a perfect sphere; no increase in capacity is possible. The Principle goes on blowing, and the sphere bursts.

There are three phases in this normal evolution. The little sphere at the beginning, the little balloon mass before expansion has started, represents the phase which precedes man's temporal realization, coming before the development of personality and the ego. In a sense the little child is *still* spherical. The second phase, that of the developed personality, corresponds to the complex balloon figure with all its individual peculiarities. In the third phase, which ends with the balloon bursting, irregularities are evened out and personality begins to fade as the mind attains a universal viewpoint, or, more accurately, frees itself from the narrowness and rigidity of the individual point of view. The individual returns to the initial spherical shape, but the difference now is that temporal realization has already occurred. So there is a resemblance between this phase and the first, although in a sense they are opposites (the words of Jesus come to mind: 'Verily I say unto you, Whosoever shall not receive the kingdom of God as a little child, he shall not enter therein', Mark 10:15).

This third phase seems to involve both progress and regression: progress from the universal point of view since the balloon increases its capacity, and draws closer to an explosion which is going to unite it with the immense cosmic sphere; but regression as far as the individual features, or personality, are concerned. At this stage those characteristics which distinguish individuals from each other are reduced: they become more and more ordinary, and distinctive features disappear. The old self weakens and begins to die as the birth of the new self, heralded by the bursting of the balloon, draws closer. (This gives us a key to understanding the words of Saint John the Baptist: 'Prepare ye the way of the Lord, make his paths straight, Every valley shall be filled, and every mountain and hill shall be brought low,' Luke 3:5.)

The culmination of the third phase, the bursting of the balloon, is the explosion of satori, the instant where all limitations vanish and the one is reunited with the all.

I have mentioned that it is our ignorance which frustrates this normal evolution. Before initiation the interior of the balloon lacks any reality as far as the individual is concerned, while its surface and its particular features seem to possess a unique, undeniable reality. In the state of ignorance, the will to be is only expressed as the will to be as a distinct and separate entity. The ignorant balloon figure, which is now rigid like a statue, rejects any reduction in its distinctive features; *it hardens into its particular shape, resisting the opening out which would increase its capacity by making it more spherical.* The excess pressure cannot be released in the normal way, so it seeks an alternative; this is provided by emotional and imaginative activity, which acts as a safety valve, releasing the excess pressure produced as the Principle goes on blowing into it. This is the process mentioned earlier, whereby energy is wasted which should instead be accumulating in order to produce an explosion.

Self-observation demonstrates that a variable excess of inner tension is present in us all the time. It can be felt in the agitation of our emotional states, whether these be positive or negative, elated or depressed. These states correspond to our unconscious resistance to the smoothing out of those features that make individuals of us. But though it may be easy to see what excess tension in our everyday psychology corresponds to, what constitutes the *normal* inner release of this tension is less obvious. This release occurs the moment I become conscious of my tension, while disregarding the circumstances that have given rise to it, and accept it within me.

As I emerge from ignorance, and understand that reality is not to be found in the external forms which are the object of my fears and cravings, but in the excess pressure which vital energy itself is generating, there is then a corresponding shift in attention away from forms towards my centre and source, the place where this vital pressure originates. This is possible if I have understood that my Principle is leading me to my true fulfilment, and that I do not have to worry about this process. Then there are instants when affect-driven imaginative activity stops and I feel the excess tension within me give way. That is all I *feel*, but I also *know* that my balloon's capacity has just increased because its shape has become simpler. This yielding of mine to the preparatory process of being 'smoothed out' is obviously fleeting and instantaneous, so this 'letting go' has to be repeated persistently as many times as necessary.

The analogy I have just used can be criticized, as can all analogies. But it can help us understand the nature of normal belief, in particular the essential idea that belief will mature of its own accord into its own perfect fulfilment, providing we can have faith in it and stop obstructing it with our anxieties and inner manipulations.

Let us take another look at the idea that ignorance entails lack of faith, and consequently lack of hope and charity. I am going to show how the normal direction of development is reversed, when faith is lacking. The normal direction takes place from above downwards: when an individual emerges from ignorance, his knowledge, which pre-existed from all eternity, dormant and unconscious, awakes in the intellectual centre. Of the three theological virtues, Faith leads the way, as the intellectual intuition of the Absolute Principle and as the certainty that it is 'my' Principle. Faith's awakening leads to the awakening of Hope: there is nothing more to be afraid of, and everything to hope for, once the Absolute Principle is acknowledged as 'my' Principle. So what began in the intellectual centre continues in the emotional centre. Finally the awakening of Faith and Hope brings about the awakening of Charity. It is a common mistake to think of Charity as an emotion, like adoring love.* It is really a love-desire, like a hunger felt by our whole organism for an existence which is no longer hidden from view by the spectres of dualism. It is a constant yearning for *every* aspect of existence. So what began in the intellectual centre and continued in the emotional centre ends in the animal or instinctive centre; what began in the head moves to the heart, and thence to the loins.

As long as ignorance prevails, this sequence is inverted. It begins with the appetite for existing, the desire to affirm oneself as a distinct entity, wishing only for the positive aspects of existence. This natural awakening of the wish to exist arouses all sorts of 'hopes' which are the inverse of Hope. They are hopes for some kind of success at the phenomenal level. What began in the animal centre continues into the emotional centre. The final stage is when the awakening of the desire to exist and of the various hopes brings about 'beliefs', which are the inverse of Faith. These create the false values, the objectives needed by the hopes,

---

* In a subsequent book, *De L'Amour,* Benoit distinguished three kinds of love: *amour-bienveillance, amour-appetit,* and *amour adorant.*

107

the image-idols required to polarize the impulses rising from below. So what began in the animal centre and continued in the emotional centre, ends in the intellectual centre. What began in the loins, rises up to the heart, and then to the head.

That these two directions are radically opposed to one another is obvious. The *natural* direction goes from below upwards: cravings for the positive aspects of existence, then hopes, then fears. The *normal* direction goes from above downwards: Faith, then Hope, then Charity or the yearning for every aspect of existence.

The natural direction exists on its own early in life. Realization consists of the appearance and eventual triumph of the normal direction. This final triumph is satori. Before satori the normal direction has to emerge in competition with the natural direction, and take over increasingly at the latter's expense. ('*It* has to increase; *I* have to diminish.')

When we study the problem of Realization, we continually meet all kinds of paradoxes. For example, the Gospel says, 'He that loseth his life . . . shall find it.' Such paradoxes no longer trouble us when we fully understand that two vital currents flow in us: one which is natural and innate, flowing from below upwards; and another, potential, 'normal' current, which flows from above downwards. One can also speak of 'natural' life as the life of the 'old man', and 'normal' life as the life of the 'new man'. ('One must die in order to be reborn.').

The new current has to appear while the old natural current is still flowing upwards, and it starts in the intellectual centre, where the natural current ends. For the new person's life originates in 'Independent Intelligence', which is pure thought, i.e. intellectual intuition shielded from affective influences. The work of Independent Intelligence gradually destroys the beliefs which polarize the ascending natural current and are essential to its upward flow. As the individual 'stops cherishing opinions', in the Zen phrase, there is a proportionate and definitive decline in this natural current. In other words, Faith increases as beliefs decrease.

But the most interesting aspect of this opposite development occurs at the emotional level, and it gives us a better understanding of what is meant in Zen by 'let go'. Both Faith and Hope are eternally present but dormant. Just as Faith stirs into life with the gradual annihilation of beliefs, so Hope awakens as the whole assembly of hopes is gradually demolished. Dawn for the new life is sunset for the old; triumph for the one is disaster for the other. The old self can only anticipate satori with foreboding as the most radical disaster imaginable.

Self-observation reveals that I am instinctively striving to *succeed* all the time; that, whether my actions are egotistical (winning, enjoying, gaining admiration, etc) or altruistic (supporting someone else, becoming 'better', eradicating my 'faults', etc), there is this continual instinctive struggle to achieve a 'good' outcome, striving towards some 'higher' objective. I am continually agitated by 'upward'-striving tensions, like a bird beating its wings without pause in order to climb, or to prevent the wind from forcing it to the ground. I behave as though my 'hopes' were valid, and as though the true good I really need (Realization, satori) might be found by fulfilling them. But the opposite is true; my hopes are deceptive and are part of an infernal circle in which I struggle uselessly and exhaust myself. All my efforts to lift myself up are just ignorant acts of resistance against the joyful, spontaneous trans- formation which my Principle is always ready to bring about. Perfect Bliss is not waiting for me on high; it is down below. It is not waiting for me in any seeming triumph: it lies in what at present looks like disaster. Perfect joy is waiting for me in the total annihilation of my hopes.

It must be understood that the total disaster, whose centre conceals satori, does not necessarily have to coincide with some practical, external disaster. The disaster which brings about realization, the 'satori disaster', is an understanding, an intellectual intuition, of the radical senselessness of our natural ascending current: in other words, when we see clearly the nothingness which lies at the end of all our hopes. The despair which triggers realization is not derived from the practical disappointment of hopes which persist inside us (that would lead to suicide, not satori), but in the destruction of the hopes themselves. When people are referred to as 'desperate', it is not usually accurate to say that they are without hope. It is more a case of being full of hopes that the world has refused to oblige, and it is this that has made them miserable. Those who have reached a state of real desperation, in other words, when there is nothing more to be hoped for from the world of phenomena, are flooded with the perfect joy to which they finally cease their resistance.

This is how I should go about promoting the destruction of my senseless and regrettable 'hopes'. There is nothing to be gained by arranging to fail at work: hoping to succeed in ruining myself as opposed to hoping to succeed in getting rich would not change any- thing. No, I allow my instinctive and emotional life to carry on as usual. But once my understanding has been introduced to reality, it begins to work in parallel. When I suffer because my hopes come up against the world's resistance, I remind myself that my former 'suc- cesses' never brought me the absolute fulfilment that my hopes had anticipated from them; intense though they may have been at times, all my surface satisfactions have disappointed me in the end at a deeper level, the level of truth.

Strengthened by the experience gained from interpreting my illusory successes correctly, I begin to think about the new successes which I crave. I imagine what they would be like if I were to achieve them in reality, and I sense again the futility of success. In fact the bad times, the times when we are distressed, are best for this work; suffering which is felt by the organism as a totality checks the illusions which point us in the opposite direction to satori. Providing the hopes that were essential have been more or less fulfilled in the past, any hope that keeps on recurring in the present is extinguished more easily if the world frustrates it. It is easier for me to 'let go' when my muscles are very tired. Zen asserts: *'Satori comes upon you unexpectedly when you have exhausted all the resources of your being.'*

None of this should be understood as a masochistic appetite for suffering. People who work according to Zen are not in love with suffering, but with the fact that suffering happens to them, which is not the same thing at all. Their suffering helps them to 'let go', and creates the moments which facilitate that inner stillness, that discretion and silence, which enables the Principle to work actively in them for their Realization.

'Progressive' doctrines which invite us to ascend a hierarchy of states of consciousness, and more or less explicitly conceive of the perfect man as a kind of Superman, are quite clearly misguided, and all they do is modify the form taken by our hopes. Zen on the other hand invites us to engage in work which, right up to the moment of satori, only seems to be taking us downwards. In a sense everything gradually gets worse until the bottom is reached, where there is nothing else to go wrong, and where everything is found because everything is lost.

We cannot imagine anything about the transformation satori brings; so we risk acquiring a new idolatry if we try to imagine what it might be like. From our present perspective, the right kind of development can only look like the progressive destruction of everything we call success, and the realized individual seems to be someone who has become absolutely ordinary. Only an individual who has achieved satori can say: *'A stray dog, begging food and pity, hounded without mercy by urchins, has changed into a lion with a golden mane whose roar terrifies the faint-hearted.'*

# Part Two

*of*

## *The Supreme Doctrine*

# *Essays on Zen and Psychology*

# Foreword to Part Two

Some readers have wondered where the ideas contained in the first volume* came from. Confronted by precise, often paradoxical, views on the human condition, they were understandably curious to discover their origin and they also wanted to know how much they owed to the Zen masters and how much to the author.

I was not particularly surprised when I learned of this reaction, though I had not anticipated it. I would like to explain why, and I want to use a Zen perspective in examining the relationship between an intellectual truth and the individual personality conceiving it.

Consider first the profound distinction made by the Vedanta between *Reality* and *truths*. There is only one Reality, the Principle underlying all manifestation, which encompasses everything (including the manifestations of intellect); being itself boundless, it cannot be contained within any formulation, and is therefore inexpressible. On the other hand there are an infinite number of truths: these are accurate perceptions of aspects of Reality refracted onto the plane of the human intellect. Every truth which can be expressed is only one intellect-mediated aspect of Reality and does not in any way exclude other equally valid aspects, since each of these truths is *limited*, existing only within its limits. A truth manifests Reality within its limits; it cannot do so outside them. So every truth has a dual aspect: valid in so far as it manifests Reality, and worthless in so far as it does not. Bearing this distinction in mind, we can see how ideas concerning the individual and the universal relate to truth.

What actually happens within me when I discover a truth, when I suddenly see a relationship connecting ideas which I had previously considered unrelated? I feel certain that I have not fabricated this new truth out of old material. I have not made it up, I have received it. There was an instant when things relaxed within me, and it *arrived* in my awareness. But where did it come from?

It came from within me, from the source of all the physical and mental

* See the Preface for an explanation of the publishing history of *The Supreme Doctrine*.

phenomena which comprise me. It came from the Principle and Origin of which I am an individual manifestation, the Principle which creates the whole Universe just as it creates me. My truth came to me from something universal. When it emerges in consciousness it takes on a form and boundaries, which reflect my particular structure and style of thought. By taking on form, it becomes possible for my truth to be conceived and expressed. But as well as the aspect which manifests original Reality and is therefore valid, it acquires the other aspect which does not manifest Reality and is valueless. My version of truth is universal to the extent that it manifests Reality; but to the extent that it does not manifest Reality it is individual and worthless. In other words, whatever is valid and worth considering in my version of truth does not come from me as a distinct and separate entity, and, strictly speaking, it has nothing to do with my particular personality.

Once I understand this, then the individual brain which gave shape to a particular truth is of no interest to me; it is simply the receiver which picked up the message. Though there is an obvious relationship between the form in which the thoughts are expressed and the individual make-up of the person expressing them, these individual characteristics have no bearing on the *truth* of the thoughts, or the extent to which they express Reality. The formal aspect of my book is my responsibility, but there is a formless truth in its matrix of words which may be able to evoke thoughts in you, and these will take shape according to your individual make-up. This formless truth does not come from me or anyone else; it comes from the universal.

Claiming authorship of any idea is irrational: the impulse to do so comes from an egotistical belief in our own divinity which lurks in the depths of our psyche, maintaining that we are the First Cause of the Universe. No individual ever really creates anything: creativity is anonymous and universal, a manifestation of the Principle. In wiser times, no artist, scholar or preacher would have dreamed of attaching their names to the works which had come into being through them.

Curiosity about the authorship of a teaching reflects a lack of confidence in the intuitive capacity of our own intellect. If I am looking for a 'faith' I can subscribe to *without sensing within me that it is self-evidently true*, and without my intelligence insisting that it ring true, then I am going to seek information about the particular sources, the 'authorities', with whom the teaching originated. This kind of search is a waste of time. However prestigious their origins, these 'faiths' can only lodge in my psyche as unassimilated inclusions, since they have not been re-constituted in a personal synthesis. So they are useless for the fulfilment of my being, and a spanner in the works as far as my machine is concerned.

But if I want to gradually develop an authentic understanding with the help of intellectual nourishment which I can digest and then reconstitute in a personal synthesis, I will search everywhere without prejudice, and the particular individual whose words I listen to or read will be a matter of indifference to me. It is quite possible that I will get nothing from some famous teaching and genuine revelations from an obscure source. I have little interest in the individual whose thoughts I engage with; I am only interested in whatever these thoughts contain which may be able to awaken my own still dormant truth. The Gospels interest me because I find in them clear evidence of a profound teaching, but discussions about the historicity of Jesus as a person leave me cold.

I wrote 'The Supreme Doctrine' in the way I did, without references, without precise documentation, without ever indicating which thoughts had originated in the minds of Zen masters, and which in mine, because I am quite unable to make these distinctions.

After I had read some of the Zen literature and experienced an intense revelation, accompanied by the sense that I was dealing with self-evident truth, I allowed my mind to continue working on it. If the mind is permitted to work without preconceptions, its inclination is to construct; it establishes an increasingly rich set of relationships between ideas which have already been assimilated. It does this in bursts of intuition, which bring the ideas together like the pieces of a jigsaw puzzle. This process of coordination and integration results in an increasingly harmonious whole in which we are quite unable to decide what has come from outside and what has developed within us. And, to repeat the point, it simply does not matter. The reader's approval of an idea in a book should not depend on who thought of it: it should depend on this inner resonance which we must learn to recognize and use as our only guide.

This preoccupation with the person behind the teaching reflects our illusory need to discover the Absolute in an aspect of the manifold. We want to find the Absolute embodied in a form. When we read about a system of ideas, our inclination is to accept or reject it as a whole; this is the easy option, because it saves us the bother of having to think about it. We find ourselves thinking about the text's author in terms of individual worth: is this someone we should take seriously or ignore? This may be the right approach if we are reading something factual, but it is unsuitable when we want to form our own ideas and discover our own truth (in other words, our own intellectual vision of Reality). When I seek my own truth, I know I will not find it outside me. What I take from outside to help my inner search for truth can seem to be a coherent whole: if I let this impress me, I will never succeed in carrying out the

*[handwritten margin note: what do I allow my mind to work on?]*

analytic process on which my personal synthesis and intellectual assimilation depend.

This warning applies even more to Part Two than it does to Part One. On the whole, I believe the old Zen masters would have given this book their *imprimatur*. But that is not important; what matters is that they would certainly have approved of the detachment with which I strive to maintain the integrity of my own thoughts whatever other thoughts I may come across. Think of the Zen master who saw one of his pupils growing pale over a Sutra and said: '*Don't let yourself be upset by the Sutra. It is you who should be upsetting the Sutra.*' This is the only way in which a real understanding can be established between pupil and Sutra.

# CHAPTER FOURTEEN

# Emotions and the Emotional State

Classical psychology, when it studies the emotions, fails to recognize a distinction which is extremely important from the point of view of the inner evolution of human beings. It provides a good description of the 'movements of the soul', the angry, loving, remorseful impulses etc., which arise in response to an image perceived in consciousness which some stimulus from the external world has provoked. But the play of emotion in us cannot simply be reduced to this, since I am often aware of an enduring emotional *state* which is clearly not triggered by whatever images I have in my head at the time. For example I may be feeling gloomy, although the things I am thinking about are insignificant. If I try to discover what images are responsible for my state of mind, there are times when I find nothing, but I can often discover some preoccupation beneath my surface associations which has triggered my sombre mood. When I was not thinking about it, it was static (like an *idée fixe)* and was triggering a persistent and apparently unchanging emotional *state*. Once I start to think about it, in other words when I generate an imaginative film about it, this sets up emotional reactions like those mentioned at the beginning. However, I sense that the static emotional *state* persists beneath these emotions and I feel that it is definitely related to the preoccupation which I have just brought to the surface of my mind.

So introspection indicates that there is a *static* emotion at a level below *dynamic* emotions. But what is meant by a 'static emotion'? The phrase has a paradoxical ring; 'emotion' implies 'movement'; can one speak of static movement? One way of resolving this contradiction and showing that *emotional states* involve both movement and immobility is to compare emotions, which are 'movements of the soul', to movements of the body, such as muscular contractions. Muscular *contractions* are dynamic, but muscles can also contract isometrically and remain fixed in a *contracture*, or cramp. Emotions linked to conscious images are the equivalent of dynamic psychological *contractions*, while the emotional state linked to subconscious images is like a persistent psychological *contracture*.

For the sake of clarity I have used approximate terms to establish the distinction I wanted to make, but now I can be more precise. Emotions represent a short circuit between our psychological and somatic poles. When we are discussing emotional activity, we should not talk in terms of *psychological* contractions and contractures, but of contractions and contractures of our psychosomatic organism. The emotional centre is midway between the intellectual (psychological/subtle) centre, and the instinctive (somatic/gross) centre. Similarly my initial account of emotions triggered by images, which are psychological, subtle stimuli, must now be qualified by the recognition that gross, somatic stimuli are just as likely to be responsible. A somatic disorder can trigger depression, which is a persisting emotional contracture of the psychosomatic organism. Anyway, whether the trigger is psychological or somatic, the resulting contracture always affects both psyche and soma, so that a psychological contracture based on a subconscious image will always be accompanied by some contracture of smooth or striated muscle, and vice versa.

The idea that emotions in general represent a short circuit between the intellectual and instinctive poles can help clarify the distinction between dynamic emotion (referred to from now on simply as 'emotion'), and the static emotional state ('emotional state' for brevity). To use an analogy from electricity, emotions correspond to a spark between two poles: the spark has some duration, but is not static because the contact it creates between the two poles is a continuously moving, changing process; it does not just move between the poles, but also darts out to the side. This contrasts with emotional states, which resemble the flow of energy between two poles in direct contact over a fairly extensive surface.

This comparison highlights one of the factors which make emotional states more harmful than emotions. Because the latter are active states, they are visible and conscious; internal cues alert the subject to their presence and bring defence mechanisms into play immediately, which first reduce then interrupt the energy-wasteful short circuit. Emotional states, however, do not activate defence mechanisms as quickly and their unhelpful consequences will already have become apparent by the time the defences are brought into operation. The defensive processes required at this stage have a very tiresome characteristic: they are 'neurotic' (using the term in its broadest sense). They reduce the amount of contact between the two poles, but they do so in a way which damages them. Another way of looking at this is to compare emotions to a visible haemorrhage which alarms the patient and gets treatment started; emotional states are like persistent, occult haemorrhages weakening someone who is sick: help will be obtained eventually, but at a stage when it will be much more difficult for treatment to bring about recovery.

But these are fairly crude comparisons and they neglect the most important considerations. They implied that the consumption of energy in the spark is similar to the destruction of energy when the two poles are in full contact. But in fact this is not so; there is a fundamental difference between the two phenomena. Where emotions are concerned, the two poles are separated; the spark which connects them should not really be called a short circuit: energy is consumed and released in it, so there is a product. But with the emotional state, both poles are in contact and there is a true short circuit, and energy passes from one pole into the other. This causes a drop in the voltage difference between the two poles, and a reduction in the subject's total energy which depends on this difference. The energy lost in this way is consumed without producing anything. Emotions form part of the manifest world, of life manifesting being, so they are normal. Emotional states are not 'living'; they destroy and provide nothing in return, and the energy they consume cannot be used for liberation. Since they cannot bring about normalization, they must be considered abnormal.

Another analogy may be helpful. If a horizontal wheel is turning round a point which does not coincide with its geometric centre, its rotation is 'eccentric'. Two kinds of forces act on this wheel: a rotational, or dynamic, force; and a centrifugal force acting on the whole wheel and tending to move it away from its centre of rotation. The second force, which never achieves its objective, can be called 'static'. Rotation, representing emotions, can be made use of; if I fit a belt to the wheel, it will be able to drive other machines. But the static force, which is trying unsuccessfully to hurl the whole wheel away from its centre of rotation, cannot be used for anything. It symbolizes the unmoving contracture of the cramped emotional state.

Realized individuals, after satori, are like wheels whose rotational centre coincides with their geometric centre. They might have emotions, but they would not have emotional states. Ordinary people, before satori, are like the eccentric wheels.

We can use the image of an eccentric wheel to clarify some important aspects of our affective life. If we apply this analogy to my inner world, there seems to be something like an elastic link between the rotational and geometric centres of my wheel, which is trying to make them coincide. When the wheel turns slowly, in other words when I am relatively free of emotion, the centrifugal force is weak, and the elastic succeeds in keeping the two centres close to one another. But the moment violent emotions arrive on the scene, the wheel begins to spin rapidly, the centrifugal force increases, and the two centres move apart despite the elastic.

This also illustrates the effect that emotions have on how the emotional state presents. When I have just experienced violent emotions, I feel as though I have 'lost my centre'. It is as though I have been shifted from my axis and a kind of displacement has occurred within me. Some time has to elapse before the elastic can have any effect and begin to draw the rotational and geometric centres closer again. Before satori the wheel's two centres never coincide exactly. Emotions in ordinary people unused to correct inner work may sometimes be relatively weak, but they are never non-existent. The wheel may turn slowly on occasion, but it turns nonetheless. There is always some centrifugal force present, preventing the elastic from bringing the two centres to a point where they coincide.

Continuing with this analogy, satori corresponds to an instant when the wheel stops turning altogether. This is an atemporal instant (otherwise the individual would die), but it is sufficient for the two centres to coincide. Once they have coincided, even for a single instant, they will never separate again; however fast the wheel spins, it can never produce a centrifugal force. Following the satori instant, during which there is neither emotion nor emotional state, the full range of emotions will return, but there will be no more emotional states.

The elastic in this image corresponds to every human being's deep longing for satori. This is not actually experienced as a yearning for true satori, since this is not something that ordinary people can imagine, but rather as a longing for something in the temporal domain or as a yearning for something we imagine to be satori. Nonetheless it is still a longing for satori. The further someone caught up in emotional states is from satori, the more tightly stretched the elastic; that is, the more intense the longing for fulfilment in some form or another. The closer one gets to satori, the slacker the elastic becomes, and the longing for fulfilment becomes less intense. On the brink of satori, in the moments preceding it, all longing for fulfilment disappears. So, being free of longing, someone who achieves satori does not experience it as a fulfilment, but can say, like Hui-neng, 'There is no fulfilment, there is no liberation': liberation only exists in the eyes of someone who is not liberated. In terms of our analogy, liberation is when the elastic is completely slack; but in satori the elastic vanishes completely and its slackening is no longer relevant.

Pre-satori man cannot really imagine what post-satori man will be like. It is more a question of imagining what he will not be like, in that there will be a profound difference in the ways emotions are experienced before and after satori, because they will no longer trigger the emotional state, the inner contracture, which is the basis of our distress. This takes us to a new way of understanding the distinction between emotion and emotional state. Emotions can be positive or negative, joy or suffering; but emotional states are always negative. In terms of our analogy, the wheel can turn in either direction, but the centrifugal force is always centrifugal. We can see this if we look at what happens in our emotional life: when something marvellous happens to me and triggers intense joy, I experience the same displacement from my centre, from the axis referred to earlier, as I do from intense negative emotions. Underneath all the joyful images there is distress, which is linked to my fear of losing the affirmation which I have just received, or to the unsatisfied demand which any affirmation only intensifies, which is that I should go on being more and more affirmed until I achieve that absolute fulfilment of myself which I am still waiting for deep within myself.

Emotional states, or deep emotional activity as opposed to the surface emotional activity of the emotions, correspond to the deep, subconscious level in the psyche where my ego pursues its 'proceedings' in response to situations where I am involved in some confrontation with the outside world. Emotional states are always related to some doubt about my being. This doubt, which is the 'being or nothingness' dilemma, is an ever-present threat, so the proceedings carry on, driven by the unrealizable hope that the case will eventually be dismissed once and for all.

The observation that there are some euphoric individuals who always seem to be possessed by a positive emotional state, might seem to contradict the above. It is worth taking a closer look at the apparent happiness of ordinary people because this can help us understand emotional states better. If I observe myself over time, I notice that I am sometimes euphoric and that this state corresponds to brief episodes during which self-doubt is dormant. If some external situation affirms me and seems likely to persist for a while, providing also that I am in good health, it has the effect of suspending my inner 'proceedings'. With nothing happening in court, judge and witnesses go to sleep and the subconscious level of my psyche dozes. This explains why the state I am in is a pleasant one. But this pleasant state is not related to any positive qualities in the currently active emotional state, but to its inactivity. In terms of the proceedings analogy, it is corresponds to a temporary adjournment, not a favourable outcome. Nor has my illusory conviction that I lack something been abolished: it is only temporarily quiescent. How is this possible? Since the ego is always in existence, how can the proceedings it is actively pursuing be suspended in this way?

People who are habitually euphoric provide the explanation. Their need for the Absolute is weak and often practically non-existent. Once their desire for egotistical affirmation has achieved a measure of satisfaction, it becomes quiescent and makes no further demands; they can be content with what they have. They have developed compensatory mechanisms: their approach to challenges from the external world allows them to register the aspects which affirm them and not see anything which negates them. They apologize for themselves monotonously, and this surface activity replaces the deep level proceedings which remain dormant most of the time. It is interesting to note that these people are particularly lacking in sensitivity and can be criticized quite strongly without their pride being wounded. It is in an anaesthetized state which is related to the soporific state of the trial.

Such people seem more or less without ego. It is in fact present but the weakness of their need for the Absolute enables the compensations which have been established to maintain their effectiveness. These people are shielded from self-doubt by defences which do not deteriorate with the passage of time, and they do not grow tired of the attitudes (compensatory mechanisms) which they adopt towards the external world. But the apparently positive quality of their emotional states is simply a reflection of the fact that these states, which are by their very nature negative, have been neutralized or inhibited. Such people may experience many moments of happiness, but these emerge against a background of sleep and absence, and their occurrence does not signify that the deep emotional state has loosened up and become supple. They are only possible because the deep level contracture is excluded from consciousness by inhibition (cf. the 'courage' shown by someone who is unaware of danger). This in turn happens because of the congenital weakness of their need for the Absolute, which allows the compensations to go on functioning effectively.

On the other hand, people whose need for the Absolute is intense will have difficulty establishing effective compensatory mechanisms, because they are too demanding and their craving for egotistical affirmation is too insistent. If they do succeed in establishing compensatory mechanisms, not much use is made of them. So their 'proceedings' are seldom, if ever, dormant. As their life progresses, the compensatory mechanisms available to them deteriorate irreversibly. So there are no more adjournments in the proceedings, and everything that happens, every confrontation with not-self, is increasingly viewed from a perspective of self-doubt. In the ever-wakeful subconscious they live their lives in anticipation of an illusory verdict upon which their final absolution or condemnation is felt to depend. Their self-esteem is endlessly involved, whether in a positive or negative sense; and they are over-sensitive in this respect. This continual excitation is directly related to the permanent activity of the subconscious emotional state, which is one of agitation and tension. While people who have little hunger for the Absolute are calm, those with a great need for the Absolute suffer from over-excitability and excessive tension. Everything concerns their ego; they see everything solely from the perspective of their self-esteem.

Let me conclude this section by stressing that an emotional state is always negative, a contracted state of anxiety; and that the activity in the subconscious where it operates is related to the need for the Absolute, and hence to the need for atemporal realization. In any given individual, there is an intimate connection between the presence of this distress and the need for satori.

Emotions may still be felt after satori, but they are no longer experienced against a background of constant distress. The change that this represents in the whole of our affective life is so enormous and fundamental that we simply cannot form any adequate idea of what the emotions will be like after satori.

Inner work with satori as its goal should be directed towards achieving that essential instant of perfect freedom from affect which I described earlier. We cannot understand how to do this and bring emotional activity under control correctly if we do not fully appreciate the distinction between emotions and the emotional state: only the latter is abnormal and an obstacle to satori; emotions are normal and do not hinder satori. But it is immeasurably easier to perceive emotions than it is to sense the existence of an emotional state. So people often believe in the value of curbing the emotions, but all their work is useless because it is misguided.

Correctly directed work will aim at controlling the emotional state. It will not aim to abolish those brief contractions of the psychosomatic organism which constitute the emotions: its goal will be to abolish the organism's contracture. What applies to the total organism also applies at a purely somatic level: pianists do not achieve virtuosity by suppressing muscle contractions, but by suppressing the contracture, the tiresome underlying muscular tightness which accompanied their muscle contractions at the beginning of their apprenticeship.

The question is, how can we resolve the emotional state, the anxiety contracture, which lies at the heart of our whole affective life? A direct approach would be useless. One might think that voluntary efforts at relaxation would help, and hope that this partial relaxation would automatically bring about a general relaxation. The fact is that such efforts, which are directed towards a partial object, are incapable of producing a global effect on the organism. The effort I make to relax a part of myself is necessarily accompanied by a central contracture. I cannot envisage any particular thing in this way without a contracture occurring. Another approach might be to struggle directly with our emotions, since they trigger the emotional state; but this would be equivalent to an attack on the very substance of our life. The problem is how to relax the emotional state without interfering with the emotions, or anything else.

We can only bring about any change in our total organism if we apply the Law of Three. This is the reason why any direct attempt to curb or minimize something in us is ineffective as far as our totality is concerned. What we should do is look directly and with respect at whatever it is that we deplore in ourselves, and then bring forward to face it the element within us which opposes and complements it. Doing this brings the conciliatory principle into play, and this makes it possible for the undesirable element to be resolved. It is reintegrated into the whole and disappears with the loss of its illusory autonomy.

Let us see how the law applies in the present instance. The deep contracture of my whole organism, although it affects my organism as a totality, is itself neither total nor absolute; it may vary in intensity, but it is always partial. In other words, at any given moment only part of the potential contracture has an effect, while the rest of it has no effect and is not manifested. Deep attention, the attention operating on this deep level, is naturally always placed on the part of the contracture which is manifested. Imbalance is located precisely in the natural bias which leads me to pay attention only to the manifested aspect of my contracture, and not to the rest of it. It follows that the necessary balance will only be obtained if I pay attention to the non-manifested as well as the manifested part of my contracture. In other words, I must not only pay attention to my interest in something, but I must at the same time pay attention to my indifference towards the rest of manifestation.

Once again there is the familiar temptation to take direct action, in this case to will myself to perceive my indifference towards everything that does not immediately concern me. But this is impossible, because the indifference needing my attention is non-manifested and, as soon as I try to think consciously that I am indifferent, what I perceive is the manifested idea of 'indifference' and not the non-manifested indifference itself. What is not manifested must inevitably elude my dualistic consciousness, comprising as it does a subject who perceives and an object which is perceived, both of which are manifested.

Once I have avoided this pitfall and mastered the temptation to *act* directly, I am brought to the fundamental article of faith in our evolution towards realization: *only pure intellectual understanding is effective.* No useful change in my inner phenomenology can ever result from any planned manipulation, however ingenious it may be. Any change which is relevant to the goal of atemporal realization has to arise spontaneously from our Absolute Principle as a result of the opening made in the screen of ignorance by intellectual intuition. Each self-evident intellectual fact we discover concerning the problem of our own realization breaches the screen of ignorance. By means of this breach the process of our transformation will take place without our having to worry about it.

*[handwritten margin note: experience shows this to be so]*

In the present case, what we need to experience as obvious through intellectual understanding is the following: we are fundamentally wrong about our deep emotions. We believe in the existence of our emotional state alone, in our contracture. We only believe in deep level emotional activity to the extent that it is manifested in a contracture, and has some living expression. We are unaware of all the rest, of all affectivity at the deep level which is not manifested or expressed in our lives. However the emotional activity expressed in life is limited, while that which is unexpressed is infinite. What is real in my affectivity every second of my existence, and what really matters, is not my emotional state, or my contracture, or my bias: on the contrary, what is real is what lies behind all that, which is my perfect detachment, my non-contracture and my impartiality. In so far as I am a sentient being, what matters is not what I am feeling, but the infinite nature of what I am not feeling. To summarize, my emotional state as it is currently manifested is really of no interest to me.

*[handwritten margin note: Key understanding]*

When I acquire this understanding as an obvious intellectual fact, it is a revelation which revolutionizes the way I look at my inner life. This illumination does not immediately destroy my affective bias towards the manifested emotional state, but it establishes a counterbalancing intellectual certainty which affirms my non-manifested emotional state, my relaxed, non-manifested serenity. This new intellectual certainty fosters the development of an attentiveness towards the infinite detachment which dwells within me beneath my finite interests. This attentiveness operates in the Unconscious and does not produce any dualistic perception; but it has a definite effect in proportion to my understanding, and, in the long run, its activity is reflected in the visible world by a progressive reduction in the intensity of my emotional states.

This makes it possible for me to progress towards the affect-free state which will bring about the release of satori.

When deep attention is functioning correctly, the effect it has on our overall development is to produce a reduction in our emotional states *over time*. I stress 'over time' because there will be temporary phases in our development during which the emotional contracture increases. We will see why this happens.

Before the distinction between emotion and emotional state has been grasped, attention functions as follows: at the conscious level, surface attention is fixed on emotions (more accurately, on emotional images); deep attention, which is subconscious, is fixed on the emotional state. Ordinary people are not usually aware of their emotional state (which is why classical psychology ignores it). They only have a 'subconscious' awareness, so, for example, if they sometimes recognize that they are particularly tense, they do so indirectly, through inference. The direct experience of anxiety and tension remains in the background, and what people experience are the images which take shape in consciousness against this background.

As our understanding of this distinction between emotion and emotional state increases, attention gradually operates at a deeper level. Surface attention, operating at the conscious imaginative film level, will now tend to operate at the hitherto unconscious emotional state level (in other words, understanding enables one to direct one's attention towards the emotional state), while deep attention will tend to operate in the Unconscious, that infinite, immutable background against which changes in the emotional state emerge.

If understanding were complete from the outset, this shift in deep attention would happen straight away and would be complete and stable. Deep attention would reintegrate the Unconscious (the Self or Self Nature of Zen), and satori would take place. But understanding is far from complete at first; between the initial moment of conception at a theoretical level and the point where experience has supplied the whole previously missing temporal dimension, there has to be a lengthy period of maturation. Obtaining theoretical understanding does not immediately remove all the previous illusory beliefs, which are maintained by powerful affective automatisms and behaviours. Faith and beliefs will co-exist for some considerable time. Understanding matures with the progressive erosion of errors as truth is acquired; the good seed gradually chokes the weeds.

While this ripening is taking place, there is conflict between understanding (which is equivalent to Faith) and the affective automatisms which maintain error. Faith tends to make us aware of our emotional state; but our automatisms put up a barrier of distress between the gaze of consciousness and the emotional state where the anxiety contracture is located. The more the emotional state is perceived, the more it will lose its illusory, toxic distress; but when my attempts to perceive it are unsuccessful, when automatisms prevent me seeing what understanding is urging me to look at, then the emotional state will be strengthened. So progress towards inducing the emotional contracture to relax can be interrupted by a potentially critical increase in its severity (there are dragons guarding the way to the treasure). People need to be forewarned of this so that they do not become frightened and discouraged; if we know what to expect, we can continue working to deepen our understanding without stopping, even when the situation seems to be getting worse. When consciousness finally makes its courageous breakthrough into the hitherto subconscious level of the emotional state, then it will be revealed that deep attention has penetrated into the Unconscious, domain of the Absolute Positivity which dispels all distress.

I have emphasized that only pure intellectual understanding is effective, and that it is not possible to devise techniques to bring about changes in our inner phenomena that would promote satori. This is an important point, and I would also stress the importance of challenging any ideas which support the belief that we can *as individuals* bring about our own metaphysical transformation. However, having duly acknowledged this, I am now going to show how an intentional inner action, designed to enable the emotional state to be perceived, plays its part at an appropriate moment in the evolving process of liberation.

When my understanding has reached a certain level and I have transcended my main compensatory attitudes, the deep emotional contracture will become more intense. As I mentioned above, my understanding will then tend to shift my attention's activity to a deeper level. This enables me to experience the usefulness of an inner action which is neither natural nor automatic, which is aiming towards the conscious perception of the hitherto subconscious emotional state. Another way of putting this is that I experience the usefulness of *not running away* from distress as I had been doing, but rather *confronting* it in a spirit of investigation. This comes through understanding alone: the decision to intervene like this flows spontaneously from understanding. I do not do it because it is advocated by some emotionally-charged, idolatrous belief system (such as a duty to seek 'salvation', or 'spiritual' ambition) wanting to take over at the expense of other tendencies. The decision to do it happens spontaneously when its usefulness has become obvious. Only when the long labour of understanding has been completed can I

127

carry out this now obviously useful action. Before that, any attempt to do so would be premature and inopportune.

Let us suppose that the requisite state of intellectual certainty has been acquired and that the *decision* to perform the relevant inner action flows purely from complete conviction; and let us also suppose that I am finally capable of performing this action effectively: I then realize that the *execution* of this action cannot flow spontaneously from understanding alone. The action is decided within pure intellectual intuition, but it is carried out on that concrete inner world level where all my automatic mechanisms operate. It is an unnatural manoeuvre performed in the realm of natural mechanisms, and against the current of automatisms which are tugging at my attention all the time, drawing it towards images.

I had to make this essential point absolutely clear, reminding the reader that any irrational affectivity which has played a part in the decision to undertake inner work condemns that work to failure as far as satori is concerned. Now that these indispensable precautionary remarks have been set out clearly, I am going to consider the kind of practical inner work which this study envisages.

The work consists of this: whenever possible, attempt to perceive the emotional state by an inward movement of the mind. But there is a paradoxical aspect to this 'perception' which needs to be appreciated right away. The emotional state affects me and my psychosomatic organism as a totality; so it cannot be the object of any dualistic perception involving subject and object. It is illusorily objective as long as I make no attempt to perceive it, but it vanishes the instant I try to do so. *The liberating action, the inward movement of the mind which I am referring to, aims at perceiving the emotional state, but cannot achieve this; what it achieves is a kind of perception of my total organism, or Self, across and through the emotional state which covers and conceals the Self, while at the same time pointing towards it. So the outcome is an instant of real subjective consciousness obtained through the partial annihilation of the emotional state ('seeing into one's own nature').*

Ordinary people with no experience of inner work believe they can perceive their emotional state; but when they observe that they are tense, for instance, what this means is that they have perceived an image which is a direct by-product of the illusory concreteness of their emotional state. All their reflexes, all their mechanisms, are governed by their emotional state. Its importance is enormous, but *implicit* and subconscious. For the emotional state which influences everything they think about, is itself never thought about in consciousness. Ordinary people live solely as a function of their ego, but this ego is something that they never ask questions about. The role played by the emotional state in human functioning is that of a fixed point round which everything turns. Another way of putting this is that ordinary people are centred on their subconscious (corresponding to the rotational centre), while their real, or geometric, centre is the Unconscious.

The emotional state is not really a fixed point; and its illusory fixity is what governs all the illusions of our egotistical life. When I deliberately direct my attention towards my emotional state (i.e. towards my total coenaesthesia, and in reality beneath that towards my ego) I sense movement and a lack of fixity in the 'object' of my attempted perception. I sense intuitively the energetic flow of life deep within me (this is an experience of phenomena, not of the noumenon: the ego cannot be Absolute, because it is not unmoving). Partially destroying the illusory fixity of the emotional centre in this way brings rotational and geometric centres closer: I become more 'normal'.

This sense that there is movement at the centre of my phenomenal being is not analogous to the impression of movement I have when a stone is thrown. It is an experience in which time, space and forms do not exist, and I sense within me 'movement' in which there is no alteration or change in position: I am in contact with the eternal instant.

In practice the work has to involve repeating the manoeuvre, this inward shift in attention, again and again, and doing it quickly and lightly. It should not be done slowly and laboriously as though one were trying to seize hold of something. There is nothing to seize. It is a question of intentionally observing, in a perfectly simple, instantaneous, split second of a glimpse, that I have a global awareness of myself for that instant (through the attempt to note *how* I feel in that instant). I succeed in this instantaneously or not at all; if not, I try again later. I can do this a few seconds later, but it must be a separate event.

It is in my interest to make the attempt as often as possible, but I must be flexible and unobtrusive in the way I do so, disturbing the flow of my dualistic inner life as little as possible. I have to interrupt what ordinary awareness I have of my dualistic life with clear-cut, decisive and instantaneous 'breaks', but I must not do anything to modify awareness directly. Normalizing changes will be brought about by the Absolute Principle through the instantaneous 'breaks' which this inner work creates.

The distinction between emotion and emotional state can be used to clarify the precise nature of how we perceive our affective life. What we call a 'feeling' is a complex phenomenon consisting of an imaginative film and a variable emotional component.

Take the imaginative film first: it is obvious that I perceive this in consciousness. The images which pass through my mind are fixed by memory and stored up inside me; they provide me with a supply of subtle forms which I can call up, bring back into the field of attention, examine at leisure, and describe in words. I can control my images; I organize and manipulate them in an active perceptual field where consciousness as subject grasps image as object.

With the emotional variable, in other words my actual feelings as opposed to the images, the situation is quite different. In a sense I do have some kind of perception of this aspect: so if I am feeling sad, and someone asks if I am happy, I can say, 'No, I'm sad,' which implies that I have some perception of sadness. But if I try to investigate my sadness and get a closer look at it, I discover that all I ever see is a film of sad or distressing images, but never my sadness itself as something irreducible. I am quite unable to take hold of my sadness and perceive it actively, as I can with my sad images. I simply cannot hold my sadness in a 'mental grip' and experience it in the same way. With images, I can get hold of them and break them down into their constituent parts. I can analyse them and discover what irreducible elements they are composed of. I simply cannot do any of this with feelings: I know of their existence (so I am not entirely unacquainted with them), but I cannot get to know and analyse them in the same way.

The fact that I do have some perception of a feeling indicates that it interacts to some extent with surface consciousness. This interaction is obviously different from the kind that exists between consciousness and images, because it does not allow me to get any purchase on the feeling. When consciousness and feeling interact, consciousness is passive and feeling active. To make this easier to understand, imagine that I pick some object up in the dark and turn it around in my hand: this provides me with an active perception of the object which gives me information about it. Now imagine an enormous giant picking me up in the dark, and turning me around and palpating me: I know that the giant exists and I will like or dislike him depending on whether he handles me gently or roughly. Apart from that, I know nothing at all about the giant and am unable to describe him.

So my experience of feelings can be described by saying that the images which form part of the phenomenon are in my grasp, but that the global emotional phenomenon to which they contribute has me in its grasp. On the image side of the interface, consciousness captures; on the feeling side, it is captured. It is as though I am conscious of the images which form part of my feelings, while my feelings are conscious of me.

But this is to look at things from the ordinary, illusory perspective where we identify our surface consciousness with our selves, with who we are. But in reality my surface consciousness is not 'me': it is not the source and principle of all the phenomena through which my psycho-somatic organism is created. This principle alone is what 'I' refers to in reality. Surface consciousness is just one particular level among the phenomena which manifest my principle. So instead of saying that my feelings capture my consciousness, I should say that my subconscious captures my surface consciousness.

My subconscious is still 'me'. Though it may feel like a loss of freedom when consciousness is taken over by the subconscious in this way, this is not because its captor is a stranger to me. It is because the subconscious, though still 'me', is unawakened and therefore completely determined by the external world. Where the feeling aspect is involved, the outside world seems to hold me in its grip. However, external influences only govern the modalities in which my unawak-  ened subconscious operates, while the real driving force behind its activity is no stranger to me, being my own principle, 'me'. It is certainly the case that I am acted upon where feelings are concerned, but only because I let this happen as a result of my present unawakened condi-tion.

At this point I realize that what I have called my subconscious is illu-sory, something that forms part of the dream of my pre-satori sleep. The force that takes hold of surface consciousness and moves it is my sole, primary driving force, my principle, the Absolute Principle which moves me as it moves all created things. This Principle is prior to all consciousness, since it gives rise to all consciousness as it manifests itself in consciousness. It is appropriately referred to in this context as Originating Unconscious (the No-Mind or Cosmic Mind of Zen). What I have called my subconscious is only a way of imagining how the mind's dormant centre affects its own superficial phenomena, these being its only awakened aspect at present. It represents the effect of the Unconscious on surface consciousness. The subconscious is an inter-mediate level without reality: the Unconscious has absolute reality (noumenal), and surface consciousness (the imaginative film) has rela-tive reality (phenomenal), but the subconscious only has illusory reality. It is simply a hybrid intermediary: if one considers it from the point of view of activity or passivity, it is either active Unconscious or passive superficial consciousness.

It will be no more possible to seize hold of feelings after satori than it was before. Satori, or the awakening of Originating Mind, dissipates the illusory hybrid representation we call feeling. *And it is precisely the fruit-less effort to take hold of feelings, to grasp what cannot be grasped, that succeeds in awakening Originating Mind.* After satori, feelings no longer exist as we know them at present. Surface consciousness experiences the direct action of Originating Mind in a cosmically harmonious response to excitation arising in the external world, a response which takes the particular external circumstance into account without being in any way controlled or shaped by it.

# CHAPTER FIFTEEN

# Sensation and Feeling

I HAVE ALREADY MENTIONED that there is a continuous, ongoing relationship between mental images and the underlying emotional activity whenever emotions are involved. The relationship between them is complex, and it is worth studying because it involves a number of particularly subtle traps which prevent us paying attention to our emotional life.

Let me remind you of the basic distinction between the imaginative film which is based on present reality, and the imaginative film which is invented by the mind. When I look at something, I observe it through the medium of the imaginative film, which provides a partial reproduction of what is visible, based on those external forms which catch my attention. When I daydream, whether I am doing something at the time or happen to be idle, I am perceiving an imaginative film invented in my mind. Emotional activity is associated in quite different ways with these two kinds of film.

We will examine them using the following terms: the film based on the external world will be referred to as 'real imaginative film' (because it derives from phenomena which, though not real in an absolute sense, are relatively real); the invented film will be called 'imaginary film'.

With the real imaginative film, the relationship with emotional activity is fairly straightforward: the nature of emotional activity varies (in terms of the degree of contraction or relaxation) according to whether the film's images affirm or negate. Images associated with a threat to my existence produce emotional contraction, while those associated with a continuation of my existence reduce contraction and produce a relative affective relaxation. This is a simple one-way relationship: the form taken by the image phenomena determines the form of the emotional phenomena. Within the context of form, the external world is active, my inner world passive. Nothing stays the same; external phenomena are changing all the time, and emotional activity changes continuously in response. There is no fixed emotional activity;

133

there are only contractions, no persistent spasms or contractures; only emotions, no emotional *state*.

It is all a great deal more complicated where the imaginary film is concerned. The relationship with emotional activity is not one-way, but operates in both directions at once. First, there is the same kind of relationship as in the previous case: emotional life responds to imaginary images just as it does to real ones (it does not distinguish between the two kinds: a jealous man who conjures up a powerful image of his wife being unfaithful is as disturbed emotionally as if the scene were real). But the emotional *state* also influences how the imaginary film develops: for instance, if some real misfortune afflicts me and darkens my mood, I begin to imagine all sorts of things going wrong, and see everything in a bad light. So a vicious circle of reaction and counter-reaction is established.

However another factor involved in the relationship between our emotional life and the imaginary film is more important. The imaginary film is like the real film in one respect: the films I invent are derived from elements which originally came from the outside world. But the essential difference between the two kinds of film is that the real film is invented by the Cosmos and it springs from the cosmic source and origin, the First Cause of the Universe. So every real film is in harmony, and in a state of equilibrium within the Whole. The Noumenon provides its fixed centre: the film itself is pure movement, and fixations at the phenomenal level cannot occur. —*Always Change—Never Static*

Contrast this with the imaginary film, which is centred on my ego, on the self which claims absolute being for itself as a separate individual. Its source and centre is not the unchanging noumenal centre of the cosmos: it is a false, eccentric centre. The imaginary film also contains a mixture of continual movement and fixated phenomena, the latter originating from the eccentric phenomenal centre. We can see this in day-dreams: they are composed of moving images, but these always tend to circle round some *idée fixe*. Day-dreams are always more or less obsessive, with scenarios organized in artificially coherent clusters or complexes, which are separate from the cosmic Whole. The emotional reaction corresponding to this phenomenal level fixation, which is the persisting affective contracture or emotional *state* referred to earlier, shows a similar fixity or stuckness.

The emotional reaction to the real film is free of any fixated component, and is *normal* or *healthy*, since it is a response to the normal relative reality of cosmic phenomena. The emotional reaction to the imaginary film always involves an element of chronic emotional spasm or contracture and is *abnormal* or *unhealthy*. It is a reaction to images which are abnormal, since their formative centre is not the real centre of the Universe.

There is then a clear distinction between the emotional responses in the two kinds of film. But, except during the earliest stages of infancy, emotional activity never occurs in response to a real film alone. There is always an imaginary film running at the same time. The emotions are never pure: there is always a co-existing emotional *state*, and this is particularly true of someone with a need for the Absolute, who craves being and whose world view gives more weight to the inner world of ideas than it does to an independent external reality ('idealists'). Very young children are unable to create an imaginary film because their intellect has not developed sufficiently for this, so their emotional life is practically pure, fluid, unstable and free of any contracture. As the intellect develops, persistent emotional spasms or contractures begin to appear in the form of emotional states. Adults with a very strong yearning for the Absolute have an emotional life characterized by potentially quite unstable contractions beneath which contractures develop and subside slowly. If they are good at self-observation they will notice two separate rhythms operating in their emotional life: there seem to be two distinct kinds of emotional activity, one which speeds along, the other tending to remain firmly in one place (dreams often allude to this state of affairs, a typical scene being one in which I want to run, but am glued to the spot).

So there are two kinds of imaginative film, two kinds of emotional response, and, in practice, within our inner phenomenological (experiential) world there are two kinds of emotional life: of these, one is *authentic*, responding to the real film, and the other is illusory or *false*, responding to the imaginary film. Authentic emotional activity corresponds to the domain of sensation (sensory perceptions of the external world), and inauthentic activity to the domain of images (imaginary perceptions). Authentic emotions, as in children, are fluid, labile, and quite irrational (in other words, they react to images in a way which bears no relationship to the importance which our 'rational' value system attributes to them). Inauthentic emotional activity is more or less rational in the above sense and moves to a slower rhythm, with the qualification that instability can also set in during periods of exhaustion. However this instability does not represent a healthy freedom from fixations: it is simply due to a contracture becoming weak through exhaustion.

Inauthentic emotional activity is related to my idealized image of myself and the world, and my wish to see myself behaving and thinking in ways which reflect beauty, truth and goodness, and my fear of appearing ugly, false and wicked. My authentic reaction to a given situation discounts 'the ideal': it depends purely on what I see in the external world. My false reaction can be fundamentally different, because it depends on the idealized way in which I see myself and is made up of feelings which I harbour because they relate more to my performance before the external world than to the external world itself. This is why it is quite possible for me to be inauthentically cheerful (within the realm of imaginary emotional activity) at the same time as I am authentically sad (within the realm of authentic emotional activity), or vice versa.

For example: I really look forward to my annual holiday for months beforehand and have a vivid image of myself having a great time in Florence. If I am someone with idealizing tendencies, am markedly egotistical, and have a strong craving for unconditional being, then I develop a compelling need to realize my fantasy. But when I get to Florence I am tired and depressed. My authentic state, which is not the least concerned with my vision of myself and is only reacting to the real situation, is tense, and beneath the surface I am fed up. But my wish to realize my fantasy of myself having a good time in Florence will not allow me to acknowledge that I am unhappy. So if someone asks about my holiday, I reply: 'Marvellous! All the museums get a bit tiring, but who cares, with so many beautiful things to see!'

If I examine my emotions in a true spirit of investigation, I see the naked truth: I am miserable, even more than I usually am on my way to work in the Metro. I can also see that it took a special effort before I was able to recognize this; or perhaps that I may have been aware of my sadness before, but mistakenly attributed it to an imaginary film which was in fact the effect of my being sad rather than its cause.

Another example: take someone who has been tyrannized for years by an egotistical father; he has been humiliated, all his projects have been sabotaged, and he has been undermined by a sadistic upbringing purporting to be in his best interests. His father dies. The son's authentic emotional response is one of enormous relief. But if he is very much an idealist, he will have such a need to perceive himself as sad that he will succeed in doing so despite the obvious evidence to the contrary. The sadness of his imaginary film can largely block his feeling of profound relief, and may prevent it altogether.

This discrepancy between emotions and imaginary emotional states is particularly striking from the following point of view: my ideal, absolute, divine image includes, among other 'divine' attributes, those of stability and immutability. The Absolute Principle, the Primordial One which is the source of everything, is immutable, beyond time and its vicissitudes. So one of the essential attributes which my desired self-image must include is equanimity, in other words stability of the emotional state. This explains why the way in which I represent my emotional states to myself throughout my life is always immensely distorted in the direction of stability. As soon as I start to investigate the variations in my authentic emotional activity objectively, I observe that they are far more frequent and pronounced than I had thought. It does not take much to produce peaks and troughs on the graph of my emotional life: a few words, an image, colic, a little wine or coffee. On the other hand, my ideal self-image implies that my emotional reactions should be *rational*, so I maintain that it takes something really significant to produce a strong emotional response in me, and that there is a direct correlation between the intensity of my emotional response and the importance reason attaches to the events which affect me.

A little child's emotions are strikingly labile and can change from laughter to tears without a transitional state; they are also irrational: take away its rattle, and it shows signs of extreme distress. There seems to be an enormous difference when I compare my emotional life with the child's: mine seems so much more stable and rational. But it is only my false emotional activity and the child's emotional activity which are different, and their difference is due to the huge lie involved in the development of my false emotional life. My need to give expression to my ideal self-image has gradually distorted my emotional life. When I make honest efforts to see its fluctuations just as they are, what I see are my authentic emotions and I then realize that there is no difference between the little child and me: my authentic emotional life is just as labile and irrational.

The kind of inner work we are discussing at present, where we attempt to get a direct, instantaneous perception of our emotional state, employs a direct, intuitive, inward gaze which penetrates through inauthentic emotional activity without being distracted by it. All inauthentic emotional activity is dissipated by this inward gaze. What remains is authentic emotional activity, which corresponds solely to the sensory, or animal, plane; the imaginal level – the 'ideal' or 'angelic' – is abolished. To discover that there is a unique reality to our irrational affective agitation and to realize how consistently we have lied to ourselves about it, comes as a strange revelation. We begin to see that the 'animal' has persisted intact within us below the imaginary constructions of the 'angelic' level; and that this is the only aspect of our whole being which has achieved realization so far; all the rest is unreal. It is to this organism that we must return in all simplicity, and seek to awaken in its centre its immanent and transcendent principle.

The inward gaze of intuition penetrates inauthentic emotional activity without being distracted by it; in other words it dispels the imaginary film's images as it passes through them. But though it may be able to dispel the film, it cannot dispel the deep contracture which determines the nature of the film. I can already understand this at a theoretical level: getting rid of whatever imaginary film is linked to the subconscious at a particular moment is not going to abolish the whole subconscious. Practising this method gives me effective proof of the deep contracture's persistence. I need to give the matter more thought, to understand how it is that the contracture, which I referred to with some justification as 'abnormal', now appears to be on the road which leads to satori.

There is an element of immobility in the contracted state of my total organism which is definitely healthy. We would evolve spontaneously towards satori if we 'obeyed the nature of things', and stopped our restless pursuit of false substitutes for satori. 'Doing nothing', where our whole organism is motionless, and there is no movement at its phenomenal centre, enables satori to ripen. Hence the deep contracture has a positive side which gives it the potential to aid normalization; and it can be considered healthy in so far as it has this tendency to immobilize our centre. The fact that it has so far failed to exercise this normalizing function for me is because I have always been protected from this immobilization by a reflex process.

Recall how the two-way relationship between emotional activity and the imaginary film operates: images initiate the contracture and then the contracted state triggers images. Images are always bound to trigger contractures and that in itself is not a problem, because this facilitates the desired state of immobility. But what is a problem, and is avoidable, is that the contracted state triggers images which continually modify it, and it is these variations in the contracture which stop me profiting from the immobility potentially contained within it.

 Why should a new imaginary film be triggered by, or rather in relation to, the contracture, and thus prevent me developing stillness? Because there is a false belief present within me, a belief that immobility is disastrous and deadly. As I lack Faith in my Principle, I am convinced that I should achieve 'salvation' by my own efforts and that I should bring about total fulfilment by action as an *individual*. While this set of beliefs is in operation, I cannot prevent the contracted state triggering a new imaginary film and the ensuing vicious circle of agitation and restless activity.

A caterpillar has to be motionless in its chrysalis before it evolves into a butterfly. When I am feverishly caught up in the vicious circle of emotional states and imaginary films I am like a caterpillar struggling furiously against the threat of immobilization when it feels chrysalis formation begin.

It makes no sense to be afraid of immobilization, because what the deep contracted state is offering me is not annihilation but just the appearance of death (chrysalis stage) in order to obtain real life at last (butterfly stage). Once I understand this, I can see that there is nothing inevitable about the emotional state triggering an imaginary film. *Sit with it* Protected by understanding and Faith, I discover that I am comfortably able to curl up within the contracture, in my fear, sadness or worry, *without generating any corresponding images of distress,* and without any related thoughts or inner activity. A moment later my sadness is replaced by a colourless immobility; I become deadened and anaesthetized, like a block of wood. In a sense I seem like a fool, but my ability to act and react appropriately to the external world is unimpaired; I am like a robot in good working order.

We have clearly come to some paradoxical conclusions. Our initial observations made us view the contracture, the emotional state, in a negative light and encouraged us to think nostalgically of the pure emotional fluidity of early childhood. But there is no going back; and the child's condition was in any case at the extreme opposite end of the spectrum to satori. We have to go forward. The regrettable consequences of our intellectual development are simply due to our intellect never having been enlightened: because of our ignorance, we fought against becoming inwardly motionless and our resistance caused fluctuations in the contracted state, waves of distress. We hurt ourselves against the restraints which held us fast.

But the cure is to be found where previously we only saw the affliction; the restraints only harmed us when we fought against them. The emotional contracture was only destructive so long as it continued to be emotional, in other words in a state of agitation. When I am no longer frightened of stillness, I become free of the imaginary film which derived from the contracture and whose power to compel was illusory; and when the contracture loses its emotional character, it immediately stops being a contracture and simply becomes stillness without suffering. Ripening into satori then becomes a possibility.

The paradox we have reached is one which always confronts the human mind at the point where thesis and antithesis resolve into a synthesis. To begin with I had the unthinking conviction that my emotional state was my true life (thesis); study and reflection have brought me to the diametrically opposite belief, that the contracture at my centre is my death (antithesis); then intellectual intuition suddenly discovers that I can, by consciously fixing attention on the contracted emotional state, free myself from it. In other words, doing this conciliates life and death, movement and fixity, contracture and suppleness. The paradox is only apparent and exists in the domain of form; behind the appearance there is the conciliation of opposites.

I will use my earlier analogy between emotional activity and muscle to explain this new state of release we obtain once we stop struggling against the immobilizing force of the contracted state; and it will be seen that this comparison is relevant at the point where it begins to cease to be applicable. When muscle contracts, it shortens; when it relaxes, it returns to its original length and is ready for a new contraction. When I am not doing correct inner work, my central contracted state will obviously still diminish in intensity from time to time. When this happens, just as with muscle, it puts me back into a state of relaxation ready for the next contracture. Up to this point the comparison is valid. But when I consciously attach my awareness to the contracted state, something happens which has no analogy in physiology: the equivalent would be a muscle which could relax without lengthening, could de-contract without returning to its previous length, and could be both shortened and supple at the same time.

For example, suppose some defeat in my life has triggered a contracted state of humiliation; in the absence of any correct inner work, my feelings of humiliation are going to fade with the passage of time and in due course I will be free of them. However, by the time my feelings of humiliation have disappeared I will have reverted to my usual conceitedness and so laid myself open to the possibility of a further humiliation. If on the contrary, in my humiliated state I really fix awareness on my contracture, my feelings of humiliation disappear without my conceitedness returning. My central 'muscle' (unlike the case with physical muscles) relaxes without ceasing to be shorter. *Humiliation* is transformed into *humility*.

The comparison with muscles expanding and contracting works well. When I am on a high with success, I feel twice as big, I take up ten times as much space; I feel my chest expand and my nostrils flare, and my gestures become expansive. When some failure humiliates me, I feel small, hunched up, diminished, my chest is tight, and my gestures cramped.

The inner work I have been describing requires us to crouch willingly inside this shrunken space. This brings about a kind of condensation of the ego: it is as though the ego were restricted in size, while its mass stays the same, a bit like the process which changes carbon into diamond. The aim of this process is not to destroy the ego but to transform and transcend it. The effect of conscious acceptance can be compared to causing carbon to become more dense, black, and opaque until it transmutes instantaneously into a perfectly transparent diamond.

Fixing our attention wholly like this on the constricting spasm is obviously not something we can achieve the moment we start trying. All our pre-existing automatisms will prompt us to act in other incompatible ways. Inner work consists of persistent attempts to carry out the right activity, albeit incompletely. I will start to feel calmer as a result, and this effect will increase progressively. So I will be moving in the direction of that complete tranquillity which will one day enable satori to be triggered.

I learn to sense my contracture, my malaise, directly beneath the imaginary film which more or less conceals my centre, and the rest of the work depends on my acquiring this new inner sensation. My attention is then able to break away from the film and settle, motionless, on this profound unease which I have now glimpsed in its purity. Previously I had always run away from it but now I do my very best to settle into it (when you are dealing with this kind of lion, the only safe place is inside its mouth!). To the extent that I succeed in doing this, my unease disappears and I find that I am at the centre of my self, where my illusory distress seemed to reside. For a long time I will only be partially successful, so the contact between my attention and my centre will not be stable and will only last for a split second. When unease disappears, attention is left without an object so it gets caught up by images once more, and everything starts all over again. Our spirit of investigation must have staying power.

This work involves despair, but it is an appropriate despair from which Hope is born. Before this my hope had been that my imaginary film's convulsive activity would eventually succeed in getting rid of my contracture; and whenever something worried me, I would perform a 'forced labour' of sterile rumination, without questioning its usefulness. I was condemned to penal servitude by an irrational faith in my own imagination.

But now I have seen imagination for what it really is, a sterile *trompe-l'oeil*; and the hope which I based on its activity is now transformed into Hope based on its non-activity. The door of my cell opens; I have won the right to suffer without ruminating, in other words without perpetuating my suffering. This means that I can take advantage of my suffering's intrinsic instability, and allow myself to be comforted by my Principle without doing anything. By no longer having to suffer for nothing, I 'sacrifice' my suffering, and I conserve the vital energy required for transformation which I had previously been squandering.

A detailed description of the inward action described above would be of considerable interest. Unfortunately words do not describe inner experience well, and become ineffective as we approach the limits of the world of phenomena and forms. There are various ways of describing what it is we seek beneath the imaginary film: a kind of deep, cramp-like feeling, a paralysing grip, a cold that immobilizes (like the cold that can stop a river by turning it into ice); and our attention has to rest on this hard, immobile, cold layer. It is as though we were to stretch out peacefully on a piece of hard, but welcoming, rock which was exactly shaped to fit our body. But descriptions like this can only provide a general indication; it is up to everyone to carry out their own inner research, in the light of their own level of understanding.

# CHAPTER SIXTEEN

# Pleasure, Pain and the Affective Response

WE ARE NOW IN A POSITION to go more deeply into the preceding investigation by considering the whole gamut of conscious emotional life, in other words all the inner phenomena through which we register pleasure or displeasure in our contact with the external world. Since these two poles, pleasure/displeasure, correspond to quantitative variations in the same thing, which is my sense of myself as a distinct and separate entity, it will simplify matters if the following analysis deals for the most part with the unpleasant end of the scale. Whatever applies to unpleasantness will be equally applicable to pleasure.

There are two kinds of sensibility involved, physical (physical pain), and psychological (mental suffering). There is no confusing the kind of pain I get from an abscess with the suffering caused by the death of a loved one. The two types of sensibility seem to correspond to my gross or somatic aspect, and my subtle or psychological aspect. One involves *sensations,* the other *feelings,* and in both cases the reaction can be pleasant or unpleasant. In practical psychology a clear distinction has to be made between these two domains.

However this soma/psyche duality only refers to two aspects of a single thing, my psycho-somatic organism. They are just two aspects – distinct only to an outside observer – of the creature I call 'me', a microcosm both composite and unitary which is one particular manifestation of the Absolute Principle. If I hold a card edge on in front of my left eye, the right eye sees it as a surface and the left as a line. But it is still only one thing; in one sense, it is both line and surface; in another, it is neither line nor surface; either way, it is just a single card.

If body and mind are two aspects of the same thing, it follows that physical and psychological sensibility are also two aspects of a single underlying sensibility. Beneath two aspects there is in reality only one organism; similarly, beneath two aspects there is in reality only one underlying sensibility.

The idea that the different aspects of sensation and feeling share the same nature at a deeper level tempts one to conclude that only one of these aspects is real, and that the other is illusory. Suppose for example that I try to reduce all perceptible phenomena to sensation. I will take the view that there are only sensations: physical pain is a sensation whose effect on my body is localized or partial, so in other words it affects my body as an assemblage of separate organs and components. Psychological suffering is a sensation which affects my whole body. It is mediated through the global image which I have of myself and thus affects my body as a totality.

But this approach, although ingenious, does not succeed. When I analyse my body into an aggregate of organs and components, I am using an approach which artificially isolates one aspect by excluding the conciliating principle which converts the assemblage into a whole. My body cannot be fully defined in terms of its constituent parts. On the other hand my ability to think of my body as a totality, complete in itself, also involves me in an analytical sleight of hand. My body only exists by virtue of its connections with the rest of the cosmos, as a particle of the cosmic whole; it cannot be described adequately as a self-contained entity. Since I cannot provide an accurate and comprehensive account of my body in this way, I cannot use it to support the hypothesis of an individual sensibility composed solely of sensations.

So a materialist approach is inadequate, but could a mentalist approach be any more successful? This would involve saying that there are only feelings: there is no such thing as 'physical' pain, because I can only perceive it in my mind, through a mental representation; every unpleasant impression must occur in the psyche, and so all suffering is 'in the mind'. But where I was unable to establish my body as a fixed entity which I could refer to in support of the materialist hypothesis, I now find myself in even greater difficulties when I try to think of the world of my mental imagery as a fixed entity. If I was unable to define *me* in terms of my body, how much more is this true of my attempts to define *me* in terms of my mind.

I cannot reduce my sensibility to either one of its two aspects any more than I could do so with my psycho-somatic organism. I am both body and mind, and at the same time neither one nor the other. Similarly my responses are both physical and psychological, yet at the same time neither of these. When I consider my psycho-somatic organism, I come to the idea of the Self, or the Absolute Principle manifesting itself in me and this concept resolves the psycho-somatic dualism. But how is the dualism implicit in my sensibility to be resolved? And what is the status of its two aspects in reality? Since I cannot locate my single sensibility solely in my gross aspect (bodily organs) or in my subtle aspect (images), where is it located?

Studying sensibility got off to a bad start when it began with the body/mind distinction; it began with an artificial discrimination, so not surprisingly it failed to reach a satisfactory conclusion. I am going to try a different approach, one which will take both physical and psychological sensibility into account.

Instead of studying perceptible manifestations when they have already developed into their final form, we will examine the process of development itself. We will begin with an ordinary, everyday experience: one day a friend comes to see me while I am experiencing moderately severe rheumatic pain in one of my arms, and involves me in an interesting conversation. After he leaves, I feel pain once more and realize that I have been unaware of it during our conversation, though it must have been present throughout. It was there but I did not feel it, because my attention was distracted from it. If instead of rheumatic pain I had been suffering from mental pain of similar intensity, perhaps low in mood because something had upset me before my friend's visit, exactly the same thing could happen.

We are not dealing here with two different kinds of suffering in their final form, but with two different stages in the development of suffering. This is irrespective of whether the suffering in question is physical or mental. What was happening when my attention was distracted? Do I really think that my pain was there but that I was not aware of it? Certainly not. I cannot claim that pain is present if I do not feel it. At the same time, something must have persisted while I was distracted, which then caused my pain to return. So what is it that persists? To explain what I experience, I need to distinguish between painful excitation and awareness of pain. While I was distracted, the painful excitation persisted, but awareness of the pain had stopped. Clarifying this enables me to see how to retrieve the body-mind distinction and use it correctly: the painful excitation is a somatic phenomenon, while awareness of pain is a mental phenomenon. Our unsuccessful attempts to approach the problem from exclusively materialist or mentalist perspectives can now be brought to a valid conclusion. The painful excitation is a phenomenon affecting the body or *soma*; and the effect can be partial or total. It is partial when the body is involved through one of its component organs (painful physical excitation), and total when my body is affected as a total entity (painful excitation of the psyche, whose effect on the totality of my body is mediated through the global image I have of myself). Painful stimuli can affect me by passing through my gross aspect (the plane of sensation), or through my subtle aspect (the plane of images or feelings).

So there are two poles: painful excitation, and consciousness of pain. The materialist account applies to the first of these: it is always my body in which the painful excitation is located, and it is affected partially or totally. The mentalist account applies to the second: consciousness of pain is always a function of mind, irrespective of whether the painful excitation has affected a part of my body or affected it as a totality.

If we try to locate pain in either one of the two poles, painful excitation versus consciousness of pain, we run into difficulties again: I cannot confine pain to the painful excitation on its own, and exclude consciousness of pain; nor can I imagine a pain which would be pure awareness without any painful excitation. So where is pain located? Because we operate within a space-time framework, the question is formulated in these spatial terms, and it is our way of asking what the nature of pain amounts to in *reality*. Or, more accurately, what is pain's *cause*, since an effect is caused by its underlying reality. In relation to my consciousness of pain, the painful excitation is causal; my mind is affected *because* my body is affected. But the injury suffered by my body is itself the effect of a cause, which is not, as one might imagine at first, the external world. The way my body is affected is in fact a *reaction* to the external world's action, which is the immediate or precipitating cause, but not the efficient cause. The real or efficient cause of my body's reaction lies within my body itself, not outside it: it lies in my vital principle, in the source of all my manifestation – in other words it lies in the Absolute Principle as it manifests in me.

So there are three stages in the genesis of conscious pain: first, the Absolute Principle; next, the somatic aspect, which is impelled by the Absolute Principle to generate painful excitation; lastly, the subtle aspect is impelled by the painful excitation to produce awareness of pain. The Absolute Principle corresponds to originating Unconscious; the painful excitation to the subconscious (while I was distracted, my pain was subconscious); awareness of pain corresponds to consciousness.

So the whole pain process is an uninterrupted flux of energy which disintegrates outwards from the universal centre towards the individual periphery. The reality, or first cause, of this whole stream of phenomena is located in the originating Unconscious. This means that conscious suffering arises out of an unconscious level of reality: the reality of conscious suffering is unconscious. In other words, we are mistaken when we think of our conscious sensibility, which is composed of end-stage phenomena, as though it were a self-contained

146

and self-sufficient entity, able to provide us with the right guidance in our lives.

Although the phenomena of feeling, like all phenomena, are not Absolute Reality, nonetheless it might be thought that they possess the relative reality of Manifestation. This would be quite mistaken, for affective phenomena are packets of disintegrating energy which go directly from infinity to zero without integrating into forms at any point. The organs of my body possess a relative reality because they represent a coarse form of integrated originating energy. The same is true of my images: they have a relative reality because they involve the integration of originating energy into a subtle form. But with pleasure, pain, joy, and suffering there is no integration into forms, either coarse or subtle. A painful injury affecting my body has a coarse form and the mental distress which corresponds to it has a subtle form: in other words both gross and subtle manifestations of my pain have forms; but my pain itself, with its dual manifestation, is formless, as formless as the Absolute Principle which alone is its reality.

Given this absence of form, it is not surprising that we can never *grasp hold of* suffering itself. As already noted, attempts to grasp sadness never succeed: we can hold on to sad images, but sadness itself eludes us. The same is true of physical pain: if my arm is hurting, and I try to get a hold on my pain by actively perceiving it, what I succeed in perceiving is my painful arm but not its pain. The pain eludes me: it can get me in its grip, but I cannot do the same to it.

We can use a different approach to clarify these ideas. My body's painful reaction to an external stimulus, on which my ensuing consciousness of pain depends, only happens because of my 'need to exist'. It is a defence mechanism which presupposes that my existence *ought* to be defended; it implies that whatever threatens my existence threatens *me*. But I only feel threatened by threats to my organism to the extent that I identify exclusively with my organism. Because of this identification, the atemporal will to be, one of the attributes of originating Being, is expressed in my organism as the will to *continue in existence*, the need to live.

This confusion between my self and the Self, in other words my exclusive identification with my organism and my belief in the absolute reality of my phenomenal existence, is the illusion which enables the external world to cause my energy to rise up out of its source and be delivered into the disintegration of pain. If I was not ignorant, if I did not identify myself with my organism, if, like Socrates, I could say, '*My enemies can kill me, but they cannot harm me,*' then I would not feel any real threat to my self from threats to my organism. I would not suffer. I would perceive the threat to my organism, recognize that the red hot iron that was burning me, was burning me, and I could then get away from it if my rational intention was to live. But I would not suffer, and I would not experience any compulsion to protect my life. I would make a free choice whether or not to protect my life, according to the circumstances. I *could* save myself, but I would not be *compelled* by suffering to do so.

All emotion is based on ignorance and on implicit illusory beliefs which represent the sleep of my Faith in the only Reality, the sleep of Cosmic Mind within me. My perception of aggressive excitation deriving from the external world is not illusory, because it provides me with appropriate information about the phenomena which are attacking my organism. But the pleasant or unpleasant affective character of what I perceive is illusory, because it is based on illusory beliefs. My mistake does not lie in thinking of something which affects me as being favourable or unfavourable to my existence; where I go wrong is in considering it 'good' or 'bad', in other words evaluating it from an affective viewpoint. There is nothing to mislead me in the sensation of being burnt, but there is in the pain of the burn. My perceptions are correct in so far as they provide me with information, but they are illusory to the extent that they *affect* me. Between my Absolute Principle which 'is' and my organism which 'exists', between my noumenon and my phenomena, my emotions neither are nor do they exist. Every affective phenomenon represents ignorance's interpretative distortion of non-affective phenomena. All my affective experience is a kind of interpretative delirium arising out of illusory beliefs. My Real Self is free of affect.

In addition, when I respond affectively to something, this always implies that I am unresponsive to all the rest of the universe at that moment. As long as my Faith has not been wholly awakened in satori, my attention lets itself be captured by my delusive affectivity and turns away from my non-affectivity.

Inner work leaves this situation as it is, and allows attention to be drawn towards affective pseudo-phenomena. However, it does more than simply permit attention to move passively in that direction: it pushes it there actively. So now I project active attention into the place where I had previously been captured by something incomprehensible and where the fact of being trapped was expressed as suffering. I move to grasp what it was that kept me in its grip, and seize hold of what I used to call my suffering. With fear neutralized by understanding I now have the courage to turn back in a spirit of investigation towards the hypothetical flames fanned by my earlier flight. This inner effort to capture my captor causes my suffering to loosen its grip and let go of me; and this is how we should understand the Zen instruction to '*Let go*'. It is an inner action which frees trapped energy, dissolving what had become congealed; it establishes me in a state of non-sensitivity, which is different from a simple absence of emotional activity: it is 'No-Feeling', the motionless principle at the heart of all affective activity. By getting rid of the affective bias, it prepares the ground for the dawn of satori; it heals *the spiritual sickness which consists, according to Zen, of 'setting what we like against what we do not like.'*

# CHAPTER SEVENTEEN

# The Rider and the Horse

THE DUALISM OF YIN AND YANG, which rules the cosmos under the conciliating influence of the Tao, exists in man as it does in the rest of creation. Our awareness of this dualism is expressed in the belief that we are made of two autonomous elements, which we refer to variously as body and soul, matter and spirit, instinct and reason, etc. A whole range of common expressions reflect this belief in our two part composition: 'I am master of *myself*', 'I cannot stop *myself*', 'I am pleased with *myself*', 'I am fed up with *myself*,' etc.

But we know that any belief in the autonomy of these two parts is illusory; there are not two distinct *parts*, just two distinct *aspects* in any one individual. We are really *individuals, divided* artificially into two by our analytic minds misinterpreting what they observe. The mistake made by our dualistic perspective does not lie in distinguishing two aspects in us – for there certainly are two – but in concluding that they are two different entities, with one, for instance, perishable and the other eternal. In fact, self-observation does not reveal two parts in us: all it shows is that *our inner world functions as if there were two parts separated by a hiatus or discontinuity*. Because our intellect is ignorant, it jumps mistakenly from this observation of how things seem to be to the erroneous conclusion that this is how things really are, and that we really are composed of two discontinuous elements. The fact is that our inner world functions in the way it does, because we believe that this is how it does function: more accurately, it does so because the universal consciousness which alone can reveal our real inner unity remains dormant within us.

Let me try to clarify this issue by means of an illustration. When we think about our two 'parts', we think of one as inferior, instinctive, affective, motor, and irrational; while the other is superior, rational, in charge, and able to decide what the inferior part should do. In other words, the relationship we have in mind is that of horse and rider.

In reality, Zen reminds us, we are not horse and rider with a gap between the two. The real symbolical representation for mankind in this context would be the *centaur,* which is a single creature composed of two aspects without any separation between them. We are centaurs but inwardly we experience ourselves as horse and rider because we believe that our two aspects really are separate, or, more accurately, because we do not perceive the unity within which they become integrated.

Our next task is to identify the elements in our make-up which seem to fall into the horse or rider category, and to try and understand why we have this mistaken idea about ourselves.

It is tempting at first to establish the boundary between horse and rider by adopting a morphological approach: the horse would be our gross manifestation or soma, while the rider would represent our subtle manifestation, or psyche.

But this would be incompatible with our present approach: we are not simply studying the *modalities* of the human machine's functioning, but are concerned with the problem of what *determines and controls* its functioning. We are looking beyond *how* our lives proceed to what gives them their *direction.* Seen from this higher level perspective, the two parts are no longer two kinds of phenomena, one physiological and the other psychological, but two *ways of being,* two different *styles,* two different *rhythms* in the way in which our being is manifested.

The horse stands for how I am when I am not thinking impartially and independently. It represents my life when it is self-centred, egotistical and biased, the life I lead when my intellect is operating under the influence of desires, fears and affective reactions in general. Only the inferior conciliating principle is functioning within me at such times, the Demiurge who presides over the processes of growth and decay on the temporal plane. Nature is expressing its will in me, accomplishing its objectives through my organism. This is me as I am when I want to be distinct and separate, and want to be self apart from and in opposition to not-self.

The rider represents how I am when my thinking is disengaged from my affective life and operates impartially and independently. It represents my Independent Intelligence, or impartial reason, when thought is characterized by purity, objectivity and universality. This is how I am when I am thinking without wishing myself to be distinct and separate, when I am free from all opposition between self and not-self.

Understood in this way the rider is not the motor which moves my machine, but is responsible for the direction its movement takes. He is the principle of my action, its source and origin, but is himself non-action. So while both horse and rider are ways of being, only the horse is a way of *living.* The rider is not a way of living, because living implies movement and the rider is non-action: it is a way of thinking which is independent of my life. In my present condition, my life is necessarily egotistical, biased, impulsive and affective; when thought functions independently of affectivity, it is independent of my life as an individual, of my life itself. Another way of putting this is that the horse stands for the way I live when my thought is biased and blinkered; the rider represents pure, non-active thought. I am the horse when life captures my attention; I am the rider when attention frees itself from the hold which life has over it and succeeds in arousing my Independent Intelligence.

Conscious attention is unitary and is unable to focus on my life and the realm of pure thought beyond life at the same time: it has to be on one *or* other of these two aspects of my being. As my attention moves from one to the other, I identify in turn with the horse (when I feel and act), or with the rider (when I think impartially). Only surface consciousness is awake in me at present –and so I can only be horse or rider at any one time – and this explains why I believe that the two parts are separate, although in reality they are not. The illusory hiatus which exists between horse and rider is not a hiatus between two parts operating at the same time: it is my mistaken interpretation of the fact that I cannot be aware of my biased, partial life and my impartial reason at one and the same time. If I had no memory there would be no such misinterpretation: it exists because memory enables imagination to evoke these two ways of being at the same time. Apart from this I am never conscious of them together. I can imagine myself as both horse and rider at the same time in memory, so I can see the image of these two aspects of myself simultaneously, though they never operate simultaneously as far as my surface consciousness is concerned. But because surface consciousness never sees them both functioning at the same time, the image which brings them together can never succeed in uniting them. It cannot be the image of a centaur; it has to be the image of a rider on his horse and they are clearly separate from one another.

Since horse and rider, defined thus as two ways of being, never operate in consciousness at the same time, the horse is never *guided*. What I mean by this is that the rider never guides the horse's movement at the time it is made. His actions do have a controlling effect on what the horse does, but it is an indirect and delayed effect. During the moment when the rider is awake, and attention therefore cannot be on the horse, memory indicates how the horse has just been behaving during the preceding moment and the rider evaluates this in the light of what he considers desirable. Whether this *judgement* is favourable or not results in an image which is correspondingly flattering or wounding for the horse in relation to its need for affirmation. When attention reverts to the horse, the way it functions will be affected by the judgement, which it will experience as a pat of approval or a blow. The horse retains a memory of it, which is recorded like a conditioned reflex. What this means, given that the horse and rider cannot both be functioning at the same time, is that the only form of control available to the latter is to *train* the horse by establishing automatic behaviour patterns. This is an indirect kind of intervention, a product of the illusory separateness of horse and rider. It is quite comparable to what happens when a real horse is being trained: its rider uses a combination of patting the horse and flicking it with his riding-crop to get it to respond automatically. But ultimately it is the horse that carries out the movements. The horse may be indirectly dependent on the rider, but it is the horse, not the rider, that directly controls its own movements.

As I am at present in my pre-satori state, my life is inevitably made up of conditioned reflexes rather than actively directed behaviour. My Independent Intelligence has no real control over my life: the effect it has can only be relative, indirect and limited. In my present state, all my attempts to direct my life amount to no more than the kind of training one gives an animal, in other words they involve the elaboration and development of automatic patterns of behaviour, or automatisms. Automatisms imply fixed, stereotyped movements. However many there may be, and however tiny the behavioural components which comprise them, the fact that they are fixed and stereotyped prevents real *adaptation* to the external world. It is like a broken line; however many times it is broken into smaller units, it will only fit approximately onto a curve; it will never coincide exactly with it. So long as I think of myself as rider and horse, my inner world will conform to this, and all I will succeed in achieving will be training for my horse. Real adaptation to the outside world will elude me.

True realization is totally different from this kind of training. It is brought about when the centaur develops a new awareness in which the illusory division between rider and horse is abolished. There is no longer trainer or trained; no more reflective thought where 'I' thinks about 'me' (subject and object); 'I live' and 'I think' are reconciled into a single 'I am'.

This realization is beyond most people, for whom it is inconceivable that the illusory division should disappear. They also confuse atemporal and temporal realization, imagining that realization is the result of successful training. This is not to say that we should dismiss the approaches which rely on training. This would make no sense and it will indeed become clear that they play an essential part in the work which prepares us for satori. The point I want to make is that it is quite mistaken to imagine that any training can bring about realization: it may follow chronologically after training, but this does not imply in any way that the training causes or produces it. Although it is true that satori may burst forth following or in association with particular phenomena, no phenomenon can actually cause it.

Failure to understand this is responsible for the widespread popularity of some systematic methods involving the pursuit of some ideal, or different kinds of yoga, or codes of conduct setting out which automatisms should be established and which eliminated: in short, all sorts and kinds of disciplines which are thought to possess some intrinsic ability to bring about realization. *The mistake does not lie in trying these methods out, nor in following them; the mistake lies in imagining that such methods can lead to satori on their own, like roads leading to the journey's end.* The problem with any kind of training is that it implies that the illusory division between trainer and trained is real, so it cannot be instrumental in getting rid of that particular illusion. Only when the illusion is destroyed does realization occur.

This misconception is also responsible for another common mistake, which is to assess progress towards realization on the basis of how much harmony and balance someone has achieved in their training. This is not a good indicator: what matters is the degree of understanding. Anyone can be my teacher in whom I sense an understanding which can enrich my own; the particular training his horse has had, which may be mediocre, is not important. In the same way, I should not worry for myself if my horse's reactions are sometimes seriously lacking in harmony and balance, perhaps even more obviously than they were before when I had less understanding: training may be very important for inner comfort, but understanding is all that matters for realization.

As we have seen, the basic requirement of all training is that I evaluate my life, judging it to be good or bad; each time I assess my external or internal phenomena, I pat or chastise my horse. And Zen reminds us insistently of the importance of transcending this partiality: '*As soon as you have good and evil, confusion results and the mind is lost.*' Zen shows us that evaluation and training of this kind is undesirable inner manipulation, and is a habit we must get rid of. This is the unfortunate 'doing' which Zen refers to when it tells us that we have nothing to do, that we must learn to stop doing.

But this is not easy advice to understand properly. If I take it to be a condemnation of training, I am wrong, because by condemning training I am still caught up in the evaluation process, so the outcome could only be a kind of anti-training. I would simply end up training myself not to do any more training, which would change nothing. I would still be on the wrong track, believing in the effectiveness of a counter-training approach which would still be a form of training. Zen tells us not to interfere with life: '*Let things be as they may.*' There is no scope for me to make a direct attempt to modify habits connected with training myself. I can only get them to disappear by indirect means, by developing a progressively deeper understanding that my efforts to train myself, which I continue, have no intrinsic effectiveness as regards realization. The goal is that my attempts at self-training, which are compensatory activities, should lose their special value. For this to happen, they have to fail and this failure must be correctly interpreted. I do not have to do anything about them failing, which will happen naturally; but I must make sure I interpret their failure correctly.

If I believe in the intrinsic effectiveness of a particular discipline, I am going to attribute its failure to everything except the discipline itself, in whose value I will continue to believe. But if I have understood its intrinsic ineffectiveness, while still allowing myself to go on practising it if I feel the need to do so, I will experience the gradual build-up of a deep weariness, which will disengage me from the discipline and enable me to really *transcend* it. At present it is natural for me to intervene intrusively in my inner world: I cannot stop myself doing this, nor should I. But if I fully understand how futile these interventions are, then, with experience and the passage of time, my emotionally-charged belief in their usefulness will gradually dissipate. Beliefs are like wheels set spinning at a great rate: if my intellect stops boosting them by justifying them, sooner or later they will run out of energy.

We know that what satori crowns is not some ultimate success, but an ultimate failure. The awareness of always having been free appears in us when we have exhausted every effort, every training which we once thought could liberate us. The various disciplines may not be capable of leading us to satori, but that does not mean we should not follow them. They lead to impasses, and they all lead to a single, final impasse: and it is precisely because satori cannot be obtained until we have come right to the end of this ultimate blind alley that we should follow them. They should be followed with the theoretical understanding that they lead nowhere, so that experience can transform theoretical understanding into full understanding, into that clarity of vision which represents arrival in the impasse, and opens us to satori.

Here is a dialogue between a Zen monk and his master. The monk, Tsu-hsin, had just experienced satori. '*Tsu-hsin approached the master Hui-nan. As he was about to bow, the master smiled and said: "You have now come into my room." Tsu-hsin was filled with joy and said: "If the truth of Zen is what I now possess, why do you make us swallow all the old stories and exhaust ourselves struggling to make sense of them?" The master said: "If I did not make you struggle in every possible way to discover their meaning, so that you eventually reached a state of no-struggle and no-effort where you could see with your own eyes, I am sure you would forfeit any chance of finding yourself.'*

So I do not have to avoid seeing myself as a rider on a horse, nor do I have to avoid behaving like a rider training a horse. But I do not forget, despite this optical illusion, that I am really a centaur and that any training, which colludes with the myth of a separate horse and rider, distances me from my true nature. However beautiful, however inspiring the outcome of my training, it still distances me from my true nature. In reality it matters little to me whether my horse is trained to be a 'saint' or a yogi with spectacular powers, or to experience 'transcendent' inner states. My true nature is not in any of these: it consists of me and my horse being one. Then will my least action in life, however commonplace, participate in the nature of Reality.

The centaur symbol is an aid to understanding before realization, but the instant the illusory gap is abolished, which is the instant the symbol achieves fulfilment, it too is abolished. 'Not being two,' according to Zen, 'everything is the same, and the whole of existence is included therein.' Rider and horse become one, but they are united in the formless Whole, in such a way that horse and rider are no more, and the centaur is transcended the moment it is attained. This is the subject illustrated by the marvellous Zen text known as *The Ten Ox-Herding Pictures.* In this Zen affirms the need to undergo training; but it also emphasizes that the final goal is not a trained ox. *'Riding the ox, the man finally comes home again. But, look, the ox has vanished, and he now sits with such serenity on his own!* Then the man disappears as well: *'Everything is empty, whip, rope, man and ox. Who has ever contemplated heaven's immensity? The fire is incandescent and no snowflake can fall upon it. It is here that the Patriarch's mind is manifest.'*

CHAPTER EIGHTEEN

# The Primordial Error or 'Original Sin'

IN THE PREVIOUS CHAPTER, we discussed discipline, or 'training our horse', encompassing all the different kinds of training in this concept. I drew a distinction between someone before satori, in whose case training is essential, and someone after satori, for whom there is no more training.

For someone like me in the pre-satori state, it is interesting to note that there are different kinds of training which I can rank, like all phenomena, along a scale from gross to subtle. This ranking cannot exist in any absolute sense since phenomena as such do not share in the nature of Absolute Reality in a graduated, *more or less*, way; it has a relative existence in relation to my affective bias. It should not be represented as a sloping ladder, which would be the obvious choice of symbol from the affective viewpoint, but rather as a road running horizontally towards a point where the vertical axis runs abruptly upwards. This corresponds to all the inner work which brings one *chronologically* closer to satori, but not closer in reality, in the sense that no creature can come closer to its Source and Origin, since it has never *been* away from it.

The horizontal scale corresponds to graded alterations in the way our Independent Intelligence functions. There is an important distinction to be made here between the fundamental source and origin of our pure thought, which is Infinite Wisdom, Objective Knowledge, the *buddhi* of the Vedanta, and the relative and limited operation of this limitless intelligence as our own Independent Intelligence. Here is a practical example from everyday psychology: on a given occasion I may feel angry and express my anger impulsively; on another occasion I am just as angry but I contain my feelings, because I have an ideal image of myself in mind which I want to express and this image includes self-control (I might be influenced in this by a variety of different reasons: I might find self-control aesthetically more attractive, or it could be a means of avoiding unpleasantness, or there might be tactical and strategic considerations, or I might anticipate 'spiritual' rewards for such deserving behaviour, etc.). In the first case my mind is driven by the most urgent affective impulse, the emotion, the affective priority, of the moment.

In the second situation I am disengaged from this impulse, but my mind is driven instead by my love for my ideal self: this amounts to control by an enduring, generalizing, affective process which has a broader perspective than those lesser individual affective impulses whose focus is the current moment. I am freed from control by short-term affective priorities, but I am now subject to a set of values which participate in the fourth dimension, persisting over time, superimposed in a way across an infinite multitude of moments. In this second case Independent Intelligence is at work since I am functioning independently of the immediate issue; but its operation is imperfect because I am now under the sway of a new, persisting concern. This involvement of the temporal dimension frees one from the tyranny of the moment, but brings its own constraints.

What is Independent Intelligence? It has something of the nature of Absolute Impartiality, of Objective or Divine Reason, and so of the Infinite, and yet it appears, in the example above, to be imperfect, relative and limited. The apparent difficulty this question presents derives from the easy mistake of confusing a source with its manifestation, so that when we speak of 'Independent Intelligence' we are tempted to confuse *buddhi* and the manifestations of *buddhi*. I contain within myself the possibility of thinking entirely with perfect impartiality: and this is *buddhi*, or originating Independent Intelligence. But, before satori, this possibility is not fully realized; it is only manifested as a relative impartiality: but this relative impartiality is *a relative manifestation of absolute impartiality*. There is no such thing as imperfect *buddhi*; there is the incomplete appearance of perfect *buddhi*.

My Independent Intelligence as it manifests itself at present has two aspects which I must not confuse: its source and origin, *buddhi*, dwells within it (immanence of the originating source or principle), so it partakes of the nature of *buddhi*; but, before satori, my manifested Independent Intelligence is not *buddhi* (transcendence of the originating source). As soon as my mind disengages to some extent, however little, from the affective activity of the moment (meaning that there is some shift from the particular to the general), *buddhi* manifests itself. But this does not mean that my mind's functioning is then identical with *buddhi* itself or 'the vision of things as they really are'. Independent Intelligence involves disengaging mind from affect, but this can happen to a varying degree; viewed qualitatively, any disengagement that occurs is perfect in itself, but it will not be complete, so it remains impaired from a quantitative point of view.

This quantitative variation in Independent Intelligence's functioning creates the whole horizontal hierarchy of disciplines mentioned earlier, producing, from my affectively biased perspective, a qualitative classification of different kinds of training on a scale from gross to subtle. I do not intend to study this whole hierarchy but will concentrate on its higher reaches. It is important to study the most subtle modality in which Independent Intelligence is expressed, the primordial training from which all trainings further down the hierarchy are derived, because we will find there the primordial incompleteness of *buddhi's* manifestation in us. This is the ultimate error which we have to transcend in our return to the origin.

We have seen that all training involves evaluating and judging how the horse is getting on in relation to the rider's ideal standards. At every moment, everyone has an idea of how their horse *ought* to be behaving, and this is expressed in an image. There is a correlation between the nature of the image and the position the training is felt to occupy on the affective hierarchy, so images which are particularized and gross belong to the 'lower' end, and those of a more general, subtle nature are felt to be subtle or 'higher'.

As my understanding becomes richer and more precise, the clarity of my mind dissipates idolatries, which means that my ideal image of myself weakens and fades. I finally understand that Reality is prior to all form, and that any ideal image must therefore be illusory. I no longer have any theoretical grounds for wanting my horse to behave in one way rather than another.

It might seem that I would stop judging myself in relation to an ideal image, once all ideal images had disappeared. It would be impossible to make judgments without criteria to refer to, so I would stop judging myself. Complete impartiality would prevail, and I would have achieved satori.

This is what would happen if the ideal image *caused* the judgment, in other words if I were judging myself according to a pre-existing ideal image. But the opposite is true: I feel the need to judge first, and then construct the ideal image which will enable me to pass judgment. My experience of my own temporal limitation distresses me and my suffering awakens in me a doubt about my 'being', and this triggers a need to judge and evaluate myself. This need to judge myself triggers the creation of an ideal image as a reference point, something for me to emulate in the hope that I will achieve absolution in this way.

The reason that being subject to time distresses me is that I have a deep, implicit belief that I ought not to be subject to it. This belief is the expression at the phenomenal level of a misinterpretation of the unconscious, primordial and correct intuition that 'I am Buddha nature.' The whole process can be summarized like this: in the originating Unconscious (the universal source), I know that I am Buddha; in my subconscious (the first individual level), I consider myself entitled to freedom from temporal constraints and contend that my existence should never be called into question by not-self; at a conscious level I experience painful uncertainty regarding these subconscious claims, and I then feel compelled to look critically at how I am in the hope of dispelling this uncertainty. So I create an ideal image which I must imitate in order to obtain absolution from the burden of these concerns.

This is why my need to judge and criticize myself does not go away, despite my having reached a level of understanding which dissipates all idolatrous images. It persists because the uncertainty about myself persists, because its causes are still present at a deeper level. There are no more individual, ideal images left to support a preference for any one particular training, but what does persist is the implicit general image which gave rise to all the individual images, namely the primordial 'I should never be negated' image. This continues to determine a form of training, a primordial version whose aim is to train my horse in such a way that it should never be negated, so that it would always triumph completely over not-self.

There is a sense in which my inner state gets worse as understanding gets rid of every particular formal ideal. While I had such ideals, they offered a supportive refuge: when negating experiences, threats to my fantasy of absolute and unconditional existence such as actual or potential failures, impinged on me from the outside world, I could reduce their impact and compensate or over-compensate for any damage inflicted by conforming to the dictates of my ideal. It meant that there was a space where I could, through my own efforts and the exercise of self-control, win as much affirmation as I needed to neutralize the negating effect produced by events in the outside world. My increasing understanding puts an end to this comforting arrangement.

So getting rid of all the individual disciplines does not lead to the complete absence of any discipline. What remains is the fundamental, universal discipline which compels me to face the antagonism of not-self without any tricks and self-deceptions to protect me: in other words I am forced to confront the image of my personal non-divinity. This last discipline is not as easy to transcend as the individual ones; the ideal form which it involves is not conscious, so my conscious mind, not having actualized and attached value to it, cannot easily dismiss it. It is a subconscious, underground form which I cannot grasp and devalue directly; I have to wait for it to gradually lose its value with a 'burning patience', watchful and impartial, truly living out the Zen expression: *'Let go; let things be as they may.'*

Let us take a close look at this fundamental, primordial discipline and the subconscious ideal image on which it is based, bearing in mind what was said above. In the universal, originating Unconscious, I know I am Buddha. On the first individual or subconscious level I claim to be Buddha as a distinct entity, as a self confronting not-self. Hence on this level I maintain that I should never be denied by not-self and I contend that I should triumph completely over the outside world for ever. Then at a conscious level I doubt the legitimacy of these subconscious claims and not-self fills me with dread (this explains why every failure is associated with a feeling of culpability). As long as I had a special ideal, I could escape from the subconscious requirement that I should always enjoy complete success; a particular territory was privileged to represent the whole and by succeeding there I was immunized against negation experienced elsewhere.

But once understanding devalues all conscious ideal forms, the primordial obligation to triumph completely over not-self all the time falls on my own shoulders. It is subconscious, so self-judgment withdraws into the shadows. Evaluating consciousness is no longer directed on me but is fixed on the external world and my struggle to live and succeed in which I demand affirmation and refuse negation. Positive or negative, affirmed or denied, my states of mind no longer depend on whether the form expressed by my mechanisms is judged beautiful or ugly on the basis of how closely it resembles some particular ideal; they now depend on fluctuations in my psychosomatic state, in other words on my successes and failures in the outside world and my coenaesthetic states of well-being or discomfort. I respond to circumstances affecting my psychosomatic organism by becoming arrogant or contrite towards not-self, without any conscious awareness of self-judgement in these attitudes. My conscious impression is that I no longer impose any requirements on myself and that my demands are solely directed towards the external world. It is clear, though, that when I insist that the outside world should yield to me, I am simply giving expression to the primordial demand hidden deep within me that I should triumph over the world. Therein lies the fundamental demand, the first *personal* manifestation of my *universal* identity with the Absolute Principle, and hence the first dualistic, egotistical error, the 'original sin'. This is an important point: we are here at the very root of the Ignorance from which all our illusory anguish flows.

Let us take a detailed look at the nature of this 'primordial training'. The horse wants to feel affirmed in its opposition to the external world. The rider requires that the horse should succeed in feeling affirmed the whole time. At first sight it looks as though they both share the same goal. The opposite is true: their preferences and inclinations differ radically in both nature and direction.

The horse's inclinations are *relative* in their *nature*. They belong to manifestation, the relative phenomenal level: it wants to be affirmed as much as possible, but accepts limits in this because limitlessness is not part of its domain. It prefers affirmation, but puts up with negation and adapts as best it can. Its wishes are *directed towards the external world*, and it desires objects that belong to the not-self.

The rider's preferences and inclinations are *absolute* in *nature*. The effect of my identity in the Unconscious with Buddha the Absolute, is to produce an *absolute* demand in my subconscious that self should triumph over not-self, rather than a *relative* wish that this should happen. My rider is the representative of the Self, the Absolute Principle of my being, and this is true however ignorant my consciousness may be. Similarly the independence of my intelligence is no less absolute by nature, however incompletely it may be manifested. My rider issues directly from the Absolute and represents it, so in the temporal plane it functions like infinity in mathematics, multiplying everything without limit: the demand the rider makes on the horse knows no limits, and it can mobilize my organism's entire available energy at any moment. So there is a radical opposition between the rider's absolute and the horse's relative tendencies.

Moreover the rider tends to be oriented towards the horse rather than the external world. It is the horse acquiring the not-self object that matters to him, not the object itself (witness the familiar saying: 'It is the principle of the thing that matters, not the thing itself'). The rider dismisses the things that matter to the horse; the horse in itself is of no interest to him. Suicide illustrates this relationship at its most extreme: when the rider realizes that the horse will never be able to meet his requirements, he condemns it to suicide. The rider only thinks of the horse as an instrument capable of embodying in some misconceived way the noumenal superiority of the Absolute Source over manifestation, through the triumph of self over not-self in the phenomenal domain. So horse and rider express fundamentally opposed tendencies: the horse is struggling against the external world, the not-self, while the rider is struggling against the horse, the self.

So primordial training involves a fundamental antagonism between my two parts, which is not surprising since antagonism is one of the aspects of the Yin Yang dualism. But within the harmonizing equilibrium of the Tao, the Yin and Yang poles, though antagonistic, are also complementary. The problem for me is that my ignorance causes the antagonism between my two parts to be *radical*, which means that I live out my life in a way which only expresses the antagonism between my two poles in my life, and not their complementarity. What I live out in my life needs to be completion, not destruction.

This fulfilment can only be brought about through understanding. It has already freed me from individual ideal images and, by so doing, purified the radical antagonism which these idolatrous illusions were masking: now it will work at a deeper level. As I develop a clear theoretical understanding of the ideas expressed in this study, they gradually penetrate into the everyday workings of my inner life and experience. Subconsciously my great ambition is to triumph completely, for ever, over the not-self, and my rider goes on making implacable demands on my poor horse: but, as I begin to recognize this at a theoretical level, a new attitude develops within me in relation to the old one, which it gradually neutralizes. It is an attitude of indulgence towards the horse, an acceptance of its feelings when it has been negated. I stop feeling fed up with myself whenever I fail, or am unhappy or unwell. I think of my horse as a friend, and stop treating it as a mere instrument to be exploited on behalf of my limitless claims. I make my peace with my brother before going to the temple, as the Gospel tells me to.

However this new attitude does not appear in consciousness, so it should not be confused with the common conscious attitude of self-indulgent lenience towards oneself which is the reassuring outcome of the individual trainings. It is like when a chemical base is thrown into acid; it is scarcely present in the mixture and stops being a base as such, and its presence is only registered by a reduction in acidity. Similarly no friendly bias in favour of my horse develops within me, simply a reduction in my unfriendly bias against it. No judgement is given in its favour, but the general process of judging which went on before and always condemned is less prominent.

My horse gets on fine when I leave it alone. Zen says: '*When the ox is well looked after, it becomes pure and docile. Even without a chain, with nothing to restrain it, it will follow you of its own accord.*'

# CHAPTER NINETEEN

# The Immediate Presence
# of Satori

My PRIMORDIAL CLAIM to being as a distinct and separate entity condi-tions all my desires, and through them my hopes and beliefs. The fact that I make this claim implies a longing and an *expectation*; and my belief that something is lacking means that I wait for something to make good my deficiency.

This longing is of a general nature, expressing itself in the fact that I seem to be waiting for my life to become different, becoming life as it truly ought to be in the sense that I would be totally and perfectly affirmed, not incompletely and imperfectly as at present. We may or may not realize this, but we all live in the expectation that a day will come when 'true life', free of all negation, will finally begin.

Each of us has a different idea of what our ideal, true life would be like, depending on our personality structure and circumstances. We all have a picture of what is needed to bring about a new era in which life's current imperfections would be abolished. I find myself thinking that everything would finally be perfect if only I possessed some particular item, or if I were different in some way, or if some particular event were to take place. Sometimes I have a very clear idea of what is needed to initiate this 'true life' for me; at other times it is not clear, and I am just waiting for something ill-defined which I am convinced would put everything right. There are times when these expectations are silent within me, but they are only briefly in abeyance and before long my yearning for a perfectly satisfying life re-emerges. It is as though I believed myself to be exiled from some paradise which really does exist somewhere; and as though I saw some change in myself or the external world as the *key* which could unlock the door to this lost paradise. I live my life in a quest for this key.

While I wait, I 'kill time' as best I can. Part of my vital energy may be invested in actually developing the 'key', so I work towards some achievement, which may be material or subtle. I can only invest some of my energy in this; the rest goes into imaginative activity, day-dreams dealing with the all-too-familiar inner proceedings, whose successful outcome would be assured by the key. I feel compelled to invest my energy somewhere, to make changes, inwardly or outwardly. I cannot just be in a state of expectancy without moving. Expectation implies movement, a straining towards what is to come, a longing for it; without this dynamic of longing I would be dead. If I cannot make changes in the external world to obtain the key I am waiting for, then I make them inwardly, creating images which make it easier for me while I am waiting.

Like everything else I can observe in my natural make-up, my state of expectation is basically sound but wrongly directed. It is sound because it is a manifestation of my profound need for that vision of things in their suchness which would mark the beginning of a *true* life for me. It is badly directed because my expectations are directed towards things as I see them at present. So long as correct teaching has not awoken my understanding, I cannot prevent my expectations being directed towards what I am familiar with and can imagine, in other words towards the dualistic world of phenomena. As long as I seek the key to the lost paradise in things which I can represent to myself, I cannot help depicting it to myself either like something I have already experienced (at least partially), or as something not yet experienced exactly but of the same general nature as things with which I am already familiar. Even when my idea of the key is imprecise and unformed, I visualize my return to the lost paradise as an inner state which will be perfectly positive and happy, similar to but better than the happy states which I have already experienced. The natural orientation of my expectations cannot help being situated along the horizontal plane of temporal dualism; *it is not directed at something new, beyond dualism, but towards an improvement in what I am already familiar with.*

This is clearly mistaken: I am waiting for something perfect to emerge from an improvement; but there is no way in which something which starts off imperfect can be brought to perfection by an improvement, however broadly conceived. No 'evolution', no 'progress', can bring one to what Zen calls 'the haven of rest.' It is also worth noting that my longing is directed towards the joy/pain, satisfaction/dissatisfaction dualism, so it is based on the ill-founded hope of being able to dissociate the two aspects of a dualism which is indissociable and can only be conciliated in the Tao. Longing directed at this dualism can only generate the same dualism and its polarities; and the stronger such longing is, the stronger my own inner dualism becomes, whether I am aware of it or not. When my thirst is managed in this way, the water I receive is like salt water which increases my thirst after briefly seeming to relieve it. Whoever expects to find 'true life' in the world of manifestation, the familiar world, will wait in vain until they die.

That aspect of my longing which is appropriate has the following effect: waiting for something different from my current life prevents me becoming completely identified with it, and protects my consciousness from being completely absorbed by forms present in the here-and-now. But at the same time the mistaken orientation of my longing means that I am swallowed up by another identification: I identify with something which I imagine, more or less clearly, as absolutely desirable; and this something, because it is a product of my imagination, still has a form (which may be the subtlest imaginable) in which my consciousness is lost. My dream of finding paradise may free up attention in the midst of life's immediate events, but this precious available attention is then handed over to imagining a chimera of perfection in the realm of phenomena.

This misguided longing of mine creates the illusion of *time* for me and the painful sense that it is forever running away from me. When I think of what I long for as an improvement in what I know (which is in the phenomenal realm, conditioned by space-time), I am necessarily projecting my state of perfect satisfaction into the future. This imbues time with an absolute, illusory reality, so that it seems to stretch forth from the imperfect present moment to the longed for perfect moment in the future.

Time is thus misleadingly endowed with an absolute value and I am ambivalent towards it: looking back I bitterly regret its speedy passage and would like to make it retrace its steps or at least prevent its further passing; looking ahead I would like time to pass with infinite speed because waiting for my lost paradise to open its gates is unbearable. Episodes in my past feel very different when I recall them from how they felt at the time; when I recall them I do so without that vertiginous yearning directed towards a better future which possessed me then, tearing me away from the present moment and preventing me from living it to the full; and this explains why I feel regret for periods in my life which I scarcely registered at the time.

When the right kind of teaching awakens my understanding, a change takes place in me. I realize that my yearning, which is primordial and boundless in nature, will never be assuaged by the phenomenal world, at whatever level of subtlety and universality this may be conceived. I understand that what I have been waiting for all this time, and have previously deluded myself into believing that I had found embodied in various forms, is what Zen calls *satori*. I understand that satori cannot be thought of as an improved version, however marvellous, of my present life; it cannot be based on dissociating the two indissociable parts of dualism, with the progressive purification of a 'goodness' which could be cleansed of all 'evil'. Satori is access to something beyond dualism which conciliates it within a tripartite Unity. Obviously I cannot represent this something to myself, other than as something unimaginable and inconceivable, something totally different in nature from everything I know at present.

If I have really understood this correctly, the result will not be a new state of conscious expectation, this time directed towards something unimaginable; because consciousness cannot operate without involving the imagination, and imagining something unimaginable still produces an image. Correct understanding does not produce a new conscious expectation different from its predecessor. The new state of expectation does not arise in surface consciousness, but originates in the depths of the mind where it has the effect of harmonizing and neutralizing the previous hopeful expectation which was directed towards something that could be imagined. Correct understanding initiates and nurtures, in the depths of my being, an expectation which opposes and complements my former aspirations. It is as though there were a growing insistence that I should no longer expect any restrictive affirmation of myself as a distinct entity, developing opposite my former original demand that I should be so affirmed. On its own, this new development is as inadequate as the situation that preceded it; but a time approaches when these two polarities, which are inadequate on their own, will come into equilibrium in the 'Great Doubt' of Zen and thus provide the conditions which will enable us to enjoy satori. It is just as though we came into the world with only one eye open and had to work hard to open the second fully, so that we could finally achieve the 'opening of the third eye'.

Although this new expectation which understanding has engendered is confined to our unconscious, where it confronts the original expectation from which all our conscious aspirations arise, this need not prevent us trying to imagine what it is like (it is not as though Zen forbids this kind of effort or any other, for that matter). At the same time let me make it quite clear that I am not recommending this as a systematic technique for bringing about realization.

The new state of expectation directed towards satori is a longing for something unimaginable, something radically new unlike anything I know already. When I try to put myself into this expectant state, my mind encounters various sorts of perceptions and images which it rejects as they push themselves forward. Because they are located within me or outside me, being either inner states or aspects of the external world, their disappearance leaves my expectation somewhere between these two situations. It is directed neither outside me nor within me, nor on some possible object of perception, nor on a possible perceiving self as subject. It is directed at the very act of perception which links subject and object but is itself imperceptible and is like a point without dimension or location. There is then virtual freedom from space, accompanied, as we shall see, by a similar freedom from time. In my former state of expectation, I was waiting for something which was not available at present but nevertheless existed for me in the realm of possibility. In my new state, I am waiting for something which does not exist for me at all because it is unimaginable. It is outside my range of possibilities and I can no more conceive of it in the future than I can evoke it in the past; it is outside time as it is outside space (unsurprisingly, as these are both aspects of the same system). When I wait on this entirely new and unimaginable consciousness of the world and of myself, and of the relationship which connects us, I am waiting for something which, existing neither in space nor time, is in the very centre and instant of my waiting, at the point where the whole Universe comes into being in the eternal instant, *hic et nunc*.

My state of expectation stops being expectation, since what I am waiting for is not separated from me by space or time. *I understand then the mistake I made when I thought of satori as a future state; my actual realization of the state of satori may be seen as something happening in the future, but this is not true of the state itself, which is already, and always has been, my state and my eternal 'being'.* I should not think of realizing the satori state as a future possibility; it is on offer at this very moment, at every moment. It is only my acceptance which is situated in time, in the negative sense that I can say as every instant passes that I have still not accepted satori, while not rejecting the possibility that I may accept it in the following instant.

I am like someone in a room whose door is wide open while the window is barred; from the moment I was born the world outside has enthralled me and I have clung to the bars of the window, clutching them tightly because I am greedy for the images from outside. My tightly clenched hands prevent me leaving the room, so in that sense I am not free. But the only thing that really keeps me prisoner is the ignorance which makes me mistake imagined life for the real thing. It is the tight grip of my own hands which keeps me trapped, nothing else. I am free; I always have been free; and I will realize this the moment I 'let go'.

It is interesting to compare these ideas from Zen with the parable of the ten virgins from the New Testament: there were five foolish virgins who took no oil for their lamps, and five wise virgins who did take oil; and they all slept until the coming of the bridegroom. Their sleep symbolizes my egotistical life's state of identification (with all the dreams engendered by my hopes and fears). The oil symbolizes the state of expectation directed towards the unimaginable, satori. Without this oil, the new expectation born of understanding, I am like the foolish virgin who is unable to receive the bridegroom. And the parable ends with the bridegroom saying: 'Watch therefore, for ye know neither the day nor the hour'. It can be each instant, it is offered each instant.

A Zen story illustrates this idea of *pure expectation* (pure in the sense of freedom from time and space), which is *pure attention,* attention without any object:

> *A man of the people one day asked the priest Ikkyu: 'Reverend Sir, would you be willing to write down some maxims of great wisdom for me?'*
>
> *Ikkyu took a brush and wrote: 'Attention.'*
>
> *'Is that all?' the man said, 'Won't you add some more words?'*
>
> *Ikkyu then wrote twice: 'Attention. Attention.'*
>
> *'That's all very well,' the man said, vexed, 'but I don't see anything particularly profound or subtle in what you've written there.'*
>
> *Ikkyu then wrote the same word three times.*
>
> *A bit irritated, the man said: 'Well then, what does this word 'attention' mean?'*
>
> *And Ikkyu replied: 'Attention means attention.'*

# CHAPTER TWENTY

# The Mind's Passivity and the Disintegration of Our Energy

THE PURPOSE OF THIS ESSAY is to deepen our understanding of satori and the inner phenomena which precede it. We must begin by drawing a clear distinction between the atemporal satori state, and the historical satori event. I have already indicated that the state of satori is not to be thought of as a new state to be accessed, but as our eternal state, existing independently of birth and death. Each of us lives in the state of satori and could not live in any other way. When Zen speaks of satori in time, as in the following quotation: 'Satori comes upon us without warning *when* we have exhausted all the resources of our being,' it is not referring to the atemporal state of satori but to that instant when we realize that we are in that state, or, more accurately, when we stop believing that we live outside that state.

This distinction between satori-state and satori-event is very important. If I only think of satori as a state I lapse into fatalism. If I only think of satori as an event I succumb to spiritual ambition and a greedy craving for Realization. This is a mistake which binds me firmly to the illusion which underpins all my distress.

The satori event is a very special kind of event in that it ceases to be regarded as such as soon as it occurs. People who have achieved satori no longer see themselves as exiled from the atemporal; they live in the atemporal and know it, and no longer distinguish between a past where they would have believed that they were not living in satori and a present where they can know that they are. This does not mean that they no longer remember the time before the satori event. They can recall everything, their distresses, their weaknesses, the inner phenomena which compelled them to act against their 'reason'; *but they see that all of that was already the state of satori,* that nothing ever has been, is, or will be outside the state of satori. Since past, present and future are now seen to be immersed in the state of satori, the satori event is obviously no longer experienced as a special historical date. Satori only exists as an event for us, with our current illusory perspective, because we have not experienced it yet. For us, those who have experienced satori are *liberated*; for themselves, they are not liberated, they are *free, free since the beginning of time.* This explains how Hui-neng can say on the one hand 'I had satori the instant I understood a certain idea', and on the other: 'There is no liberation, there is no realization.'

The state of satori, being atemporal, is obviously unconditioned; it is especially not dependent on the satori event. But our present perspective limits us: we are only able to conceive of satori as an event, and one conditioned by the kind of inner processes we have been investigating.

There are some general considerations which are relevant to the question of what conditions are associated with the satori event. The idea of conditions and conditioning should not be understood as causality, particularly in this context. No event is *caused* by a preceding event, but it is conditioned by it according to the Buddhist formulation: '*This being so, that happens.*' So our purpose is not to discover what inner processes are capable of causing or generating satori, but rather what processes necessarily precede it.

It will also become clear that the concept of conditioning, even if purged of any suggestion of causality, remains a very inexact approximation. In fact the very special way in which attention functions prior to satori cannot really be called a process: it brings about the abolition of a process which is inherent in our present condition. It is really my non-perception of the state of satori which is conditioned by certain processes; the 'conditioning' of satori is only negative, in the sense that it is the ending of the conditioning which maintains my non-perception of satori.

So this study will concentrate on analysing the inner processes which are currently responsible for our illusion of not living in satori. We will see that these are our *imaginative–emotional processes* – which our vital energy disintegrates into – and we will try to get a precise idea of the defect in the way our attention functions that creates the conditions which make these imaginative–emotional processes possible.

I will begin with a concrete example: someone treats me with disrespect, and I am angry and feel like hitting him. If we analyse what goes on within me at the time, we will see that my inner phenomena can be divided into two different reactions, which I will refer to as primary and secondary.

The *primary reaction* involves the activation within me of a certain amount of vital energy. This energy was latent in my central source of energy until it was activated by my perception of energy manifested against me in the not-self. This extraneous aggressive energy evokes a reactive force in me which balances the not-self force. At this point the reactive force is still not an impulse of anger. It lacks precise form, like a substance waiting to be poured into a mould. Just for an *instant* without duration, as it is mobilized in my source, it remains a force *in statu nascendi*, not yet a force of anger. In that instant, it is a pure, vital force, still without form. This primary reaction corresponds to a particular perception and *knowledge* of the external world. So it corresponds to a particular *consciousness*, but one which is quite different from what we usually understand by that term. It does not possess the clarity and accessibility of ordinary consciousness, and it does not involve the intellect. It is obscure and deep, operating at the level of reflex: it is *organic*. It is the same consciousness which governs the patellar reflex, or knee-jerk. Every reflex depends on this organic consciousness which 'knows' the external world at a level which does not involve the intellect. There is a subjective observation which supports this: I feel anger *rising up into my head* where it proceeds to generate a lot of images; I feel it coming up from below, from my organic being. This primary reaction is very fast and I will not notice it unless I pay close attention; but I can examine retrospectively what went on inside me when I was angry and can then recognize that there was a brief instant when a pure, impersonal, organic force rose up from an organic level of awareness and that this happened before intellectual consciousness came into operation and created the images of anger.

Note that organic consciousness releases a discharge of energy in response to my perception of not-self. What this means is that organic consciousness operates in a way which implies acceptance of not-self existing in opposition to self. This in turn indicates that it is in harmony with the cosmic order and the nature of things as they are. It governs exchanges of energy between self and not-self, and conciliates these two poles; it is in harmony with the Tao.

Let us turn to the secondary reaction. When the primary reaction mobilizes energy in response to energy in the outside world, this causes a dynamic alteration in my being that initiates a second reaction. Just as some shift in the external world triggered a reaction in organic consciousness, so this reaction manifesting as changes within me will trigger a reaction in intellectual consciousness. This secondary reaction will tend to re-establish the original state of immobility in me by disintegrating the mobilized energy.

Why should this happen? The reason is that intellectual consciousness, unlike organic consciousness, does not accept the existence of not-self. Recall our primordial demand, which I have also referred to variously as our fiction of divinity, our insistence on absolute being as a distinct and separate entity, and our claim to absolute existence. Underlying our intellectual knowledge of the Universe is the irreducible discrimination between self and not-self, a taking for granted that 'I *am* and consequently not-self *is not*.' We invoke this discrimination when we speak of ego, and of identification with our psychosomatic organism. As an organic consciousness, I do not discriminate, but as an intellectual consciousness, I do. In the former, I am identified equally with not-self and self; in the latter, I am only identified with the self, and affirm its separate existence. Intellectual consciousness only knows self; I may think that I know the external world through intellectual consciousness, but in reality I only know the modifications taking place in my self through contact with the external world. Philosophers call this 'the prison of subjectivity'. They ignore organic consciousness, which does not discriminate between 'subject' and 'object', and in virtue of which I am already to all intents and purposes free.

Let us look at how the nature of intellectual consciousness affects inner phenomena. During the primary reaction my organic wish to exist was frustrated by the external world, hence a force developed in me which counter-balanced the external force. During the secondary reaction my intellectual need to 'be' is thwarted by this mobilization of energy, because it implies acceptance of the external world and thus separates me forcibly from the immutability of the Origin. When intellectual consciousness is active I function as though I required my organism's energy source to possess the same attributes as Absolute Origin: immutability, non-action, permanence, and an unconditioned state. So activation of this energy is bound to produce a secondary response in me which rejects and opposes this development. However this opposition to the cosmic order can never succeed; the force which has been mobilized in me cannot return to non-manifestation. My resistance to the activated energy can only succeed in bringing about its destruction through disintegration.

The law of equilibrium in the Tao operates in these two reactions. The primary reaction brings the forces of not-self and self into balance. The secondary reaction counterbalances the mobilization of my vital energy by causing the energy to disintegrate. The primary reaction aims to maintain the balance between self and not-self; the secondary to maintain the balance within the self, between constructive and destructive manifestation, between Vishnu and Shiva.

Disintegration of activated energy is brought about by the imaginative–emotional processes. It has already been noted that they are like short circuits in which energy dissipates into the production of organic phenomena and mental images. These mental formations are known to Buddhist philosophy as *samskaras*.* They have substance and form; their substance is simply my vital energy in the process of disintegration; while their forms, which are infinitely varied mental images, are extraneous to *my form*, my organism's form. Because of these alien forms, *samskaras* can be compared to foreign bodies which should be rejected by my organism. They are mental formations with something unnatural and ill-formed about them: they are heterogeneous, they lack inner structural harmony, and they are non-viable. None of this is surprising because they manifest energy in the process of disintegration.

When these images appear in my mind, they initiate a vicious circle. They stimulate my organic consciousness, just as the images perceived in the external world did a moment before, so they trigger a new primary reaction, mobilizing energy which disintegrates in its turn. This is how a sustained imaginative–emotional rumination develops, which takes some time to run its course, like a pendulum which, once set in motion, only stops after a certain number of oscillations.

In addition the rumination is kept going by further changes in my perception of the external world, in this case of the man who has been disrespectful. These explain my inclination to hit him. My secondary reaction, which is striving to abolish the mobilized energy, uses the image of me harming my enemy in an attempt to neutralize the image of me being harmed which is responsible for mobilizing my energy. This aggressive external reaction would not happen if it were not for disintegrating energy giving rise to images which produce the vicious circle mentioned above; the secondary reaction would be wholly absorbed inwardly in an adequate disintegrative process. This does not happen, because the process of disintegration does not achieve completion, but releases new packets of energy which disintegrate in their turn, so that the secondary reaction spills out of my inner world and impels me to annihilate the external object which is negating me. However, my aggressive inclinations towards the external object are incidental: the process fundamental to the task of disintegrating mobilized energy is the imaginative–emotional process. This may seem paradoxical, but it is obvious that external signs of anger can be suppressed, while anger

---

* Sanskrit term referring to the tendencies and latent states present in non-conscious levels of the mind. They function as dispositional traces built up by the action of thought waves and they create new thought waves in their turn. Our character can be thought of as the sum total of our *samskaras.*

could not be present without the corresponding imaginative–emotional processes. I may not lay a finger on my enemy but I might break the first vase that I come across: I use this representation of the self harming not-self to neutralize the image of not-self harming the self. It does not really matter that my external enemy is unaffected; *the real target of my secondary reaction is not external, it is within me, and its real purpose is to annihilate the energy mobilized from my source.*

This should come as no surprise, knowing as we do that we have no really objective perception of individual objects. The external object does not exist in itself for me and I never really deal directly with it. Even during the primary reaction I am not really dealing with the particular external object involved. Although the force mobilized in me is certainly reacting to the external world, it is still a pure vital force, formless and anonymous. It is the force which activates me in all my dealings with the external world, but, although it has objective knowledge of the Universe in general, it has none of the individual external object.

If during this hypothetical scene an outsider were to ask me why I was angry, I would get twice as angry. Their question has the effect of increasing my perception of activated energy; and my secondary reaction increases with the triggering perception. This is further proof that my secondary reaction is solely directed against the internal mobilization of energy, and not against my external enemy; for the comment has nothing to do with him and does not in any way modify the excitation in me attributable to him.

What we have just seen in relation to anger is equally true of all our contacts with the outside world; and it makes little difference from this point of view whether the contact is negative or positive. If the external force is positive and brings me a positive affirmation, it will induce a primary reaction which will still involve the mobilization of a certain amount of pure energy. This will be followed by a secondary reaction with the objective of bringing about the mobilized energy's disintegration in an imaginative–emotional rumination. On this occasion the associated images and emotions will be positive and pleasing.

Nor does it matter much whether contact with the external world takes place through psychological or somatic channels. In the example given of anger, the psychological route was involved; but my energy can equally well be mobilized by contacts which affect my centre through the somatic route: toothache is a negation of self by not-self. When the pain disappears, the self is affirmed; both experiences are accompanied by the mobilization of central energy, which is then disintegrated in correspondingly agreeable or disagreeable imaginative–emotional processes.

The process involving this double reaction is quite general: it governs our *vital metabolism*, with the primary reaction representing *anabolism*, and the secondary *catabolism*. The primary reaction corresponds to the *reflex*, and is centrifugal. The secondary reaction corresponds to *reflection* (though not in the ordinary sense of the word), and is centripetal, directed against an inner phenomenon, so the energy wave is 'reflected' towards my centre. In physiological terms one might associate the primary reaction with mid-brain nuclear activity and the secondary with cerebral cortical activity. Surgical interventions which destroy some of the connections between these two areas of the brain produce a considerable reduction in the secondary reaction, in emotional life and imagination, and in the experience of distress which is dependent on their integrity. Freud's life- and death- instincts correspond to the primary and secondary reactions respectively: mobilization of energy is *life*, and the need to disintegrate it represents resistance to life, a refusal of life, hence a tendency towards death.

If we set Freud's formulation to one side and think of the distinction made earlier between 'existing' and 'living' – the former discounted, the latter highly valued – it is clear that the primary reaction corresponds to 'existing', and the secondary to 'living'. For ordinary people, the processes which disintegrate their vital energy are experienced as 'living' and are highly regarded. But they do not attach any value to their vital energy itself, prizing instead the sparks which are produced by its disintegration.

As already noted, two different types of consciousness correspond to the two reactions: organic consciousness to the primary reaction, intellectual or imaginative consciousness to the secondary (the latter kind of consciousness being what one usually refers to when speaking of 'consciousness' without additional qualification). Ordinary intellectual-imaginative consciousness is dualistic, and the imaginative–emotional processes which unfold in it can affirm or negate, please or displease. This contrasts with organic consciousness which is not dualistic, since the vital force which arises in it is formless, impersonal and unchanging, and independent of the dualistic forms which it will subsequently activate. The role it plays in relation to imaginative consciousness is that of a conciliating principle, or hypostasis. We have seen that it does not discriminate between self and not-self, and that it functions in a way which implies the essential identity of these two poles and consequently a truly objective knowledge of the Universe in general, in its unity. These characteristics, together with its origin in the very depths of being, support the view that organic consciousness represents the first individual manifestation of the impersonal originating Unconscious. The possibility that we may one day recognize for ourselves that our present state is already that of satori is linked to the activity of organic consciousness; and our Faith that satori is our state even now is intimately connected with our observation that this consciousness is present within us.

To summarize, only my organic consciousness knows the Universe. Its activity is triggered by the Universe and it reacts to this by mobilizing my energy. My ordinary consciousness only knows my private inner world, and my mobilized energy: its activity is triggered by dynamic inner changes, to which it reacts with imaginative–emotional processes, the *samskaras*.

Contrary to what one might think, it is the concept of organic consciousness which is easy and satisfying, while what I usually refer to simply as 'my consciousness' is difficult to conceptualize and therefore name. I have referred to it as 'intellectual', 'psychological', and 'imaginative', but none of these terms is satisfactory. Why this should be so will become clear as this investigation proceeds; the consciousness associated with the secondary reaction will be shown not to be a real consciousness, but simply a resistance to the activity of organic consciousness (which is the only real individual consciousness). Ordinary consciousness expresses the failure of organic consciousness to achieve completion. This failure to complete obstructs my machine's functioning – it is 'a spanner in the works' of my machine. My everyday 'pseudo-consciousness' is alluded to when Zen says that satori is '*the removal of the bar*'. What we speak of ordinarily as consciousness refers to the mass of inner phenomena which result from the fact that organic consciousness before satori is not functioning fully as No-mind.

These observations contradict what is generally accepted, but they help me understand the strange kind of machine that I am. If I take an ⚡ *Key point* impersonal and universal view of the processes described above, I see that it is all perfect, and in perfect balance. Both kinds of reaction establish an exact equilibrium, even though the process of balancing the secondary reaction can involve terrible suffering and even result in suicide. Both reactions also balance one another exactly. After its mobilization, energy disintegrates and so completes a perfect spiral in the course of which I am connected to not-self by an exchange of energy and so participate in the two aspects of cosmic creation, construction and destruction.

On the other hand these processes seem less than perfect if I look at *Common Reaction* them from an individual perspective, in other words from the perspective of my subjective emotional life. As energy flows between self and not-self, it ceases for a time to be pure and formless. Between the instant when it arises from the source and the instant when it is returned to the external world after disintegration it takes on mental forms alien to my own, 'foreign bodies' which are coarse and damaging, and cause suffering while they are being expelled. These *samskaras*, 'complexes', and accretions are all experienced by me as a negation of my being. They are chimera, participating in both self (since my energy sustains them) and not-self (since their elements derive from the external world), and from a subjective viewpoint they represent a *fusion* of the two poles of self and not-self which seems to contradict and negate the three-fold unity. This gives rise to an apparent Nothingness refuting Being.

So *for me*, as far as my emotional life is concerned, my inner processes are imperfect and I look for ways of not suffering. I ask myself where the problem lies. I see it in the domain of imagination and emotion, in the *samskaras*; so then I look for ways of enabling energy to pass from my source into the external world without harming me. To achieve this I need a better understanding of what conditions the formation of *samskaras*. I have already realized that it results from my identifying with my organism alone and not with the rest of Manifestation. But that is not enough and I need to uncover the underlying process whereby identifying with my organism alone results in the formation of *samskaras*.

The process responsible is the *passive* way in which my attention functions: because it operates passively it is alerted by energy which has *already* been mobilized, and this happens at a late stage where the only option is to disintegrate it. At present my attention is not in a state of autonomous, unconditioned watchfulness; it is only aroused by energy mobilized within my organism and its arousal is dependent on these mobilizations. So I am always confronted by a *fait accompli*. As soon as the timeless instant is over, in which my energy emerges, formless, from non-manifestation, it is effectively seized by the formal world. So there is no opportunity to store it up, still in its formless state, against the future explosion of satori; disintegration into imaginative–emotional forms is inevitable.

By this stage my energy has entered the territory where my egotistical identification reigns supreme, and this identification is the barrier it comes up against as it disintegrates. It seems as though I am afraid to contain my mobilized energy when I am confronted by it. Exclusively identified with my organism, I believe implicitly in its 'being', and that it is permanent, immutable and invariable. But when my energy is activated, this presents me with a contradictory view of my organism as something which is moving, impermanent, and limited. So I reject the mobilized energy which invokes this unbearable prospect; for my exclusive identification with my organism has the paradoxical effect that I reject the idea of being this limited organism (Saint Paul: 'Who shall deliver me from this body of death?' Romans 7:24).* I have no wish to be aware of it. (Note that the body seems to lose its density in psychologically or pharmacologically induced ecstatic states.) I lose no time in disintegrating the mobilized energy which is filling my organism and giving it substance.

Disintegrative processes are inevitable when attention is functioning passively and is then alerted by energy which has already been activated. These processes should not be thought of as bad, or as something to be prevented. What they express is not some 'bad' condition of my manifested being, but one which is imperfect, incomplete, and unfinished. The same is true of the identification with my organism on which these processes depend; it is not mistaken, it is simply incomplete in that it excludes my equal identification with the rest of the Universe. The egotistical illusion does not consist in my identifying with my organism but in the exclusive form which this identification takes. When satori bursts upon me, it will not destroy this identification, which represents what is already realized in my present egotistical condition, but it will destroy the sleep which at present affects my identification with the rest of the Universe. In other words it will awaken the part of me which lies beyond the illusory limits of the ego and is still asleep at the present moment. That is when my identification with the totality of Manifestation will come to life.

These ideas are essential if one is to understand correct doctrine and avoid giving one's allegiance to useless 'methods' of realization. As long as I thought of my imaginative–emotional processes and my exclusive identification with the self as 'bad', I was compelled to struggle against the ego, and against my egotistical condition, and so against my own machine, involved as it is in this condition; and this led to perpetual inner disharmony. When I understand that the condition of being identified with the self is not 'bad', but simply incomplete, I also understand that I must live out this stage of development to the full in order to transcend it. My misfortune at present is not that I am living in this stage, but that I am not living it to the full, in its wholeness.

Let us look at how all this applies in practical terms to what we are studying. When I see how much energy is wasted in my imaginative–emotional processes, I am tempted to suppress them. Because of

---

* This is a literal translation of the French, which compares with the Authorized Version: 'Who shall deliver me from the body of this death?' The Revised English Bible (1989) gives 'Who is there to rescue me from this state of death?'

the connection between them and the resistance which consciousness puts up against energy being mobilized, it is tempting to try and put an end to this resistance. But such efforts do not cause my inner state to change direction, they just complicate it. Attempts to stop resisting are just resisting a resistance, and counteracting a contracted state with a contraction cannot lead to relaxation; unlike what happens in algebra, responding to this kind of negative with another negative does not produce an affirmative. So it is impossible to suppress my resistance to energy being mobilized. In any case, it would not be desirable: as we have already seen, this resistance is part of a process which is not in itself 'bad', simply incomplete.

*The problem is not that I resist my energy being mobilized, but that my resistance is incomplete,* comes too late, and is therefore useless. It is not a real, effective resistance, but a useless protest in the face of a *fait accompli* because it *follows on* after the rejected inner phenomenon. My ordinary consciousness is functioning reactively rather than actively at present, and its activity cannot balance that of organic consciousness because it is only responding to the latter's manifestations.

In reality, ordinary consciousness is not intended to function reactively: it is active and masculine, rather than reactive and feminine. Organic consciousness on the other hand is feminine; it is intended to *react* to excitations originating in the external world (primary reaction). At the same time, ordinary consciousness is not designed to react to the primary reaction in a secondary reaction. Rather than following on after energy has been mobilized, my resistance to its mobilization should come into operation the very *instant* that my energy emerges from non-manifestation. The activity of ordinary consciousness (male) should directly balance the activity of organic consciousness (female), not its energetic sequelae. Only then will the two antagonistic and complementary kinds of consciousness be brought into a state of conciliation. This will make it possible for energy to be mobilized without being trapped by the domain of form.

When a fully developed resistance to energy mobilization is redirected to the very instant when mobilization occurs, the effect is not to suppress it (which would mean death), but to counter-balance exactly the organic will which is producing it. Creating a state of equilibrium like this results in energy being produced which remains formless, escapes the process of imaginative–emotional disintegration, and accumulates until it explodes into satori. When resistance to energy mobilization changes from passive to active, it continues as resistance in the sense that it works effectively against energy being 'poured' into forms and so disintegrating; but at the same time, it stops resisting in the sense that it does not prevent formless, non-manifested energy being actualized.

What is actually involved when attention is transformed from reactive female to active male functioning? The point has just been made that attention comes into play *too late* in relation to the actual mobilization of my energy. Would it help if it managed to function earlier, and react more quickly? No; however fast the reaction, it will always be too late because it is a reaction, not an action. 'Too late' in this context does not have its ordinary meaning; no time interval, however minute, separates these primary and secondary reactions. 'Too late' does not refer to a second or a fraction of a second, but to the fact that the reaction of ordinary consciousness, despite being instantaneous, is always late, *because it is a reaction when it ought to be an action.* Attention should not be alerted by energy being mobilized, but before it happens; and this will be brought about when, instead of *seeing* the imaginative–emotional processes as they emerge, I *look at* them as they are about to emerge. This is achieved when I actively direct attention at perceiving my energy's actual moment of birth, instead of remaining passively attentive to mobilized energy and its subsequent disintegration. A new watchfulness keeps the mobilization of energy under surveillance. Put more simply, active attention watches out for emerging inner movements of energy. My emotions themselves no longer interest me but their birth does. Their activity is unimportant: what matters is that formless activity which gives rise to their subsequent activity in the formal domain.

This active functioning of my consciousness, which is so contrary to the automatic way in which I function naturally, cannot be attained by direct effort or any explicit discipline aiming at Realization. This important issue will be developed later; the reason for raising it early on is to warn the reader against the persistent and misleading quest for enlightenment 'recipes'.

First I want to explain that when attention is functioning actively it is pure attention, attention without any manifested object. Mobilized energy itself cannot be perceived; all that can be perceived are the products of its disintegration, the images. This disintegration only takes place when attention is operating in passive mode; active attention prevents it. Consequently, when attention is operating in active mode, there is nothing to perceive. Energy is still mobilized; organic, female consciousness goes on working; but the energy stays formless, non-disintegrated, and unmanifested. This explains why Zen advises us *to awaken the mind without fixing it on anything*; and we can indeed understand how there must be nothing for the mind to fix on if it is awakened within itself rather than in response to organic energetic reactions. The Zen saying could then be modified as follows: 'Awaken the mind in itself, and it will then not be fixed on anything.'

The idea that active attention to my inner world is object-free can easily be verified. I need to adopt an attitude of listening actively to my inner monologue, and giving it permission to say what it wants, however it wants. My attitude needs to be as though I were saying: 'Speak, I am listening to you'. If I do this, I observe that the monologue stops, and only begins again when I no longer maintain my attitude of expectant watchfulness.

Some people may be reluctant to suppress the imaginative film in this way, fearful that this would be to suppress 'life'. But the imaginative film is not really life. It is produced by the disintegration of energy which should instead be accumulating for the future birth of the 'new person' in satori. So the imaginative film is actually an *abortive* process: the 'birth' of what I call my inner world is really the repeated abortion of the 'new person'. Suppressing this abortive process does not go against my life and my true development. By observing and thus postponing the birth of so-called living within me, I am preparing for the consciousness of existing to be born within me, preparing for perfect existential bliss.

Ordinary consciousness has been shown to have both male and female modes of functioning, which I have described and distinguished from one another. The next step is to see that both kinds of functioning are going to co-exist within us.

Any direct efforts, active attention 'exercises', specific attempts to observe the birth of emotions, would be quite misguided. The successful outcome of all such efforts would consist of perceiving nothing at all. At present we are attached to our imaginative film – *our primordial attachment is there*, and death terrifies us because it represents the ending of our precious consciousness – and the purpose of such exercises would be to break this attachment. The complete 'masculinization' of attention brings total detachment in satori, and rupture of the ego's boundaries. Direct attempts to achieve this complete 'masculinization' would amount to striving to 'seize', to 'get hold of', total detachment, and this approach contains an obvious internal contradiction which condemns it to failure. As I have observed repeatedly, there are no 'recipes' for Realization.

The processes on which the satori-event depends, or more accurately the suppression of the processes which maintain our present ignorance of our atemporal state of satori, are simply a matter of *understanding*, and nothing else (the Tibetans call this *penetrating vision*). This understanding works by devaluing images: not any images in particular or any particular sequence of images, but the imaginative–emotional process in its entirety.

For many years my attitude towards my inner cinema has been one of great credulity and it took me in completely. I believed in it and I believed in the supposed reality of what the disintegrative process showed me. As I progress in intellectual work and understanding, I become less credulous, am less likely to be taken in, and am less and less convinced that this is where my real interests lie. The fascination which the images have held for my attention begins to weaken, and with it their ability to keep it in passive mode. As my attention begins to disengage from my imaginative world, it returns spontaneously, in line with its *normal* orientation, to the source of my being and to the formless energy which is my life's reality (and it stops going back to the formal images which represent the continual abortion of my life). This process of 'conversion' is unconscious, since my attention is object-less when it operates in active mode. What I do notice is a gradual decline in the apparent reality of my inner world of imagination (I have noted elsewhere that the changes that lead to the satori event seem like a descent, an apparent regression).

This brings us back to an idea which I have already mentioned, that ordinary consciousness, whether one calls it reflective, psychological, or intellectual, is not a real consciousness; and that our only real consciousness at present is organic consciousness. When attention functions in its active mode, it is object-less and unconscious, and forms stop manifesting in the mind. What I used to refer to as my consciousness disappears, and the male mental principle which lay behind it (*buddhi*) joins the female mental principle of organic consciousness in the tripartite unity of *No-mind* or the *Unconscious Origin*.

The accounts provided by Zen masters who have experienced satori make it possible for us to picture the final stage in this evolving process. A point is reached where the mind functions as much in its male as in its female mode: unbelieving lucidity and blind credulity are in balance. This is the *Great Doubt*. Organic consciousness can be compared to an eye which has been open since we were born, with ordinary consciousness as a second eye closed by a persistent spasm. Ordinary consciousness is essentially male and in this analogy the contracture symbolizes its operation in female mode. As male functioning begins to come into balance with female functioning in ordinary consciousness, the eyelid's spasm is balanced by increasing relaxation. At the moment of Great Doubt, complete equilibrium is attained. An instant later, the Great Doubt is shattered; the second eye opens, and the combined vision of both eyes is something entirely new, providing access to a hitherto unknown depth. This is called *'the opening of the third eye'*.

What is interesting about this analogy is how it illustrates the point that there is really no third eye to be opened, in other words there is no third 'supernormal' consciousness. Nothing 'new' has to appear in us. The satori event is the instant when our present dualistic being, just as it is right here and now, discovers its normal functioning by arousing attention to a state of autonomous and unconditioned activity.

# CHAPTER TWENTY-ONE

# Concerning 'Discipline'

HELPED BY THE LIGHT WHICH ZEN SHEDS on these matters, we have come to understand that there can be no 'recipes' for attaining Realization. No systematic way of living one's life can trigger the synthesis of all possible ways of living; no conscious activity can reintegrate us into originating Unconscious; no training, no discipline involving a struggle can enable us to transcend the dualism in which this struggle takes place. And so we reach the conclusion that understanding is the only means of dissipating our present state of illusion and bringing us to satori.

We also understand now that the satori explosion presupposes the accumulation in us of non-disintegrated energy. This accumulation in turn implies that we not only have a theoretical understanding but that this understanding finds practical expression in the form of a special kind of activity on the part of our attention. Given that understanding is the only means of obtaining satori, it is clearly not enough for it just to be expressed as a guiding theory: it must also be realized in the form of inner phenomena which give practical expression to the theory. The phenomena in question cannot be generated correctly in the absence of the understanding whose practical extension they are. This is the reason why they do not constitute a recipe for realization which can stand on its own. However, they do constitute a kind of *practical inner work* suitable for daily life, distinct from the abstract vision obtained during moments of withdrawal into the ivory tower of the intellect.

So we arrive at two apparently contradictory conclusions: on the one hand, there is no effective method, no system requiring us to impose methodical changes on the inner or outer phenomena of our lives, which can help us on our way to satori; on the other hand, achieving satori requires practical inner work during the course of our daily life. We came to these conclusions by different routes, but in both cases we had the same persuasive impression that we were dealing with self-evident facts.

Any contradiction of this kind provides a valuable opportunity for us to deepen our understanding and challenges us to discover a more encompassing viewpoint where the two previous points of view are conciliated and their apparent opposition resolved.

In this particular case we have to understand inner work in such a way that it does not represent a methodical attempt to impose change in our lives. We can break this down into two assertions: first we must understand inner work as something which does not involve some kind of intervention in our life; next we have to understand it as not subjecting us to the constraint of some system or method. I will spend most time on this second point as I have not dealt with it at all so far. But before doing so, I will remind you of some ideas I have already expressed which relate to the first point.

Inner work with satori as its goal must not be an intervention in our life. 'Intervention' means what happens when something 'intervenes' between elements on a particular level, modifies their pre-existing relationships, and disturbs that level's basic organization. Zen declares: '*Don't meddle with life's flow*'; and the master illustrates this to his disciple with the example of the torrent which flows unchecked. There will be satori for us when we finally stop going against 'the nature of things', which includes our own nature as well as that of the cosmos in general. Inner work towards satori must not involve any ill-considered and presumptuous interference in the flow of our personal phenomenology. This does not mean that no change ought to take place in our phenomenology as we move closer in time to the satori event; but appropriate changes can only be produced by our Absolute Principle, the Unconscious in us – not by our presumptuous consciousness.

When there is 'intervention', that which 'intervenes' between elements belonging to the same level is the same kind of thing as the elements themselves. Any intervention in my behaviour brings some new behaviour into play, but it is still a form of behaviour; any intervention in my inner life, in my psychological mechanisms, brings a new mechanism into play, but it is still a mechanism. When an intervention takes place on a particular level, nothing new comes into effect which does not belong to the same level. The harmonious synthesis of being requires the operation of the Conciliating Principle alone, which does not belong to the plane of phenomena, but transcends that level. When the Principle manifests on this level as a harmonizing influence, this should not in any way be understood as an intervention. Only the Principle can modify our phenomena and our lives without interfering in our life.

I have already mentioned on a number of occasions the inner act of de-contraction or relaxation which is not an intervention since it does not directly modify the mental film: it interrupts it without causing any particular image to intervene. I have described how this action occurs at a level higher than that where everyday inner phenomena occur, and have compared this to the action causing muscles to relax which takes place in the brain at a level above the spinal cord centre responsible for contraction. The 'doing' of this action corresponds to a 'not doing' of our usual phenomena. Should this action of releasing attempt to interrupt the imaginative film directly by using a particular image – for instance an image of the film being interrupted – this would be an inappropriate intervention which would not succeed in stopping the film. It would simply generate a fixation on the idea of stopping (it would be an exercise in concentration leading to a kind of auto-hypnosis, trance or black-out).

If the act of relaxing is carried out in the right way, it will only release the constricting process indirectly: it does not target it directly nor does it evoke any image of de-contraction. *On the contrary it requires us to relinquish control over consciousness and all its active and perceptual functions; and when we authorise consciousness to function autonomously in this way, we must do so completely, impartially and unconditionally.* This act is a moment in which everything which directs and controls my life comes to a halt, during which it as though I were trying to open myself up to my very existence, the unchanging presence beneath all the activity of my life. But I do not evoke the image of 'existence'. With my inner world at this instant functioning autonomously, wholly independently of my control, this action is like a gaze directed right into its centre, and then penetrating beyond this level towards the unknown. Because it is a gaze with no preference for any particular object, directed without preconceptions at nothing in particular, it meets nothing and consequently succeeds without my having actively willed this in stopping my imaginative film. It is wholly a questioning. It takes no particular form; it gets no response because it requires none. It is a challenge without object or recipient. It is an attentiveness to everything, an attentiveness which has no object.

I interrupt my imaginative film in this way without actively seeking to do so. The interruption only lasts for an instant. It is without duration, a timeless flash of lightning in the depths of time: it has nothing in common with the sort of states which concentration exercises induce in me. Because it has no duration, this attempt to 'see into my own nature' does not result in sight with the 'third eye'. It simply prepares for it. Each act falls short, but it is the repetition of these failures – and they need to condense into one final failure – which will one day banish the illusion in which I live at present, the illusion that I am not already in the state of satori.

The instantaneous act of releasing prepares the satori-event because each of these split-second interruptions in the imaginative film's activity breaks the vicious circle which links images and emotions. I have previously referred to this vicious circle as 'imaginative–emotional rumination', which corresponds to what I have also described as 'emotional state' or 'contracture' or 'spasm', and as 'intellect driven by affect'. It is an internal automatism whose activity is maintained by a powerful inertial force.

Imaginative rumination does not operate continuously at the same level of activity; its effect and influence vary according to our stage of development. Its potential is gradually exhausted and undermined by instants of letting go. The vicious circle linking images and emotions becomes less and less substantial, and there is a progressive modification of our internal life and of how we see things in general. Though we cannot have even the slightest hint of 'seeing things as they are' before satori, the way we see things as they are *not* begins to lose some of its clarity, depth and colour.

The indirect changes which inner work brings about in how we see things can be explained with the help of the following analogy. Our imaginative film can be compared to a film projected in the cinema, where there is a projector, a screen and a pyramid of light connecting them. When the film is properly focused on the screen, I see sharp images with good contrast. If I move the screen closer and closer to the projector without making any changes in the latter, the images will gradually lose their clarity and contrast. A point comes where they are difficult to recognize and the blacks have become grey. Next, only pale, vague shadows are left, while the overall luminosity of the screen increases. Finally, when I get right up to the projector, the screen is completely white and sparkling.

The projector symbolizes the originating Unconscious or No-Mind, the source of our consciousness; the beam of light symbolizes the subconscious, the screen our conscious mind. It is our individual egotistical determinism which keeps the screen of consciousness at the right distance for the images to be in focus. Our insistence on being separate and distinct keeps our attention fixed there. This corresponds to our biased and partial internal attitude which is one of strongly contrasted opposition between likes and dislikes. Composed of vividly contrasting light and shade, the images provoke strong emotions which release new images in their turn; and the film's progress in sharp focus represents my imaginative–emotional rumination.

In the instant of letting go, of de-contraction, when there is object-less attention, the screen touches the projector and is bathed in pure, image-free light. I do not see this pure light because this happens in an instant without duration, and I can only perceive within durational time, as all perception is based on memory. But this image-free instant lessens the power of the vicious circle which maintains the distance between screen and projector, and the screen moves closer. If the action of letting go is repeated with sufficient perseverance, the screen moves closer and closer. Light and shade in the imaginative film lose their distinctness; the outlines of the forms which separate them blur, and blacks become greys. This does not mean that my thinking becomes less rigorous but that my value judgments, opinions and beliefs become less rigid and constricting. The growing brightness of the screen represents a lessening of my fundamental distress, an alleviation of my whole affective state.

The 'Great Doubt' which precedes satori corresponds to the final stage of this process. The screen is then very close to the projector. The conscious inner state is very luminous, and free of distress. The negativity at the heart of our emotional life is almost completely neutralized; distress has gone from it, although there is still no awareness of positive existential bliss. Mental formations, the *samskaras,* have disappeared; and the individual describes himself as being 'like an idiot, an imbecile'. Because there are no shadows, the world seems to be transparent, 'like a palace of crystal'; 'mountains are no longer mountains, and waters no longer waters'. Attention is now very close to the source of the Unconscious: it takes one final movement for it to become established there once and for all. This is the 'haven of rest'. For an instant all distinction between screen, projector and beam of light is abolished. Then, everything comes back into separate existence, but working in a way that is simple and perfectly harmonious – and quite impossible for us to imagine as we are at present.

This illustration helps us understand how the metabolism of vital energy within us changes during inner work. As the screen gets closer to the projector, less light energy is broken up into black and white shapes. At the end point where the beam leaves its source, there is only whiteness, pure light. I mentioned previously that our own energy arises, still formless, from the source where it was non-manifested; and I claimed that an energy exists which is both manifested and formless. Metaphysically speaking, this seems nonsensical: manifestation without form is inconceivable. But this absurdity derives from the words we use which seem to freeze the flow of emerging energy. When I refer to it as both manifested and formless, I am using this questionable terminology to indicate the timeless instant where energy leaves its source. I am referring specifically to energy when it is at the hypothetical boundary between non-manifestation and manifestation, at the instant where it is already manifested relative to its source, but still formless in relation to manifestation. The 'accumulation of formless energy' mentioned earlier should be understood as an endlessly available possibility for withholding energy from the imaginative–emotional vicious circle.

After this reminder that inner work should be understood as a letting go, a total, instantaneous relaxation of our conscious being, we come to a point which is central to this study: when is it right for us to do this 'not doing', this 'letting go?' There is a potential pitfall here: if I think of satori incorrectly as something to be accomplished by me as a distinct and separate entity, which is the misleading 'superman' model, I am going to *covet* satori. It will become a positive object of desire, something I want. If I am going to make a bid for satori on this basis and have also understood that 'letting go' is the effective way to achieve it, I will *have to* achieve letting go. So a constraint, arising logically from my claim to be separate and distinct, from my primordial contracture, impels me to impose the act of de-contraction on my organism, whether it likes it or not. It is quite obvious that no real de-contraction can be achieved like this: a contracted mental evocation of the image of de-contracting would be generated and that would be all.

This is not to say that there is no *discipline* involved when inner work is carried out correctly; but it has to be properly understood. In all inner work 'something' directs the functioning of my psychosomatic machine; but what is this something which correct inner work requires?

To answer this, I will first explain what it should not be, which I will do by analysing the usual ways in which we think about 'working on oneself', 'self-mastery', and 'willpower'.

I will not start by investigating willpower, which is a fine idea, but a source of confusion. I will use this term in its usual sense while we examine the first concept. 'Working on oneself' can mean work on one's external behaviour: 'good' actions or 'good' abstentions (asceticism); or work on one's internal behaviour: 'good' feelings or 'good' thoughts, or mental exercises to get the mind functioning in a 'good' way (concentration, meditation, emptying the mind, etc). All these procedures can be shown to rely on the same primary mechanism, the intentional evocation of an image or a system of images. This is clearly true of meditating (even though the image evoked may be that of an absence of images); and just as true of any external action, since the decision to carry out an action occurs in response to the development of a mental image.

So all work one does on oneself consists essentially of intentionally evoking something in the mind, in a *manipulation* of the imagination which gives expression to my *partiality* towards one image to the detriment of all other possible images. This bias in favour of one particular form of my manifestation and against those forms which oppose it prevents my work on myself from achieving a synthesis of my whole manifestation. This kind of 'doing' excludes what I do not do: unification of my being is not possible under these circumstances. The favoured images are just as much *samskaras* as the rejected ones. This approach cannot modify the imaginative–emotional process as a whole; it can only modify the forms which the process creates. The preferred *samskaras* are reinforced; they tend to become 'encysted'; and the imagination develops fixed habits. I can train myself like this to feel loving towards the whole universe, to the detriment of my aggressiveness. This would represent the modification of a mental form, but going beyond the form, *transforming* it, would not be possible.

I have already indicated that these methods of training are not in themselves an obstacle to obtaining satori. Reinforcing certain *samskaras* to the detriment of others cannot make the internal situation worse as far as an eventual transformation is concerned. Something which does not contribute to satori does not work against it, because nothing can: ignorance has no active reality in relation to the Timeless or its eventual realization. It is only so much time lost as far as the satori-event is concerned.

There is a possible objection to all this. The correct inner act of letting go gives a blanket authorization to all images without exception, so there can be no more question of evoking a preferred image and I have to give up all bias in my dealings with my internal world. But suppose I decide to practise letting go systematically because I covet satori, and want to do it each time I think of it without taking account of my current internal state. Then I would be bound to evoke the *preferred* image of permitting all images without exception; and so I would fall back into the same absurdity.

This is the first time that we have come across an idea of fundamental importance, which is that *we should take account of our current internal state*. The fact that the usual idea of discipline ignores this aspect is precisely what brings it into conflict with the correct approach which I am trying to define.

Let us examine what happens when one attempts to change oneself in some way. There will always be a struggle between two tendencies. Take trying to slim by fasting, for aesthetic reasons: there is a struggle between the tendency to satisfy the appetite, and the tendency to reduce one's size and look better. Fasting in order to progress 'spiritually' is not fundamentally different. The desire to progress 'spiritually' is obviously self-centred; so, just like the desire to eat, it represents a tendency to affirm oneself as a separate and distinct entity. In both cases we see a struggle between two essentially similar tendencies, like two men pulling a rope or pushing against a bar in opposite directions.

This conflict or *opposition* should be distinguished from the *composition* or *combination* in which tendencies normally interact. When I am not working on myself in some way, my behaviour will never be the outcome of any one tendency on its own. Any perception will cause multiple tendencies to interact and combine with one another in my subconscious before they manifest at the behavioural level as a single unit of spontaneous behaviour like the resultant of a parallelogram of forces. What makes my tendencies behave in such different ways, so that there are times when they organize themselves without my being aware of them, while on other occasions the conflict between them tears me apart?

This is where bias comes in: conflict arises when I am biased in favour of one tendency and against its opposite. The affective preference with which I respond to the activity of a particular tendency, when my mind is operating passively, creates the conditions for an intellectual bias, a *value judgement*, which functions like a 'belief' on my part that the tendency 'is' and therefore ought to exist, while the contrary tendency 'is not' and so ought not exist. This is how an identification with the preferred tendency is produced (there is a transference from my 'being' onto the tendency which I perceive as 'being').

Here as elsewhere the problem does not lie in the identification itself but in its exclusive nature, which means that the opposite tendency is repudiated. Failure to identify fully with my microcosm is mirrored at the macrocosmic level. As soon as I identify with self in a way which excludes not-self, I cannot be identified with my whole self and my microcosm divides into self and not-self. This happens for example when it splits into those tendencies which I acknowledge as mine and those which I consider alien. A lodestone may be broken up into innumerable fragments but each piece will still have two poles. Every dualism yields an infinite number of dualisms.

When there is this combination of identification with one tendency while its opposite is disowned, it feels as if one's *self* were involved in the struggle against the repudiated tendency. Forces which *combined* in the subconscious are now *opposed* in consciousness. Dualism has lost its complementarity, and only antagonism remains. The two forces can no longer act as though they belonged to one harmonious whole: bias makes them act as though they belonged to two different 'wholes'.

*'As soon as you have Good and Evil, confusion follows and the spirit is lost.'*
The way we usually think about 'will-power' is misleading: we imagine it to be some special internal power, distinct from all our various tendencies and able to maintain some kind of order among them. When we identify with some preferred tendency this way of thinking is inevitable. Take again the case of someone who fasts in order to slim: he identifies with his aesthetic tendency and he also stops being aware of it. So if he lapses and does not stick to his regime, he is not going to say, 'My greed was stronger than my wish to look good,' but he does say, 'My greed was stronger than *me.*' In the opposite case, he says, '*I* was stronger than my greed.' Though he no longer experiences the tendency which has triumphed on this occasion as something separate, he does feel that some force has overcome his greed, so he calls this his will-power.

The situation can sometimes be more complex than this but it will still amount to the same thing: people who feel pride in the success of their will-power or shame at its failure will want more and more will-power. From this a bias develops which favours a tendency to frustrate other tendencies. This is what the urge for 'self-mastery' amounts to.

While it is true that exercising control over tendencies does not necessarily mean thwarting them, nonetheless any form of control, even when it is giving permission, implies the possibility of opposition. If someone exercises control over what I do, I rightly feel that my freedom is infringed. If we take the example of someone who fasts to prove that he can, he will claim that he has imposed a fast on himself quite freely, and will deny that it has been imposed on him by a tendency within him which is at war with his greed. He does not appreciate that there is in him a tendency to exercise iron control over his internal world, and that he is himself subject to its tyranny. He wanted to stop being a slave to his desires, but he is now enslaved by his focus on a single desire, his desire to be free of all other desires. Overall the internal state stays the same, unchanged for better or worse as far as the possibility of satori is concerned. Striving to become a 'better' person can lead to 'holiness', which in this context means the harmonious unification of a positive part of the individual which is the only aspect permitted to express itself. But it does not lead to satori, the unification of the whole being. From the point of view of atemporal realization, this so-called will-power is useless.

Note that these 'voluntary' attempts to work on oneself are made without giving any thought to the current internal state; they tend to be made whenever they are thought of. When they are not being made, all this means is that the 'task' has been forgotten. If there are occasions when thinking about the task fails to produce the intended effort, this is not because internal conditions have been taken into consideration. To imagine making the effort because it is thought to be desirable in terms of some system, already in itself represents an activation of the effort in question. The fact that this sometimes comes to nothing is because the opposing tendency was stronger at the time.

Once I recognize the uselessness of my attempts to work on myself, I am tempted to sympathize with somebody who has an easy-going approach to life, makes no effort to improve himself, and invests his energy in getting what he wants from the external world. But it is fairly obvious that this reaction is illogical. If it were true that working on oneself actually made the situation less favourable for achieving satori, giving up this sort of work should improve one's prospects. But we have already seen that these efforts are not in themselves an obstacle, and cannot be so. So the fact that one gives them up cannot remove an obstacle which was never there in the first place.

The main reason for rejecting inertness and passivity in response to these issues is a much weightier one. Someone who does not undertake inner work may seem to have a relaxed and non-interventionist approach to life, but in reality this is not the case. His mind may not be consciously aware of interfering with how his tendencies are operating, but this is happening subconsciously. Though there may be no conscious opposition between tendencies and they may seem well inte-grated with one another, this appearance is deceptive and largely conceals subconscious conflict between them. People like this do not subscribe to consciously held, theoretical ideals: their ideals are subcon-scious and practical. Inwardly they make practical judgements about their tendencies on the basis of the positive or negative affirmations which these give rise to. Because there is an obvious causal relationship between tendencies and their practical consequences, and because people care about the latter, they are bound to develop a bias in favour of some tendencies and against others. In other words they develop a secondary tendency to control their primary tendencies. So people whose struggles in life seem entirely devoted to controlling the external world will also conceal an internal struggle in response to the tyranny of their practical ideals.

The situation here is more complex than it is with those who advo-cate will-power. Their internal controls are always evident because the assessment which determines whether tendencies are to be permitted or repressed takes place in consciousness. In fact their tendencies are never simply *given permission*. Those that are not repressed are *activated* by the secondary controlling tendency. With someone whose conscious striving is solely directed against the external world, internal controls are only evident in their repressive aspect. When the controlling tendency does not repress one of the primary tendencies it does not activate it either, it simply lets it take its course. In other words the controlling tendency disappears. This person's mechanisms intermittently enjoy a kind of 'spontaneity'.

To summarize, people who are not doing any conscious inner work are not 'letting go' in the sense we have been discussing. Their internal world is not governed by impartiality. Even the relative spontaneity noted above is not real spontaneity. When I act *impulsively*, my subconscious attitude towards the world of my tendencies, of my selves, is not a 'yes' addressed to the whole of this world. It is a 'yes' to whatever tendency is active at the time, but this is a selective 'yes', accompanied by a 'no' to all my other selves. In other words, my subconscious attitude is a 'no' to my machine as a totality.

So where does this leave us in relation to a method which would consist of keeping a supervisory eye on all my tendencies but giving conscious approval to the one which is currently active? It is the logical approach for anyone to adopt who has ever consciously believed in some ideals and then worked through the process of understanding the limitations from which all such ideals suffer. People who have reached this stage understand that all internal mechanisms are equivalent when considered from the only real viewpoint, that of atemporal realization; whether or not their tendencies are aesthetically pleasing is a matter of indifference to them. This relative impartiality invests them with a relative freedom. Tendencies do not stop existing because bias withdraws its investment in them, but they lose their power to compel. Dream and reality are more and more clearly distinguished; my feelings accord with my dreams, but my behaviour with my reason.

So this method, which involves giving conscious approval to whatever tendencies are present, gives me relative freedom in the external world. But it is not the 'letting go' of Zen. Consciously permitting a tendency resembles letting go, but it is not the same. Letting go, as we have seen, is achieved when I give permission to all my tendencies *before* any one of them has appeared in consciousness; and this results in none of them appearing. On the contrary, when I authorize my current tendency, my letting go is restricted to that one, and all my other tendencies are unaffected. Observing my internal phenomena with impartial approval can contribute nothing to the possibility of achieving satori.

Coming back to our present understanding of 'letting go', we need to move on from defining the nature of correct inner work to clarifying *when it should be done.* At any rate this is how the question looks at first if we express it in a way which would be appropriate if we were dealing with an ordinary action, a contraction in the usual meaning of the word. If I have decided to take up physical training, it makes sense to ask when I should do it: my exercises may produce a better effect at a particular time of day, in which case I can insist that my muscles perform them at that time, whenever it may be. The situation is different with the inward action which relaxes all tendencies at once by authorizing them all in an instant of impartial detachment. This can be *attempted* at any time but it cannot be *carried out successfully* at any time. My consciousness can request, but cannot compel my machine to do it. It can only be accomplished if two conditions are satisfied: thought *proposes, and the machine accepts.* If I meet some resistance in myself to letting go, any attempt to overcome this resistance this will prevent success: it would be like grafting a contraction onto a contracture, and tightening something which is already in spasm.

Let us consider these two conditions. Thought must *propose* the action. This presupposes that my mind is active and watchful; and this watchfulness presupposes a clear understanding of the inner work and its significance. It is in this, the active mind's state of watchful invitation, that true *will-power* is to be found, which, as Spinoza has observed, *is nothing else than understanding.* My machine must then accept the mind's invitation and open up to it of its own free will. This good will on the part of the machine comes into being when it feels that thought is asking for its co-operation persistently but without in any way constraining it: in other words, when it feels that thought is treating it with *consideration.*

We are now in a position to understand what correct inner discipline is. Earlier on, we accepted that there is 'something' directing the machine during the course of all internal discipline, and wondered what this factor might be. Can we now say that it is the active mind? In one sense yes, but in another sense no, since the effective guiding activity of the mind depends here on an agreement between it and the machine, and the mind has no direct control over this agreement. The guidance which my machine has during letting go is channelled through the active mind, but its real source is the Conciliating Principle which brings my two parts together in harmony. *It is only the Principle itself that is able to undertake correct inner discipline, which is free from any kind of constraint or internal struggle.* The only effort we have to make consists of forgetting as little as possible that our true well-being depends on letting go, on object-less attention, and on 'being available to the experience of nothingness' in our minds; and on never trying to impose de-contraction, this shared opening to the Principle, on the machine, but only ever putting it forward as a proposal.

If de-contraction is proposed in this way, the machine will grow tired of refusing after a while and from time to time it will accept, though, as I mentioned above, this will take place in a split second without duration.

The process seems to suggest that I am afraid that my ego might burst apart. If I want to win the confidence of a child who has been badly frightened, I hold my arms out to it without getting too close, inviting it to come closer without compelling it to do so. A time may come when the child will throw itself into my arms, but for a long time all I may see will be fleeting moments of relief in its eyes when it briefly accepts the idea of moving towards me, before being gripped by fear again. In a similar way my inner acts of de-contraction, my 'letting go's', are really just infinitely brief imaginings of the real letting go which would be satori. Even if my inner discipline is based on a correct understanding, all these actions it leads to are failures. But they are a special kind of failure experienced by the whole of my being and it is their accumulation which creates the conditions for the ultimate failure of my present state, when the whole dualism of success and failure is transcended in satori.

This way of looking at discipline conciliates the ideas of 'training' and 'not-training'. There is not-training in the sense that no one part of me imposes itself on another. Yet there is also training in the sense that my understanding is able to obtain a letting go from the machine which it would never have achieved on its own. The trainer gets the trainee to do something which is good for both of them during the moments when the machine cooperates willingly; and this is possible because trainer and trainee are but one in the conciliating presence of Absolute Reality.

Satori can be understood as a letting go which endures. It is an instant in which a definitive double de-contraction is established: the machine opens itself up to active mind which unites with it; and the pair so formed opens itself up to the Principle, which unites with it in a tripartite Unity. Only then does it become obvious that machine, mind and Principle were never separated.

# CHAPTER TWENTY-TWO

# *Compensations*

PEOPLE WHO HAVE NOT ACHIEVED REALIZATION are driven by the need for absolute being as separate and distinct entities and are therefore unable to accept existence as it is. At first sight this might seem to be due to the fact that individual existence takes place under the constant threat of partial or total destruction. However mankind's *essential* need is for absolute 'being', not for perpetual 'existence'; it is a need for infinite eternity, not indefinite duration. Even if sickness and death could be avoided for ever, the unrealized individual would still be just as driven to reject existence in its present form by the need for absolute being.

It is not the fact of one's existence being under threat from the external world that is unacceptable. What is intolerable is that the perceptible world does not depend on our individual existence, nor do we as individuals exist unconditionally. Because we are potentially able to experience our identity with the Absolute Principle and Origin, we find the dormant state of this identity unacceptable. We cannot accept not being the First Cause of the Universe; but we cannot see our real essential unity with the First Cause of the Universe as long as we believe that we are nothing more than our psycho-somatic organism and are solely identified with it.

Nonetheless we clearly do accept our existence in practice, since we do our best to keep it going. This is because, while we *know* that our organism is not the prime mover of the universe, our imagination protects us from *feeling* this by creating a subjective universe which is centred on us. The imaginary film protects us from what we cannot bear to see by concealing it from us. But this only works while the film is running; the threat remains and only by the imagination's continuous activity can it be kept at bay. Imagination can alleviate the distress but it cannot get rid of it completely.

*Imagination creates an imaginative film which is not based on present reality. So it is our compensatory function. It is the function which manufactures compensations.*

Compensations are image systems which we create from sensory and mental perceptions – in other words, from the image material stored by our memory – and organize in our own way, according to the structure of our individual psychosomatic organism. They constitute our personal inner world. Obviously they are not a pure creation; they are 're-created', using non-personal components, to form a personal representation of the world. This process is organized along lines peculiar to the individual, producing one particular cross-section of the Universe (although each personal representation is unique to the individual it is not created by the individual, but should be understood as one particular aspect chosen according to our personal structure from among the cosmic order's infinite array of aspects).

Our compensations are an individually re-fashioned universe which can be compared to an artist's drawing. No designer could create a form whose prototype did not already exist in the Universe, which was conceived without reference to any pre-existing image based on external reality. The designer's act of 'creation' is confined to choosing some form in the external world in preference to all the others, and also on occasion to combining forms in a way which he has never seen in reality. Similarly the personal element in how we create our imaginary universe will not be found in the basic forms we use in its construction, but partly in how we select its particular components and partly in how we put universal forms together in a style which is personal to us. A compensation develops as an *ingenious artifice* of the imagination.

There is a direct correspondence between our compensations and our value system. Each of us sees certain things as being especially real and important, and these are the things which give life its *meaning*. If I want to know what my compensations are, all I have to do is ask myself: 'What gives my life its meaning?'

Before taking this further I want to go back to the question: 'What do compensations compensate for?' It is often thought that they compensate us for those aspects of existence which negate us, but this is mistaken. If this were the case, our compensations would always be positive and affirming images; but we will see that they can equally well be negative. The essential characteristic of a compensation is not that it should please me, but that it should provide me with a view of the universe which places me at the centre. That is the only thing that matters, and whether the universe which is centred on me happens to be affirming or negating is irrelevant. Compensations compensate for our illusory belief that we are separated from Reality, in other words for the non-appearance in subjective experience of our identity with the Absolute Principle and Origin. Another way of putting this is to say that our compensations constitute a private imaginary version of the universe which compensates for the dormant state of our latent ability to see the Universe in its total reality. Since we cannot see things in their suchness, we are compelled to see them as we do at present, incompletely, mediated through the imagination.

It is not that our compensatory way of seeing the world is wrong, it is simply incomplete. The problem lies in our belief that the way we see things is wholly adequate. The importance we attach to particular aspects of the world is not wrong, nor is it illusory. It is the selective nature of our vision which deceives us, because it attaches importance to some aspects and denies comparable importance to everything else. To see things in their suchness would be to grant equal importance to all aspects of the Universe; everything would be important, and consequently nothing would be 'important' with its present connotation of 'preferable'. Illusion only resides in the partial nature of our imaginary vision, not in the vision itself.

We must be quite clear about this: our compensations may cause problems in other respects, but they do not get in the way of satori nor do they prevent us seeing things as they really are. In themselves they are not illusory nor are they opposed to satori. Idols do not in themselves bar the way to Reality; the reality we see in an idol is no obstacle to our reunion with Reality. What does obstruct us is the ignorance which prevents us seeing the same reality in everything else that we see in the idol. *The only obstacle is ignorance, and ignorance is partiality.* Our compensatory vision of the world is not something bad which we must get rid of; it is something incomplete which needs to be expanded and made whole by dispelling what is restrictive, selective, and biased about our ignorance. Incompleteness itself is not bad; what is wrong is partiality or bias, meaning our ignorant belief in the totality and all-inclusiveness of something which only expresses a part of the whole.

These points had to be established before we could proceed to investigate compensations in any depth. When compensatory mechanisms are spoken of as though we were completely under their control, it must be understood that what really controls and makes slaves of us is our ignorance, the bias which ensures that we implicitly deny whatever we are not actively affirming. No compensation ever enslaved us of itself, but it is our biased attitude towards it which makes slaves of us. To see Reality in the image of Jesus or Buddha is not enslavement, but it is if one only does so by denying Reality to the rest of creation.

Compensations are necessary if we are to achieve realization, because we would not be able to accept existence without them and would destroy ourselves very quickly. They have a part to play in the evolving process which leads to satori, though achieving satori presupposes that we will eventually transcend them. Transcending our compensations should not be understood to involve the loss of the creative energy contained within them. It is rather that the excluding formal 'membrane' which confined it is shattered: the reality seen in the idol is not destroyed but radiates forth from it once its restrictive shell has disintegrated.

There are advantages and disadvantages to compensations as far as progress towards satori is concerned. Their *affective* aspects are helpful, because they nurture me and protect me from suicide; but they hinder to the extent that they involve an *intellectual* belief in the Reality – or absolute value – of the compensatory image. For example, one of my compensations is to have a healthy child: the image of me having a healthy child makes me feel happy, so this compensation favours my development towards satori because it plays a part in helping me accept existence. What is unhelpful about it, however, is my belief that this state of affairs is *absolutely* good, while my child's death would be *absolutely* bad. The problem here is a form of belief where my investment in the compensatory situation is such as to exclude any investment in its contrary. The effect of this exclusion is to limit what I can perceive of cosmic reality and it even prevents me seeing what I do see properly because it severs its connections with everything else. I cannot perceive anything as it is in reality as long as even one of its connections with the rest of the Universe is cut – and all connections are concentrated in the relationship which something has with its antagonistic and complementary contraries.

Hui-neng repudiates this damaging belief implicit in our compensations when he proclaims: *'From the beginning not one thing is.'* When he says this, he does not condemn pleasure arising from compensations. This is a dynamic phenomenon which only 'exists' and makes no claim to 'be'. *What he repudiates is belief in the Reality of a fixed image which lays claim to 'being' by excluding the contrary image. Idolatry's affective basis is not condemned by Hui-neng: what he repudiates is idolatrous intellectual belief.*

This is belief which takes an image and isolates it by excluding its counterpart in the cosmic Yin Yang equilibrium, in a vain attempt to endow it with the unchanging Unity of the Absolute Principle and Origin. Once the image has been artificially isolated in this way it becomes a compensatory idol. It is not the image itself but this way of seeing it as an idol which Hui-neng is attacking when he reminds us that 'not one thing is'.

Hui-neng's admonition is in no way intended to warn us against living out our compensations, so he is not telling us to stop attributing value to particular things. But we are being invited to transcend compensations by using understanding to shatter the tyrannical exclusivism which our idolatrous opinions impose on us. Only the restrictive intellectual forms are disrupted by this, not the living affective substance contained within them. Understanding enables me to go on feeling that individual objects are valuable without implicitly maintaining that their contraries have a contrary value. It enables me to appreciate that there are no such things as 'value' and 'anti-value' when these things are seen from the only real point of view, the perspective of atemporal realization: everything can be used for realization.

*Hui-neng's phrase quoted above is not a curse on all things in their particularity; on the contrary it is an undifferentiated, impartial blessing on them. The same idea is expressed repeatedly in a remarkable Zen text known as 'Treatise on the Believing Mind':\**

'The Perfect Way knows no difficulty,
'Save that it refuses any preference.'

'If you want to see the Perfect Way made manifest,
'Entertain no thought for it or against it.
'To set what you like and what you do not like in opposition,
'Therein lies the sickness of the human spirit.'

'Do not try to find the truth,
'Simply stop attaching yourself to opinions.
'Do not linger in dualism.'

'As soon as you have good and evil
'Confusion follows and the mind is lost.'

'When the single mind is not disturbed,
'The ten thousand things cannot offend it.'

'When no discrimination is made between this and that,
'How should bias and preconception arise?'

'Let go, let things be as they may.'

'If you desire to follow the Mahayana way,
'Do not have any prejudice against the six sense objects.'

'Whereas the Dharma itself does not treat of individuals,
'The ignorant become attached to particular objects.'

* *Hsin-hsin Ming*, attributed to Seng-ts'an, the third Zen Patriarch.

# Compensations

*'The enlightened have neither attachments nor enmities.'*

*'Gain and loss, justice and injustice,*
*'May they disappear once and for all!'*

*'The ultimate end of things*
*'Is not defined by rules and measures.'*

*'Everything is empty, clear, and illuminated from within;*
*'There is no work, no effort, and no waste of energy.*
*'This is beyond the reach of imagination.'*

*'In not being two, all is the same,*
*'And everything that exists is comprehended therein.'*

*'It matters little how things are conditioned,*
*'Whether by 'being' or by 'not being'.*

*'The thing that exists is the same as that which does not exist;*
*'What does not exist is the same as what exists.'*

*'If only this is realized,*
*'You need torment yourself no longer about your imperfection!'*

All compensations are idolatries, attempts to see Reality embodied in a particular image, an illusion of fixity and permanence outside the cosmic vortex. When a compensation is transcended, what is destroyed is not the image but its artificial fixity: when an image loses its particular value as an idol, it is put back into the multitude of other images, into the ceaselessly moving flow of cosmic life in its suchness.

The actual process whereby compensations are transcended and idols lose their value takes place in intellectual intuition. It presupposes that the right theoretical understanding has been achieved, which unmasks the idolatrous and illusory belief system. It also presupposes that I have experienced through suffering the intrinsically unsatisfactory nature of compensations. This distressing failure to achieve satisfaction is inevitable. We have already seen that compensations only alleviate my distress while they are active. Deep down, however, I am expecting them to cure my distress *permanently*. Sooner or later, I am forced to realize that the nature of compensations is such that this expectation is bound to be disappointed. It is when I am experiencing the pain of this disappointment that understanding will manifest itself by correctly interpreting my suffering. Abstract understanding and concrete suffering are both necessary; neither is sufficient on its own.

I will come back to this, but we need to understand the structure of the different types of compensation before we can go any further with the question of how they are transcended.

The essential constituent of all compensations is an image involving my ego, which resembles a nucleus around which innumerable satellite images cluster. Like everything in the domain of form, this central image is bi-polar, which is why there are both positive and negative compensations. People have an innate preference for the positive – the good, the beautiful, and the true – and always try at first to construct a positive compensation; but failure can trigger its inversion into a negative compensation. For example, if I try to have an affair with someone but am unsuccessful I may begin to hate them instead, with the result that hatred then gives my life the meaning to which love used to.

Having indicated the way in which compensations can be 'inverted', I will now confine myself to describing the main positive compensations which we can observe in ourselves and other people.

First, there is the 'being loved' compensation. In this the nuclear image is of me being served by the external world. Then there is the 'enjoying' compensation which has a central image of me actively grabbing hold of food in the external world (in this scenario I am affirmed by eating the external world; love of wealth is included, because it makes consumption of the external world possible).

Next there are many compensations arising from a central image of me serving and nourishing the external world: 'loving', 'giving pleasure', 'giving one's life', 'helping', 'serving' one's country/a political cause/a just cause/humanity/the oppressed/the weak, etc.). Other compensations which fall into this category are pleasure in doing one's duty, in being faithful to a moral code, in living up to some ideal.

There is another group of compensations in which the central image is of me engaging with the external world by *perceiving* rather than through *action*. Here the compensatory image is of me perceiving the external world, as when pleasure is gained from participating in beauty, art, intellectual truth, or knowledge in general. Or the image may be of me being perceived by the external world: pleasure is derived from attracting attention, being admired, or being feared.

In other cases there may be a central image of me as the 'creator' of some work in the external world, responsible for imposing some change on the world around me, which I think of as a distinct and separate entity, such as a work of art, or some scientific or intellectual work, a political movement, or a society or religious order, etc.

Or the central image might be of me creating something in myself: developing myself, realizing myself, discovering who I am, developing my potential, showing what I am capable of, improving my mind, working hard, or doing research, and becoming rich in the process, etc. This is a huge category and an important one; it includes all the different kinds of ambition, which can be material, subtle or so-called spiritual. (I will devote some time to the question of spirituality later on, in so far as it relates to obtaining 'higher' states of consciousness, and 'spiritual powers', in a more or less disguised form of the superman cult).

Finally there is a very remarkable compensation in which the constituent elements of all the compensations listed so far are merged together and lose their separate identity (just as all colours are present but indistinguishable in white). This is the *adoration* compensation, in which my ego is projected onto some gross or subtle external form, and the central image is of me interacting with my ego's projection. The dualities of self/external world, acting/being acted on, nourishing/ being nourished, perceiving/being perceived, and creating/being created vanish because of the identity existing between subject and object. The relationship between subject and object is a greatly simpli- fied one: I experience joy which is no longer derived from agency, or from seeing myself perceiving, *but simply from perceiving in a unitive contemplation.* My gaze rests on the image onto which my self has been projected in a selective act of identification, and in it I believe that I see my Principle and Origin.

Different compensations can be found in combination with one another. Adoration in particular combines most frequently with 'loving and being loved', in the sense of 'affirming and being affirmed', and of 'serving and being served.'

Every compensation, or imaginative constellation, introduces an element of fixity into the way an individual functions. However, this is a dynamic fixity, like a stereotyped gesture which has become habitual and represents a fixed element in my pattern of movement. It is this fixed aspect of compensations which favours the expression of partic- ular groupings of dynamic, living phenomena. In this sense all compensations represent a stereotyped form of living. It is important to draw a distinction between the compensation itself, with its tendency to make me live in a particular way, and whether or not I actually do live in that way. It is possible for me to have a particular compensation active within me without expressing it in my life, without engaging in the kinds of interactions which it promotes.

This can be seen clearly in the neuroses; and neurotics can be defined as people who are poorly compensated, and unable to live out their compensations. Take for example someone with the love/be loved compensation, which requires one to participate in society on the basis of an exchange of services. Suppose they come up against the world's wickedness and undeserved misfortune strikes them: if their compensation inverts fully, they could then have the possibility of living it out in its inverted form. Their life would find its meaning in hatred and vengeance, and this would provide the compensation. But the inversion in such cases is often only partial, and affects the practical but not the theoretical aspect. So the individual refuses to engage with the external world in response to particular events, while still wanting to engage at the level of generalities. He might want to act by hitting or injuring someone on a particular occasion but is prevented from doing so because he still persists in wanting to follow the general rule of love and service.

It is often said that people like this have still not found their compensations in life. In fact this is incorrect, because everyone always has compensations: neurotics have compensations but they cannot express them in their lives. Their compensations are split and separated, and unliveable. Caught between hate and love of the same object, the neurotic is paralysed. Vital energy cannot be invested in objects, and this has the effect of disturbing the metabolism of internal energy. Aggression is turned against the self, and there is a build-up of distress. This distress is an experience which originates and is felt at a stage before the compensations come into play, since the neurotic has not yet succeeded in establishing them as functioning elements in his life. But it is essentially the same as the distress experienced when established compensations have been exhausted without the help of understanding. In both cases, 'decompensation' takes place; but these two kinds of crisis have to be resolved differently. People whose compensations are fully enacted in their lives need to move beyond this stage, while those who have failed to integrate their compensations into their lives still have to enter it.

When compensations are fully integrated into life the psycho-somatic organism is brought into a harmonious and adaptive state. If someone thinks they have found Reality in something – whether it be money, honours, power, or some high endeavour – they have a guiding purpose which gives their lives structure and effectiveness. For them Reality appears to be focussed in a single image and this gives them an apparent inner unity by simplifying the dynamics of their personality. This *simplification* means that some tendencies have been rendered dormant and it should not be confused with the *simplicity* of someone who has achieved satori, in whom everything is united without distinction into an all-inclusive synthesis. But the resemblance between the two states is like that between a two-dimensional image and the three-dimensional object it portrays. If an adoration type of compensation is developed to a very high degree of subtlety, the simplification of inner dynamics which this induces can generate unusual and apparently supernatural powers within the psycho-somatic machine, such as mind-reading, clairvoyance, the ability to influence others psychically, precisely adapted unconscious behaviour, healing powers, etc.

Well-compensated individuals are *idolaters* in the precise meaning of that term to the extent that they believe the compensatory image to be responsible for the harmonising effects of their compensations and identify this image with Reality. This belief treats a subjective value as though it were objective and has the all too obvious effect of impelling the idolater to think that everyone *must* see things the same way. With the positive kind of idolater this leads to proselytism, evangelism, and missionary work; with the negative type, to intolerance and the persecution of non-believers. Belief in the Reality of a particular form also brings with it the need for formal manifestations; for the idolater, rituals, instead of just being an optional means of expression, which is all they really are, become a compelling necessity.

Compensations form an integral part of that period of human development which stretches from birth to satori. Before satori we are maintained in a state of unstable equilibrium by our compensations. Hence it is impossible to transcend compensations completely before satori; complete transcendence only comes with satori. Satori is a 'transformation' in the sense of going beyond form and it is a unique, instantaneous event; but it is preceded by a number of changes at the formal, or phenomenal, level which reflect the progressive development of the necessary inner conditions. This is what I will be referring to when I speak of transcending compensations as a progressive process.

Let me illustrate what I mean as follows: when a fox wants to get rid of his fleas, so the story goes, he holds a bit of moss in his jaws and climbs down into a stream backwards; the fleas abandon the submerged bits of the fox and escape to areas still above the water. The area they occupy gradually shrinks, becoming at the same time more and more densely infested. Finally all the fleas are concentrated on his snout, and then on the tuft of moss, at which point the fox releases the moss and it floats off in the current. Until the moment when the fox abandons all his fleas at once, he has not freed himself from a single flea; but he has gone about things in a way which altered their distribution and prepared the ground for their complete and instantaneous disappearance.

Understood in this way as a reduction in extent and an increase in intensity, the progressive transcendence of compensations corresponds to a purification of the compensatory image, which evolves from the particular towards the general. Since every compensation is an image of the Universe centred on my ego – in other words a constellation whose central star is my ego orbited by various satellite images – the process of purification I am referring to involves the satellites becoming more and more subtle, while the central star increases in density. But what happens next is something unique and no illustration can convey it: the ego has no reality, neither absolute nor relative, so the density which accumulates in it does not give rise to any manifestation. Progressive *detachment* is a purification of the attachment to oneself which is at the centre of all attachments in general. But the progressive purification and condensation of this central attachment to an image which is no more than a figment, an illusory hypothesis, can proceed and intensify without this becoming manifest to the senses.

When Saint John of the Cross transcends his mystical compensation, and disengages from the image of God after it has already become as depersonalized as possible, he does not feel attached to the image of ego from which the God image drew its apparent Reality. He does not feel attached to anything, he does not feel anything. It is the 'Night' where nothing is left for feelings or thoughts. But there is still a final attachment to the ego as the structure which integrates all the individual's resources and faculties. The ego is the ultimate, invisible compensation. Transcending this invisible compensation brings true detachment, and it is total and instantaneous. 'Night' is followed by what Saint John of the Cross calls 'the theopathic state', and Zen calls 'Satori'.

*Detachment*, or the transcendence of compensations, is often poorly understood. It is thought to involve destroying the affective preference felt for the compensatory image, and to require that all desire should be expunged from oneself. This is to forget that attachment does not reside in the desire itself, but only in our demand that it should be satisfied. The desire does not have to disappear, only this insistence on its satisfaction. Abandoning the desire is not the result of an inner struggle: it is something which happens once we correctly understand that disappointment is inevitable, whether or not our insistence on having our desires fulfilled is met. Distress, demand, and a belief that the sought after image is Reality, these form the scaffolding of errors which understanding undermines and will bring crashing down one day. Detachment is not a painful inner event; on the contrary, it is one which brings relief.

Sometimes our understanding is too weak and for a long time does not enable us to transcend some particular compensatory situation. Our inner growth seems to be blocked by this obstacle. But, let me repeat, what we love, what we are attached to, is never itself the obstacle. It is only our ignorance, our mistaken identification of the image we cherish with Reality, which provides the obstacle.

The possibility of transcending any compensation depends on the power of intellectual intuition. It also depends on the compensatory image's level of subtlety. In the first place, the more subtle it is, the less chance there is that it will fail us; every image loses value over time but the more subtle it is, the stronger it is and the longer it takes to lose its effect. If fatigue and disappointment do occur, however, then the more subtle the compensatory image, the more difficult it is to interpret our disappointment correctly. Instead of doubting the image's reality, I am more inclined to criticize myself for being inadequate, unskilful, idle, or cowardly in the way I relate to it.

In this connection I must draw attention to a very subtle kind of compensation usually referred to by the term 'spirituality'. In 'spiritual' compensations, people love and serve a lofty cause: an infinitely good and just 'God' whom they attempt to know directly through a state of union; 'superior', 'exalted' states of consciousness which they seek to acquire; total realization which they conceive of as something to be conquered; an 'ideal' whose goal is the kingdom of love and justice for all mankind, etc.

What do these spiritual values really amount to? Three kinds of value are commonly distinguished: material, intellectual, and spiritual. The spiritual values obviously form part of Manifestation, since they can be defined, loved and obeyed; but, while Manifestation clearly has a gross or material aspect, and a subtle, psychic or intellectual aspect, it is hard to see what a third, or spiritual, aspect would consist of. Those who adore the spiritual say that it is the Absolute (which is what all idolaters say of their idols). According to them this third aspect would be 'Spirit' ruling over and conciliating 'soul' and 'body'. But the Absolute cannot be contrasted with other values existing in Manifestation because this treats it as though it were in the same category as Manifestation. The Absolute cannot be defined or loved or obeyed like some object positioned in front of the self as subject. Spiritual values cannot be the Absolute. The various guises in which these values appear always conceal an idea of something perfectly positive, which simply represents the positive principle of temporal dualism. It can be called God or Creative Principle of the world, or Principle of Good, contrasted with the Devil or Destructive Principle, or Principle of Evil; it is the Principle of Light set against the Prince of Darkness.

It is normal for mankind to love creation and hate destruction, to love God and hate the Devil. Spirituality only begins to be idolatry when the intellect misleadingly identifies God with the Absolute, or with Reality, or the Atemporal. When this mistake is made, God is identified with the Absolute Principle, and the Devil with Manifestation. Satan becomes the Prince of this world, and spiritual and temporal goods are set in opposition. When Metaphysical Unity is forgotten, the result is inner dualism and the synthesis of being becomes impossible. This is seen in every idolatrous compensation.

I have made a point of drawing attention to so-called spiritual compensations because they are the most subtle of all. The mental image of God, the positive principle of temporal dualism, is the most powerful of all compensatory images, and the one most resistant to devaluation. Consequently it is the one most difficult to transcend. We cannot choose our compensations; if our psychic structure is such that we have a sense of the sacred and a love of God, then this is how we are. But we then have a special interest in reminding ourselves that nothing which is conceivable is Reality. Our own nature is the Absolute itself; nothing which we can conceive of, contemplate, or love, can be transcendent to the domain of images which we have created ourselves, we the Absolute.

Zen is categorical on this matter and in no respect could it be considered a spiritual doctrine. It is radically atheist, if by 'God' is understood a Reality which our minds are supposed to be capable of conceiving. *'From the beginning not one thing is.'* Rinzai* said: 'IF YOU MEET BUDDHA ON YOUR WAY, KILL HIM . . . . OH YOU DISCIPLES OF THE TRUTH, STRIVE TO DELIVER YOURSELVES FROM ALL OBJECTS . . . . OH YOU WITH EYES LIKE MOLES! I SAY TO YOU: NO BUDDHA, NO TEACHING, NO DISCIPLINE! WHAT DO YOU SPEND YOUR TIME LOOKING FOR IN YOUR NEIGHBOUR'S HOUSE? DON'T YOU UNDERSTAND THAT YOU ARE PUTTING ANOTHER HEAD ON TOP OF YOUR OWN? WHAT DO YOU LACK IN YOURSELF? WHAT YOU ARE USING AT THE MOMENT IS NO DIFFERENT FROM WHAT BUDDHA IS MADE OF.'

---

* Chinese Zen master Lin-chi (d. 867), founder of the Rinzai school. The quotation comes from the *Rinzairoku*, the chronicle of Lin-chi.

# CHAPTER TWENTY-THREE

# Inner Alchemy

ANYONE WHO WANTS TO UNDERSTAND ZEN must bear in mind that it is essentially concerned with the doctrine of *sudden awakening*. According to this view we do not have to acquire liberation, nor do we have to be raised to a higher level. Zen therefore does not admit the possibility that our condition might gradually improve until we finally became *normal*. The satori event is no more than an instant separating two periods in our temporal life. It has no more reality in existence than the line which separates shadow from light. Either I do not see things as they are, or I do; there is no period of time during which I might *gradually* come to see the Universe in its Reality.

But although the idea of gradual progression may be unrelated to Realization itself and 'transformation' be unequivocally abrupt, Zen teaches that transformation is preceded by successive changes in the character of our inner functioning. I say 'successive', not progressive, as a reminder that the development which takes place before satori is not a gradual emergence of Reality, but simple, gradual alterations in the nature of our blindness.

Bearing this qualification in mind, it is worth taking a closer look at the gradual, non-progressive evolution which precedes satori. As understanding, or 'penetrating vision', becomes more profound, we observe changes taking place in our spontaneous inner life – in our emotions and imagination. Hindu wisdom teaches us: '*What you become proceeds from what you think.*' This process of evolution and change is like *distillation*, the purification and refinement of matter. When mashed up fruit is distilled, the alcohol obtained from it is the result of changes which make the original material less substantial and raise it to a higher level. There is less matter, but it is finer. It has less of a physical presence (alcohol is not as heavy as the fruit from which it is derived), but at a subtle level its effect is greater (drinking alcohol produces effects which cannot be matched by eating fruit). Successive distillations accentuate these changes in substance. Mediaeval alchemy, with its retorts and stills and its quest for the 'quintessence', was a symbolic representation of the inner process we are studying. With increasing refinement a

211

substance is rendered more subtle and its essential characteristics become less visible: the way a fruit looks tells us what to expect when we eat it, while the properties of alcohol, despite its enhanced potency, are less obvious from its appearance. In ordinary usage the French word *subtiliser* can mean 'to make something disappear'. To refine something, to make it more subtle, is also to purify it; and the more subtle a substance, the simpler its structure.

The evolution of understanding is like a distillation of our inner world, of our great store of images. This material is purified, refined, and simplified, as are all the imaginative–emotional processes associated with them. For example, when I was a child I believed in a little Jesus, a perfect child who loved me and wished me well, who watched over me and whose feelings about me were the same kind of feelings that I had. This is a 'gross' image, seen clearly and full of concrete detail. As an adolescent I came to understand God as a Being without a visible body, but still as a personal God with thoughts and feelings, though these were vaguer and less easy to imagine. The image had become more refined and 'subtle', and no longer manifested with its previous clarity. With a larger non-manifested element it was now vaster and more powerful in the sense that it encompassed more. As I grew older and understood more, the idea took shape within me of an impersonal Principle which I thought of as uniquely good and constructive. Next I came to think of this Principle as something beyond the creation/destruction duality, with Not-doing ruling over all phenomena. I drew a distinction between this Principle and its Manifestation and believed in the reality of this distinction. I understood that this Principle is my Principle, I saw my identity with it, but I also distinguished between my Principle and my manifestation, and believed in the reality of this distinction.

Finally I came to understand that the distinction between Principle and Manifestation is just an analytical construct which my mind needs in order to express itself. I realized that I went off on the wrong track the moment I set up an opposition between any of the elements I distinguished from one another. The image of Reality, originally represented by the concrete image of the Infant Jesus, had become refined to a level of subtlety where it became the abstract image of the *Void* described by traditional metaphysics, which contains all conceivable phenomena in their plenitude. This 'distillation' of my imagination is accompanied by similar changes in my affective responses to my ideas about Reality, and they too become more refined and subtle. Inwardly and outwardly, changes take place in the way my machine functions when I stop believing in a personal God, whom I love and fear, and start to think in abstract terms of my Buddha nature beyond all thought and feeling.

This process of 'distillation' which results from work by intellectual intuition relates to an idea which I have expressed frequently in this book that *the right kind of inner development destroys nothing but fulfils everything.* The 'old' person may seem to die but nothing is really destroyed. When alcohol is extracted from fruit, the fruit's essence is not destroyed: it is purified, concentrated, and brought to fulfilment. Similarly my conception of Reality is brought to fulfilment when I evolve from my image of the Infant Jesus to an image of the Void. Something seems to have died in the sense that there is less to see, less for the mind and senses to perceive; but the fact that there is no longer belief in the Reality of a perception does not imply that something has been destroyed. It is necessary for our fulfilment that illusory Reality should be expunged from all the images perceived by our mind and senses.

We are born feeling fundamentally unsatisfied. Something seems to be lacking. What we are and what we have does not meet our needs. We are waiting for something else to turn up, for real life to begin. We feel that we have a problem and go on looking for a solution. We feel we have a right to expect existence to provide us with various different situations.

This dissatisfied, demanding attitude of ours is the source of all our suffering, but it has to be fulfilled, not destroyed. When we looked at compensations, we saw how the demands we make and the attachments we have developed can become more subtle and refined. All our attachments are derived from the central attachment we have to the image of our ego, which is the image of ourselves as distinct and separate entities: they develop through a process of association through identification between individual images and the central image. As understanding deepens, the associations so formed are destroyed; my attachment to the central image is purified, refined and concentrated, becoming less apparent, and increasingly non-manifest. The demand associated with this attachment shows no signs of decreasing before satori, but it is purified and fulfilled as the instant of sudden transformation draws near, where attachment and detachment will be conciliated.

My self-esteem, my pride, is an aspect of my demanding attitude. This also becomes purified with increased understanding. I seem more modest to people observing me from the outside. But I am well aware that this impression is misleading. My self-esteem is less visible to others because it has become more subtle and concentrated. It approaches fulfilment, tending in one direction towards the zero of perfect humility, and in another towards the non-manifested infinity of my absolute dignity.

The distress associated with our basic egotistical demand undergoes the same gradual modification. It is a serious mistake to imagine that understanding can make our distress worse. The wrong kind of information can do this, by implanting restrictive beliefs in our minds. But the intuitive understanding of truth refines distress, reducing its manifested aspect and increasing its non-manifested aspect. The profound distress from which all manifested individual distresses are derived is not reduced at all before satori; but it becomes less and less manifest, so that, as Zen students evolve (without 'progressing'), they experience less and less distress. When distress has become almost completely non-manifest, satori is close.

Our inner agitation reflects the conflict between the life force and our rejection of the temporal constraints within which it operates. Confronted by life as it is, we both want and do not want it. Our agitation is purified as understanding brings with it a lessening of our rejection of temporal constraints. The life force is not affected, but negative attitudes towards it are lessened. So it too is purified; agitation disappears; and my machine runs more and more smoothly.

As I mentioned earlier, the main feature of the process of development and change under consideration is the growing refinement and subtlety of our image material. Images gradually lose their apparent density and illusory objectivity; they become increasingly subtle, spacious, general and abstract. There is a decline in their ability to activate vital energy and lock it into contracted emotional states. The whole imaginative–emotional process loses its intensity and compelling force. Our imaginative film shows less contrast, and our inner dream world weighs on us less heavily.

Satori can be thought of as an awakening, in relation to which our current condition is a kind of sleep whose dreaming is our conscious thought. There is an element of truth in this view but it is also a potential source of misunderstanding. My natural inclination to picture things in my mind is coupled with a tendency to forget that satori, which is an unimaginable inner event, cannot be likened to anything I am acquainted with. So I am tempted to imagine that there is an analogy between the ultimate awakening of satori and what I experience every day as I emerge from sleep into the waking state. The idea of progression slips back insidiously in this misleading analogy. So just as ordinary waking seems to represent an advance on the sleeping state, satori comes to be seen as a state of 'super-wakefulness', true awakening, the ultimate in progress relative to my current waking state. Just as waking up restores a level of consciousness which is unavailable when I am asleep, so satori would supposedly endow me with the 'super-consciousness' which I lack at present. This way of thinking is mistaken, because each one of us has been in a state of satori since the beginning of eternity and despite all appearances we lack nothing as we are. Thinking along these lines leads to erroneous assumptions about the inner process which precedes the satori event.

*All is well*

Between deep sleep and waking comes dream sleep. The emergence of conscious activity during sleep represents a shift in the direction of waking; the more compelling and intense my dreams are, and the more they portray a deceptively objective reality, the closer I am to waking. If I were to accept the misleading progressive analogy, I would expect satori to be preceded similarly by an intensification of conscious thought and the imaginative film. I would expect that a phase of mental hyperactivity, in the form of ecstasy or nightmare, would build up to a critical level of tension and succeed in bursting through the final barrier into a state of cosmic superconsciousness.

All this is completely incompatible with Zen's 'sudden' teaching. Notice how ego-centred identification turns up again in the fantasy of incremental progress, and deceives us into worshipping our own consciousness: our imaginary inner universe, centred on our individual self, lays claim to being the true Universe, and our consciousness, creator of this universe, comes to be thought of as though it were the same as the Universal Mind; which is not surprising, since we were relying on this same consciousness to conquer Realization.

In reality, asleep or awake, I am in the state of satori right here and now. Sleep and waking are equally immersed in this state, and satori functions in relation to them as the third element, the hypostasis which conciliates them. Immersed in the Atemporal, sleep and waking are two extreme modes in which my psycho-somatic organism functions; and I oscillate between them.

Dream sleep occupies an intermediate position between deep sleep and the waking state, and is shown on the diagram as a projection downwards from the apex of the triangle onto its base. Hence comes the transcendental wisdom of the dream. In symbolic dream thought, situations relating to our private microcosm can be expressed in a form from which all the illusory objectivity of the external world has been stripped. This is the only kind of thought available to us as we are at present which is capable of seeing certain things as they really are, in their suchness. This is the reason why dream thinking is expressed in symbols: direct forms of expression cannot give an adequate account of things as they really are.

Let us now apply the correct approach to these issues and try to understand how consciousness, our 'waking dream', is altered by the gradual non-progressive evolution which precedes satori. Like everything else in us, our waking dream comes to fruition through a gradual process of refinement. Far from becoming more intense, more apparently real and hallucinatory, it actually becomes lighter and more volatile, less dense, less opaque; it is less clinging, less viscous. The affective charge associated with particular images becomes weaker, and our internal universe begins to level out and lose its peaks and troughs. In a waking dream which is becoming lighter and lighter, we bring the sleep of our current egotistical condition ever more completely towards fulfilment. In short, the approaching fruition of conscious thought brings it closer in a sense to deep sleep. But conscious thought is also differentiating from sleep while this is going on, as it develops its full subtle intellectual potential. At the non-manifested level the two states draw closer; at the manifested level they seem to become more distinct. There is a hermetic aphorism: 'As above, so below; as below, so above.'

Imaginative activity becomes more subtle, tending towards non-manifestation, although the mind remains awake and continues to function. A 'concentration on nothing' develops beneath the level of attention which is still caught up by images. At this stage my state resembles that of the absent-minded professor; but unlike the latter, who is absent-minded because his attention is concentrated on something in the formal domain, I am absent-minded because my attention is concentrated on something which is formless and neither conceptualized nor conceivable.

The whole imaginative–emotional process becomes lighter. This shows in the way I feel happy for no apparent reason; I am not happy because existence seems good, but existence seems good because I feel happy. The changes which precede satori do not make distress worse; on the contrary they bring about a gradual alleviation of manifested distress. Our fundamental distress is brought into a state of balance and harmony and is neutralized; and this precedes the instantaneous moment when we will see directly and for ever that our distress has always been based on illusion. This is in keeping with the idea that our yearning for fulfilment disappears as we draw near to 'the haven of rest'.

The Western mind often has difficulty understanding the expression 'the Great Doubt', which Zen uses to refer to the inner state immediately preceding satori. It is thought to be a stage where uncertainty and agitation, and hence distress, are at a maximum. In fact it means exactly the opposite.

This needs clarification. We enter the world with a doubt concerning our 'being', and this exercises a controlling influence over all our reactions to the external world. Although I am not often aware of this, the question whether 'I', my self, has 'being' lies behind all my endeavours. I am looking for some definitive confirmation of my own 'being' in everything that I pursue. I treat my metaphysical concerns and the issue of temporal success as though they were identical, and as long as I do so, and try to resolve the metaphysical problem within the realm of Manifestation, I will continue to suffer distress because I am a creature bounded by time. As long as the question is formulated like this, there is always the threat that the answer to my question will be in the negative.

However, as my understanding becomes deeper and the way in which I represent the Universe becomes more subtle, the identification between my metaphysical doubt and the possibility of failure within the framework of time breaks down; my distress diminishes. My uncertainty about my own 'being' is purified and its manifested aspect grows less. It does not diminish in reality but it becomes increasingly non-manifested. By the time the process of distillation has finished, my doubt has become almost perfectly pure. It has become 'Great Doubt' and at the same time it has completely lost its distressing character. Maximum confusion co-exists with maximum clarity, clarity in the absence of any formal object, accompanied by calm and peacefulness. *'Then the individual has the impression of living in a crystal palace, transparent, life-giving, exhilarating and royal;'* at the same time, he is *'like a fool, like an imbecile.'* The great, illusory, question about my being becomes purified, and, with this, it is nullified; and when I finally escape its hold over me, I do so not by finding a satisfactory solution to the 'problem', but by seeing that there never was a problem in the first place.

Let us finally observe how the process of development, which refines our inner world and makes it more subtle, also modifies our perception of *time*. I mentioned earlier that we believe in the reality of time because we are *waiting for* our phenomenal life to be changed in a way that will make good our illusory sense that we are lacking something. The more

217

we yearn for some future change, the more grievously are we troubled by the time problem. We reproach ourselves for letting time slip by, for not knowing how to fill the passing days. As my impulse towards change becomes more subtle, and increasingly non-manifested, my perception of time is modified. Time manifested in the events of my day-to-day life slips away from me at an increasing rate, and I allow it to do so and attach less and less importance to it. My days are less and less filled with things that I can recount or even call to mind. In parallel with this I sense that my impression of time lost is fading away; I am less and less inclined to be frustrated by the clock's inexorable progress. Here as elsewhere the less I strain to grasp, the more I possess. However, let us be clear that this is nothing to do with turning time into a possession, but with a gradual reduction in our poignant sense that time is something we do not have. When we enter the Great Doubt we do not possess time at all, but neither is it something whose loss we feel, because we no longer lay claim to it. Time for us is suspended, and this heralds our reintegration into the eternity of the instant.

Let us now look at why there has to be a gradual process of simplification and refinement, of 'subtilization', before satori occurs. When we read the accounts of their own satori which some Zen masters have left, they describe an inner event which seems to occur in response to an external stimulus. This could be something they see or hear, or it might be something like a fall, or a blow; it is not necessarily an intense experience but it is always something which happens suddenly and alerts attention. Just as any sudden perception will usually arouse the attention of our passive mind, on this occasion its effect is to arouse active mind and bring into consciousness the ability to see things as they really are, to see them in their suchness.

When we try to understand this, there are a couple of mistakes to avoid. First, if I am very attached to the idea of causality, I will imagine that the sound of a bell has *caused* the Zen master's satori. I will speculate about how that might happen and I may be tempted to believe that there are special bells producing special sounds which can reveal their Buddha nature to those who hear them. Second, if I am not interested in childish explanations of this kind, I may conclude that the bell's sound played no part at all and that the Zen master noticed it quite independently of what was taking place inside him.

In reality a perception responding to the external world does play an essential part at the instant of satori, but it does so as a perception of the external world *in general*, while the particular modality involved is irrelevant. The fact is that every perception, at every moment of our life, contains the possibility of satori.

One day a Zen disciple reproached his master for concealing the essential teaching of Zen from him. The master led him into the mountains; the oleanders were in full bloom and the air was heavy with their fragrance. 'Do you smell them?' asked the master. When his disciple answered in the affirmative, he continued: 'There you are then, I have kept nothing hidden from you.'

The possibility of satori is implicit in every perception of the external world because each perception brings into being a *bridge* between self and not-self, *and implies and manifests an identity between the nature of self and not-self*. I have mentioned on a number of occasions that our perception of an external object is the perception of a mental image generated by our contact with the object. But behind the external object and the internal image is a single perception which links the two together. In the Universe everything is vibrating energy. My perception of an object arises when the object's and my own vibrations are combined and united. This can only happen because our vibrations share the same essence; and when they combine, they manifest this essence which is the oneness underlying the multiplicity of phenomena. The perceptual image is produced 'in me', but originates in the Unconscious, or Cosmic Mind, which is not located in any particular place, being present in both the perceived object and the self which perceives. The conscious mental image may belong to me as an individual but the perception which is the principle and origin of the image belongs neither to me nor to the object. At that level there is no distinction between subject and object. It is the conciliating third state, the hypostasis which unites subject and object in a tri-partite synthesis.

So why is it that satori is not released in me by every perception of the external world? Because at present the image in my mind captures my whole attention. In my present belief, my faith, that individual objects *have being*, I am mesmerized by the purely personal aspect of universal perception. I have still failed to understand with all my being Hui-neng's declaration: '*Not one thing is.*' I still believe that *this* is essentially different from *that*. Bias and partiality remain. In this state of ignorance the multiple images which are the elements of my inner universe remain clearly separate and distinct, standing in contrast to one another. Each image is given definition in my eyes by the ways in which it differs from the others. From this perspective no one image can represent, in its 'anonymity' and equivalence to every other image, the totality of my inner universe. This means that no image is 'self', but only an aspect of self. So, under these conditions, everything takes place without apparent union between self and not-self in perception, only a partial identification. Because self has not been integrated, it is only

219

partially identified with not-self. Hence the revelation of total identity, which is satori, does not occur.

This revelation only becomes possible when the process of refinement and simplification has been completed. As my images become more refined and subtle they become less obviously separate and distinct. I still see the ways in which they are different, but these differences no longer seem oppositional; it seems as if I were gradually beginning to sense the unity beneath multiplicity. Discrimination based on opposition and contrast moves increasingly into the non-manifested. In my inner universe true unity is not realized before satori, but as multiplicity becomes non-manifested, my inner state shifts towards simplicity, homogeneity, and mathematical unity (which must not be confused with metaphysical or originating Unity). As impartiality towards my images is realized, it accomplishes the integration of my self. Partial identification with external objects diminishes; and I feel myself increasingly distinct from the external world. Total identification is not preceded by a process of gradually increasing partial identification but rather by its progressive disappearance. To use a spatial analogy, the manifested self gets smaller and smaller, tending towards the dimensionless *point* of geometry. As I approach this point, my representation of the external world is also following the same pattern; it is as if a common area of interpenetration between self and not-self was becoming purified, as though self and not-self were becoming more separate at the same time as their apparent opposition grew less. So two enemies, as their hate for one another diminishes, become increasingly aware of each other as strangers while their opposition to one another is disappearing.

At the end of this gradual evolution my inner universe has achieved homogeneity, not by getting rid of forms, but by abolishing the opposition between forms. Everything becomes equivalent. Now any image can represent the totality of my inner universe adequately. I have become able to experience, in a single perception, not just a partial identification with the not-self, but my total identity with it. All that remains is for not-self to manifest itself; and this is what takes place with the triggering perception reported by those who have experienced satori. In the presence of the self, which is now integrated in a non-manifested totality, not-self makes its appearance, represented by a single phenomenon in which it is totally integrated. A perception then springs forth in which is manifested the totality of self and not-self without any discrimination between them. The totality of the self becomes manifest, but this occurs in the Unity where all things are conciliated and where this self seems to vanish utterly in the very instant of its fulfilment.

# CHAPTER TWENTY-FOUR

# *Humility*

I WANT TO END THIS BOOK by stressing a most important aspect of this theoretical and practical *understanding* which is uniquely able to deliver us from our distress. I refer to understanding the precise nature of *humility* and seeing that it contains the key to our freedom and to our greatness.

Here and now we already live in the state of satori; but we are prevented from experiencing it by the incessant activity of our psychological mechanisms which lock into a vicious circle within us: imaginative–emotional agitation prevents us seeing our Buddha nature, so, believing that we lack our essential reality, we are compelled to *use our imagination* to make up for this illusory deficit.

I believe that I am separated from my own 'being' and I seek to be reunited with it. Because I only know myself as a distinct individual I look for the Absolute as an individual and I want to affirm myself in absolute terms as distinct and separate. The attempt to do this creates and maintains in me the fiction of my own divinity, *my fundamental claim to be omnipotent as an individual, on the phenomenal plane.*

I have compensatory psychological automatisms which operate when I represent things to myself in imagination by selectively attending to my successes and avoiding anything that suggests my impotence. In situations where the evidence for my powerlessness is inescapable they withdraw my claim to omnipotence. I organize things so that I never recognize the equivalence between the external world and myself. I maintain that I am different from the external world, removed from it, above it whenever possible, but below it if necessary. An indisputable requirement of the fiction that I personally am the First Cause of the Universe is that the world depends on me: as far as I am concerned the external world either depends on me or it does not. There is no question of me admitting that the relationship is one of co-dependence. Hence the not-self illusion; if the external world depends on me, it is self; if it does not, it is not-self; I never want to acknowledge it as 'Itself', because I am not aware of the third element, the hypostasis which unites us.

My present inability to experience my own nature, my Buddha nature, as a universal being and not as a distinct and separate individual, compels me to fabricate a continuous and fundamentally deceptive representation of my place in the Universe. Instead of seeing that I am on a level with the external world, I see myself above or below it, 'up on high' or 'down below'. Given this way of looking at things, where above is *Being* and below is *Nothingness*, I am always compelled to strive towards Being. By direct or indirect means, I must struggle to *raise* myself, whether this be in gross, subtle, or 'spiritual' terms.

Before satori all my natural psychological mechanisms are based on my pride, the claims I make for myself as an individual, and my insistence that I should move 'upwards' in some way; and it is my insistence that any progress I make should apply to me as an individual which prevents me recognizing my infinite universal dignity.

It is sometimes difficult to recognize it for what it is, this underlying demand for a privileged status which drives *all* my efforts and *all* my aspirations. I can see it easily enough when other people are the not-self that I want to distinguish myself from. In such cases, a little honesty with myself is enough for me to acknowledge what I am doing. It is quite a different matter when inanimate objects are the not-self from which I wish to maintain my separateness and distinctness, and this is especially true when not-self is represented by that mysterious and illusory entity known as 'Destiny'. But it is fundamentally the same thing: I am exalted by good fortune and humiliated by misfortune.

The same applies to what I perceive as positivity and negativity in the Universe: I am exalted by the one and cast down by the other. When the external world is positive and constructive, this is how I want it to be and it then seems to be dependent on me. When it is negative and destructive (even without affecting me directly), this is how I do not want it to be, and it then seems to be refusing to let itself be dependent on me. *If we really see how deep the foundations of our pride and self-esteem go down, we understand that anything we can imagine enjoying satisfies our pride, while any kind of suffering wounds it.* We understand then that our insistence on our separate individuality and the claims we make on that basis dominate all our affective automatisms, in other words our whole life. Only Independent Intelligence escapes its control.

These egotistical pretensions of mine which direct me 'upwards' have to find expression in incessant imaginative activity, because they are delusive and fly in the face of reality. If I take an objective look at the whole of my life as an individual, it resembles the fiery trajectory of a rocket: its ascent corresponds to intra-uterine life where everything is in a state of preparation and as yet unmanifested; the point where the firework explodes is birth; the expanding fountain of light represents life's 'ascent', during which our organism develops its fullest potential; falling back to earth in a shower of short-lived sparks represents old age and death. At first sight the rocket's life seems to be growth followed by decline. But in fact its whole span is one of disintegrating energy; it is in a state of *decline* from start to finish.

This is how it is for me as an individual. From the moment of conception my psycho-somatic organism is the manifestation of a process of disintegration, a continual descent. The moment I am conceived, I begin to die. The energy I start with gets used up in a variety of more or less spectacular manifestations, and decreases all the time. Cosmic reality completely contradicts my inflated claims on what is 'above'; as an individual being, all my dealings are with 'below'.

The whole problem of human distress is summed up in the problem of humiliation. To be cured of distress is to be freed from all possibility of humiliation. When I am humiliated, what is the source of my humiliation? Is it recognizing my own impotence? No, that is insufficient on its own. It is derived from the fact that I try in vain to avoid seeing my real impotence. *Impotence itself does not cause humiliation; it is caused by the blow to my fantasies of omnipotence when they collide against the reality of the world.* I am not humiliated because the external world repudiates me, but because I fail to annihilate its negation of me. The real cause of my distress is never in the external world: it only lies in the claims I put forward which then smash up against the barrier of reality. I fail to understand this when I complain that I have been injured by the barrier throwing itself at me. But I have hurt myself against the barrier; my suffering is a result of what I did. When I no longer insist on making misguided claims, nothing will ever injure me again.

I may add that the distress I experience from humiliation expresses the painful tension generated by the inner conflict between my tendency to see myself as omnipotent and my tendency to acknowledge the concrete reality in which my omnipotence is denied. Humiliation and distress occur when I am torn between subjective demand and objective observation, between lie and truth, between biased and impartial ways of representing my situation in the Universe. Only when my objectivity triumphs over my subjectivity, and reality vanquishes dream will I be rescued from the permanent threat of distress.

*In our desire to escape from distress we look for doctrines of salvation and seek out gurus. But the true guru is not far away, our guru is right in front of our eyes, continuously offering to teach us: it is reality as it is; our guru is our daily life.* The evidence we need to save us is right in front of our eyes, in the obvious fact that we are not omnipotent and that our claim is fundamentally absurd and impossible, hence illusory, non-existent. It lies in the obvious fact that there is nothing to fear for hopes which are without reality, in the fact that my feet have always been planted on the ground, so there is no possibility of falling, nor any reason for vertigo.

If I am humiliated, it is because the automatisms controlling my imagination succeed in neutralizing the vision of reality and keeping the facts at bay. I do not gain anything from the beneficial teaching with which I am constantly provided because I am adept at contriving to avoid the experience of humiliation. Should some humiliating circumstance arise, concealing within itself a marvellous opportunity for my initiation, I perceive it as a threat and my imagination immediately makes strenuous efforts to ward it off. It struggles against the illusory displacement 'downwards' and strives hard to restore my usual state of complacent arrogance in which I find temporary relief, accompanied, of course, by the inevitability of new suffering. In short I am constantly defending myself against something which offers me salvation and I fight every inch of the way to protect the very source of my misfortune. All my inner work tends to obstruct satori because it is directed towards a loftier plane, while satori is waiting for me down here. With good reason, Zen maintains that '*satori comes upon us without warning, when we have exhausted all the resources of our being.*'

All this seems to suggest that humility is the 'way', and in a certain sense this is true, though not if we mean by this a systematic discipline. As I am at present I cannot make any effort which will not, directly or indirectly, aspire to something higher. All efforts to master humility can only result in a false humility in which I am still engaged in egotistical self-exaltation by means of the idol I have created for myself. *It is absolutely impossible for me to humble myself, in other words to reduce by my own efforts the intensity with which I claim 'being' for myself.* What I can and must do if I want to put a definitive end to my distress, is reduce my resistance to what concrete reality has to teach: I have to let myself be humbled by the unavoidable facts of the cosmic order.

Even in this there is nothing direct which I can *do* or *stop doing*. I will stop opposing the constructive and harmonizing benefits of humiliation in so far as I have understood that what is truly good for me is paradoxically to be found where I have hitherto thought to find harm. As long as I have not understood, my gaze is directed upwards. When I have understood, my gaze is not directed downwards – for, once again, it is impossible for me to aspire downwards, because any efforts directed downwards would transform 'down' into 'up' – but what happens is that I aspire 'upwards' with less intensity and to that extent benefit from my humiliations. I resist less, so I recognize when I am

224

humiliated more often. I recognize that all my negative states are really humiliations, and that I have managed so far to call them by other names.

I am then able to feel humiliated and unhappy with my mind free of all images except the image of the state itself, and I am also able to hold myself unmoving in this state, since my understanding has abolished my reflex attempts to escape. Once I can do this I realize to my surprise that this is 'the haven of rest', the only safe harbour, the only place in the world where I can be perfectly safe. My holding on to this state confronts my natural inclination to reject it, and this enables the Conciliating Principle to come into play: opposites neutralizing one another; my suffering vanishes, together with part of my fundamental demand. I feel close to the ground, to 'below', to real humility (which is not accepting inferiority, but giving up 'vertical' thinking in which I always saw myself as being above or below).

These inner phenomena are accompanied by a feeling of sadness, of 'night'. This feeling is very different from distress because a great calm prevails within it. It is during these sombre moments of tranquillity and freedom from tension that the processes of what I have called 'inner alchemy' take place. The 'old' person disintegrates, making way for the 'new' one to develop. The individual dies so that the universal may be born.

It is not possible to master humility by direct means; this can only be achieved by making use of humiliation. All suffering changes us by humiliating us. However, there are two fundamentally different ways in which this can happen: if I fight against humiliation this will be destructive and make my inner disharmony worse; if I let it act without resisting it, its effect will be to create inner harmony. Letting it act is simply a matter of acknowledging to oneself that one is humiliated.

From our present viewpoint Being presents as the unconciliated pair, zero and infinity. Our nature drives us to identify primarily with the infinity, which we try to attain by continually moving ever 'higher'. This is a hopeless enterprise; however high we rise within the realm of the finite, infinity will remain forever unattainable. The way to 'Being' is not infinity, but zero, which, being nothing, is not a way.

The idea that humility is not a 'way' is so important that I want to take one last look at it. Should I fail to understand this point, I am bound to make the mistake of suppressing some manifestation of my fundamental demand in my everyday life. I might for instance confine myself to some mediocre situation in society, etc. In other words I would be avoiding humiliations instead of making use of them. Simulated acts of humility are never more than just that. The point is not that I should be altering the way my fundamental claim operates, but that I should be using the factual material which comes my way from the humiliating disappointments which are its inevitable consequence. If I use artificial measures to avoid struggling against not-self, I deprive myself of those indispensable teachings which I would otherwise gain from my defeats.

It does not always say so explicitly, but Zen is centred on the idea of humility. Throughout Zen literature we can see how the masters, with ingenious kindness, subjected their students to intense humiliation when they considered the time to be right. In any case, whether humiliation comes from a master or from the ultimate experience of failure in oneself, satori is always triggered in an instant when humility comes to fruition, confronted at last with the obvious absurdity of all striving in pursuit of misguided and illusory claims. Let us remember that the 'nature of things' is our best, fondest, and most humbling of teachers; it surrounds us with its attentive help. The only task incumbent upon us is that we should understand reality and let ourselves be transformed by it.

# THE REALIZATION
# OF THE SELF

# Introduction

*The Realization of the Self* is essentially about the human condition, the possibility of its metaphysical transformation, and the conditions on which this transformation depends.

You may be surprised to find that the book begins with ideas about how the cosmos comes into being, which take their inspiration from traditional metaphysics. But mankind is part of the cosmos and has the same origin. It will become apparent as we proceed that knowledge about these matters can shed unexpected and paradoxical light on human functioning (in other words, it contradicts current beliefs).

The issue that interests us most – in our present condition – is what concerns us as individuals, and in particular what can deliver us from our painful bondage.

So I hope that you will not be put off by the abstract metaphysical concepts with which this book begins, because they are essential for insight into our present condition.

**Part One**

*of*

*The Realization of the Self*

*Traditional Metaphysics*

# 1. Metaphysical Insights

Over the millennia people have sought to understand the nature of the universe. Of these the most intelligent realized that they perceived everything within the constraints imposed by the structure of their sense organs and not as it was in reality. So they applied the term 'phenomena' (from the Greek verb *phainein*, to appear) to everything that they could see, hear, touch, etc., and then went on to speculate about '*That*' which revealed itself through these 'appearances', about the nature of the Invisible which manifested as the visible.

Many of these seekers, those whose metaphysical intuition was most highly developed, thought that the origin of all things was One, that a single Principle was the source of the multiplicity of phenomena, and that this multiplicity was its manifestation. This discrimination between Principle and Manifestation forms the basis for traditional metaphysics, the sacred science of what lies beyond the physical world.

The first texts we know of which deal with metaphysics in its pure form, traditional metaphysics, were compiled in India so long ago that we are unable to date their origin precisely. These are the texts known as the Vedanta.


# 2. The Validity of Intellect in the Domain of Metaphysics

Once we discriminate between Manifestation, what we can perceive, and the One Principle from which it originates, we are faced by a question: is reflective thought capable of reaching beyond what we can perceive, beyond what we can experience concretely? Our intellect can only know things through the medium of language, which is formal in the sense that it is composed of verbal forms, and is therefore clearly an instrument well suited to our knowledge of the perceptible phenomenal world, which is itself also formal. But can we legitimately use our intellect to explore the non-formal metaphysical world?

I believe we can, providing we know how to treat the conclusions we come to in this domain.

We say that every word *expresses* something; and in itself a word can be likened to a piece of fruit from which the juice has been expressed, when what remains is the skeleton, the structural component which gives it its form. In a sense, every word is the skeleton of what it designates; it indicates, but does not show. Where the perceptible domain is concerned, words behave as though they portray what they refer to because memory has forged a link between the verbal skeleton of the word and the flesh of lived experience. But this does not apply to words expressing metaphysical ideas because we have never experienced directly in our lives what it is they refer to, so memory cannot alter their nature and they remain verbal skeletons. It is easy to look at a metaphysical text and see nothing more than an exercise in verbal juggling where the words have no true content.

Yet it is still possible to speak validly about the metaphysical domain. Though the words used do not refer to anything we can *represent* to ourselves, we are nonetheless able to *conceive of* their meaning. Intellect can conceive of what we cannot perceive. People reading metaphysical texts who are sufficiently endowed with *metaphysical intuition* will grasp their meaning through their verbal expression even though they cannot represent it to themselves. When Jesus says: 'He that hath ears to hear, let him hear,' he is inviting his listeners to understand what his words could only suggest; and when he says: 'Blessed are they that have not seen, and yet have believed,' he is affirming that we can sense intuitively the self-evident truth of certain ideas which are accessible to the intellect but cannot be represented by any perceptible image. Metaphysical ideas can be dealt with using words from this domain, but symbols are also often necessary, or parables, of which there are many examples in the Gospels.

Intuition, however, is a very individual faculty, so it is impossible for two people to have exactly the same intuitive idea. Such ideas present themselves but cannot impose themselves on everyone in the same way, and they cannot be demonstrated logically by starting from premises which everyone accepts, as happens in the physical sciences. So there will always be differences of opinion where metaphysical ideas are concerned and many people will consider them worthless.

Ch'an* uses an excellent symbol, a finger pointing at the moon, which both shows us where it is and invites us to look. This is an allegory in which the moon represents Absolute Consciousness, which is non-formal and so inexpressible, while the finger corresponds to the formal

---

* The name 'Zen' is often mistakenly applied in the West to this initiatory teaching originating in the Far East. When Boddhidarma travelled to the Far East towards the beginning of the 7th century AD to convey the Buddha's teaching, he went to China. There Buddhism was understood and adapted to the Chinese character under the name of Ch'an, which is the purest form of this teaching. In due course, Ch'an reached Japan via Korea and gave rise to numerous Japanese Buddhist sects, whence Zen. The fact is that those we refer to as 'the old masters' were Chinese and lived in China. Zen soon became degraded and when Europeans go nowadays to a Zen monastery they do not come across the pure teaching of Ch'an. So in this book I prefer to speak of Ch'an rather than Zen. HB

presentation of the initiatory teaching, which can be expressed in spoken or written words. Ch'an has always affirmed the usefulness and even necessity of formal teaching. At the same time it has always warned its disciples against the all too human tendency to 'mistake the pointing finger for the moon' and idolize words and texts, in other words to believe that what they set forth is Absolute Truth.

So when you read any text dealing with metaphysical ideas, you need to be aware that nothing you read is true from the point of view of the Absolute. Every statement you read should be preceded by: 'Given the limitations of our understanding, this is how things seem.'

It is essential to be reminded at this stage that we should be aware of the dangers of language. There will be other reminders later on, such are the dangers inherent in our use of words and the multiplicity of meanings we attach to them. This is particularly true in relation to the Absolute Principle: it is non-formal, beyond the domain of form, so no word, being formal, can convey an adequate idea of it. Nonetheless we can still investigate this subject without the use of such terms hindering our work providing we have a metaphysical intuition of what it is that they are hinting at.


## 3. The Noumenal Domain

The central concept in traditional metaphysics is that of 'Being' as opposed to 'existence' (which comes from the Latin *ex(s)istere*, meaning to emerge, appear, be visible or manifest). But the Vedanta* goes beyond Being to an ultimate which it calls 'Non-Being' (in other words, the Principle and Origin of Being) or *Emptiness*. R. Guénon[†] defines Emptiness as 'the infinitude of possibilities of manifestation and non-manifestation' and Being as 'the infinitude of possibilities of manifestation'. So Being is not the creator, but the creative potential at a level above creation. Below Being is the Creative Principle, to which many names have been given: Brahma, God, Jehovah (from the Hebrew, meaning 'that which must not be named'), Allah, etc.

This hierarchy is not composed of three distinct entities, but represents three aspects of the Absolute, decreasing in fullness from

---

* The end texts of the Hindu scriptures known as the Veda. They include the *Upanishads*, the *Brahma Sutras*, and the *Bhagavadgita*.

[†] René Guénon (Abd al-Wahid Yahya) (1886–1951). French writer whose work spans a wide range of subjects from metaphysics and symbolism to the critique of the modern world and traditional sciences.

Emptiness to the Creative Principle. I will often combine these three ideas into one, that of the *Noumenon*, which means 'that which can be conceived of but not perceived'. This term refers equally to Emptiness, Being, and Creator. The following diagram represents the situation schematically:

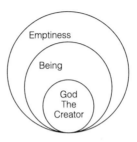

Metaphysical transformation of the human psyche is the individual becoming aware of identity with the Noumenon in its totality, in other words not just with God, but also with Being and Emptiness. Meister Eckhart distinguished God from the Godhead which for him was infinitely superior, and he affirmed that each one of us can realize our identity with the Godhead. Is not the liberated Buddha said to have exclaimed:' I am infinitely superior to Brahma'?

I had to say a few words about Being and Emptiness, but from now on our main concern will be the Creative Principle while we consider the origins of the cosmos. Mankind is part of the cosmos, and the human state forms part of the multiple states of existence. I intend to give an account of the human psyche in its usual, non-liberated state, and describe the obstacles to liberation and how we can reach our goal despite them.

I will now discuss the Noumenon in its inferior aspect as God the Creator. Then I will turn to the phenomenal world and we will see how Creator and creation are linked and the way in which this affects us as human beings.

## 4. The Creative Principle

God is the Unknowable and it is impossible to speak directly of him. But we can conceive of some of his infinite attributes.

He is *formless*: form reflects the spatial relationship between points and cannot exist in the noumenal domain, which is non-spatial.

He is not *located*: by virtue of his immanence he is present throughout his manifestation and nowhere in particular. Through his immanence and transcendence, in other words in his totality, he is the divine nature of man, his Absolute Reality. He is what we refer to as the Self to distinguish him from the individual self. Ch'an expresses this by saying: 'You seek God in vain throughout the whole cosmos if you do not seek him in man.' This despite the fact that the Self is only present in man as a potential state before realization has been achieved.

He is *apersonal*: God can be described as the One Absolute Personality but, given the way we use the expressions 'a person' and 'several persons' in which each person is limited, God has to be considered apersonal.

God is *limitless or infinite* in a precise sense. The term 'infinite' is used wrongly in mathematics, which belongs to the world of phenomena, because every mathematical value is limited. All one can do is pursue an unending succession of expanding or diminishing numbers, but this just amounts to pushing a limit further back without ever eliminating it. So one should really speak of the *mathematical indefinite*, but not of the infinite in mathematics. We can conceive of divine infinity but we cannot represent it. The liberated individual does not see the infinite Noumenon but knows that he or she is it.

God is *eternal*: this introduces the question of Time. We have two words available, 'time' and 'duration', which we tend in practice to use as synonyms with a clear preference for 'time'. India also has two words but they are used differently and kept separate: *Kali* is eternal Time and *kala* is duration. God *is* in eternal time; he had no beginning and will have no ending. In manifestation created things necessarily come into being and disappear, and their existence takes place in duration. But the total cosmos is eternal, with neither beginning nor end. God did not create manifestation on a particular day nor will a day come when he will stop creating it.

Duration consists of the past, the present instant and the future. Time itself is the eternal instant and we therefore sometimes speak of the eternity of the instant.

These attributes I have described apply to all three aspects of the Noumenon. I am now going to speak about the specific nature of Being as creator, in other words of God.

## 5. The Nature of God

'God' is the name we have given to the Creative Principle. It represents Being as it manifests itself. It is a mistake to speak of God's existence; God '*is*' and transcends everything in manifestation, which exists. As

Hui-neng said, 'Not one thing is', in other words created things only exist but *are* not; only the Noumenon *is*.

The problem with the word 'God', as with all the other names which have been given to the Creative Principle, is that it evokes the idea of a person and so tends to personify the Metaphysical Principle and Origin. All religions have fallen into this trap and they are all misguided because of it. Every 'religion' (the word comes from *re-* plus *ligare*, to bind) invites us to bind ourselves to God as though God and man were two things being or existing in the same way and only separated from each other as different aspects of the same nature. But since God is the Absolute Whole, nothing *is* except Him; and if one thinks of mankind as *existing*, as emanating from God, it is inconceivable that it could make its way back to God against the direction of the creative outpouring by means of any kind of upward movement in direct relationship to the Divine Source.

We will see that it is possible for us to become aware that the immanent Self within us is identical to the absolute Self and that we are in that sense ourselves God. But *identity* is not the same as *relationship*, nor is it *union*. This mistake is very obvious in Christianity in which man stays other than God in Paradise, permitted only to contemplate Him, and indeed resurrected in his previous bodily form from the phenomenal domain.

When people believe in God, however subtle their image of Him, the God they imagine is an anthropomorphic figure, a being with all the characteristics of a human psyche, thinking, feeling and intending just as we do.

I have been reluctant to use the word 'God' in this book precisely because of the totally erroneous meaning which we have given it in the Judaeo-Christian West. But I finally decided to use it in the hope that there are people for whom 'God is not dead', who will be able to restore this word to its correct metaphysical meaning.

God is 'That' who said to Moses, '*Ego sum qui sum*,' 'I am That I am (or That which is).' The definition of God is there, in all its simplicity. We can express this in everyday language by saying that God does nothing except Be, that He is sufficient unto Himself in Being. Immutable, unchanging in Himself, He does not act; He is what Chinese metaphysics refers to as 'Non-action'.

What I have just said about God, God as He is and not God as He manifests Himself through creation, might well suggest the image of a supreme 'Thing', something fixed which, being in Itself and by Itself, would be hovering in splendid isolation above and unrelated to the movement of the cosmos. This mistaken view, like so many others, originates in the fact that language is constructed to indicate, study and understand the phenomenal world and its formal appearances, this apparent multiplicity in which we experience the illusion of things being separate entities. In reality the Noumenon is the one and only Entity. It cannot be described as distinct and separate because there is nothing not included in it from which it could be distinguished.

Once again, however, we can use our intellect to conceive of the Noumenal world and enable us to speak of it. But you must remember that whatever I go on to say about God can only express intellectual views which are based on discriminations. Abstract ideas which rely on a discriminating process to give them a separate identity should not be taken literally and thought of as referring to distinct entities. Nothing in a correct initiatory teaching, no phrase, can claim to be a fragment of Absolute Truth, because that is One, just as the Absolute is One. Absolute Truth is the intellectual attribute of the originating One, the Absolute Whole. It is the *Cosmic Mind* of Ch'an. Because it is an aspect of the Whole, it is not made up of constituent elements and so it cannot be broken down into fragments. But when we reflect on these matters we can only understand the issues they raise by analyzing them into subsidiary concepts and the relationships between them.

So any phrase we use to express what we have understood intuitively is a product of this analytic process and the representation it provides is not endowed with Absolute Reality but reflects a reality which relates to the way our intellect functions verbally and formally. Though this is a relative reality, it is not without value and we can build on it with confidence in our search for knowledge. This is how the finger accurately pointing at the moon gradually emerges, and it is the completion of this guiding structure which may one day enable us to experience the inexpressible reality of our Buddha nature, our divinity. This experience is strictly individual and it is incommunicable because there is no possible way of expressing it in words. As you read what follows do not imagine that I am describing the way things are in the Absolute, but simply that my account contributes to the formal knowledge which is a pre-requisite if there should ever take place one day that sudden transcendence of our mind and the irreversible experience of the fact that we do not know Absolute Truth, but that we *are* it.

Please forgive me for these further precautionary comments but they are necessary before we explore what metaphysical intuition can reveal to us about the nature of Absolute Being or God within the constraints imposed by the use of language.

I have said that God is One, though One is not used here in a quantitative sense but to indicate the quality of uniqueness, the One Alone.

The Vedanta prefers to use the expression 'Not-Two'. When we say that God is One we mean that there *is* nothing outside of or other than Him. 'One' means the Absolute Whole.

If we were only to imagine God as an all-comprehending Wholeness our intuition could add nothing to its revelation of Him as the One which contains the All. But God has infinite attributes or aspects and it is from this point of view that our intuition will teach us about Him to the best of our limited means. The divine attributes are not elements or parts of God as an aggregate since God is the All, not a total. They are divine aspects which present themselves to our mind according to the way we represent God to ourselves.

## God is His Own Cause

Since there is nothing outside or apart from God, He is not caused. In other words nothing created Him. He is sometimes referred to as the *Uncreated*, though Spinoza* said that He is His own cause, that He is *That whose essence necessarily implies existence*, in other words *That for Whom non-existence is inconceivable.*

## God is Spirit

These two equivalent concepts of God as *causa sui* and *uncreated* lead us to see Him as *self-created*. In other words, above and prior to what we call Creation, the divine, originating source of creation is God Himself. 'Uncreated' and 'self-creating' are not incompatible attributes: one means 'not created by anything else' and the other 'created by Himself'. This inevitably raises the question of how God creates Himself.

When we think about *how* things are created in general, there are two components involved: one of these comes immediately before the thing created appears, and consists of some kind of constructive activity. This activity at first sight seems responsible for creating the product. But 'how' also contains a second element which is *conceptual*. Creating something depends on having some prior idea of what is required and it is this idea which is really responsible for what is produced by the activity.

If God is conceived of as a Being sufficient unto Itself, Non-Acting, He is self-evidently not engaged in creation of a kind which would

---

* Baruch Spinoza (1632–77). Dutch Jewish philosopher who made crucial contributions to every major philosophical topic. His *Ethics,* published posthumously, is described as one of the most influential works in Western philosophy.

require some kind of intermediary activity. This is inconceivable because it would imply the existence of a mechanism between God and Himself. Divine Creation does not involve any activity of the kind we envisage in our own acts of creation. *It consists of a pure conception of the thing created.* God creates through thought without action. In other words, God is Absolute Consciousness aware of itself. God is pure and absolute spirit.

## God is Absolute Consciousness aware of itself

I want to emphasize this point. When it is said that God is His own cause, this means that He is thought into being by Himself, and so is aware of Himself. Since everything is caused (created) in the mind of God, God is His own cause by the same process of divine conception. This line of reasoning leads us to the obvious conclusion that God must be absolute Consciousness aware of itself.

## God is the only free cause

God is the unique self-creating cause from which all things take their origin. He is the unique *free* cause because he exists by the mere necessity of His own nature. So Spinoza said *'God is the only free cause.'* *

## The Divine Triad †

God causing or caused by Himself, and God bringing Himself into being or being brought into being by His thought illustrate the active and passive aspects of God. The divine Absolute, however, incorporates both aspects and conciliates them within a triangular unity. The following two diagrams clarify this:

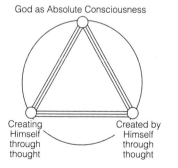

God as Absolute Consciousness

Creating Himself through thought

Created by Himself through thought

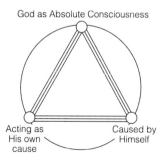

God as Absolute Consciousness

Acting as His own cause

Caused by Himself

See p. 240 for the * and † footnotes.

The annotations at the corners of these triangles require no further comment. The circles surrounding the triangles represent the fact that the Divine Absolute, which incorporates all Its aspects or attributes within Its unity, also incorporates all the active and passive aspects of God which are accessible to our understanding. These aspects of the One God are identical with one another inasmuch as they share in the divine identity. The divine Triad is grasped by our minds as tri-partite but *exists* as One. The triple lines which connect the corners represent the algebraic triple line of identity ($A \equiv A$).

A third way of looking at the divine Triad is expressed by Spinoza when he says *'God loves Himself infinitely'*.* It is difficult at first for us to understand his use of the word 'love' here because it is a word which evokes the human forms of love with which we are familiar, and these are relative loves because they have the relative nature of the phenomenal world in which they occur. God's love for Himself is an aspect of His absolute nature so Spinoza is referring here to Absolute Love. The question is, how are we to understand this?

We will start by considering what we imagine ideal love to be. Love is essentially *attraction*; the lover is attracted towards the beloved. More accurately it is love as a cosmic force which moves the lover towards the beloved. Where human love is concerned, the impulse towards the other takes the form of wanting the other's existence, of wanting to confirm their existence (either by observing it or contemplating the idea of their existence), and of affirming their existence by encouraging and supporting it in every possible way. It is obvious that someone who loves like this wants for the other what the other wants for himself. Jesus said *'Thou shalt love thy neighbour as thyself.'*[†] Two people in love often dream of becoming one. Identity being impossible in this situation, the force of love drives the lover to identify with the beloved.

We will now turn from the restricted domain of human loves and

---

*Notes from page 239*

* *Ethics, First Part, Concerning God Prop.18, Corollary 2:* 'Hence it follows that God alone is a free cause. For God alone exists from the mere necessity of his own nature (*Prop. 11*; and *Coroll. 1, Prop. 14*), and by the mere necessity of his nature he acts (*Prop. 17*). And therefore (*Def. 7*) he is the only free cause. Q.e.d. (from *Spinoza's Ethics*, 1967, London, Dent).

[†] This is a triangular triad which should not be confused with the linear Holy Trinity of Catholicism. HB

*Notes to page 240*

* Op. cit.: *First Part, Concerning the Power of the Intellect or Human Freedom.* Prop. 35. 'God loves himself with infinite intellectual love.'

[†] Romans 13:9; Gal. 5:14; James 2:8.

consider the attractive force of love as a general cosmic factor. The law of gravity or attraction is a cosmic law in which the idea of love as a generalized phenomenon is manifested. In French the word for a magnet, a piece of metal which attracts iron filings, is *aimant*, 'loving', just as if the magnet wanted to be reunited with the filings. All the celestial bodies are drawn to another, to be united, and it is only the centrifugal force of their rotation which prevents this happening.

Absolute love is love as an attribute of the divine Absolute. It is difficult for us to have an adequate idea of it because 'infinite' is an ambiguous word. When Spinoza speaks of the infinite love which God has for Himself, 'infinite' does not refer to its intensity because the word is not used quantitatively in this phrase. When 'infinite' refers to a divine attribute its meaning is always purely qualitative as in the Infinite nature of God and it has nothing in common with the mathematical indefinite.

This is a metaphysical fact which invalidates the idea of attraction, despite its fundamental explanatory power in relation to the investigation of love in the phenomenal domain. All attributes or aspects of God the One, because they share in this oneness, form a single Whole and each one of them, together with all the others, only make one Whole. They are all of the same nature, and this nature is always identical to itself. We may describe them in different terms but these differences only reflect the viewpoint from which our intellect studies the Divine Identity. So 'God loving Himself' and 'God loved by Himself' are identical though they are formulated differently. We can express this by saying that there is a metaphysically infinite attraction between these two aspects which are separated by our analytic thought processes. This infinite attraction is equivalent to identity and it re-establishes the identity of what analytic thought had artificially divided.

A similar process makes us draw a distinction between these two aspects and the 'God as Absolute Love' who conciliates them in their identity within the Trinity.

Our formal intellect functions in a way which makes these discriminations unavoidable and they are therefore artificial, but they are not unreal. They are real relative to how we are constructed and we are right to use them in our quest for understanding.

Divine love can be represented as as in the diagram overleaf.

We will now consider the Divine Triad in general and the various modalities in which it presents to us. We have distinguished three terms – active, passive, and the Absolute which conciliates them – and these make it clear that God, Being which is sufficient unto Itself, is not a sort of inert and motionless block. At first we are inclined to approach God's non-immobility with the same ideas that we are used to in the world of phenomena, which reflect our experience. So we attribute a special role to each of the three terms of the Triad, with the active aspect engaging with the passive and the latter welcoming this movement towards it. Meanwhile the Divine Absolute would be keeping them together in absolute harmony.

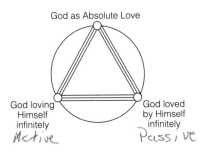

God as Absolute Love

God loving Himself infinitely
*Active*

God loved by Himself infinitely
*Passive*

This approach is strictly justifiable only if we were to introduce each description with the phrase 'It seems to us as if. . . ' and only providing we do not assume that 'active' and 'passive' mean the same as they do in the phenomenal world. From a strictly metaphysical viewpoint we can only speak of the *non-immobility of divine immutability*. If we also replace the negative 'Not-Acting' with its corresponding positive 'All-Powerful', we see God as Infinite Energy, originating, contained in Himself. When we then come to consider Creation we will see that this is in some sense a shining forth of this Divine Energy.

But we have to make the best use we can of the imperfect instrument which is language, and so we will speak of the active and passive aspects of God while striving to maintain a purely abstract usage and not fall into the pitfalls inherent in imaginative representation.

The passive aspect of God presents as immobile and not dynamic. It is the principle underlying what I will later refer to as the *immanence* of God in all things created, immanence signifying 'residence', hence non-movement. The active aspect of God is dynamic and is the principle underlying what I will call God's *transcendence* in relation to His manifestation. Obviously if one thinks of God in Himself, dwelling in Himself, then He is not yet immanent or transcendent in relation to anything, but immanence and transcendence already form part of His attributes, latent attributes which will become actualized in cosmic Creation. If we think of the active and passive aspects of God in relation to Creation, they can be referred to as masculine and feminine because it is the marriage of these two aspects which is the source of cosmic Creation.

**Part Two**

*of*

*The Realization of the Self*

*Cosmic and Human Phenomenology*

## 6. Are Phenomena Real?

Manifestation consists of the totality of all phenomena. Let me remind you that 'phenomenon' signifies 'appearance' and that our perceptions depend on the structure of our sense organs. It can seem a small step from this to the claim that our perception is illusory since the thing perceived is illusory, and we may be tempted to take it. In fact a number of people have misinterpreted the Hindu concept of *Maya* and maintained that phenomena are unreal. But how can we suppose that any kind of unreality could issue out of Absolute Reality? Maya certainly signifies illusion, but what is illusory? It is not the phenomenon which we perceive, but our unqualified belief in the absolute reality of our perceptions. The true choice here does not lie between *reality and unreality* but between *Absolute Reality and relative reality*. What I perceive and the thing perceived are real for me, relative to me. Even if I dream of a tiger when I am asleep, that tiger is not unreal, but is as real to me as if I saw a tiger when I was awake. After all we only perceive anything through the intermediary of the image which our brain generates when we see it or imagine it, and this image certainly exists. In our everyday practical life we have good reason to modify our behaviour in the light of the information provided by our sense organs.

## 7. Why Does God Manifest Himself?

That Creation exists is an obvious fact not open to dispute, known to us through our senses. But we can reasonably ask why God manifests Himself. If we think of God in Himself, He is One alone, the All, and perfectly sufficient to Himself, so in other words He has no need of anything which might form an extension of Him, as for instance the sun's rays represent a kind of extension of that body.

> *Midi là-haut, Midi sans mouvement*
> *En soi se pense et convient à soi-même,*
> *Tête complète et parfait diadème, . . .*
> P. Valéry*

---

\* Noon above, Noon without movement
  In itself conceives itself and is sufficient to itself,
  Complete head and perfect diadem . . .
  From *Le Cimetière Marin* in *Charmes* (1922)

Yet if Manifestation *is* not, it certainly *exists* as an emanation from Being and is intuited through the senses by mankind. Does the phenomenal world originate contingently or necessarily from God? Is it possible that Creation is dreamed up by God, and need not be?

God is One and, though the concept of God may incorporate the idea of three elements in the Absolute Principle and its active and passive aspects, these are reunited in Him by an infinite attraction or love. So the divine Triad includes an infinite noumenal energy which represents a potential outpouring of radiant energy, and every noumenal possibility or potential must of necessity be realized. This means that the divine outpouring of energy into the Cosmos which manifests it is necessary and not contingent. In other words, it cannot not be.

In any case the reasons people ask 'Why does God manifest Himself' are generally irrational, pre-supposing that divine and human psychology are similar! Why do we do things? Because we wish to do them for some reason or other. But it makes no sense to attribute any kind of wish to God because that would imply that He might lack something. Given that He is the All, the Whole, this would be completely illogical.

God creates Manifestation because His nature entails that he do so. This in brief is the best way of replying to a question which should not have been asked in the first place.

## 8. Two Ways of Thinking About the Cosmos

When we speak about Manifestation, we immediately think about the created things which we perceive around us. Because of our egotism we see ourselves as the masterpiece and sovereign of all creation. We make use, often foolishly, of whatever we find for our personal convenience as if it had been created expressly for this purpose.

But Manifestation, which includes Mankind, is above all the way in which the Absolute Principle manifests itself, and we should begin by asking ourselves what its purpose is for God, what it is 'in His eyes'. This needs to be done before we investigate how we see it and what scientific research reveals. These are two entirely different points of view.

The Absolute Principle becomes manifest through the Universe or Cosmos. What it creates directly must be something absolute, perfect and eternal like itself. I will call this 'thing', which has the same noumenal nature as God, the Noumenal Cosmos. (I will deal later with how the phenomena contained within the Cosmos are created mediately or indirectly).

The Noumenal Cosmos* is eternal. From our point of view, in which time has duration, we would say that it had no beginning and will have no ending, that it always has been and always will be like the Principle of which it is the necessary Manifestation.

It shares in divine perfection. It is a perfect equilibrium among an indefinite number of disequilibria whose conciliatory principle it is. Everywhere and always the phenomenal world is in movement. All movement presupposes an imbalance of energy: waterfalls need a difference in level; electricity will only flow with a voltage difference, etc. All these states of disequilibrium occur everywhere all the time and the world could not survive as it does unless they were perfectly conciliated. We also observe that there are two forces at work in the world of phenomena, constructive and destructive respectively. If they were not in perfect balance the world not survive, and yet it does. This is true of the eternal Cosmos, not of the created things it contains such as our little earth, which appeared one day and will disappear in due course on some other day.

So in God's eyes Manifestation is the Noumenal Cosmos, perfect and eternal. It is a divine attribute, an aspect of noumenon. It is Being as it is manifested. We can now understand that God's view of His Manifestation is totally different from how we see it as humans. For God the Cosmos is His own splendour, formless and one.

For mankind the Cosmos is an immense aggregate of phenomena among which we ourselves are numbered. We are only able to perceive created things through our sense organs. The mistake most people make is to believe that things *are absolutely* as perceived.

Manifestation may be His absolute splendour as far as God is concerned but it is radically different for mankind. Ch'an illustrates this with an ingenious allegory:† it invites us to imagine a piece of brocade made of silk and embroidered with gold and silver. The material has two surfaces, front and back, which are quite different from one another, and it symbolizes Manifestation presenting its right side to God and its

---

* HB's expression is *le Tout Cosmique Un*, which translates literally as 'the One Cosmic Whole'.

† Compare p. 56 in *The Zen Doctrine of No-Mind* (D. T. Suzuki, 1979, Rider, London): '*It is like appreciating a fine piece of brocade. On the surface there is an almost bewildering confusion of beauty, and the connoisseur fails to trace the intricacies of the threads. But as soon as it is turned over all the intricate beauty and skill is revealed. Prajñā consists in this turning over. The eye has hitherto followed the surface of the cloth, which is indeed the only side ordinarily allowed us to survey. Now the cloth is abruptly turned over; the course of the eyesight is suddenly interrupted; no continuous gazing is possible. Yet by this interruption, or rather disruption, the whole scheme of life is suddenly grasped; there is the 'seeing into one's self-nature'.*

wrong side to mankind. Its right side is divine splendour but the wrong side is composed of threads which seem to be arranged chaotically – it represents the life of human beings as a 'tale told by an idiot, full of sound and fury.' However in places the threads on this side show beautiful and terrible forms next to one another. It is a chaos whose contrasts are particularly striking from a moral perspective, ranging from the sadistic torturer to the saint who devotes her life to the service of others.

What does the human intellect consider things to be made of? The constitution of matter has been investigated in increasing depth by contemporary scientists but to consider their discoveries further would take us outside the present frame of reference. I will simply comment that Hindu sages maintained that the Universe is entirely composed of unevenly distributed energy waves and vibrations. This energy originates in the infinite, divine source, the energy potential mentioned earlier which is the infinite Love or attraction of the divine Triad. In the atom (a misnomer since this manifestation is indefinitely divisible) what scientists refer to as 'particles' are minuscule energy fields whose wavelike trajectories depend on the underlying presence of the *Ether*. One cannot imagine waves formed in nothing, though this is what light waves appear to be when they cross what scientists call empty space. Even so the ether must be present if waves are formed. Sound waves require the presence of air which itself is composed of atoms ultimately dependent on the ether. The Ancients thought that the ether was a weightless, indefinitely elastic fluid and I find myself concluding that they were right when I reflect on this subject. There is no empty space anywhere in the universe just as nothing neither is nor exists.

## 9. The Genesis of Creation

God the Absolute Creator can only be the direct or immediate source of something that is also absolute, and is one of his infinite attributes, such as the Noumenal Cosmos which is an attribute of his made manifest. Indirectly He is the Creator of all phenomena through two intermediaries, one being the Purusha–Prakriti duality and the other the Law of Interconditioning. They are both noumenal in terms of their origin but act in the phenomenal world as relative principles and they are responsible for the appearance and evolution of its constituent phenomena. So there is a break or discontinuity between the noumenal origin of these two intermediaries and their action in the phenomenal domain. This same discontinuity can be seen between the noumenal Cosmos, and the manifold phenomena it contains. There has to be this discontinuity because there can be no conceivable progressive transition between Absolute Reality and relative reality.

It corresponds to the *abyss* which the old masters invited their disciples to throw themselves into.

Note that this abyss-discontinuity is only an obstacle when viewed from below upwards, not the other way round. It is the final obstacle which stands in the way of our realizing our divine nature but presents no barrier to divine omniscience in relation to the phenomenal world in its entirety.

## 10. The Purusha–Prakriti Duality

The phenomenal world is founded on duality. According to the Vedanta two relative principles, *Purusha* and *Prakriti,* give rise to all created things. They are relative principles because they act in the phenomenal world of relative reality. Purusha is active and masculine; Prakriti is passive and feminine. They correspond to the concepts of *essence* and *substance* in scholastic philosophy.* A thing's essence is the totality of characteristics which make it what it is. Substance is what underlies or sustains the thing created ('substance' comes from *sub-* + *stare*, to stand). It can be compared to the screen onto which a film is projected: the screen underlies the images and they would remain invisible if it were not there. Purusha initiates the formation of an object, but forming an object entails the use of Prakriti: without this primordial duality nothing could be formed.

There is a well known Hindu parable about a potter shaping clay into various objects. The potter symbolizes Purusha, the active force which changes; the clay symbolizes Prakriti, the passive force or inertia which resists change. Purusha models the clay into all kinds of bowls, cups and vessels. The human eye can only perceive shapes and colours so it sees the shapes and colours of the objects, but not the clay itself. It is the same for everything we refer to as substance. Prakriti is undifferentiated primordial substance. It is self-evidently invisible and it remains invisible in all its various modalities.

God gives the Purusha/Prakriti duality the task of creating things in their suchness in each instant, where 'Time and eternity intersect', in Louis Lavelle's[†] phrase. The Law of Interconditioning, however, is

---

* The philosophical tradition developed in mediaeval universities, whose major exponents were Aquinas, Scotus, and Ockham.

[†] Louis Lavelle (1883–1951) Professor of Philosophy at the Sorbonne.

responsible for creating things in durational time, in other words for their becoming.

I will spend more time on this law than I have done on the Purusha/Prakriti duality because it governs the evolution and destiny of created things to which we attach particular importance when they concern us or our interests.

## 11. Divine Indifference

Before we examine the creation of things in durational time and the law which governs this, I want to return to the question of what creation is for God, what it is 'in His eyes'.

I have already said that Creation for God is His splendour manifested (the right side of the piece of embroidery) and that it is in this respect direct or unmediated Creation. On the other hand, what we see is the underside of the embroidery and this constitutes indirect or mediated divine creation. God is indeed the only true Creator of the phenomenal world but He is so through the intermediary action of the Purusha/Prakriti duality and the Law of Interconditioning. These are mechanisms which have their own dynamism and they carry out the task for which God has made them responsible.

This does not prevent God knowing the whole world of phenomena in Eternal Time. How does the Absolute Reality of God see the relative reality of phenomena? To Absolute Reality it is all the same in all its aspects. The side that we see, the embroidery's under-surface, presents different aspects to us, some terrible, some marvellous. God knows them all but they are all equivalent to Him and they do not move Him in any way. For Him nothing has a special value: as Ch'an says 'Everything is the same.' The divine perspective alone is real. This is how we should understand divine indifference, as a non-differentiation between phenomena which mankind's dualistic discrimination regards as opposites.

We represent things to ourselves in such a way that the images formed affect us. So we attribute something similar to God, making the assumption that He can be affected by and experience feelings, which is senseless. Then how do we reconcile this with talk of *Agape*, God's infinite love for mankind? Let us not forget that we have two natures: one of these, the self, is phenomenal, while the other, the Self, is divine; and the Self which is God loves Himself infinitely. We have already seen that this love is not a feeling but it is how we refer to the identity which unites the divine Triad into One. The distinction between Self as a potential state and the realized Self has a subjective meaning for us but has no objective meaning for God. So Jesus said: 'For, behold, the kingdom of God is within you' (Luke 17:21)

## 12. The Law of Interconditioning

People with enquiring minds want to understand what gives rise to the phenomena they observe. The first impression is that phenomena are produced by other phenomena in a chain of cause and effect, but this is an over-simplification. For a start we must use the word 'cause' correctly if we are to understand the question properly, and this implies using it differently from how we do in ordinary, everyday language. For the present discussion the correct meaning of 'cause' is *'Source and Origin'* or *'Primordial Principle'*, so I am using it to signify the Absolute Principle, the Source and Origin of the Noumenal Cosmos, the unique cause of the created Universe. Mediaeval scholasticism distinguished the first Cause from innumerable 'second causes' but this is an unhelpful terminology which leads one to believe that the Cause and causes share the same nature, whereas the first is noumenal and the rest are phenomenal, and their two natures have nothing at all in common.

I will avoid this difficulty by saying that phenomena intercondition one another sequentially in a series of chains, which is compatible with the Buddhist phrase 'This being so, that happens' (and not 'This produces that'). This Buddhist formulation gives a good account of conditioning in the phenomenal domain but we will see shortly that this conditioning is really an *interconditioning*. The Buddhist *Law of Dependent Origination*\* makes the same point.

I want to emphasize that there is a radical difference between the Cause–Effect relationship and that which exists between conditioning and conditioned phenomena, because the word 'causality' which is commonly used in this context introduces confusion by implying that a phenomenon could be the Cause of something else. We can only clarify matters by restoring to the word 'Cause' its true meaning of One and Only Principle or Unique Cause. I write Cause with a capital 'c' to indicate its noumenal or absolute nature and remind you that it stands for That which we in the West call God.

In the relationship between Cause and Effect, the Effect is an attribute of the Cause, sharing in its Oneness and Absolute nature. This is how

---

\* The doctrine of *Paṭicca-sammuppāda* (Pali).

the Noumenal Cosmos is a divine attribute because it is simply the Unique Cause manifested.

On the other hand, when there is a conditional relationship between phenomena, i.e. when one phenomenon is dependent on another, the two phenomena are not identical in nature. Two phenomena may resemble one another but they are never identical; and conditioned phenomena which depend on particular conditioning phenomena never occur in their absence.

A simple example will clarify the relationship between phenomena: if I light a match under some dry straw it will set fire to it. It is obvious that setting fire to the straw depends as much on the nature of the straw as it does on the flame provided by the match. If I had tried to do the same with an equivalent piece of iron it would not have caught fire. So two conditioning factors were involved in interconditioning this particular phenomenon.

We can go further up the chain of conditioning than the match and the straw because they are both the end result of numerous conditioning factors. In fact all phenomena in the space-time continuum are interrelated. One way of visualizing this important point is to imagine a net like the kind used by fishermen, but one which stretches towards infinity in all directions and dimensions. Each one of all its innumerable knots is continuously affected by every movement that sets the other knots in motion, while its own movement affects all the other knots in return, and so on. *'If Cleopatra's nose had been shorter, the whole face of the world would have been different'* (Pascal*).

This is how the coming into being of created things is governed. The conditioning factors are often so many and so subtle and hidden that we attribute events to 'chance', and use this word to draw a discreet veil over our irremediable ignorance. But it does not refer to anything real: everything which happens does so because it has to. At the roulette table, once the croupier has set the roulette wheel and ball in motion, the winning number is already chosen. The ball cannot come to rest at any other number. It is not a question of chance versus necessity: there is only necessity and the choice lies between its foreseeable and its unforeseeable workings.

Every phenomenon occurs through the operation of a single Law which I call the *Law of Interconditioning*. (I prefer this expression to the *Law of Interdependent Origins* because 'origin' in this context might be associated misleadingly with the Originating Principle i.e. the Unique

---

* *Le nez de Cléopâtre: s'il eût été plus court, toute la face de la terre aurait changé.* From *Pensées* by Blaise Pascal, French mathematician, philosopher and writer (1623–62).

and Only Cause). This Law can be thought of as the mother Law of all the numerous daughter laws, such as those of chemistry, physics, thermodynamics, biology, psychology, etc. which are the ways in which the mother Law is expressed in the human mind. This Law is a thought and creation of the Divine Mind and it must be distinguished from its practical operation, just as one draws a distinction between the legislature and the executive powers which put its laws into effect. It might be compared to an unimaginably complex computer created and programmed by the Divine Mind which puts the programme into effect impeccably and so governs the whole phenomenal world and does this in Eternal Time.

'Law of Interconditioning' is an awkward phrase and I will often use the more practical term Demiurge in its place, though not with the same meaning as its original Greek one. Demiurge is derived from *dēmiourgós,* which meant 'craftsman, artisan', from *dēmios,* 'public', and a stem *erg-* 'work'. In Platonic philosophy the term referred to a kind of Creator God. I am going to use it as synonymous with the Law of Interconditioning. The Demiurge can also be thought of as a representative created by God with the task of governing the conditions whereby phenomena arise, but it must be borne in mind that this image should not be anthropomorphized. The Demiurge is a mechanism, a sort of robot which carries out its work impeccably, distributing good fortune and misfortune and doing so without the slightest hint of benevolence or malign intent.

Where the two intermediaries between the Creator and the phenomenal world are concerned, in other words the Purusha–Prakriti duality and the Demiurge, it is only the latter's role which concerns us human beings. I am not particularly interested in the fact that Purusha–Prakriti has created me as a specimen of humankind, but what does concern me are the incidents, accidents and misfortunes arranged by the Demiurge which lie in wait for me in the days ahead. This is the territory where my hopes and fears are engaged, for I do not know what is programmed for me and is therefore fated to happen to me.

'Fated' is a word which conjures up the idea of *passive fatalism* and the fear that we might be reduced to that state by what we know of the computer-like Demiurge. The same can be said of the Islamic saying *'What is written is written'.* But I might just as well be conditioned to face difficulties with fierce determination and that too would be inevitable because it would also have been written. If you understand fate in the right way there is no reason to be passive.

It is very difficult for us to accept the role of the Demiurge because of the immense value we attach to what we call 'free will', our freedom to exercise choice. This is such an important question that it needs to be considered in greater depth.

## 13. Our Total Conditioning as Human Beings

God is immanent in everything created but transcendent to His phenomenal manifestations. There is one exception to this divine transcendence and that is the human being. The divine nature (the Self) dwells integrally in every individual human (the self) but as a general rule it is only present as a *potential state* and remains so throughout the whole of life. Only in rare cases where very special conditions are present does the Self pass from a state of possibility to one of realization.

Although the Self is only present as a potential, its effect is to make man the only intellectual animal on earth. Intellect endows us with many possibilities which we sometimes make good use of but all too often waste or abuse.

After this brief introduction concerning human nature, let us consider how the Law of Interconditioning operates within it.

We are conditioned by three groups of factors, hereditary, biological and circumstantial.

### Hereditary Factors

We are conditioned by these from the moment of conception. When we consider how the chromosomes divide and what genes are passed on, we are inclined to assume that the process is governed by chance, though this simply reflects our ignorance of conditioning factors which are beyond our understanding but must be involved in producing these phenomena.

The innate or congenital essence of a human being is determined in this way. 'Essence' suggests the essence/substance pair, Purusha/Prakriti, but in this context its meaning is less general: Purusha refers to all the characteristics which make a created thing what it is in the instant now, but innate essence means all the characteristics which an individual being will manifest in the course of normal development. It determines those features that gradually emerge as persistent character traits as well as differing levels of ability across the range of human activity.

The issue of ability or talents is particularly important in relation to intellect. This is a very complex field because the intellect is a kind of optical device with numerous functions which are relatively indepen-dent of one another. On the one hand there is intellectual intuition which is a direct and unmediated kind of vision and can be sub-divided into various levels of ability depending on the domain in which it is operating; and then there are a whole number of intellectual operations such as deduction, induction, differentiation, etc. which are intermediary in the sense that they provide the intellect with conclu-sions acquired indirectly rather than directly. As far as getting rid of false and illusory opinions is concerned, what matters is the ability to understand psychological mechanisms. This starts from observing oneself and others and leads on to the interpretation of the mecha-nisms observed and the discovery of the general laws governing the human psyche. This whole process is illuminated by the revelations of traditional metaphysics.

This is not the place to develop this topic further, but I want to clar-ify the difference between theoretical understanding and Knowledge. I have used these terms before but now I want to indicate what an enormous difference in meaning there is between them. Only Knowledge in this special sense is able to get rid of what the Buddha called Ignorance, the source of all our suffering. Someone who has an accurate and exhaustive theoretical understanding, and nothing else, is learned but ignorant, and will go on living according to all the illusory opinions which in theory should have been revealed for what they are. This is a kind of understanding which can be expressed formally, and it can be spoken or written about, unlike Knowledge. This is because illusory opinions are not replaced by correct opinions once they have been abolished. True Knowledge is inexpressible because there is no longer anything to express. How could one express the solution to an illusory problem? One could only say that there never had been a problem: there is no solution to a false problem, so how could it be put into words?

Innate essence is like a seed which will, providing it grows normally, produce a particular plant. But how this plant grows will vary according to the environmental conditions.

## Biological Factors

Biological factors affect the development of the human psycho-somatic organism from birth to death, with its component organs showing char-acteristic changes at particular stages. This is sufficiently obvious not to require further discussion.

## Environmental Factors

The human psycho-somatic organism develops for about twenty years and then it stops growing. Thereafter it may go on to achieve its potential or it may undergo changes for the worse, but early childhood, when the child is weak from every point of view, is the time when unfavourable circumstances can present the greatest obstacle to the unfolding of essence. When the young being grows up in an unfavourable environment, one which negates it, potential aspects of its essence are inhibited to a greater or lesser extent while psychic mechanisms develop which do not belong to essence and must be termed neurotic. Since no one's circumstances are ever entirely favourable it is fair to say that every human being is more or less neurotic, though one only talks of true pathological neurosis at a level where the impairment is sufficient to hinder adaptation to what we know as 'reality'.

When we examine the part played by the Demiurge it is particularly relevant to consider it in relation to our three functional centres. Let me remind you where and what these centres are:

- the instinctive centre is situated at the lower extremity of the vertebral column and it controls the mechanisms which we share with animals.
- the affective centre lies in the cardiac region at the epigastric level and governs our affective mechanisms.
- the intellectual centre is situated in the brain, where it controls conscious and unconscious thought.

I intend to show that the phenomena which arise from these three centres are the inexorable result of the demiurgic Law and that the individual freedom which we think we have does not correspond to anything in reality.

*Instinctive Centre*: This is already partially active at birth. The question of free will does not arise at this point because awareness is lacking.

Later, at puberty, erotic desire awakens and it is obvious that this does not appear as the result of the individual exercising free choice in the matter.

*Affective Centre:* This is also in operation from very early on in life. Here it is also obvious that our feelings, our likes and dislikes, are not decided on the basis of freely made decisions. When we love or detest something, we do not do so because we have made a free decision to do so. We can conceal our feelings but we cannot generate them at will. Everything affective is subject to interconditioning.

*Intellectual Centre:* What about our minds? Are we at least free and unconditioned in our thoughts? The answer has to be 'no', no more than we are in the other centres.

Whenever we are engaged in some automatic activity or are doing nothing, our imagination always plays an imaginary film which is most often about something completely useless and therefore silly. It is seldom about anything useful or beneficial. In every case, ideas *come* to us: we do not create them freely.

I am well aware that we can direct our attention to a particular subject and bring it back despite associations which have a tendency to distract us. But why do we engage in introspective activity like this which requires some tiresome effort on our part? We do so because our wish to resolve some problem or other prevails over the disagreeable quality of the effort we have to make. All wishes are affective, in other words they are conditioned.

We can strive to obtain mastery over the mind and achieve inner silence in this way. But fighting against the mind's activity like this is obviously itself the expression of an intense desire to escape this enslavement; so once again we find that the source of these efforts is affectivity, and totally conditioned affectivity at that. In other words, what we discover is another form of bondage.

The problem of *choice* is connected to how the intellect functions. When we have difficulty choosing between two solutions, we subject them to intellectual scrutiny and analyze their pros and cons (at least we do so if we are not slaves to our impulses). Intellect can function independently of affectivity, with the same impartiality towards our own situation that we could show towards someone else's, functioning in other words like a disinterested judge. When we consider matters in this way and exercise our potential for this kind of deliberation, does this amount to what we popularly call 'free will'? Note that I am only referring to the deliberation that precedes the choice. So what happens at the actual moment of choosing? If one of the alternatives will produce a reasonable and agreeable outcome while the other will result in something unpleasant and disagreeable, we are conditioned to choose the former. But there are other situations where one choice seems reasonable and disagreeable while the other is attractive but irrational. If we opt for irrational pleasure, our choice is obviously determined by affective factors and these are not free. If we choose to do what is rational but disagreeable, we can have the impression that we have freely come to a decision and freely put it into effect. But we can only maintain this if we fail to recognize a conditioning factor of great importance, which is that we need our self-image to be morally pleasing. Our moral narcissism can urge us towards the satisfaction we derive from doing our duty and prompt us to avoid acts of moral laxity which would be a stain on our image and cause us to suffer the pangs of remorse. This concern we have for our image can be seen at work in many situations. An example would be someone who does something unreasonable because they want to: their intellect is then influenced by emotion to produce dishonest rationalizations which legitimate their choice by lending it a false veneer of rationality. Does not every one of us want to be 'in the right' about what we do?

If we are honest with ourselves and search in good faith for the origin of our acts, we will always find an affective component at work and beyond that we will detect the influence of conditioning factors which operate at the demiurgic level.

The emotions in general tend to have a dynamic effect, in the sense that they are associated with feelings of attraction or repulsion. The intellect, however, simply delivers information and, providing it is operating honestly, tells us what the right and useful course of action must be without taking our feelings into account. Its sphere of activity is that of information-gathering and deliberation but it is powerless when action is required. This is where our emotions take over and these, of course, cannot in any way be free.

What we call 'will' is in fact the resultant of the forces of desire, and these may be numerous and indeed at times may be in conflict with one another.

Is there anything to be surprised at in this? Because the Absolute Self is only present in us as a potential state, the person that we are, our psycho-somatic organism, amounts in practice to an aggregate of phenomena. We have already seen that all phenomena in the Universe are subject to the mother-Law of Interconditioning through its intermediary daughter-laws. Realization of the Self is called 'Liberation' precisely because we are not free until it takes place, but remain slaves of the Demiurge.

To summarize, ordinary people, those in whom the Self has not been realized, which means practically everyone, can reasonably be compared to puppets in which body and mind are controlled by an unimaginably complex system of wires. Since the wires are invisible, we cannot help being convinced that we do what we do because we choose to do so freely and think freely about whatever we chose to think. Readers may be somewhat shocked by what I have just said about 'puppets' and they may be inclined to dismiss it, but nonetheless this is how things are.

The presence or absence of free will is a question of fundamental importance which is obscured by a failure to discriminate between interior and exterior freedom. Everyone wants to be free from oppression by others, and this is something which can be achieved in principle. What about freedom in relation to our interior mechanisms? In the days of slavery, slaves had to do as their master commanded but considered that they were free to think silently just as they wished. But, though they thought the thoughts that came to them or that they chose to think about, were they in fact free to create their own thoughts? The reality was that their minds were conditioned. However we look at this question, however hard we try to find some example of physical or mental activity free from conditioning, we will always be disappointed if we think things through honestly. We will always find that conditioning has played a part in governing our behaviour.

If this is the case, how can we still believe in 'responsibility'?

## 14. The Role of the Demiurge

I have compared the Demiurge to a computer programmed by God and it carries out this program rather like someone given an assignment to carry out. The task in question is infinitely complex and we will only deal with the aspect which concerns us humans.

Its mission involves the whole of humanity and I want to consider this in the light of the Hindu concept of endlessly repeating cycles of creation and dissolution, each of which is divided into four phases. According to René Guénon the whole of recorded history has taken place in the fourth and last phase, the *kali yuga*, of the current cycle, and we are even now close to its apocalyptic end. Guénon's book *The Reign of Quantity and the Sign of the Times*\* deals with this subject and I cannot recommend it too highly, though the reader is warned that the first part of the book takes for granted an acquaintance with traditional metaphysics. When *kali yuga* has ended, a new cycle begins which starts with a golden age.

Man is a most complex creature. In the first place he consists of a psychosomatic organism similar to that of animals (with the huge difference that the human psyche contains an intellect which animals lack). This organism has a relative as opposed to absolute reality and it is what we refer to in general as the 'self'. It constitutes the experience of 'me' and we define ourselves by it because we are mistakenly identified with it. But the Divine Noumenon also dwells within corpo-

---

\* *Le Règne de la Quantité ou les Signes des Temps.*

real man. This is our Absolute Reality and we refer to it as the *Self* as opposed to the *self*.

The self is obviously individual while the Self is universal. When we reflect on the Self as it is objectively in itself, its universality is apparent. However, we see individual differences in the Self-realized personality (an exceedingly rare phenomenon) as it is expressed in different people. The fact is that abrupt or sudden Self-Realization requires many years during which changes take place in the individual's conditioning and eventually give rise to a very special form of conditioning ('spiritual death') in which the potential for Self-realization is actualized into Realization itself. As far as the Self is concerned, there is no difference between being in the state where Realization is a possibility as yet unfulfilled and being Realized: they are both one and the same state. The difference is purely subjective and consists of an upheaval in the psyche of the individual in whom this state of Illumination suddenly arises.

But we must move on from this topic since the role of the Demiurge does not include liberating man from his bondage to demiurgic conditioning. Its primary task is to bring about and maintain life. It implants in man the conviction that life, even a wretched life, is a treasure of inestimable value. It is the source of hunger, thirst, sleep, and erotic desire (conservation of the species). I am well aware that some people maintain in good faith that their death is a matter of indifference to them. But they imagine death in the abstract and if they were threatened by imminent death in reality they would be deserted by this relaxed attitude which they claim to possess. The fear of death dwells deep within the human psyche. If we really succeed in imagining the destruction of our own body, we experience an organic feeling of horror which is so powerful that such a thing, quite irrationally, seems unlikely or at least improbable. Because we are conditioned like this, each of us is compelled to protect our life. When the Demiurge acts on us in this way, it is not however working against the possibility of Illumination, because, as the proverb counsels, *'primum vivere, deinde philosophari.'** It takes an exceptionally wise person to say as St John of the Cross did: *'Come, Death, so stealthily that I do not sense your approach lest I be restored to life by the joy of dying.'*

Our attachment to life goes hand in hand with our *compensations*. I want to take a closer look at these, and what it is they compensate for. Although in the vast majority of people the Self is only present as a potential state, they are intuitively aware of this possibility at an uncon-

---

* 'Live first, then philosophize.'

scious level. There is evidence for this in the fundamentally unsatisfactory nature of our compensations, whatever they may be. We always want more: if money is the object of our desire, we will not stop with our first million but strive to acquire another, then another, and so on. Don Juan has never conquered enough women. The politician deceives himself when he believes he would finally achieve fulfilment by becoming head of state. These are just a few examples but they make their point. What is being compensated for in these and other cases is the absence of that Divine Beatitude which is eternal and indestructible. This is the yearning in the depths of our being which is common to us all. But our response is not to try and discover the diamond in its purity; instead we chase without discrimination after all kinds of fakes and substitutes in the belief that they represent our supreme value. It is an endless pursuit, and all the time the pure diamond is within us. In this respect we are like someone riding around on an ox and looking for it all over the place.

Since ordinary people are ignorant in the sense that they take illusory beliefs to be true and since they consider other people's compensations satisfying and desirable, they expect to find in false substitutes that Beatitude which is ultimately their true need. If we take Christians, who among them lives according to the words of Jesus, that only one thing is necessary and that is the Kingdom of God within?* Ordinary people spend their lives playing and hoping to win; in that respect they remain children and only the realized individual is an adult.

I would like to return to the role of the Demiurge and the nature of its mission by relating one of the allegories told by Gurdjieff.[†] The earth was struck by an enormous meteor whose impact caused part of it to break away. Gravitational forces caused both the fragment and what remained of the earth to become spherical again, thus forming the earth and moon as they are at present. The Great Cosmic Individuals gathered together to decide what radiations the earth would provide to nourish its satellite as the sun nourishes the earth. They realized that a very special kind of radiation was required which could only come from human suffering. 'This may be true,' commented one of the Great

---

* 'But seek ye first the Kingdom of God, and his righteousness; and all these things shall be added unto you.' Matt. 6:33; 'for, behold, the kingdom of God is within you.' Luke 17:21.

[†] G. I. Gurdjieff was born in Tsarist Alexandropolis (now Gyumri, Armenia) and lived in France from the early 1920s until his death in 1949. He was a charismatic teacher who taught that we are asleep and our personalities fragmented, and that 'ordinary man has no soul and no will'. His pupils engaged in 'conscious labours and intentional sufferings' to promote inner development.

Cosmic Individuals, 'but a creature which can only suffer, and is unable to hope for anything else, will simply kill itself.' So the council decided to graft a special organ onto the base of the human spine. This was a compensatory apparatus whose function was to blind us to our situation with the result that we wrongly accept false substitutes in place of our sole true need.

What would our fate be without this compensatory device? Because the Divine Self is hidden from us, being only present within us as a potential state, and because we do not know the way to Realization, we would suffer the pain of divine abandonment which is the anguish of Hell itself. The present situation is that we are all in hell but do not realize it, because we cannot recognize the difference between various forms of imitation jewellery and the pure diamond itself. (Rodin,* who was writing about sculpture at the time, said to a friend: "Whenever I have to write the word 'sculpture' I feel like writing 'God'".)

Because of our compensations and our own blindness, we are able to experience what we call pleasures, joys and even happiness, though our experiences of happiness are quite different in nature to Divine Beatitude, which we cannot conceive of. We also tend to experience inner states as though they were eternal, so we often forget that these substitutes are always transient and we spend our lives beneath a whole cluster of Damoclean swords held up by fragile threads.

The demiurgic programme is only concerned with the phenomenal world and has nothing to do with the Realization of the Self. God has not instructed it to either favour or hinder Realization. What happens is that it endows some individuals with an intelligence that is lucid and independent of their emotional life, and is associated with an intense need for truth and an ability to develop an accurate, intuitive understanding of metaphysical issues. These characteristics are seldom found in the same person. Most people in our present kali yuga epoch are distracted by the Demiurge's programming into compensatory activities and beliefs in which they imagine that the meaning of their lives is to be found. Realization remains an unfulfilled possibility.

Parallels can be drawn between the idea of a Demiurge and the myth of Satan. There are really two aspects to Satan, one relating to God and the other to Man. Towards God he acts as a faithful servant: in the book of Job, God summons him and charges him with the task of testing Job, which Satan does in many ways, fulfilling his mission impeccably. In relation to mankind, Satan is the Deceiver, the Negater, and the Tempter who turns us away from the true path by offering us compensations-

* Auguste Rodin, French sculptor (1840–1917) whose best known works include *The Kiss*, *The Burghers of Calais*, and *The Thinker*.

what Pascal referred to as 'divertissements'* – such as gold, sensual pleasures, power, etc. This is the Satan who leads us all in a dance, Satan the Prince of this world. The Demiurge behaves in this respect as if it wanted to prevent Realization of the Self, yet it is God, or the Self, which has programmed it in this way. To us this seems incomprehensible, but it cannot be understood from a human perspective. This would require an understanding of the cosmic order, which we clearly do not have. Everything that exists in the Cosmos has its cosmic reasons for existing there and this also applies to the human condition.

## 15. God and Man

Omniscient God knows everything which has been, is and will be on this earth. All phenomena, as I have already mentioned, possess relative reality and are equivalent in the eyes of Absolute Reality. God loves infinitely the Self which is in each one of us since the Self is God Himself, and we only use the term 'Self' to draw a distinction between it and the little self or 'me'. This little self in the eyes of God is equivalent to any other created thing. What we call good and evil are equivalent for God, as are all the opposites generated by our dualistic viewpoint.

We relate everything to ourselves and we think of God as some infinitely superior person, but a person nonetheless. When people pray, they imagine that God listens to them and takes account of their prayers. Most prayers take the form of requests as if God controlled events in response to emotional considerations, even though He is free of all affect. Imagine a mother whose beloved son is seriously ill, who begs God for her son's recovery. The fact is that her son's death or recovery will depend on biological laws which are themselves expressions of the Law of Interconditioning, and the outcome will determine whether the mother is filled with grief or joy. But in the eyes of God, the boy's recovery or death and the mother's joy or grief amount to exactly the same thing. The Cosmos is like an enormous machine whose operation God is watching. He may observe a tiny wheel turning in one direction while another turns in the opposite direction. The directions in which they rotate are equivalent, both participating equally in the machine's perfect activity.

Human morality is simply a set of aesthetic responses. Deeds may be beautiful or ugly but what we call sins and virtues are equivalent: the

---

* The particular significance of 'divertissements', meaning diversions or distractions, for Pascal was that they prevent us thinking about our true condition.

word 'sin' should be replaced by 'error' and it is undeniable that error is a human characteristic since we are conditioned to get things wrong. Merit and demerit merely correspond to different kinds of conditioning for which man the puppet is in no way responsible. Hitler was conditioned to destroy while someone like the Curé d'Ars* was conditioned to be constructive, but in this perspective they were both equally not responsible for what they did. God is amoral, pure Spirit without affective involvement in phenomena, for whom the beautiful and the ugly are equivalent.

The kind of petitionary prayer mentioned above, where a request is made of God, is useless. However it can influence the person praying in the sense that they become more hopeful and this subjective emotional effectiveness is all it can achieve.

When prayers are 'granted', believers are convinced that their prayers have succeeded. When on the contrary they are unsuccessful, they think that the ways of Providence are unfathomable, but this will not stop them turning their thoughts to prayer again on another occasion.

There is another kind of prayer, contemplative or meditative prayer, where the individual contemplates and adores the divine perfections. This kind of prayer can lead to ecstasy, but that is a transient state in no way comparable to Realization. It is still a compensation, though the most perfect of them all. So it is still an obstacle to Realization, though one which will disappear providing Knowledge continues to progress. It has the advantage, however, of ensuring unshakeable faith. Instead of being something which is only *thought*, the divine splendour is *seen* in a quite new light which is devoid of forms and colour. It is of infinite intensity though the eye of spirit can sustain its brilliance. It is not beautiful, it is Beauty itself. One might contemplate it for ever and never tire of it.

The illusory idea that there is a direct relationship between man and an anthropomorphized God is found in the belief that God rewards good deeds and punishes evil ones even in this life. We must all have heard expressions such as 'What have I done to God that He should send me such trials and tribulations?'

We must not forget the abyss which separates the Noumenon from phenomena. Despite all their striving towards God, believers cannot cross this abyss. At best they achieve a mental image and, though it may be considered perfect in every respect, it is still formal in nature, belonging to the phenomenal order. Beliefs which are founded in emotion can never give rise to Realization.

* Jean-Marie Vianney (Saint), priest at Ars near Lyons for forty-one years, celebrated for his holiness and the crowds who came to hear him. He is the patron saint for *curés de paroisses*, parish priests, in France.

**Part Three**

*of*

*The Realization of the Self*

*The Agony and Death of
Human Egotism*

## 16.  A Critique of Systematic Methods

The Self which dwells within us can make the transition from being a potential state to the Realized state. Realization occurs abruptly and instantaneously, but it must be preceded by changes in our conditioning which take place over time. The length of time required will vary from individual to individual.

At the beginning of its existence, the little child is still incapable of metaphysical intuition so it cannot avoid falling into what Buddha called Ignorance. 'Ignorance' as used by Buddha does not refer to a lack of knowledge or understanding but to a mass of illusory convictions which are taken to be obvious truths. How, for instance, can the child not fail to take it for granted that his organism, his body and mind together, constitute his true identity? How could he not believe in his freedom to obey or disobey, to do good or evil in keeping with the moral values of his family circle, and to deserve praise or blame from them accordingly? It is simply not natural to observe in one's own person the workings of a totally conditioned puppet.

To progress from these early conditioned states to the state which enables Realization to occur requires some very considerable changes.

The first stage in this development occurs if, as an adolescent or adult, the individual obtains a correct initiation into the theoretical understanding of traditional metaphysics. In this, as subsequently, the most favourable conditions are provided by a Master who has already obtained Realization. In practice nowadays the search for such a Master and teaching would be unlikely to succeed because of the lack of *true* Masters. There are many who pretend to be such in India and Nepal, but the role is all too attractive. A further difficulty is that Realization is not susceptible to proof. Fortunately a great deal of written material has survived which has preserved the Vedantic texts and the teachings of the first Ch'an Masters. Boddhidharma* arrived in China during the sixth century AD. and his teachings were assimilated and adapted by his pupils according to the style of Chinese thinking, which was influenced by the Taoist religion. Between 600 and 800 AD. the teaching remained pure, based uniquely on the understanding that mankind should abandon its illusory beliefs. It remained faithful to the Buddha's teaching which affirmed that all human suffering arose from Ignorance

---

* The legendary founder of Zen, an Indian monk who was supposedly the 28th Indian Patriarch in direct succession from Buddha and the first Chinese Zen patriarch.

and that Realization could therefore only arise when Ignorance had been dispelled.

Unfortunately, and this is an implacable law, all initiatory teachings gradually lose their true meaning, as indeed have those of Jesus Christ and Mohammed. They become debased until they amount to no more than a mass of superstitions. This is what happened to Ch'an Buddhism which arrived in Japan via Korea and fragmented into a number of different sects.

About two centuries after Boddhidharma arrived in China, the Ch'an Masters observed with sadness that their pupils were engaged in endless wrangling over theoretical points. They wanted to re-direct this activity in quite the opposite direction and this they did by advising their students to engage in the practice of the *koan*. Here the task involves understanding a cryptic dialogue.

For example, the question 'Why did Boddhidharma come to China?' was answered by 'The cypress in the courtyard', and the student's task was to fix his attention on this strange dialogue until he had understood it. The koan cannot be resolved by the rational intellect. It acts as a kind of wall and the student's mind continually comes up against it, sometimes for as much as eight consecutive hours without sleep. The purpose of the koan is to exhaust the subtle cerebral 'musculature' engaged in this mental work, just as carrying a load without respite would exhaust the muscles of the body (always assuming that the student has the courage and determination to go through with this kind of torture). The outcome is that the intellect reaches a point where it can no longer function, and has transcended the domain in which the rationality versus irrationality dualism applies. Since this dualism is the aspect of the mind's habitual functioning which prevents access to Absolute Truth, transcending it enables the Truth which is beyond all form to become accessible. For a moment formal thought is extinguished and the mind functions as though the Self were awake; and the Self does awaken and the student has an experience of Divine Beatitude. But this achievement is transient because the vital principle re-establishes the brain's ordinary modes of functioning, together with all its habitual conditionings. The Self returns to its previous state of merely being a possibility. Even if the student were to begin the process again by using some other koan, the results would always be temporary.

The practice of using koans is still recommended today. A young woman told me of her reception in a Zen monastery in Japan. She was told right away that the intellect was of no use and that there was nothing to be understood intellectually, and she was given a koan to solve. People who achieve a temporary pseudo-liberation are in any case few in number, and she was not one of them.

The koan was the first of the *methods* which must have been recommended in order to obtain what the Japanese call *satori* (Realization), and there are many others. An old Zennist squatted before a wall for thirty years. Getting no results, he sought out Hui-neng, the sixth Patriarch, who convinced him in a few sentences that he had wasted his time.

Shen-hui* recommended *thought without dwelling*, meaning that the student should not let the inner monologue develop in relation to any particular subject. Unfortunately it would take too long to explain why this approach is bound to fail, because to do so would require a lengthy account of the complex mechanisms responsible for our daydreams.

Many different methods were, and still are, recommended. They involve fixing the attention on a single, unchanging object such as one's breathing and are referred to as *meditation techniques*, though it is a little strange using the term 'meditation' in this way given that it really means a state of deep reflection, of profound thought. In the West today another recommended method is practised under the name of *Zazen*, in which the student is required to adopt a very precise posture. This has to be observed and maintained faultlessly, with the obvious effect of making it more difficult for the mind to wander. None of these methods is more likely than any of the others to lead to Realization but some at least have the virtue of promoting greater mastery over one's behaviour and a greater degree of inner tranquillity.

I am also open to criticism in this respect: towards the end of my book *Lâcher Prise*[†] I recommended a method which I called 'divergent language' and in due course this turned out to be as ineffective as all the others. The mistake, which is all too human, is to imagine that there is some procedure, some method, some kind of 'trick', and that this is the direction in which we should be looking.

We should rather listen to Hui-neng:

---

* Meditation master at Ho-tse monastery, who lived from 668 to 760 and was a famous disciple of the Sixth Patriarch, Hui-neng. He emphasized the particular importance of not thinking about what was aimed at i.e. enlightenment. In *The Way of Zen* Alan Watts quotes a dialogue between Shen-hui and another meditation master, Ch'eng, which suggests that Shen-hui's approach was not dissimilar to Benoit's. The dialogue concludes with Shen-hui observing: 'All practice of *samadhi* is fundamentally a wrong view. How, by practising *samadhi*, could one attain *samadhi?*'

[†] *Lâcher Prise*, 1954, La Colombe, Paris. First English version: *Let Go*, 1962, George Allen and Unwin, London.

*I, Hui-neng, do not know of any method;*
*My thoughts are not suppressed;*
*The objective world excites my mind for ever,*
*And what would be the point of making Illumination come to ripeness?*

Illumination has ripened in Hui-neng but he has not *made* it ripen by some kind of systematic work. He has not *done* and there is nothing to *do*.

I want to say something about *hatha yoga* despite its having come to us from India rather than the Far East, because it is enjoying a certain vogue over here. I was talking to Professor Suzuki one day and the topic of hatha yoga was raised. Professor Suzuki said to me: 'You have to be human to think of such bizarre postures. Look at animals: none of them do anything like it.'

It is perplexing that people who seek Realization have such an uncritical predilection for systematic methods. The fact is that people who are brave enough to think by themselves are unusual. Take an everyday example of someone has lost something in his flat: often he will prefer to turn everything upside down rather than sit down and ask himself calmly where and when he used the missing object and where he might have left it. We seem to be very reluctant to think things over by ourselves. We will read a whole number of books uncritically and attend lectures which shed little light. We will go to them because they are given by an Oriental, without taking into account the possibility that they may be worthless. If Realization was guaranteed for everyone who had moved ten thousand paving stones over a distance of one kilometre, then no doubt a lot of people would set to work at this agreeably stupid task. But working things out on one's own is a different matter! This might be explained as a fear of being mistaken and getting things wrong. But our error would be revealed sooner or later and so there would be progress towards the truth as a result. So what is there to be afraid of?

I have mentioned and criticized some methods but what is far more relevant is to recognize that any method whatever which our intellectual mechanisms can conceive of will be produced under the control of the Demiurge. No method could therefore function outside the Demiurge's realm, which is the realm of phenomena. No method could change 'puppet man' in any way other than into a puppet whose conditioning may be different but who is still located on the phenomenal side of the afore-mentioned abyss, without ever being able to cross it.

Recommending a method also suggests that there is an *ascending* path to follow, a progressive route where one improves every day and advances towards Realization, like some traveller who would find Shangri-La at the summit of some mountain, providing he had the requisite courage and perseverance. As one climbed, so would life become progressively truer until finally one attained that True Life of which Rimbaud spoke when he wrote: 'True life is absent; we are not in the world.' This is to forget what Jesus told Nicodemus:* 'In truth I say to you, if a man does not die, he cannot be reborn.'

The true way, which I will shortly be considering, is a *descent* which leads down until, at the lowest point, the individual touches and takes possession of the *axis or tree of Heaven*, and is then borne aloft into the infinite heights of the Void.

## 17. Theoretical Understanding at the Intellectual Level and 'Lived Knowledge'

What part does the intellect play in the inner developments which precede Realization? There are those who maintain that pure intellect has no part to play, and is in fact more of a hindrance than a help. For them only Knowledge experienced by the whole being is fruitful. There is some truth in this claim but it raises the question of how this trans-rational Knowledge would emerge if ignorance had not first been dispelled in the rational domain, and if unchallenged beliefs based on illusory and misleading convictions were still held to be true because at an unconscious level they were considered unchallengeable?

No, the ordinary, everyday opinions which surround us have a para-lyzing effect and it is absolutely necessary to subject them to a critical analysis. The dangers that lie in theoretical intellectual understanding are not intrinsic to it but arise from its misuse. Purely intellectual under-standing must be penetrated and worked through until its essential truths have been mastered. Among these is the truth which shows us that we are somnambulistic puppets by nature, dreaming our lives away.

When we finally reach this point, we observe that the way we live our lives does not accord with our new clarity of mind and we realize that the situation will never change as long as we continue to approach the problem posed by our condition through the intellect. Intellectual work is necessary but after a certain point it becomes an impasse. Our

---

* This is something of a misquotation, though it captures the sense of the story. 'Verily, verily, I say unto thee, Except a man be born again, he cannot see the king-dom of God' (John 3:3).

yearning for the True Life is then transmuted into a questioning attitude without form, in which we are like a question mark which is neither preceded by a question nor, as yet, followed by an answer. We live our ordinary lives as though they were the true koan and this mysterious 'thing' for which we yearn is felt to be beyond the everyday.

The difference between lived Knowledge, which will be an instantaneous accompaniment of Realization, and purely theoretical understanding is *qualitative*. It is not that the Intellect becomes less active, but that it no longer operates as a philosopher. It simply functions in the awareness of each lived instant.

## 18. Dying in order to be Re-born

Ch'an and Zen literature is disappointing on this subject, giving accounts of a number of cases of Realization which are very different from one another, and it often has little if anything to say about how individual Masters achieved their liberation. This is in keeping with the ineffectiveness of all techniques and methods. If this were not so, liberated individuals could give an account of how they set about achieving their goal and how long it took them to attain it.

All we can claim to know is that people destined for Realization are in the first place, at some point or other in their lives, free from all compensations and wholly devoted to this single objective. Their minds do not ever seem to be distracted towards anything else. This detachment seems to be something which they all share, but the paths they  follow are extremely varied. One thing, however, they have all experienced and that is failure, or a succession of failures if they have pursued a number of different ways. This is the *downward way* of repeated failure culminating in the final failure. Here I would like to quote Dag Hammarskjöld's remarkable intuition about this:

> Drawn into the labyrinth of life, I come to a moment and a place where I understand that the way leads to a triumph which is a catastrophe and to a catastrophe which is a triumph . . . and that the only possibility of our being raised to a higher level lies in the depths of humiliation.*

Death of the ego and rebirth happen simultaneously. The moments which precede this 'death' are the same for everyone who undergoes it. The inner state is one of complete humiliation, fully accepted; in other words a vision of oneself being nothing, not being. Thought becomes

* Dag Hammarskjöld, *Markings*, 1964, Alfred Knopf, New York.

unimportant and stops. Emotional activity also ceases because the individual experiences two feelings of equal intensity: on the one hand there is despair about the possibilities open to oneself, on the other there is total confidence in the Self in whose favour the little self is abdicating. This is the point where the individual finally stops *doing* anything towards Realization while desiring it with all his being.

Let me quote a Zen saying:

*Satori comes upon us unexpectedly when we have exhausted all the resources of our being.*

The resources referred to are the powers with which the Demiurge endows us, and they are constantly directed towards earthly happiness, compensations, affirmations of self, and success. Together these forces amount to the desperate centrifugal orientation which directs us into the labyrinth of life. They also ensnare the intellect when it sets itself up to develop practical ways of resolving the enigma of the human condition (these are the methods and techniques discussed earlier).

The instant when all the resources of our being are exhausted is the instant of Realization. Here is an account from the Ch'an literature: '*A taut thread, a light touch, and an explosion shakes the earth to its foundations; everything hidden in the spirit explodes like a volcanic eruption or bursts forth like a flash of lightning.*'

The labyrinth in Greek mythology can be used as a symbol to help one understand the individual's evolution towards the death that precedes rebirth, though not without some important qualifications.* Our labyrinth is horizontal and built on the surface. It has no exit on this level. The only way out is at its centre, where the Minotaur is. It goes vertically through the middle of the Minotaur and it corresponds to what traditional metaphysics calls the axis or tree of Heaven.† Right from the moment we are born we are in this centre but without the ability to be aware of it. With the emergence of intellect, we start to explore the external world in search of compensations. Sooner or later, without exception, these centrifugal excursions turn out to be dead ends. As each of these possibilities is ruled out, the subject is gradually driven towards the centre. For the Greeks, who readily humanized their gods and deified their heroes, the Minotaur was killed by Theseus. But in our symbolic and metaphysical labyrinth, the Minotaur devours Theseus. It is this that enables Theseus to rediscover the axis of Heaven, and he is then drawn up to the Divine Absolute and freed from the

---

* Cf. *De l'Initiation* by Jean d'Ecausse, Le Courrier du Livre, Paris. (HB)

† Cf. Réné Guénon, *The Symbolism of the Cross*, Ch. XXIII. (HB)

prison which the labyrinth represents. From our usual point of view, this account of exploring the labyrinth and going from one dead end failure to another before finally being devoured by a monster has to be a *descending* path. The way to infinity passes through zero.

In summary, at the microcosmic level Realization is indeed a strange revolution: in the ordinary, unrealized individual, the affectivity that dominates all our behaviour is under the control of the Demiurge; Realization effects an about-turn, bringing the intellect, which has now become Cosmic Mind, above affectivity, and giving it infinite bliss. The Demiurge is now limited to controlling the animal or vegetative part of the individual. It is the disappearance of the whole dominant ego structure of the self that justifies the term 'spiritual death'.

The length of time required for the inner evolution which takes place from the first desire for Realization to the final moments of dying into rebirth is extremely variable. It may only have taken two years for Sri Ramana Maharshi, but it is much more usual for it to be a matter of decades. Perhaps this is what Buddha had in mind when he was asked to name the greatest virtue in man, and replied that it was *patience*.

The first stages in the *descending path* are characterized by the compensations becoming less attractive. When we picture ourselves engaging in some compensatory activity, a voice within us immediately says: 'And then what?' or 'What is the point?' and the illusory pleasure we have considered is no longer attractive.

As the psychic screen on which our compensatory fantasies are projected begins to lose its opacity, what the eye of spirit perceives beyond it is profound night, meaning that fundamental yearning arising from our abandonment by God. This is what the crucified Jesus expressed when He cried: 'My God, my God, why hast thou forsaken me?'* To speak in Plato's terms, it is when we are born, when the soul falls into a human organism, that we really seem to have been abandoned by God.

As we begin to become aware of this fundamental yearning – and this is a slow, gradual process – we feel a new sadness which seems to be without cause. We try to discover its source, but we either cannot or we come up with reasons which are out of keeping with our deep sense of sadness.

For this suffering to be of any use,† we have to start by purifying it, which means clearing our mind of these associations. This will not have

---

* Matthew 27:45.
† It should be quite obvious that the idea of using suffering carries no implications of asceticism, let alone masochism. (HB)

the effect of diminishing the presence of suffering and we will be able to experience it consciously *without thinking*. It is a diffuse disquiet, experienced throughout the whole being, in the whole body, and sometimes localized to some extent at the level of the heart. What makes this initial purification possible and ennobles it is the understanding that *all spiritual suffering, whatever its degree, expresses our yearning for God.* Those who live in a state of liberation, in whom this yearning is objectively no longer present, are invulnerable to suffering, and this is precisely because the source of suffering is no longer present.

This is true acceptance of suffering, which has nothing in common with resignation. It is perfectly expressed in the words of Jesus: '...not my will, but thine, be done).*

When the individual reaches the depths of *the night of the senses and of the spirit,*[†] feelings and thought are moving towards a state of complete cessation, which will, once it is reached, release Realization.

When a disciple asked what is the ultimate word in Ch'an Buddhism, his Master replied: 'It is YES.' The attitude of ordinary people when they are faced with suffering is one of 'No,' and they fight against their situation. When they do so, their struggle is often ineffective, and they bring more suffering on themselves. Let us learn, in all circumstances, to have an attitude of 'Yes,' and to accept our misfortunes as equably as we do our good fortune. Happy events provide very useful moments of release, but let us also be grateful for and experience to the full our sufferings and boredom, since only by maintaining this attitude will we enable our egotistical condition to suffer the blows which will bring about its eventual disappearance. This approach will allow work to take place within us at an unconscious level which our intellect would be quite incapable of undertaking, and which can only be accomplished by the Self.

What do we mean by our misfortunes? We rightly draw a distinction between *psychological suffering* and *physical pain*. People who are liberated are no longer susceptible to mental pain, but will still experience

---

* Luke 22:42.

[†] 'In order to reach perfection, the soul has to pass, ordinarily, through two kinds of night, which spiritual writers call purgations, or purifications, of the soul, and which I have called night, because in the one as well as in the other the soul travels, as it were, by night, in darkness.

The first night is the night, or purgation, of the sensual part of the soul, which is the privation of all desire, wrought by God . . . The second night is the night of the spiritual part, which is for those who are more advanced, when God wishes to bring them into union with Himself.' From *The Mystical Doctrine of St John of the* Cross, ed. R. H. J. Steuart, sj (1946), Sheed & Ward, London.

physical pain. However they will not experience it in the same way that ordinary people do: they feel it but are indifferent to it. This indicates that physical pain affecting ordinary, non-realized people is always accompanied by mental suffering. In effect what people want for themselves, and even feel entitled to, is a permanently pain-free body and, when this demand on life is thwarted, they fight against their situation, experiencing mental pain in the process because their protest is often powerless to achieve anything.

I want to focus on mental pain in particular. Why it should present is less easy to understand than is the case with physical pain where sensitive nerves are irritated and their activity communicated to the brain and hence to consciousness.

In order to explain mental suffering we need to go back to Hamlet's fundamental question, to that *uncertainty about the nature of our being* which dwells in each one of us. We rightly have an intuitive awareness of our divine nature, of the Self which is our Absolute Reality, but at the same time our self-definition is construed in terms of ourselves as separate persons, and in this respect it is an obvious and enduring fact that we do not possess any divine attributes. Nonetheless our intuition of our own divinity is irrefutable because it is correct (despite the fact that the Self only exists as a possibility in our ordinary, unrealized state). The simultaneous presence of these two conflicting facts within us leads inevitably to our uncertainty about the nature of our being, and once the problem has taken this form, it is insoluble. Yet we go on seeking to resolve it all our life in favour of our claims to personal divinity, in other words by means of successes which provide the self with affirmation.

Unrealized people make continuous internal and external efforts to be 'happy' and strive after compensations. If they are struck by misfortune, they either rebel more or less ineffectively against their lot and in the process suffer intensely or they resign themselves and take refuge in an attitude of silent, passive protest which results in less suffering and allows the passage of time to give some relief.

When we suffer psychological pain, this indicates the presence of disharmonious energy within us. This is characterized by a marked bipolarity and it develops into a vicious circle, forming a loop between emotion and imagination. How this happens is that energy escapes into the imagination and triggers the release of more disharmonious energy from the affective centre. The effect is that this energy is not available to be used for achieving Realization unless the vicious circle, the feedback loop, is interrupted at the level of imagination, in the conscious mind, and so no longer forms a mass of formal energy, like a foreign body which should be rejected by the organism. The raw material from which this polarized energy is derived is a portion of the individual's own homogeneous vital energy. Once I begin to devote my attention to what my body feels, without accompanying thought, the energy of suffering loses its disharmony and no longer tears me apart between two poles. It becomes available to the Self which draws closer to its awakening as the self's claims to its own divinity grow less.

If we know how to make use of our suffering, the self becomes less conceited and importunate. Our inner state moves downwards in the direction of that fundamental yearning to which Rimbaud alluded when he wrote:

'O mille veuvages
De la si pauvre âme' . . . '*

We also begin, with increasing frequency, to experience the inclination to feel in our body that malaise which our sense of being abandoned by the divine induces. Our compensatory mechanisms usually disguise this malaise, as though it lay in a direction which should at all costs be avoided. But this invaluable malaise is easily revealed if the gaze we direct towards it is clear and free of bias. It is invaluable because it will gradually lead us towards that fundamental yearning which is a hell that suddenly transforms into paradise the moment it is reached. The way to the Divine Kingdom within us must truly be preceded by the illusory fact of its absence; and the way of true Happiness, infinite and eternal, must pass through the loss of all hope in it.

All our sufferings are humiliations. Once they are accepted, they are transcended in true humility, in visions of our self having less and less *being*. Then, just as we finally see it as being nothing, the Self is realized and wholly takes us over, revealing that, without having been aware of it until that moment, all along we had been the Self in the full splendour of its Absolute Reality.

* 'The thousand widowhoods of the poor soul . . . ' Extract from *Chanson de la plus haute tour.*

# PART FOUR

*of*

## *The Realization of the Self*

# *Humility and Deliverance*

Part Four was added in January 1984 as a supplement to the original text published in 1979.

## 19. The Search for Happiness

Everyone seeks happiness. In the vast majority of cases, their search takes place in the phenomenal world, in other words in the domain of what ordinary people take to be the sole Reality. Metaphysics, if it is encountered in a book or in conversation, which is already a very rare event, is taken by ordinary people to be an intellectual game, an activity which does not correspond to reality in any way and is completely useless. Anyone who makes an attempt to study metaphysics is simply a dreamer whose mental health is more or less compromised.

Yet all of us, in the depths of our psyche, yearn unconsciously for absolute happiness. For want of anything better, the happiness we seek in practice is relative and partial and quite insufficient. People often make do with this if they are 'philosophical'. There is a proverb which expresses this: 'You can't have everything.' The English have another saying which expresses a more extreme pessimism: 'Life is just one damn thing after another.'* The partial happinesses which we experience are sometimes very great, but they are always under threat and death will in any case will put an end to them.

A lot of people are not 'philosophical' in the popular sense and they are driven by a burning ambition to find some kind of success from which they anticipate enormous happiness. Sometimes they achieve their objective but with the passage of time they grow weary of it. Solomon possessed everything a man might desire but at the end of his life he concluded that all was vanity and the pursuit of the wind.† To seek absolute happiness, total and eternal, in the plane of phenomena makes no sense at all, because success is impossible.

Someone who studies metaphysics knows that Realization alone is able to grant that inward awakening of the Self, and thus of Absolute Happiness and all the aspects of the Divine. The individual who lives in a state of Realization is immortal and eternal. It will be objected that this person's body will die and with it the self. This is certainly the case, but the phenomenal body, the self, has already died at the instant of Realization. Let us remember again what Jesus said to Nicodemus: 'In truth I say to you, if a man does not die, he cannot be reborn.'‡ In

---

* Or 'As one door shuts, another one closes.'

† Cf. Ecclesiastes 1:2, 3: *Vanity of vanities, saith the Preacher, vanity of vanities; all is vanity. What profit hath a man of all his labour which he taketh under the sun?* and 5:16: *'and what profit hath he that hath laboured for the wind?'*

‡ See footnote, p. 271.

the instant of Realization (or Deliverance, or Liberation, or Wakening, or Illumination) it matters little that the animal body will have to die later on, because what dies then does not affect the Living Enlightened one; an abyss separates the illusory body, the self, from the Self which is the Liberated person's unique Reality.

Realized individuals have a body like you and me, but in their eyes their body is not an individual self. They have achieved Selfhood, and the Self does not differentiate between one body and another, or even between the body and any other phenomenal object.

Here is an example: I was visited by a doctor who had been to India and had had the privilege of meeting Sri Ramana Maharshi. (Bear in mind that everything we know about Sri Ramana Maharshi indicates that he was Liberated). At that time the Maharishi was approaching the end of his life on earth: one of his arms had been amputated because of cancer and he was suffering bouts of acute pain from a metastasis affecting ganglia at the base of his neck. While the two men were conversing, the Maharishi's face changed abruptly. Now there is an acknowledged relationship between the upper and lower parts of the face (above and below the nose), such that the lower part expresses emotional states while the upper is expressive of intellectual and spiritual states. When the visitor noticed the sudden change in the Maharishi's face, he observed that the lower part contracted in pain, while the upper part kept its habitual expression of perfect serenity. One of the Maharishi's disciples said: 'Master, you seem to be in pain?' The Maharishi replied: 'Indeed, this body is suffering.' The disciple went on: 'But you seem to be suffering terribly!' 'Yes,' replied the Maharishi, 'you might indeed say 'terribly'.' Then, as the disciple expressed his distress at seeing his Master suffer in this way, Sri Ramana ended the exchange by saying: 'But how is that important?' What this anecdote demonstrates is that the Maharishi might continue to appear as a body, but was no longer that body. His brain *felt* and, since what it sensed only concerned the body, he did not *experience* anything consciously (except absolute and eternal Happiness).

Let us take another look at the incomplete and partial forms of happiness known to ordinary people who are not liberated. They are happy when their desires are met. They are often aware in advance of what it is they want, though this tends to be an approximation because, when people desire something, they frequently paint an unrealistic picture of the satisfaction which they think they will feel when they succeed in their wishes. Sometimes circumstances combine to bring satisfactions which were not anticipated and so had not been wished for in advance.

The quest for happiness is expressed as the search for the satisfaction of one's desires. Desires are forces which impel us to strive as effectively as we can for their satisfaction. The situation is complicated by the complexity of the human psyche which often contains opposing desires operating at the same time. Psychologists who appreciate this are also aware of the senselessness of the general belief in an internal force independent of our desires, an imaginary force referred to by ordinary people as the 'will'. What we so name is only the resultant of the various competing forces of desire. So, for example, simply saying that a child lacks will-power is wrong. To understand a child properly, one must have a clear idea of the forms taken by its various desires. Psychologists even write books about 'the education of the will' without first trying to discover what 'the will' might be.

Let us finish with this non-existent will and get back to desires, which do exist. What is their origin? And what gives rise to their particular forms? As with all our tendencies and inclinations, they are conditioned by heredity and the circumstances of our lives.

## 20. Duality and Dualism.
## The Possibility of Perfect Humility

In Part Three of this book, I introduced two essential ideas, humiliation and humility, and I stated that perfect humility was the road to Deliverance. To justify this claim would require us to examine and understand many more issues. Although it is the axial question which is central to this whole work, I will have to seem to neglect it in favour of other subjects for the moment. But in fact, though I may seem to be diverting away from the one topic which is the most important one for us to understand, I am only doing so in order to come back to it later, armed with the ideas which I need to prove it.

The concept of humility will become clear if we understand its inverse, pride. You may be surprised that I use the word 'inverse' instead of 'opposite', and it is true that the phenomenal world is constructed in terms of dualities (hot/cold, light/dark, big/little, good/bad, intelligent/stupid, etc.). But duality is not the same as dualism. The fact that we contrast what we like with what we dislike, and what we admire with what we despise, is due to the workings of our subjective affectivity. But our pure, objective intellect, which is independent of our emotional life, recognizes no opposites. Take a stick, for example: it has certainly got two different extremities, but, although they have an inverse relationship, it is no sense an opposition. Both are equally necessary for the stick's structure and use. The notion of inverse/complementary relationships can be represented schematically by the following diagram, which shows two oxen turning a vertical pole which is boring into the ground. The two oxen are attached in an inverse direction to either end of the horizontal bar which is fixed to the drill. At a given moment, one might be moving to the north, while the other would be moving south. Obviously they are compelled to walk in a circle by the transverse bar, but at any given moment their efforts are directed towards the tangent of the circle. One might imagine that by going in the opposite direction to one another, each would neutralize the force that the other was exerting. This does not in fact happen and the two forces combine in causing the central post to rotate. In other words, the two oxen work together and their actions, far from being opposed, are 'inverse-complementary'. The things that we refer to as opposites in the phenomenal world are in reality inverse-complementary pairs.

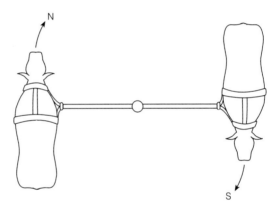

Pride and humility fall into the same category: they are not opposites but an inverse-complementary pair.

There is another very important idea in this respect which relates to duality. I mentioned Perfect Humility earlier and this might seem to contradict the widely held view that 'nothing is perfect in this world'. To understand that humility can be perfect, it must be recognized that the extreme points of a dualistic pair in the phenomenal world are qualitatively different. I will take the phenomenon of heat to illustrate this. We distinguish hot from cold; they form an inverse-complementary pair. They are obviously different in a way that everyone is aware of, but there is an additional difference between them which is at first sight rather surprising. When physicists study temperature, they realize that the top end of its range is impossible to determine. The maximum temperatures they produce are regarded as provisional limits, because there is nothing in theory to prevent them exceeding these limits at a later stage. When a substance is heated, it volatilizes and turns into a gas. If new methods of heating this gas further are discovered, a point will never be reached where one can say for certain that an impassable limit has been reached which represents 'absolute heat'. Hot though the surface of our sun may be, there are other larger stars which are doubtless hotter. On the other hand, a scientist researching cold (and we must bear in mind that cold and hot are only opposites in subjective experience) can, under laboratory conditions, almost reach minus 273.15° C, which is known as 'absolute zero', but can never get below that or even reach it exactly.

We can use this example symbolically. The manifestations of pride are limitless. There have been 'great men' who have attempted to subjugate all of Earth's inhabitants, and it is easy to imagine that this same arrogant madness would drive someone to conquer any heavenly body which men or analogous creatures could inhabit. The complementary inverse of pride is humility. There is an impassable lower limit to the latter which we might call 'absolute simplicity' (or absolute Humility). Perfect humility is attainable and is equivalent to the death of the self. Someone who reached this level, Pride's absolute zero, would have achieved perfection and from then on their ego would be a matter of indifference to them. Let me add that the objective observation of oneself and others enables humility to nearly achieve perfection, but that a final leap is necessary to transcend this nearly absolute humility and convert it into absolute, perfected humility. The acceptance of death (which Sri Ramana Maharshi realized) would be absolute humility. The final leap in question comes like grace from on high, from the Self, and the ego plays no part.

In the early part of this chapter I have used symbolic examples belonging to the domain of phenomena. It is important to recognize their limitations, but there is nowhere else to take examples from, since by their very nature they must either exist on the phenomenal plane or in our minds. In fact they can help us understand the difference between dualism (opposites) and duality (inverse-complementary pairs), as well as the possibility of perfect humility. These qualifications will be indispensable as our discussion proceeds.

## 21. Good and Evil

In the first part of this book, we saw that human life was ruled by two laws, heredity and interconditioning. Both are expressed through a multitude of inherited and circumstantial factors whose possible combinations are incalculable. Even though identical twins share the same heredity, their life circumstances will be different and their psychological resemblance will decline gradually throughout their lives. We have already looked at the non-existence of free will and responsibility, and it is now time to consider the senselessness of fatalism. A fatalist has desires and dislikes like everyone else. If his fatalism takes the form of doing nothing to satisfy the former or neutralize the latter, he is still intervening to modify the normal course of human reactions. He thinks he is doing nothing while the fact is that he is actively going against the current of human nature.

Next I want to examine the idea of 'sins' and 'virtues'. This will lead on to a much vaster concept, that of good and evil.

'Sin' implies free will and responsibility neither of which really exists. It is a word that needs to be banished from our vocabulary if we are to understand truth. It should be replaced with 'error', whose inverse-complementary is the action that is exactly appropriate to the situation. The fact that morality has such a fundamental place in Christianity can be attributed in part to the extreme insistence with which St Paul preached about it, though the tendency to develop moral systems seems to have been a basic human characteristic since the beginning of time. Genesis tells of the tree of knowledge of good and evil in Paradise, whose fruit Jehovah forbade our first ancestors to eat. Led astray by the Serpent, first Eve, then Adam, disobeyed Jehovah's edict, and were severely punished. This was the 'original error' that was unjustifiably reformulated by morality as 'original sin'. Genesis may be a myth but it expresses great truth in symbolic form.

When Moses imposed 'God's Commandments' on the Jewish people, he gave morality a powerful impulse. Once something is forbidden by law, good and evil are affirmed according to whether or not the prohibition is observed. Note that different societies have different moralities, and what may be forbidden by some societies may be approved and customary for others. Hitler promoted a morality which preached the denunciation of Jews and their execution. The extent to which some actions are seen as good while others are considered evil is entirely relative because the actions arise out of what people believe. According to the translations we have of the Gospel, Jesus said to the woman taken in adultery: 'Go, and sin no more'.* I do not know the languages spoken by the Jews at that time but I think it very likely that what Jesus said was: 'Go, and do not make this mistake again.' Morality has changed

* John 8:11.

since then and no one now thinks of stoning adulterous women. Let me quote another Ch'an statement: '*As soon as you have good and evil, confusion results and the mind is lost.*'*

Let us consider the list of what we wrongly call 'the seven deadly sins': Pride, Envy, Lust, Gluttony, Avarice, Wrath, and Sloth. I do not know whether Pride was put first intentionally, but it deserves this position. It deserves the name 'foundational sin' or rather 'foundational error'. Let us look at this more closely:

Envy: we envy someone else because they possess something which gratifies their pride while at the same time humbling us in our own eyes and in the eyes of others. So someone who is envious hates the person who humiliates them.

*Lust*: all our pleasures affirm us; at least those pleasures do which overstep the mark.

*Gluttony*: the same is true of Gluttony.

*Avarice*: Avarice is the love of money, its pursuit and accumulation. Money is a source of power for affirming the self.

*Wrath*: when what we regard as one of our prerogatives, in other words something that we are proud of, comes under attack, we react with anger.

*Sloth*: this is opting for inaction instead of doing something that we know we should be doing, so we feel ashamed of our idleness and not proud of ourselves.

To summarize, everything which affirms us in our own eyes and in the eyes of others is a product of pride, at least when we compare ourselves to others, which is what happens more often than not.

So someone who is progressing towards humility is gradually escaping from the other 'deadly sins' as well.

'Deadly sins' are really '*deadly errors*' or '*illusory opinions,*' and pride is at the root of these illusions.

It is essential to understand its causes. Ordinary people are selves which exist while the Self which IS is immanent in them.

As we have seen, although the Self seems to be asleep in us, we have an intuition of it at a profoundly subconscious level and its attributes of omniscience, omnipresence, omnipotence, eternity and absolute happiness act as a magnet to us and we want to claim them for our own. I had a friend who remembered believing that he was God when he was four,

---

* Cf. D. T. Suzuki's version of this couplet in the *Hsin-hsin Ming*, quoted by Alan Watts, op. cit.: '*The conflict between right and wrong is the sickness of the mind.*'

and assumed that his family did not refer to this in case he became excessively vain as a result.

Although the immanent Self is dormant in the individual, it becomes confused with the self. Despite the compelling evidence that we do not possess divine attributes, lacking anything better we strive to draw as near to them as we can. People differ greatly in the extent to which this dim intuition of the Self exists within them, so the intensity of their efforts towards the divine varies correspondingly, with many making a minimal attempt while others engage passionately in the struggle.

What, therefore, the original error amounts to is the misleading viewpoint which fails to see the difference between the self and the Self. Subjectively speaking, each one of us is 'the centre of the world'. Other people have no real value in our eyes other than in terms of their closeness (through ties of friendship, family or love).

'Original sin' is basically a mistaken attitude (or error) which did not deserve to be punished. What it needed was a correct and appropriate instruction in traditional metaphysics. In any case, even if this error had in fact been a deliberately sacrilegious act, it is hard to see why all the descendants of the first man should then be condemned to suffer.

No, we were so created that we were destined to fall into the trap which the original error represents. This, like everything else, results from how the Universe is constituted, and this was conceived by God Himself from the beginning of time, and its causes will forever remain beyond our reach.

Let us take another look at the myth in the Book of Genesis, which has so much to teach us. The Serpent, the Tempter and Liar, assures the naïve pair, Adam and Eve, that *they will be as Gods* if they eat the fruit of the tree of knowledge of good and evil, and that Jehovah's threat that they will die if they do so is an empty threat. But they were punished and so were all their descendants: death will be their lot and they will know many misfortunes in the course of their fleeting lives. The idea of the self and its senseless conceits makes its appearance: Adam and Eve conceal their nakedness in the belief that what they hid was ugly. The Self was now transcendent to them and all that remained of their divine potential was the Self's immanence within them, but in a dormant state. It was inevitable that they should develop ideas of good and evil with all their unhappy consequences: evil is attended by remorse and good by pride.

Let us note that pride did not wait for the 'original error' before appearing in the human psyche. In fact, Eve's error, when she fell under the serpent's influence, occurred in response to its promise: 'You will be as Gods.' It is easy to see how such an enticing promise pandered to the pride of our first parents. Jehovah had created man in his own image and likeness but had not made him his equal.

I have considered the symbolism of the Genesis myth at some length because it sheds light on man's resemblance to God and on the original error which renders man infinitely inferior to God because of his Ignorance and all his mistaken opinions. It also shows how pride is not only a 'deadly error' but also one which plays a fundamental part in the origin of the others.

The moment we fall into illusory and mistaken points of view as a result of pride, the way in which our intellect functions undergoes a complete change. It confuses a correct appreciation of the phenomenal world's duality with a dualism which generates wrong views on everything. People in their diversity see everything differently and their lives are such inextricable labyrinths that Socrates came to the conclusion that the only thing he could be certain of was that he knew nothing.

In conclusion, pride is the fundamental error, the source and origin of all the other 'deadly errors', and it has a pervasive effect on how ordinary, non-realized people function. We are always engaged in some kind of activity, except during deep sleep, and everything we do, even our thoughts and our internal monologue, affirm us, because they all give substance to our illusion of being, and blind us to our real role, that of conditioned puppets who simply exist. Descartes took 'I think, therefore I am' as his starting-point and developed his whole philosophy on the basis of this famous statement, which is totally false. As far as self-affirmation is concerned, walking is just as good. Whatever I *do*, however trivial, affirms me.

If we call pride by the seemingly more modest name of self-esteem, the extent to which pride permeates the human psyche becomes even more obvious (think how hard it is to imagine someone totally devoid of any form of self-love). Pride brings varying degrees of Ignorance in its train, using that term in Buddha's sense of the totality of misleading and illusory opinions which are at the root of suffering. If the quest for happiness is undertaken in the right way, it can only be brought to a successful conclusion through the hard-won disappearance of illusory opinions and beliefs, and, above all, by getting rid of the pride which is their chief source and origin.

## 22. The Conditions which Precede Realization

In the next section I will be discussing how one achieves perfect humility, and it is possible that you will see a contradiction between the idea that one can do this and the idea that we are 'conditioned puppets' without free will or responsibility. I must now explain this apparent contradiction. With the exception of Sri Ramana Maharshi who only had to simulate his own physical death (which he did in the full acceptance of his death) in order to begin a spontaneous evolution which continued until he achieved Realization two years later, all the Great Masters had to undergo time spent engaged in approaches which turned out to be dead-ends, which they then had to extricate themselves from so that they might continue their search in different ways. Buddha himself wasted years studying philosophy without success, and then spent further time as an ascetic during which he nearly died, before he finally sat beneath the Bodhi Tree and suspended all thought, thus finally achieving Realization.

Four factors are the main pre-conditions for Realization:

1. Knowing about it as a theoretical possibility;
2. A tenacious desire to obtain it and thus be sheltered from all suffering;
3. Finding correct teaching;
4. The strength and sensitivity of the individual's metaphysical intuition.

It was the destiny of those who achieved Realization during their lives to be provided with these conditions. They would otherwise have remained like every other ordinary person. This is not a question of injustice; we are all the product of different conditions and some us are beautiful and others ugly, while some are intelligent and others stupid. I mentioned earlier that conditioning takes an infinite number of different forms. This is an area in which there is no equality of opportunity.

Let us now take a closer look at some aspects of the four kinds of conditioning mentioned above:

Most people are completely unaware that it is theoretically possible to achieve Realization and that this would deliver them from all suffering and confer eternal, absolute happiness.

The tenacious desire to achieve the Realization that one knows about in theory is a matter of some complexity. I refer to 'tenacious desire' because no one learns about the possibility of Realization without at the same time gathering that it is extremely rare and very difficult to obtain.

However, those people who do achieve Realization are not absolutely exceptional, though their motives can be very different.

Professor D. T. Suzuki has proposed a motive in one of his books which I do not find persuasive: he suggests that many people seek Realization so that they can communicate it to others. But I question whether they know that they are going to behave like converts once they have achieved Realization. Ch'an is not a religion greedy for conquests and realized individuals see everything as equal in the phenomenal domain where their fellow humans live.

Does the desire for absolute happiness motivate people? We cannot have the slightest idea what eternal, absolute happiness would be like. More to the point might be the desire to be delivered for ever from all possible suffering. But even here the conditioning factors that we are trying to understand are absent. Every desire presupposes the ability to conjure up some particular inner state in our imagination, and we cannot when we are happy imagine and desire its opposite; neither can we, in misfortune, conjure up and desire the happiness which might come back to us any day. Our inner states seem eternal to us in the immediate moment that we experience them.

Some people are motivated by pride and arrogance, because they believe that Realization would enable them to be superior to ordinary people. Pride lurks everywhere.

The fact is that the four conditioning factors mentioned at the beginning of this chapter cannot provide a completely satisfactory account of the pre-conditions necessary for Realization, which is not to say that they are completely without effect nor is it to deny that their presence is indispensable. But it is beyond our powers to fully understand an individual destiny in all its aspects. Let us simply say that all the individuals who achieved Realization did so of necessity by following the twists and turns of a predestination which remains as closed to us as does every 'future'.

I want to say something about our present times: it is obvious nowadays that scientific research in the domain of phenomena is triumphant, having altogether vanquished metaphysical enquiry. We are intoxicated by the claims that are made for progress achieved in the phenomenal plane. Some of these claims are justifiable to a degree but, even so, can one say in general that people are any happier or wiser because we can move ever more rapidly between places, or because we can now disintegrate and fuse atoms? So-called progress of this kind is irresistible to our more degraded inclinations. The improvements which some advances bring into daily life may briefly surprise and impress but they do not improve the way we behave. From time to time idealists such as the late Aldous Huxley believe that we should be making progress in wisdom and kindness, etc. They actively promote their viewpoint in what they say and write, and by getting groups of wise people together. But it is all too obvious that all these good intentions are but a drop in the ocean!

Our 'progress'-oriented development at the phenomenal level suggests that the contemporary cultural environment is becoming increasingly unfavourable to human spirituality and the emergence of realized individuals. Present-day humanity's pride in the progress it has made on the material plane is causing it to sink deeper and deeper into Ignorance; and the frequency and intensity of hostilities between and within nations results from this. It is obviously not impossible that one or more individuals in some remote and isolated part of the world (more likely to be in Asia than anywhere else) might have achieved Realization and be living in their realized state without having any reason to draw attention to themselves. Those people who are known about and claim to be realized are relatively numerous in India and Nepal but everything that I have been able to find out about them makes me doubtful about their claims. The way in which humanity is developing at present comes as no surprise to anyone who knows that ours is the age of kali yuga. This catastrophic age seems to be drawing to a close, and its ending will herald the return of the first age, the age of gold.

These are events which belong to the cosmic order of things and, even should we realize that we have had the misfortune to be born at the end of kali yuga, there is nothing we can do to remedy the situation. In any case, it has to be acknowledged that the obstacles confronting anyone seeking Realization nowadays are particularly formidable.

## 23. How to Bring About a Progressive Reduction in One's Pride

Here we come back to a question of central importance, how to move from theoretical or intellectual understanding to that Knowledge which is lived and expressed in practice. I have already discussed this in Part Three, but there are certain points which I need to consider in more detail.

Once we have grasped that perfect humility is the key to Realization, our first thought is that we should actively cultivate humility in ourselves. But this approach is out of the question: self-love exists as a constant presence in ordinary people and truly humble behaviour is an impossibility for them. Before Realization, from the earliest age, from the moment intellect appears, we identify with our self. Even if an attempt were made to explain about the Self to a child, it would be impossible for it to understand. Only when adolescence is reached can a master or a book sometimes convey the idea of the Self, though this will obviously only be understood at a theoretical level. So the Self is always present, constantly present and active from the moment intellect develops in the baby with its initiation into language; and we can summarize the situation by saying that we never experience a single moment of true humility before Realization. So how could we cultivate humility when no trace of the real thing exists in us?

You may find what I have just said surprising and you may even be repelled by it. You will start to think of many people you know who display no signs of their self-love, and it is true that it will not be particularly obvious in polite, 'civilized' individuals. But the non-manifestation of pride, the pride which judges others and disparages them, is not the same thing as humility. When I was quite small, I remember being carried by a female relative who stopped at a farmhouse and chatted with the elderly farmer's wife, who had no teeth. I suddenly said: 'Look, the lady's got no teeth,' and the poor old woman responded: 'Aren't children naughty!' I had not been trained how to behave, had not been 'civilized'.

Social life would be impossible, full of strife and hatred, if people went around saying what they thought of each other to their face. However, behaving discreetly like this in order to maintain peaceful relations in society has nothing to with humility. What it does show is that we treat each other's self-esteem considerately and try not to upset it in order not to make an enemy who might be able to harm us. What a lot of friendly remarks fail to prevent those who make them from thinking rather less charitably of those to whom the remarks are addressed! What a lot of pious lies! It is their self-love, not true humility, which makes polite people think and behave like this.

To summarize, pride or self-love, which is the fundamental preoccupation with oneself, is established so deeply and firmly from the very beginning in our psyche that pure humility is impossible as long as the spiritual death of the self has not taken place. Realization alone brings the only true, pure humility into being.

It is useless intending to consolidate true humility gradually if we do not possess it in the first place. We should devote our attention to our self-love, in order to flush it out and identify it in the certain knowledge that this is what brings so much suffering into our lives, suffering which alternates with those precarious moments of happiness derived from self-satisfaction.

Realization brings about a total and instantaneous upheaval in the psyche, and humility in its only true and perfect form enters abruptly and totally. However, the fact that this is a sudden event does not mean that it cannot be preceded by the progressive development of a partial and imperfect humility.

When people have understood deeply and repeatedly that humility is the only desirable goal, and that their self-love and its manifestations are silly and vulgar and are distancing them from absolute happiness, they become loath to waste time on anything that feeds their vanity. To love humility because it alone can lead us towards happiness and to hate pride because it achieves the opposite, this is the correct attitude.

Theoretical understanding will gradually be transformed into lived Knowledge if, during the course of our life, we do our best to watch out for external or internal manifestations of our pride, and condemn them as disagreeable and harmful.

The appearance of partial humility in oneself cannot be observed because it has no observable manifestations. What can be noticed is that events which are usually a source of flattery and considerable pleasure hold less attraction for someone who has made progress. But I hesitate to recommend this observation because the danger is that it will stimulate pride in having made progress in becoming humble. The idea of 'pride in being humble' reminds me of an amusing story about a bishop who was heard to say: 'As far as humility is concerned, I have nothing to fear from anyone.' St Francis of Assisi is a typical example of someone who took pride in being humble.

Let me summarize by saying that all our efforts to observe ourselves and others should focus on pride and its various modalities, self-esteem, vanity, conceit, presumption, touchiness, boastfulness or self-promotion, etc.

Why does right understanding enable us to watch out for our congenital pride without being able to observe whatever partial humility has been attained? Unfortunately it is because pride is the norm when the self is struggling to produce at least a simulation of Realization. When I say it is the norm, I mean this in the sense of 'usual', 'habitual', a general finding across the whole of mankind subject to the consequences of the 'original error'. Because in practice pride is the rule, its manifestations are familiar and easy enough to recognize; humility on the other hand is only a momentary breach or an overall lessening in one's usual attitude of self-love so it is easy to be aware of the pride which remains, and not of any evidence that it has diminished. Basically one can define humility as a reduction in one's usual self-love, or, as in the case of a liberated person, its total disappearance.

Humiliations are another excellent way of striking blows against pride. To make use of a humiliation, one must strive to accept it by acknowledging without reservation that the circumstances of one's humiliation were completely deserved. On the other hand, one will try not to ruminate about one's suffering and its cause and will endeavour to fix one's attention on any other matter, but without forgetting in the process that one has received a very important piece of helpful information. Welcoming a humiliation in this way and guarding its valuable memory is not something one usually does. I have often had to say to one of my patients: 'In other words, you were angry,' and got the reply: 'Angry? What do you mean? It was nothing of the kind, it was just that I was very upset.' This is such a common response that I always expect it. Sometimes an individual who wants to get rid of his pride will recognize for himself that he has been offended by someone else's attitude, and it will benefit him to undertake this same labour of acceptance, which may need a great deal of patience.

Perfect humility is a characteristic of Realized individuals. What this means is that their self is spiritually dead and in a spirit of simple acceptance they welcome what would previously have wounded the self that has now become a matter of complete indifference to them.

I need to add something to round off what I have just said about pride being reduced. It might be thought that humility would advance as pride diminished. This is not quite right and I will use a diagram to clarify the matter. Perfect humility, as we have seen, is zero pride, which I indicate by a point at the bottom of the diagram. A line runs vertically down to this point and this represents diminishing pride. As it approaches zero it is separated from the point by a tiny gap and this represents what Ch'an calls the *abyss* separating the phenomenal and noumenal domains. I have already spoken a bit about this and about the instantaneous leap brought about by the awakening of the Self in someone who has reached this stage. What it means is that everything we can do to reduce our pride belongs to the phenomenal world and cannot have the slightest effect on the leap which crosses the abyss and attains the noumenal. We cannot conquer Realization; we can only open ourselves to the awakening of the Self through nearly perfect humility.

The diagram (overleaf) and the discussion which it illustrates shed some light on the so-called *Via Negativa*.* If we were aware of the extent to which we had developed partial humility and could perceive it existing on the fringes of the self-love which is always busy at work within us, then we could direct our efforts towards increasing it. That would be a *via positiva*. But, as we have already seen, it is impossible for us to perceive our level of humility. We can only increase it by destroying our pride through a slow process of attrition. Let me illus-

* The Negative Way.

trate the situation with the following analogy: let us imagine a piece of land covered with a lot of buildings (these symbolize pride). I have a passionate wish to make use of the bare earth (humility). Directing my efforts at the land itself is not an option. It cannot help me achieve my desire because the whole area is cluttered up with buildings. So I will have to strive to get rid of all these dreadful buildings. I will have to demolish them and get rid of the rubble. At that point I will have achieved my goal and will not have to do anything else. I will have achieved the flat, bare land I wanted without having had to bother in any way about what was happening to the land itself. Since to demolish is negative, the way I have followed must be called a *via negativa*.

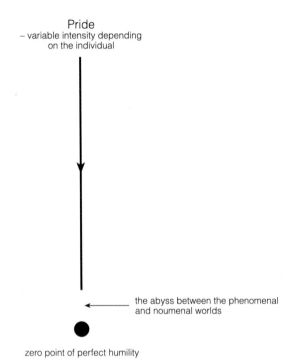

Pride
– variable intensity depending
on the individual

the abyss between the phenomenal
and noumenal worlds

zero point of perfect humility

So I will conclude this chapter as follows:

'Destroy your pride progressively. Your true goal is humility, but let it take care of itself and let it grow without even attempting to be aware of it.'

# Benoit's Technique of Timeless Realization

## Translated by Aldous Huxley

### Translator's Note

*Dr. Benoit is the author of "Métaphysique et Psychanalyse" ("Metaphysics and Psychoanalysis"), which was published last year in Paris. Himself a psychiatrist, he has attempted in this very interesting, but rather difficult book, to relate the findings of Freud to the philosophy of Vedanta and Zen Buddhism. And since theoretical psychology and abstract metaphysics are never enough, has gone on, in the following notes, to discuss a technique of realization.*

*Of particular importance, it seems to me, is what Dr. Benoit says of the imagination as being simultaneously the screen which separates us from objective reality, spiritual and material, and the compensatory mechanism which alone makes tolerable the life of unregenerate humanity. If we lacked our compensatory fancies, we should be so completely overcome by the misery of our condition that we should either go mad or put an end to our existence. And yet it is just because of these compensatory and life-saving fancies that we are incapable of seeing into reality as it is. What is ultimately our worst enemy is proximately our best friend. It is interesting, in this context, to compare what Dr. Benoit says with some of the recorded statements of the Zen Masters of China and Japan. "Allow a flash of imagination to cross your mind, and you will put yourself in bondage for ten thousand kalpas." And this applies even to the imagination of ultimate reality. For the imagination of Suchness, or Emptiness, or Brahman, is just as much of a home-made impediment to the actual experience of that reality as is the most mundane fancy. By exercising oneself in the imagined tranquillity and perfection of the Void one may produce a kind of quietistic samadhi; but, for the Bodhisattva, such a samadhi will be no better than hell, since it guarantees the enjoyer of it against the actual experience of Suchness in the Ten Thousand Things, of Eternity within Time.*

*And here is an anecdote which I quote from Dr. Suzuki's most recently translated volume, "The Zen Doctrine of No-Mind":*

*"A Vinaya master called Yuan came to Tai-chu Hui-hai and asked: 'When disciplining oneself in the Tao, is there any special way of doing it?' "Hui-hai: 'Yes, there*

Original Publication: *From Vedanta and the West* (March–April 1950).

is.' "Yuan: 'What is that?' "Hui-hai: 'When hungry, one eats, when tired, one sleeps.'
"Yuan: 'That is what other people do; is their way the same as yours?' "Hui-hai: 'Not
the same.' "Yuan: 'Why not?' "Hui-hai: 'When they eat, they do not just eat, they
conjure up all kinds of imagination; when they sleep, they do not just sleep, they are
given up to varieties of idle thoughts. That is why their way is not my way.'"

In a word, the realization of Eternity in Time, of Suchness in the world of appearances, is possible only when we put away our all too human gift of compensatory fancy
and learn to see Reality as it is.

In order to enter the Kingdom of Heaven we must become not merely like children,
but like animals – reproducing the immediacy and spontaneity of instinct upon a higher
level.

The average sensual man is without the consciousness of the Self as a
self-sufficient totality. He is unceasingly aware that something is
lacking. He comes into the world bearing with him a negation of Self-
consciousness, or a negative consciousness of self (original sin).
Consequently all his pleasures are of a negative character; they are but
the impressions, on the physiological or imaginative plane, of a partial
and momentary appeasement of his sense of original lack, of congenital
defect. If we study human sensibility from the point of view of the realization of Being, we shall find that it is pointless to concern ourselves
with pleasure; for all that we experience is only the increase or decrease
of a fundamental pain. Suffering is not an act of Self-consciousness, but
rather an act of the absence of Self-consciousness.

But the absence of Self-consciousness is illusory. Man possesses
everything needed for the existence of Self-consciousness; but these
prerequisites for Self-consciousness are not in the right state. It is like ice
and water; ice possesses the nature of water, but possesses it in a state
in which the properties of water are not apparent. Man is of the nature
of God, but in a state in which this is not apparent. Apparently he is not
divine, and because of these deceptive appearances, his present
consciousness is limited to a knowledge of appearances; he is not aware
of his divinity, he is not Self-conscious. We can put the matter differently and say that he possesses Self-consciousness, but does not know
it or have the enjoyment of it.

We see then that, inasmuch as it produces in man the illusion that he
lacks Self-consciousness, suffering is illusory and deceptive; it misleads
man and is the explanation of his illusory servitude.

But here an important distinction must be drawn between physical
suffering and moral suffering. Physical suffering works on the gross
plane of manifestation, a plane divided by the barriers of space and time.
Here a part of the Not-I affects a part of the 'I'. This partial negation by

a partial object is not illusory, since it does not negate anything real. (From the standpoint of 'being' there is no 'reality' except in wholeness.) From the standpoint of 'being' such a negation is not illusory, but merely null. Of itself and directly, it does not constitute an impediment to the realization of Self-awareness.

'Moral' suffering, on the other hand, works on the subtle plane of manifestation – the plane of images, unlimited by space or time. There the image of the totality of the Not-I (a totality which is merely represented, symbolically, by some concrete object) affects the image of the totality of the 'I'. Such suffering is illusory and deceptive; for it causes a man to believe in the non-reality of the Total-Self, divine, infinite, sufficient, non-discriminated. Hence it is that only 'moral' suffering constitutes an impediment to the realization of Self-awareness.

'Moral' suffering working on the image-plane is closely bound up with the play of the *imagination*. It is in the failure to master the imagination that human servitude resides.

The play of imagination is a necessary corollary of 'original sin.' Man is born with the potentiality of Self-awareness, but without the immediate possibility of enjoying it. (He is ice and not yet water.) He is also born with the need for this enjoyment – the need to become 'water,' the thirst for the absolute. Man cannot achieve realization (the melting of ice) except by the most penetrating comprehension. The years which precede the full development of the intellect are a period during which man must accept his situation as a non-realized being. But man would refuse to go on living, would do away with himself, if this inability to enjoy Self-awareness were not compensated by something else – by some ersatz enjoyment which imposes on him and so makes him bear his lot with patience. Man, one can say, is born head downwards, and he would fall into the horizontal position (which is incompatible with his true nature and therefore fatal to him), if it were not that a kind of gyroscope came into play. This gyroscope is the imagination. To use another metaphor, imagination is a kind of inner cinema-film which creates an appearance of Wholeness. This appearance gives man the consoling illusion of possessing true 'being.' Its only and irremediable defect is that it lacks a dimension and that, consequently, the totality of the Self and the totality of the Not-I remain unreconciled.

Imagination does not bring realization, but only the fallacious hope of realization. (In imagination, man conceives of realization as the victory of the Total-I over the Total-Not-I.) It is this fallacious hope that gives man the patience to bear his lot and protects him from suicide. In this way man finds himself moving in a vicious circle. Imagination assuages the craving for the absolute, but through the 'moral' suffering which flows from it, imagination constitutes the chief impediment to realization. It is like the case of one who scratches himself because his skin itches, and whose skin itches because he scratches himself. Imagination is not the primary cause of man's failure to realize Self-awareness. But inasmuch as it is the necessary compensation for non-realization, it acts, when the possibility of realization presents itself, as the bolt that bars the door. It helps a man to await the possibility of realization; but when this possibility comes, its automatisms hinder him from achieving Self-awareness.

The automatisms of man's physiological life are not a bar to realization. The impediment is created by the automatisms on the image-plane. This being so, the work of liberation must consist in an unremitting struggle against these automatisms on the image-plane.

This work must be carried out as a practical exercise undertaken at times when the subject can withdraw from the immediate excitations of the outer world.

**The exercise.** Alone, in a quiet place, muscularly relaxed (lying down or comfortably seated), I watch the emergence within myself of mental images, permitting my imagination to produce *whatever it likes*. It is as though I were saying to my image-making mind, 'Do what you please; but I am going to watch you doing it.'

As long as one maintains this attitude – or, more exactly, this relaxation of any kind of attitude – the imagination produces nothing and its screen remains blank, free of all images. I am then in a state of pure voluntary attention, without any image to capture it. I am not paying attention to anything in particular; I am paying attention to anything which might turn up, but which in fact does not turn up. As soon as there is a weakening of my voluntary effort of pure attention, thoughts (images) make their appearance. I do not notice the fact immediately, for my attention is momentarily asleep; but after a certain time I perceive what has happened. I discover that I have started to think of this and that. The moment I make this discovery, I say to my imagination, 'So you want to talk to me about that. Go ahead; I'm listening.' Immediately everything stops again, and I become conscious of the stoppage. At first the moments of pure attention are short. (Little by little, however, they tend to become longer.) But, though brief, they are not mere infinitesimal instants; they possess a certain duration and continuity.

Persevering practice of the exercise gradually builds up a mental automatism which acts as a curb on the natural automatisms of the imagination. This curb is created consciously and voluntarily; but to the extent that the habit has been built up, it acts automatically.

The principle of the liberative method is now clear. Man triumphs over his imaginative automatisms, not by pitting himself against them, but by *consciously* allowing them free play; his attitude towards them is one of *active neutrality*. His final triumph is the end-product of a struggle in which his voluntary attention does not itself have to take part. (Such participation, it may be added, is incompatible with its pure, impartial nature.) Man rules by dividing; refusing to take sides with any of his mental forces, he permits them to neutralize one another. It is not for Divine Reason to overthrow nature, but to place itself above nature; and when it succeeds in taking this exalted position, nature will joyously submit. (It should be noted that the curb which is imposed by the exercise on the automatisms of the imagination is not imposed by the opposition of Divine Reason to automatic nature, but by the opposition of one pole of our dualistic nature to the other pole.)

During the exercise the subject, insofar as he practices it successfully, feels himself relieved from his fundamental distress. After the exercise he falls back into this distress, which may be momentarily greater than usual. The reason for this is that he has fallen back into his ordinary state of inner passivity, so that there is nothing to neutralize his distress; at the same time his imagination, curbed for a moment, does not at once recover its compensatory power. On the whole, however, the longer the exercises are repeated, the more the subject finds himself relieved of his basic distress.

The aim of the exercises is to deliver men from their ordinary condition of wretchedness; but they do not achieve this directly. Directly they achieve the progressive development of a curb on the automatisms of the imagination. Liberation will come – and will come abruptly – only when the construction of the curb is complete and is as strong as the automatisms of the imagination. At that time we may expect the ultimate neutralization which will reconcile man's inner dualism.

In this context it is interesting to study the state which, according to the Zen masters, precedes *satori* (enlightenment). At this moment the curb on the imagination has become so strong that it holds in check all the affective reactions to the stimuli of the external world. All the illusory significances which the subject used to attribute to things (significances which depended on his affective reactions) now disappear, and the subject is permanently divided into actor and spectator – but the actor has become unapparent. 'It is like two flawless mirrors reflecting one another.' No longer is there any distress (*angoisse*), and the subject experiences a kind of pure and total alleviation – which is not, however, the state of positive blessedness. There is now a condition of unstable equilibrium between the forces that delude and stupefy and the forces that tend to awake us to reality. The subject no longer has the old, false consciousness; but he does not yet possess the new consciousness. (In Zen, this state is called *tai-i*, literally 'great doubt.') Hence the subject who is in this state says of himself that he is 'like an idiot.' The screen separating him from objective reality has worn thin and lost its opacity. Finally, in response to some sensory stimulus, *satori* breaks through. In the past, stimuli from the outside world reached the subject through this screen and had the effect of stupefying him; now that they reach him directly they awaken and enlighten. The screen is imagination, is associative and discursive thinking. And it is this screen that separated the subject from objective reality and prevented him from realizing the absolute identity of the 'I' and the Not-I. ('The eye with which I see God is the same,' says [Meister] Eckhart, 'as the eye with which God sees me.')

The work of liberation cannot be carried out by one who is in immediate contact with external stimuli. It is not that I am incapable of achieving a state of pure attention in the course of everyday living; but I cannot maintain such a state under the continuous assault of my affective reactions to external stimuli. My efforts cannot achieve more than instantaneous flashes of pure attention. These infinitely brief instants fail to neutralize our basic distress. Indeed, my efforts may increase this distress by hindering the compensatory action of the imagination. Pure attention is a two-edged sword; if I succeed in achieving pure attention, I am working for my future liberation; but if I strive for it without success, I merely intensify my bondage. It is therefore essential that we should work upon ourselves only when we know clearly what we are doing, and only under conditions in which the work can be carried through successfully.

Between the exercises, as my training in them goes forward, I notice in the course of everyday life a certain spontaneous working of the curb which the exercises have built up. This manifests itself by the appearance within me of a certain 'active neutrality,' which runs parallel to my normal and natural attitude of passive partiality. This does no harm because it comes gradually, in proportion to my capacity for tolerating a weaning from compensatory imagination. It is in this 'normal' way that the exercise must penetrate little by little into the heart of life. We must refrain from making deliberate efforts to jerk ourselves into a state of pure attention during the course of everyday life. Such efforts must be reserves for the times when we retire from life into our exercises.

What a man can and ought to do in his everyday life, between his periods of exercise, is to undertake a persevering labour of theoretical understanding by means of his discursive reason. It is impossible for a man to understand that the exercise is well founded, impossible for him, above all, to refrain from making a direct effort at realization in the course of everyday life, if he has not uprooted from his mind, by patient intellectual work, all the erroneous ideas which have been inevitably implanted during the first part of his life – ideas of affective 'morality,' of a God and a Devil whom one loves or fears as persons, of 'spiritual' ambition, of a belief in the usefulness of direct struggle against one's instincts, etc.

This uprooting of erroneous ideas should also have made it possible for a man to establish in his life the most positive of possible compensations, involving the least possible distress, and poising himself in the best equilibrium of which his constitution is capable. This equilibrium will be achieved, of course, in the head-downwards posture which is congenital to man; but it is necessary, none the less, for the work of liberation. The man who is badly compensated and imperfectly balanced, is fascinated by concrete existence and is unable to absent himself from life, even momentarily, in order to perform the exercise. The intelligent man will therefore accept the necessity of finding his equilibrium head downwards; but he will recognize that this is not an end, but only a means. The Gospel tells us that we must be reconciled with our brother before we pray; the balancing of our being in the conditions of everyday life represents this reconciliation. This means that a man may have to work long and laboriously on his ordinary nature before undertaking the work of transcending it. It is in this sense and only in this sense, that it may be necessary for a given individual to give up certain temporal satisfactions, if the procurement of these satisfactions must ineluctably be paid for by an increase of his basic distress. Asceticism has in itself no efficacy – at any rate where timeless realization is concerned. Nevertheless a certain asceticism may be necessary for the achievement of the inner state of maximum calm, without which the exercise cannot be properly carried out.

# Buddha and the Intuition of the Universal

In the story of the life of Buddha it is told how his quest for total real-ization began. Buddha was as happy as a man can be in his usual state of development. The precariousness of his happiness had not yet become clear to him. But one day, upon emerging from his palace and from his dream, he met suffering, sickness, and death. The revelation of the impermanence of human joys shattered his "happiness," that is to say, the illusion of immutability and stability which had up to that time coloured his joys. He resolved to obtain true happiness and he applied himself solely to the solution of this problem.

It is important to understand that Buddha's whole search developed not from an objective standpoint as the fulfillment of a duty, but from a subjective one, as the quest for individual happiness. Buddha was an intelligent man in the most profound sense of the word; that is, he was endowed with a penetrating intuition of the universal. It was evident to him that all things equally manifest the perfection of the cosmos and that they are therefore absolutely, i.e., from a cosmic point of view, perfect. Everything is perfect in the world which is perfect. The immutable stability of the cosmic equilibrium manifests the infinite; and all the vortices of energy, which in Hindu tradition are called "the ten thousand things," are of equal value in that they all manifest the eternal play of that energy. Further, everything that happens is, strictly taken, equivalent. The simple fact that an event occurs, that the cosmos is mani-fested in it, is its complete legitimation.

This equality of all things in perfection was for Buddha an intellec-tual truth so clear, an axiom so certain, that his teaching could be based upon it without even having to mention it. The whole Orient is profoundly aware of objective universal perfection. A doctrine intended

Original publication: *The Hibbert Journal* (1959), Vol. LVII, pp. 113–16.

for the Hindus need not enunciate this point. It can be taken for granted as common knowledge and a teacher can build solidly upon it as an implicit premise.

But it is not the same for us in the Occident. That which Buddha did not need to say, that underlying faith which gives his message its real tonality, must be formulated clearly for us if we wish to understand the essential attitude which is the truly effective agent in the search for realization.

The universe, in itself, is perfect in the sense that it is complete, and that everything in it participates in this perfection. Therefore no objective importance attaches to whether I obtain total realization or not. It is objectively indifferent whether I live in one way or another, whether my life goes in one direction or another, whether it ends up here or there. Some Occidentals have said, "Buddhism is not a religion but a moral philosophy." In reality Buddhism is neither a religion nor a moral philosophy. Buddha knew that nothing can occur which is not absolutely in accord with the laws of universal perfection. An objectively "bad" act, in the sense of an act contrary to the cosmos, is inconceivable, since nothing exists outside the cosmos and its will.

The teaching of Buddha is expressed from a purely subjective standpoint. He shows us that the way we set about seeking happiness is erroneous. He does not teach that it is our duty to find happiness. The obligations of which he speaks to us are not absolute but relative, conditional. He tells us what we should and should not do *if* we wish to be rid of suffering. When he states that "all is suffering," he does not say that this state of affairs is absolutely "bad," nor that it *ought* to be modified. He tells us only that it can be modified and he offers to help us to do it.

Buddha pointed out the illusory bases of suffering. This apparently so real evil is not real. Thus it is not necessary to remedy this unreality. But since in our incomplete state of development we have the unhappy impression of the reality of our suffering, and since we cannot prevent ourselves from seeking a remedy for it, it is a good idea to seek in a manner which will be efficacious. That is all. The necessity for this search is purely subjective. Each one of us has an interest in working for his realization, a self-interest. And that is sufficient.

Under the influence of my affectivity I habitually think of good as opposed to evil, but if I have a clear metaphysical intuition of the equality of good and evil, all that has just been said about the Buddhistic point of view becomes evident, and it is obvious that I should make an effort to understand the error which I make in my usual Occidental way of thinking about realization. Western man in general is not very gifted for the intuition of the universal. He has, to be sure, an intuition of the One in the Many, but this distinction ends up in a split in which God and creation are opposed. He does not understand that the Principle of the cosmos and the manifest cosmos are simply two aspects of one single reality seen through the prism of our minds. Western man *says*, to be sure, that God is immanent as well as transcendent, but actually he conceives of God only as transcendent, distinct from his creation which whirls beneath him. He taxes the oriental metaphysical conceptions in particular with pantheism because they do not shut the Absolute Principle away from its manifestation.

When Western man considers the world of phenomena, he repudiates metaphysics. He becomes mistrustful and ironical when he encounters "the point of view of Sirius," as he calls it. "All that is very nice," he says to himself, "but we live on earth." His subjective vision is "real" for him. He centres his representation of the world upon his own appreciation of things, that is to say, upon his affectivity. Lacking the intuition of the universal, he builds up intellectual constructions in which he "universalizes" his ego-centred vision. Since he experiences things as good or bad for him (that is, as constructive or destructive toward his own person or toward those others with whom he is identified), he jumps to universalized notions of good or bad. He sees order and disorder in the world. He sees some things which participate in the universal harmony and others which disturb this harmony. The universe thus becomes a gigantic battlefield upon which the proponents and opponents of universal duration meet – an agonizing duel in which Light and Darkness vie with each other. In this tortured cosmology, the individual need to persist in existence is expressed by the idea that the forces of cosmic order must triumph and prevent catastrophe. For example, it is well known that many people are in anguish at the idea that a possible blunder on the part of atomic scientists might set off the explosion of the earth. "It would be the end of the world," they cry out in terror. The use of the word "world" instead of "earth" is significant. Man confuses himself with the planet on which he lives and then he confuses this planet with the cosmos. (In reality, the explosion of the earth would be a tiny incident in the cosmos, an incident which, moreover, would be a part of the eternal equilibrium of the universe and would constitute a link in the infinite chain of the cosmic order.) According to the usual occidental view my individual actions suddenly assume an absolute importance since they are able to help the forces of order or those of disorder and thus to influence cosmic destiny. I see myself called by "God," the Cosmic Manager, to collaborate with him against the Powers of Darkness. From this follows an absolute moral philosophy. My acts are good or bad in themselves according to whether they serve the will of God or run counter to it. This vision is obviously very flattering, since it raises me as an individual to the level of God himself, but it charges me with a terrible responsibility.

Further, in virtue of the analogy existing between the macrocosm and the microcosm, the conception of an objective good and an objective evil engenders in me the idea that my own evolution can go either in a good or in a bad direction objectively speaking, and that, consequently, I *ought* to strive to evolve properly. When we look at a young animal we think that it is made to develop, to grow as completely as possible, to perform the actions corresponding to its nature, to procreate creatures like itself, etc. In reality, this animal, like everything else, has no other end than cosmic manifestation; and it can realize this end just as well by a premature death as by the fulfillment which I have dreamed for it. From the cosmic point of view, which is the *real* one, miscarriage is equal to fulfillment. As popular wisdom puts it, "It takes a little of everything to make a world." Nevertheless, if I think of man, and in particular of myself, I have the impression that this creature is made for perfect happiness, for total realization, for he will have no respite until he has attained it. This impression is valid subjectively, but not at all objectively. The fact that a man dies without having attained his realization is inscribed like everything else in the infinite order of the cosmos. I have an interest in being rid of suffering, but it matters little in itself whether I succeed or not.

In short, realization can be conceived of from a superstitious standpoint, which implies a divinity of some sort or other who wants me to obtain this realization, or a free standpoint, from which I have no duty whatsoever. This latter is the perspective from which the search and the teaching of Buddha developed. Buddha's attitude was never submissive. In seeking realization he followed only his own will. Since he saw the precariousness of the happiness he had known up to that time, he wanted perfect happiness. To attain it, he tried philosophy. Perceiving that philosophy failed, he rejected it and directed himself to asceticism. When asceticism failed, he rejected *it*. He saw that none of the traditional disciplines would lead him to his goal. It was then that he sat down under the Bodhi-tree, resolved to remain there until realization should come to him. A decision of this kind indicates a fierce personal will, audacious and in revolt against all enslavement. It is clear that Buddha never sat down under the Bodhi-tree with the idea of accomplishing a *duty*, but only with the idea of realizing a will.

This comprehension of Buddha's inner attitude is necessary to us if we too wish to escape one day from our suffering. Indeed the beliefs, falsely objective, which present to us the duality of existence as an unreconcilable dualism are precisely at the root of our illusory problem. So long as we believe that we *ought* to free ourselves, that the cosmos expects this of us, our search will imprison us in an impasse. True and effective courage consists not in submitting to the pressure of duty, but in rejecting this reassuring crutch and assuming our liberty.

# Glossary

**Atemporal**

Refers to what is beyond characterization by any concepts which depend on the idea of time or its negation. Realization is said to be atemporal because it is a form of union with the Source and Origin, which itself can strictly neither be said to be in time or outside time.

**Coenaesthesia**

There is a detailed discussion of this concept in Chapter 11. Total coenaesthesia is the instantaneous inward perception of one's total physical and psychological state. Cultivating this fleeting perception plays a key role in Benoit's approach to the problem of how to achieve realization, insight into one's true nature.

**Conditioning**

Conditioning is not the same as causality. An event is conditioned by a preceding event according to the Buddhist formula: This being so, that happens.

**Determined**

When this term is used in relation to causality, it means 'not self-caused', 'not self-created'.

**Direct versus mediate knowledge**

Immediate, or direct, knowledge, as opposed to mediate, or indirect, knowledge, or knowledge which has been reached through the mediation of the special senses. Broadly overlaps with esoteric knowledge. Western science tends to ignore the possibility that direct knowledge of this nature exists or might have any relevance, and modern Western thought does not usually question the belief that all knowledge must come indirectly through the special senses. Bertrand Russell expressed this viewpoint strongly in his *History of Western Philosophy*, where he affirmed that there is no method of attaining knowledge other than that used by the scientist.

**Ego**

For Benoit, the ego is the image one has of oneself in the ordinary, pre-realized state. It is therefore an image of oneself as separate and distinct from the rest of the universe and ignores the individual's essential identity with the Whole. Developmental factors result in the individual projecting ideal characteristics onto the self-image.

### Emotional State versus Emotions

Emotional states are persistent conditions, largely outside consciousness, which Benoit likens to persistent muscular contractions or spasms. They are maintained by a feedback loop operating between images and emotions. Benoit also refers to them as 'imaginative–emotive ruminations', 'inner contractures', and as 'intellect driven by affect'.

Interrupting the vicious circle between image and affect which maintains these states is achieved for an instant by each inner act of de-contraction or 'letting go'.

### Existential State

Before realization, one only has access to fleeting glimpses of one's existential state or *total coenaesthesia* (q.v.). Realized self-awareness (*subjective* conscious in Benoit's terminology) implies that awareness of one's self, of one's existence, is a continuous, enduring process.

### Imaginative Film

The images which pass through our mind in an almost uninterrupted stream are divided by Benoit into a 'real imaginative film' and an 'imaginary film'. The former reproduces and occurs primarily in response to what is happening outside the individual. The latter arises primarily in response to internal stimuli such as memories, fantasies and preoccupations and gives rise to day-dreams and musings which are largely independent of the external world.

### Independent Intelligence/Intellectual intuition/pure thoughout

These concepts describe the human mind's potential ability to function as a channel for Absolute Truth. Independent Intelligence appears with the young person's emerging capacity for reasoning, and thinking in general and abstract terms, as well as for more inclusive forms of ethical and aesthetic response.

### Law of Three

In traditional metaphysics, fundamental processes such as creation and destruction are mutually antagonistic but complementary. Their resolution requires a higher level principle, the conciliating principle. Chapter 2 begins with a discussion of this concept in relation to the continuing creation of the universe.

## Letting-Go: The Inner Act of De-Contraction

An indirect means of interrupting the imaginative film by relinquishing control over consciousness: it involves a total, instantaneous relaxation of one's conscious being in object-less attention. It cannot be forced. It requires a harmonious co-operation between the intellect which has clearly understood the nature and importance of the work and the 'machine' (q.v.).

## Machine

The 'machine' or 'horse', i.e. the ego-centred individual functioning under the influence of automatisms, is effectively established by the end of the first two years of life, by which stage the individual is functioning at a level comparable to that of a non-human animal.

## Organic

This term usually refers to the total organism, i.e. body and psyche. *Organic consciousness* is a level of inner experience and activity not directly accessible to normal consciousness. It is the level at which reflex reactions occur, and all those instinctual and physiological activities universally present in human beings. Its particular interest to Benoit is that he sees it as non-dualistic, unlike ordinary consciousness, not discriminating between self and not-self in the sense that it accepts and responds even-handedly to these two aspects of the Universe, and to that extent it is already in a state of satori. Benoit sees organic consciousness as the first personal manifestation of the originating impersonal Unconscious.

## Principle

The fundamental source and origin of all manifestation. Benoit works with the Platonic distinction between phenomena, i.e. things that are accessible to the senses, and noumena, which belong to an underlying, primary Reality which is inaccessible to the senses, but can be grasped by intellectual intuition. Benoit repeatedly contrasts an originating Reality which is beyond form and time, with the domain of phenomenology which it creates as it takes on form and enters the realm of time and space.

## Self/self

The Self is the Absolute Principle as it manifests in the individual self, the 'me'.

## Vegetative

Applies to physiological functions responsible for growth, repair and maintenance of the organism. Does not include procreation.

# Index

# Index

# Index

sleep, 104; and emotional component, 129ff; and compensations, 199
imaginative film, reactive and active operating in parallel, 89; real and
imaginary, 133
imaginative film, stopping the, 187
imaginative–emotional processes, 171ff,
221
immobility as a threat, 138
Independent Intelligence, 36, 37, 39, 222;
and the Rider, 151; and *buddhi*, 157ff
initiation through humiliation, 224; by
realized master, 267
initiatory teachings lose their meaning,
268
inner work, 87, 89, 94ff
inner work and vital energy, 98; and
fourth modality thought, 92
inner work in practice, 18, 140, 148; when
it should be done, 196
inner work, an analogy, 188
Instinct, 298
intellectual centre, insulated, 55, 56
intellectual intuition as direct vision, 255
intellectual work, 52, 77
intelligence, discursive, 29; abstract i., 105
interventions, 186
inverse-complementary pairs, 284

*jivan-muktas*, xiii
Jesus, 36, 212, 232, 240
Jesus and the Kingdom of God within, 261
Jesus, historicity of, 115; images of, 200;
teachings of, 268; crucifixion of, 274

*koan*, 99, 99n, 268ff; life lived as the true *k.*,
271
*kali yuga*, 259, 262, 292
Kingdom of Heaven, 298
Knowledge, different from theoretical
understanding, 255

labyrinth, 273
language and metaphysics, 232
language and the illusion of things as
separate entities, 237
language, dangers of, 233
Law of Interconditioning, 248, 251ff
Law of Three, 15, 124
'letting go', 107, 189ff, 195
liberation, 120
life, compared to a rocket, 222
life, meaning of, 75
light of the Origin, 74
Lin-chi, 210n
looking inwards, 84
love, 69ff
love as a general cosmic factor, 240ff

*Maya*, 245
machine, the, 36, 60, 97,196
macrocosm and microcosm, 307
*Mahayana*, xi, xiv, 202
Masters, lack of true, 267
materialist and mentalist approaches to
experience, 144
meaning, 199
mechanisms, 88
meditation, 190
meditation techniques, 269
Meister Eckhart, 234, 302
metaphysical distress, 80
metaphysics and Realization, 281
methods for achieving satori, 269
microcosm and macrocosm, 96, 192
mind as a 'formative' instrument, 53
mind as sixth sense organ, 232
Mind, the Cosmic, Unconscious, 95
mind, transcendence of, 237
mind's passivity, 55
mini-satori, 54
Minotaur, 273
Mohammed, teachings of, 268
moral philosophy, absolute, 307
morality, 19, 303

neuroses and neurotics, 205ff
neurosis, pathological, 256
neurotic, 73, 118
neurotic mechanisms and essence, 256
Newton, xiii
Nicodemus, 36, 271
Night, 76; n. of the senses and the spirit,
275, 275n
night, feeling of n. and sadness, 225
No-Mind, 59
Non-action, God as, 236
Normality, xii, xiv
Noumenon, 234, 237
noumenon of my existence, 33

objectal, 73
obsessional, 59
original error, 288
original sin, 286, 298

*Purusha Prakriti*, 248ff
pain, 47, 145ff; after liberation, 276
pain, psychological, 276
Parable of the potter and the clay, 249; of
the ten virgins, 169
Pascal: Cleopatra's nose, 252; *divertissements*, 263
patience, the greatest virtue according to
Buddha, 274
Patriarch's mind, 156
penetrating vision, 183, 211

314

# Personal Notes

*Personal Notes*